Forgotten Books

The Peasants War in Germany, 1525-1526

By

Ernest Belfort Bax

Published by Forgotten Books 2012
Originally Published 1899

PIBN 1000466518

Social Side of the Reformation in (

THE PEASANTS WAR

IN GERMANY

1525—1526

The Social Side of the German Reformation.

By E. BELFORT BAX.

I. GERMAN SOCIETY AT THE CLOSE OF THE MIDDLE AGES.

II. THE PEASANTS WAR, 1525—1526.

III. THE RISE AND FALL OF THE ANABAPTISTS.   [*In preparation.*

London: SWAN SONNENSCHEIN & CO., Lim.

New York: THE MACMILLAN CO.

THE PEASANTS WAR
IN GERMANY
1525–1526

BY

E. BELFORT BAX

AUTHOR OF " THE STORY OF THE FRENCH REVOLUTION," " THE RELIGION OF
SOCIALISM," " THE ETHICS OF SOCIALISM," " HANDBOOK OF THE
HISTORY OF PHILOSOPHY," ETC., ETC.

*WITH A MAP OF GERMANY AT THE TIME OF THE
REFORMATION*

LONDON

SWAN SONNENSCHEIN & CO., Lim.

NEW YORK: THE MACMILLAN CO.

1899

B2
cop. 2

ABERDEEN UNIVERSITY PRESS

PREFACE.

IN presenting a general view of the incidents of
the so-called Peasants War of 1525, the historian
encounters more than one difficulty peculiar to
the subject. He has, in the first place, a special
trouble in preserving the true proportion in his
narrative. Now, proportion is always the crux
in historical work, but here, in describing a more
or less spontaneous movement over a wide area,
in which movement there are hundreds of different centres with each its own story to tell, it is
indeed hard to know at times what to include
and what to leave out. True, the essential
similarity in the origin and course of events
renders a recapitulation of the different local
risings unnecessary and indeed embarrassing
for readers whose aim is to obtain a general
notion. But the author always runs the risk of
being waylaid by some critic in ambush, who
will accuse him of omitting details that should
have been recorded.

Again, the approximate simultaneity of the risings over a wide extent of territory makes it impossible to preserve chronological sequence in the general survey. Yet again, here, even more than elsewhere, discrepancies are to be found in different accounts of the same event, and the historian, writing for the general reader, must either reconcile them to the best of his power or choose between them. He cannot well give a wealth of *variorum* versions or enter into elaborate disquisitions justifying the view he takes. To do either would change the character of such a work as this from a volume designed for the average reader of history to a dissertation for the benefit of a specialist student of Reformation history.

I mention these difficulties as there is always a field in a work of this nature for the ingenuity of a hostile reviewer *qui cherche les puces dans la paille* to hunt out *minutiæ* on which two opinions may be held. By enlarging upon them, he attempts to disparage the work as a whole. A former volume, dealing with German Society in Reformation times, received favourable recognition, I believe, in every quarter save one. The one hostile review appeared anonymously in a literary journal, which, if I mistake not, was then making a special point of signed reviews. Internal evidence identified the critic as a gentleman who has been believed, rightly or wrongly, to have been for some years preparing material for a work on German Reformation History. Of the somewhat laboured attempts in the article in question to prove the inadequacy of my book, I will only mention one. Quoting a narrative passage, the reviewer stigmatised it as in the style of Zimmermann, which, he observes, "belongs to an obsolete method of writing history". Now, Zimmermann's method was to bring an historical event, as realistically as his power of language would go, before the mind's eye of the reader. This method our superfine and would-be up-to-date critic describes as obsolete! I need only point out that, if so, the late Professor Freeman and the late Mr. J. R. Green, not to speak of other leading historians, English and foreign, must be reckoned as exceedingly "obsolete" persons. That Zimmermann possessed in an exceptional degree the gift of such descriptive writing has been remarked by all who have read him. Personally, I make no claim to the power, and do not wish to excuse my own shortcomings, but I can only say that if such writing be obsolete, the sooner it be revived the better. Surely the faculty of reproducing the past as a living present remains the ideal of historical literary style!

The literature of the Peasants War is considerable in German-speaking countries. An immense amount of exceedingly careful research has been applied to the collection and elucidation of documents relating to the movement in different places and districts. Just as in Paris there are many retired scholars whose hobby it is to spend their lives in collecting every scrap of information concerning the French Revolution and the lives of the actors in it, so here, although perhaps on a smaller scale, there are many German bibliophiles who have devoted years to investigating in elaborate detail the facts in connection with the events and persons of the 1525 revolt. Instead of cumbering the text with a multitude of footnotes, I give here a list of some principal authorities consulted :—·

Zimmermann's *Allgemeine Geschichte des grossen Bauernkrieges.*
Do., 1891 edition, edited by Wilhelm Blos.

Bezold's *Geschichte der deutschen Reformation.*

Janssen's *Geschichte des deutschen Volkes.*

Egelhaaf's *Deutsche Geschichte im 16ten. Jahrhundert.*

Lamprecht's *Deutsche Geschichte.*

Ranke's *Deutsche Geschichte im Zeitalter der Reformation.*

Weill's *Der Bauernkrieg.*

Hartfelder's *Geschichte des Bauernkrieges in Süddeutschland.*

Amongst the collection of contemporary documents and early sources that have been found useful may be mentioned :—

Schreiber's *Der deutsche Bauernkrieg gleichseitige Urkunden.*

Baumann's *Akten zur Geschichte des deutschen Bauernkrieges aus Oberschwaben.*

Zimmersche Chronik.

Villinger Chronik.

Rothenburger Chronik.

Schwäbisch Hall, Chronika, etc.

Sebastian Franck's *Chronik.*

Melancthon's pamphlet on Thomas Münzer, and other documents in Luther's *Sämmtliche Werke.*

b

*Tagebuch des Herolds Hans Lutz von Augs-
burg*, published from the original manuscript in *Zeitschrift für die Geschichte
des Oberrheins.*

Lorenz Fries's *Geschichte des Bauernkrieges
in Ostfranken.*

Gotz von Berlichingen's *Lebensbeschreibung.*

Haarer's *Eigentliche Warhafftige Beschrei-
bung dess Bawrenkriegs.*

The various pamphlets by Thomas Münzer.

Amongst monographs on special subjects
connected with the events of 1525 may be
mentioned :—

The chapters relating to the revolt in Thuringia, by Kautsky, in the *Geschichte des
Sozialismus*, Band i.

Seidemann's *Thomas Munzer.*

Blos's *Pater Ambrosius.*

Barthold's *Georg von Frundsberg.*

I give the above partial list to obviate the
inconvenience of crowding up the text with
references. Of all the works on the Peasants
War, that of Zimmermann still holds the first
place, alike for comprehensiveness of view and
accuracy. Many details, it is true, have been
corrected and expanded by later research, but

for sympathetic understanding of the movement, combined with historical insight, Zimmermann has yet hardly been equalled and certainly not surpassed.

To render the present volume complete, a map of Reformation-Germany (from Spruner-Menke's *Historischer Atlas*) has been included.

E. B. B.

CONTENTS.

CHAPTER   PAGE

   I. THE SITUATION DURING THE FIRST QUARTER OF THE SIXTEENTH CENTURY   I

  II. THE OUTBREAK OF THE PEASANTS WAR . . .   36

 III. DEMANDS, IDEALS AND APOSTLES OF THE MOVEMENT.   59

  IV. THE MOVEMENT IN SOUTH GERMANY   96

   V. THE PEASANTS WAR IN FRANCONIA   154

  VI. THE MOVEMENT IN THE EAST AND WEST . . .   187

 VII. THE THURINGIAN REVOLT AND THOMAS MÜNZER .   231

VIII. THE SUPPRESSION OF THE INSURRECTION THROUGHOUT GERMANY   275

  IX. THE ALPINE GLOW IN THE AUSTRIAN TERRITORIES .   326

   X. CONCLUSION   349

THE PEASANTS WAR.

CHAPTER I.

THE SITUATION DURING THE FIRST QUARTER OF THE SIXTEENTH CENTURY.

In a former volume[1] we considered at length the condition of Central Europe at the close of the period known as the Middle Ages. It will suffice here to recapitulate in a few paragraphs the general position.

The time was out of joint in a very literal sense of that somewhat hackneyed phrase. Every established institution—political, social, and religious—was shaken and showed the rents and fissures caused by time and by the growth of a new life underneath it. The empire—the Holy Roman—was in a parlous way as regarded its cohesion. The power of the princes, the representatives of local centralised authority,

---

[1] *German Society at the Close of the Middle Ages*, by E. Belfort Bax (Swan Sonnenschein & Co., London, 1894).

· was proving itself too strong for the power of the emperor, the recognised representative of centralised authority for the whole German-speaking world. This meant the undermining and eventual disruption of the smaller social and political unities,[1] the knightly manors with the privileges attached to the knightly class generally. The knighthood, or lower nobility, had acted as a sort of buffer between the princes of the empire and the imperial power to which they often looked for protection against their immediate overlord or their powerful neighbour—the prince. The imperial power, in consequence, found the lower nobility a bulwark against its princely vassals. Economic changes, the suddenly increased demand for money owing to the rise of the "world-market," new inventions in the art of war, new methods of fighting, the rapidly growing importance of artillery and the increase of the mercenary soldiery, had rendered the lower nobility, as an

---

[1] It should be remembered that Germany at this time was cut up into feudal territorial divisions of all sizes, from the principality, or the prince-bishopric, to the knightly manor. Every few miles, and sometimes less, there was a fresh territory, a fresh lord, and a fresh jurisdiction.

itution, a factor in the political situation which was fast becoming negligible. The abortive campaign of Franz von Sickingen in 1523 only showed its hopeless weakness. The "*Reichsregiment*" or imperial governing council, a body instituted by Maximilian, had lamentably failed to effect anything towards cementing together the various parts of the unwieldy fabric. Finally, at the "Reichstag" held in Nürnberg, in December, 1522, at which all the estates were represented, the "*Reichsregiment*" to all intents and purposes, collapsed.

The Reichstag in question was summoned ostensibly for the purpose of raising a subsidy for the Hungarians in their struggle against the advancing power of the Turks. The Turkish movement westward was, of course, throughout this period, the most important question of what in modern phraseology would be called "foreign politics". The princes voted the proposal of the subsidy without consulting the representatives of the cities, who knew the heaviest part of the burden was to fall upon themselves. The urgency of the situation, however, weighed with them, with the result that they submitted after considerable

remonstrance. The princes, in conjunction with
their rivals, the lower nobility, next proceeded
to attack the commercial monopolies, the first
fruits of the rising capitalism, the appanage
mainly of the trading companies and the mer-
chant-magnates of the towns. This was too
much for civic patience. The city representatives, who of course belonged to the civic
aristocracy, waxed indignant. The feudal orders
went on to claim the right to set up vexatious
tariffs in their respective territories whereby
to hinder artificially the free development of
the new commercial capitalist. This filled up
the cup of endurance of the magnates of the
cities. The city representatives refused their
consent to the Turkish subsidy and withdrew.
The next step was the sending of a deputation
to the young Emperor Karl, who was in
Spain, and whose sanction to the decrees of
the Reichstag was necessary before their pro-
mulgation. The result of the conference held
on this occasion was a decision to undermine
the "*Reichsregiment*," and weaken the power of
the princes, by whom and by whose tools it
was manned, as a factor in the imperial constitution. As for the princes, while some of

their number were positively opposed to it, others cared little one way or the other. Their chief aim was to strengthen and consolidate their power within the limits of their own territories, and a weak empire was perhaps better adapted for effecting this purpose than a stronger one, even though certain of their own order had a controlling voice in its administration. As already hinted, the collapse of the rebellious knighthood under Sickingen, a few weeks later, clearly showed the political drift of the situation in the *haute politique* of the empire.

The rising capitalists of the cities, the monopolists. merchant princes and syndicates, are the theme of universal invective throughout this period. To them the rapid and enormous rise in prices during the early years of the sixteenth century. the scarcity of money consequent on the increased demand for it, and the impoverishment of large sections of the population. were attributed by noble and peasant alike. The whole trend of public opinion, in short, outside the wealthier burghers of the larger cities—the class immediately interested—was adverse to the condition of things created by the new world-market, and by the new class embodying it. At present it was a small class, the only one that gained by it, and that gained at the expense of all the other classes.

Some idea of the class-antagonisms of the period may be gathered from the statement of Ulrich von Hutten, in his dialogue entitled "Predones," that there were four orders of robbers in Germany—the *knights*, the *lawyers*, the *priests*, and the *merchants* (meaning especially the new capitalist merchant-traders or syndicates). Of these, he declares the robber-knights to be the least harmful. This is naturally only to be expected from so gallant a champion of his order, the friend and abettor of Sickingen. Nevertheless, the seriousness of the robber-knight evil, the toleration of which in principle was so deeply ingrained in the public opinion of large sections of the population, may be judged from the abortive attempts made to stop it, at the instance alike of princes and of cities, who on this point, if on no other, had a common interest. In 1502, for example, at the Reichstag held in Gelnhausen in that year, certain of the highest princes of the empire made a representation that, at least, the knights should permit the gathering in of the harvest and the vintage in peace. But even this modest demand was found to be impracticable. The knights had to live in the style required by their status, as they declared, and where other means were more and more failing them, their ancient right or privilege of plunder was indispensable to their order. Still Hutten was right so far in declaring the knight the most harmless kind of robber, inasmuch as, direct as were his methods, his sun was obviously setting, while as much could not be said of the other classes named ; the merchant and the lawyer were on the rise, and the priest, although about to receive a check, was not destined to speedily disappear, or to change fundamentally the character of his activity.

The feudal orders saw their own position seriously threatened by the new development of things economic in the cities. The guilds were becoming crystallised into close corporations of wealthy families, constituting a kind of second *Ehrbarkeit* or town patriciate ; the numbers of the landless and unprivileged, with at most a bare footing in the town constitution, were increasing in an alarming proportion ;

-- the journeyman-workman was no longer a stage between apprentice and master-craftsman, but a permanent condition embodied in a large and growing class. All these symptoms indicated an extraordinary economic revolution, which was making itself at first directly felt only in the larger cities, but the results of which were dislocatin the social relations of the Middle Ages throughout the whole empire.

Perhaps the most striking feature in this dislocation was the transition from direct barter to exchange through the medium of money, and the consequent suddenly increased importance of the *role* played by usury in the social life of the time. The scarcity of money is a perennial theme of complaint for which the new large capitalist-monopolists are made responsible. The class in question was itself only a symptom of the general economic change. The seeming scarcity of money, though but the consequence of the increased demand for a circulating medium, was explained to the disadvantage of the hated monopolists by a crude form of the "mercantile" theory. The new merchant, in contradistinction to the master-craftsman working *en famille* with his apprentices and assistants, now often stood entirely outside the processes of production as speculator or middle-man ; and he, and still more the syndicate who fulfilled the like functions on a larger scale (especially with reference to foreign trade), came to be regarded as particularly obnoxious robbers, because interlopers to boot. Unlike the knights, they were robbers with a new face.

The lawyers were detested for much the same reason (*cf. German Society at the Close of the Middle Ages,* pp. 219-228). The professional lawyer-class, since its final differentiation from the clerk-class in general, had made the Roman or civil law its speciality, and had done its utmost everywhere to establish the principles of the latter in place of the old feudal law of earlier mediæval Europe. The Roman law was especially favourable to the pretensions of the princes, and, from an economic point of view, of the nobility in general, inasmuch as land was on the new legal principles treated as the private property of the lord, over which he had full power of ownership, and not, as under feudal and canon law, as a *trust* involving duties as well as rights. The class of jurists was itself of comparatively recent

growth in Central Europe, and its rapid increase
in every portion of the empire dated from less
than half a century back. It may be well
understood, therefore, why these interlopers,
who ignored the ancient customary law of the
country, and who by means of an alien code
deprived the poor freeholder or copyholder of
his land, or justified new and unheard-of exactions on the part of his lord on the plea that
the latter might do what he liked with his own,
were regarded by the peasant and humble man
as robbers whose depredations were, if anything, even more resented than those of their
old and tried enemy—the plundering knight.

The priest] especially of the regular orders.
was indeed an old foe, but his offence had now
become very rank. From the middle of the
fifteenth century onwards the stream of anti-
clerical literature waxes alike in volume and
intensity. The "monk" had become the object
of hatred and scorn throughout the whole lay
world. This view of the "regular" was shared,
moreover, by not a few of the secular clergy
themselves. Humanists, who were subsequently
ardent champions of the Church against Luther
and the Protestant Reformation—men such as

Murner and Erasmus—had been previously the bitterest satirists of the "friar" and the "monk". Amongst the great body of the laity, however, though the religious orders came in perhaps for the greater share of animosity, the secular priesthood was not much better off in popular favour. whilst the upper members of the hierarchy were naturally regarded as the chief blood-suckers of the German people ii the interests of Rome. The vast revenues which both directly in the shape of [*pallium*] (the price of "investiture") [*annates*] (first year's revenues of appointments), *Peter s̨ pence*, and recently of [*indulgences*]—the latter the by no means most onerous exaction, since it was voluntary, though proving as it happened the proverbial "last straw"—all these things, taken together with what was indirectly obtained from Germany, through the expenditure of German ecclesiastics on their visits to Rome and by the crowd of parasites, nominal holders of German benefices merely, but real recipients of German substance, who danced attendance at the Vatican—obviously constituted an enormous drain on the resources of the country from all the lay classes alike, of which wealth the, papal chair could be plainly seen to be the receptacle.

- If we add to these causes of discontent the vastness in number of the regular clergy, the "friars" and "monks" already referred to, who consumed, but were only too obviously unproductive, it will be sufficiently plain that the Protestant Reformation had something very much more than a purely speculative basis to work upon. Religious reformers there had been in Germany throughout the Middle Ages, but their preachings had taken no deep root. The powerful personality of the Monk of Wittenberg found an economic soil ready to hand in which his teachings could fructify, and hence the world-historic result. As we saw in the former volume of this history, the peasant revolts, sporadic the Middle Ages through, had for the half-century preceding the Reformation been growing in frequency and importance, but it needed nevertheless the sudden impulse, the powerful jar given by a Luther in 1517, and the series of blows with which it was followed during the years immediately succeeding, to crystallise the mass of fluid discontent and social unrest in its various forms and give it definite direction. The blow which was primarily struck in the region of speculative thought and ecclesiastical relations did not stop there in its effects. The attack on the dominant theological system—at first merely on certain comparatively unessential outworks of that system—necessarily of its own force developed into an attack on the organisation representing it, and on the economic basis of the latter. The battle against ecclesiastical abuses, again, in its turn, focussed the ever-smouldering discontent with abuses in general ; and this time, not in one district only, but simultaneously over the whole of Germany. The movement inaugurated by Luther gave to the peasant groaning under the weight of baronial oppression, and the small handicraftsman suffering under his *Ehrbarkeit*, a rallying point and a rallying cry.

In history there is no movement which starts up full grown from the brain of any one man, or even from the mind of any one generation of men, like Athene from the head of Zeus. The historical epoch which marks the crisis of the given change is after all little beyond a prominent landmark—a parting of the ways—led

up to by a long preparatory development. This
is nowhere more clearly illustrated than in the
Reformation and its accompanying movements.
The ideas and aspirations animating the social,
political and intellectual revolt of the sixteenth
century can each be traced back to, at least,
the beginning of the fifteenth century, and in
many cases farther still. The way the German
of Luther's time looked at the burning questions
of the hour was not essentially different from
the way the English Wycliffites and Lollards
or the Bohemian Hussites and Taborites viewed
them. There was obviously a difference born
of the later time, but this difference was not, I
repeat, essential. The changes which, a century
previously, were only just beginning, had,
meanwhile, made enormous progress. The
disintegration of the material conditions of
mediæval social life was now approaching its
completion, forced on by the inventions and
discoveries of the previous half-century. But
the ideals of the mass of men, learned and
simple, were still in the main the ideals that
had been prevalent throughout the whole of
the later Middle Ages. Men still looked at the
world and at social progress through mediæval

spectacles. The chief difference was that now ideas which had previously been confined to special localities, or had only had a sporadic existence among the people at large, had become general throughout large portions of the population. The invention of the art of printing was of course largely instrumental in effecting this change.

The comparatively sudden popularisation of doctrines previously confined to special circles was the distinguishing feature of the intellectual life of the first half of the sixteenth century. Among the many illustrations of the foregoing which might be given, we are specially concerned here to note the sudden popularity during this period of two imaginary constitutions dating from early in the previous century. From the fourteenth century we find traces, perhaps suggested by the Prester John legend, of a deliverer in the shape of an emperor who should come from the East, who should be the last of his name ; should right all wrongs ; should establish the empire in universal justice and peace ; and, in short, should be the forerunner of the kingdom of Christ on earth. This notion or mystical hope took increasing

root during the fifteenth century, and is to
be found in many respects embodied in the
spurious constitutions mentioned, which bore
respectively the names of the Emperors Sigmund and Friedrich. It was in this form that
the Hussite theories were absorbed by the
German mind. First of all, it was the eccentric
and romantic Emperor Friedrich II. who was
conceived of as playing the *role* in question.
Later, the hopes of the Messianists of the
" Holy Roman Empire" were centred in the
Emperor Sigmund. Later on still the *role* of
the former Friedrich was carried over to his
successor, Friedrich III., upon whom the hopes
of the German people were cast.

The Reformation of Kaiser Sigmund, originally written about 1438, went through several
editions before the end of the century, and
was many times reprinted during the opening years of Luther's movement. Like its
successor, that of Friedrich, the scheme attributed to Sigmund proposed the abolition
of the recent abuses of feudalism, of the new
lawyer class, and of the symptoms already
making themselves felt of the change from
barter to money payments. It proposed, in

short, a return to primitive conditions, It was
a scheme of reform on a Biblical basis, embrac-
ing many elements of a distinctly communistic
character, as communism was then understood.
It was pervaded with the idea of equality in
the spirit of the Taborite literature of the
age, from which it dated its origin. The so-
called *Reformation of Kaiser Sigmund* dealt
especially with the peasantry—the serfs and
villeins of the time ; that attributed to Friedrich
was mainly concerned with the rising population
of the towns. All towns and communes were
to undergo a constitutional transformation.
Handicraftsmen should receive just wages ;
all roads should be free ; taxes, dues and levies
should be abolished ; trading capital was to be
limited to a maximum of 10,000 *gulden ;* all
surplus capital should fall to the imperial
authorities, who should lend it in case of need
to poor handicraftsmen at five per cent. ; uni-
formity of coinage and of weights and measures
was to be decreed, together with the abolition
of the Roman and Canon law. Legists, priests
and princes were to be severely dealt with.
But, curiously enough, the middle and lower
nobility, especially the knighthood, were more

tenderly handled, being treated as themselves victims of their feudal superiors, lay and ecclesiastic, especially the latter. In this connection the secularisation of ecclesiastical fiefs was strongly insisted on.

As men found, however, that neither the Emperor Sigmund, nor the Emperor Friedrich III., nor the Emperor Maximilian, upon each of whom successively their hopes had been cast as the possible realisation of the German Messiah of earlier dreams, fulfilled their expectations, nay, as each in succession implicitly belied these hopes, showing no disposition whatever to act up to the views promulgated in their names, the tradition of the imperial deliverer gradually lost its force and popularity. By the opening of the Lutheran Reformation the opinion had become general that a change would not come from above, but that the initiative must rest with the people themselves—with the classes specially oppressed by existing conditions, political, economic and ecclesiastical—to effect by their own exertions such a transformation as was shadowed forth in the spurious constitutions. These, and similar ideas, were now everywhere taken up and elaborated, often in a still more

radical sense than the original ; and they everywhere found hearers and adherents.

The "true inwardness" of the change, of
which the Protestant Reformation represented
the ideological side, meant the transformation
of society from a basis mainly corporative and
co-operative to one individualistic in its essential
character. The whole polity of the middle
ages, industrial, social, political, ecclesiastical,
was based on the principle of the group or the
community—ranging in hierarchical order from
the trade-guild to the town corporation ; from
the town corporation through the feudal orders
to the imperial throne itself ; from the single
monastery to the order as a whole ; and from
the order as a whole to the complete hierarchy
of the Church as represented by the papal chair.
The principle of this social organisation was now
breaking down. The modern and *bourgeois* conception of the autonomy of the individual in all
spheres of life was beginning to affirm itself.

The most definite expression of this new
principle asserted itself in the religious sphere.
The Individualism which was inherent in
early Christianity, but which was present as
a speculative content merely, had not been

strong enough to counteract even the remains
of corporate tendencies on the material side of
things, in the decadent Roman Empire; and
infinitely less so the vigorous group-organisation
and sentiment of the northern nations, with their
tribal society and communistic traditions still
mainly intact.   And these were the elements
out of which mediæval society arose.   Naturally
enough the new religious tendencies in revolt
against the mediæval corporate Christianity of
the Catholic Church seized upon this individualistic element in Christianity, declaring the chief
end of religion to be a personal salvation, for
the attainment of which the individual himself
was sufficing, apart from Church organisation
and Church tradition. This served as a valuable
destructive weapon for the iconoclasts in their
attack on ecclesiastical privilege ; consequently,
in religion, this doctrine of Individualism rapidly
made headway.   But in more material matters
the old corporative instinct was still too strong
and the conditions were as yet too imperfectly
ripe for the speedy triumph of Individualism.

The conflict of the two tendencies is curiously
exhibited in the popular movements of the
Reformation-time.   As enemies of the decaying

and obstructive forms of Feudalism and Church
organisation, the peasant and handicra. tsman
were necessarily on the side of the new Individualism. So far as negation and destruction
were concerned, they were working apparently
for the new order of things—that new order of
things which *longo intervallo* has finally landed
us in the developed capitalistic Individualism of
the nineteenth century. Yet when we come to
consider their constructive programmes we find
the positive demands put forward are based
either on ideal conceptions derived from reminis-
cences of primitive communism, or else that
they distinctly postulate a return to a state
of—things—the old mark-organisation—upon
which the later feudalism had in various ways
encroached, and finally superseded. Hence,
they were, in these respects, not merely not in
the trend of contemporary progress, but in
actual opposition to it ; and therefore, as Lasalle
has justly remarked, they were necessarily and
in any case doomed to failure in the long
run. This point should not be lost sight of
in considering the various popular movements
of the earlier half of the sixteenth century.
The world was still essentially mediæval ; men

were still dominated by mediæval ways of looking at things and still immersed in mediæval conditions of life. It is true that out of this mediæval soil the new individualistic society was beginning to grow, but its manifestations were as yet not so universally apparent as to force a recognition of their real meaning. It was still possible to regard the various symptoms of change, numerous as they were, and far-reaching as we now see them to have been, as sporadic phenomena, as rank but unessential overgrowths on the old society, which it was possible by pruning and the application of other suitable remedies to get rid of, and thereby to restore a state of pristine health in the body political and social.

Biblical phrases and the notion of Divine Justice now took the place in the popular mind formerly occupied by Church and Emperor. All the then oppressed classes of society—the small peasant. half villein, half free-man ; the landless journeyman and town-proletarian ; the beggar by the wayside ; the small master, crushed by usury or tyrannised over by his wealthier colleague in the guild, or by the town-patriciate ; even the impoverished knight, or the soldier of fortune defrauded of his pay ; in short, all with whom times were bad, found consolation for their wants and troubles, and at the same time an incentive to action, in the notion of a Divine Justice which should restore all things, and the advent of which was approaching. All had Biblical phrases tending in the direction of their immediate aspirations in their mouths. As bearing on the\development and propaganda of the new ideas, the existence of a new intellectual class, rendered possible by the new method of exchange through money (as opposed to that of barter), which for a generation past had been in full swing in the larger towns, must not be forgotten. Formerly land had been the essential condition of livelihood ; now it was no longer so. The "universal equivalent,' money, conjoined with the printing press, was rendering a literary class proper, for the first time, possible. In the same way the teacher, physician, and the small lawyer were enabled to subsist as followers of independent professions, apart from the special service of the Church or as part of the court-retinue of some feudal potentate. To these we must add a fresh and very important section of the intellectual class which also now for the first time acquired an independent existence—to wit, that of the public al or functionary. This change, although only one of many, is itself specially striking as indicating the transition from the barbaric civilisation of the Middle Ages to the beginnings of the civilisation of the Modern World. We have, in short, before us, as already remarked, a period in which the Middle Ages, whilst still dominant, have their force visibly sapped by the growth of a new life.

To sum up the chief features of this new life : Industrially, we have the decline of the old system of production in the countryside in which each manor or, at least, each district, was for the most part self-sufficing and self-supporting, where production was almost entirely for immediate use, and only the surplus was exchanged, and where such exchange as existed took place exclusively under the form of barter. In place of this, we find now something more than the beginnings of a national-market and distinct traces of that of a world-market. In the towns the change was even still more marked. Here we have a sudden and hothouse-like development of the influence of mone . The guild-system, originally designed for associations of craftsmen, for which the chief object was the man and the work, and not the mere acquirement of profit, was changing its character. The guilds were becoming close corporations of privileged capitalists, while a commercial capitalism, as already indicated, was raising its head in all the larger centres In consequence of this state of things, the rapid development of the towns and of commerce, national and international, and the economic backwardness of the countryside, a landless proletariat was being formed, which meant on the one hand an enorm increase in mendicancy of all kinds, and on the other the creation of a permanent class of only casually-employed persons, whom the towns absorbed indeed, but for the most part with a new form of citizenship involving only the bare right of residence within the walls. Similar social phenomena were of course manifesting themselves contemporaneously in other parts of Europe ; but in Germany the change was more sudden than elsewhere, and was complicated by special political circum-stances.

The political and military functions of that

for the mediæval polity of Germany, so important class, the knighthood, or lower nobility, had by this time become practically obsolete, mainly owing to the changed conditions of warfare. But yet the class itself was numerous, and still, nominally at least, possessed of most of its old privileges and authority. The extent of its real power depended, however, upon the absence or weakness of a central power, whether imperial or state-territorial. The attempt to reconstitute the centralised power of the empire under Maximilian, of which the *Reichsregiment* was the outcome, had, as we have seen, not proved successful. Its means of carrying into effect its own decisions were hopelessly inadequate. In 1523 it was already weakened, and became little more than a "survival" after the Reichstag held at Nürnberg in 1524. Thus this body, which had been called into existence at the instance of the most powerful estates of the empire, was "shelved" with the practically unanimous consent of those who had been instrumental in creating it. But if the attempt at imperial centralisation had failed, the force of circumstances tended partly for this very reason to favour state-territorial centralisation.

The aim of all the territorial magnates, the higher members of the imperial system, was to consolidate their own princely power within the territories owing them allegiance. This desire played a not unimportant part in the establishment of the Reformation in certain parts of the country—for example, in Würtemberg, and in the northern lands of East Prussia which were subject to the Grand Master of the Teutonic knights. The time was at hand for the transformation of the mediæval feudal territory, with its local jurisdictions and its ties of service, into the modern bureaucratic state, with its centralised administration and organised system of salaried functionaries subject to a central authority.

The religious movement inaugurated by Luther met and was absorbed by all these elements of change. It furnished them with a religious *flag*, under cover of which they could work themselves out. This was necessary in an age when the Christian theology was unquestioningly accepted in one or another form by well-nigh all men, and hence entered as a practical belief into their daily thoughts and lives. The Lutheran Reformation, from its inception in 1517 down to the Peasants War of

1525, at once absorbed, and was absorbed by,
ll the revolutionary elements of the time.   Up
o the last-mentioned date it gathered revolutionary force year by year.   But this was the
turning point.   With the crushing of the
peasants' revolt and the decisively anti-popular
attitude taken up by Luther, the religious movement associated with him ceased any longer to
have a revolutionary character.   It henceforth
became definitely subservient to the new interests of the wealthy and privileged classes, and
as such completely severed itself from the more
extreme popular reforming sects.   Up to this
time, though by no means always approved by
Luther himself or his immediate followers, and
in some cases even combated by them, the
latter were nevertheless not looked upon with
disfavour by large numbers of the rank and file
of those who regarded Martin Luther as their
leader.   Nothing could exceed the violence of
language with which Luther himself attacked all
who stood in his way.   Not only the ecclesiastical,
but also the secular heads of Christendom came
in for the coarsest abuse ; " swine " and " water-
bladder" are not the strongest epithets employed.
But this was not all; in his *Treatise on Temporal*

Authority and how far it should be Obeyed
(published in 1523), whilst professedly maintaining the thesis that the secular authority is
a Divine ordinance, Luther none the less expressly justifies resistance to all human authority
where its mandates are contrary to " the word
of God ".   At the same time, he denounces in
his customary energetic language the existing
powers generally.   " Thou shouldst know," he
says, " that since the beginning of the world a
wise prince is truly a rare bird, but a pious
prince is still more rare."   " They (princes) are
mostly the greatest fools or the greatest rogues
on earth ; therefore must we at all times expect
from them the worst, and little good."   Farther
on, he proceeds : " The common man begetteth
understanding, and the plague of the princes
worketh powerfully among the people and the
common man.   He will not, he cannot, he pur-
poseth not, longer to suffer your tyranny and
oppression.   Dear princes and lords, know ye
what to do, for God will no longer endure it ?
The world is no more as of old time, when ye
hunted and drove the people as your quarry.
But think ye to carry on with much drawing of
sword, look to it that one do not come who

shall bid ye sheath it, and that not in God's name!" Again, in a pamphlet published the following year, 1524, relative to the Reichstag of that year, Luther proclaims that the judgment of God already awaits "the drunken and mad princes". He quotes the phrase: "*Deposuit potentes de sede*" (Luke i. 52), and adds "that is your case, dear lords, even now when ye see it not"! After an admonition to subjects to refuse to go forth to war against the Turks, or to pay taxes towards resisting them, who were ten times wiser and more godly than German princes, the pamphlet concludes with the prayer: "May God deliver us from ye all, and of His grace give us other rulers"! Against such utterances as the above, the conventional exhortations to Christian humility, non-resistance, and obedience to those in authority, would naturally not weigh in a time of popular ferment. So, until the momentous year 1525, it was not unnatural that, notwithstanding his quarrel with Munzer and the Zwickau enthusiasts, and with others whom he deemed to be going "too far," Luther should have been regarded as in some sort the central figure of the revolutionary movement, political and social, no less than religious.

But the great literary and agitatory forces during the period referred to were of course either outside the Lutheran movement prop or at most only on the fringe of it. A mass o broadsheets and pamphlets, specimens of some of which have been given in a former volume (*German Society at the Close of the Middle Ages*, pp. 114-128), poured from the press during these years, all with the refrain that things had gone on long enough, that the common man, be he peasant or townsman, could no longer bear it. But even more than the revolutionary literature were the wandering preachers effective in working up the agitation which culminated in the Peasants War of 1525. The latter comprised men of all classes, from the impoverished knight, the poor priest, the escaped monk, or the travelling scholar, to the peasant, the mercenary soldier out of employment the poor handicraftsman, or even the beggar. Learned and simple, they wandered about from place to place, in the market place of the town, in the common field of the village, from one territory to another, preaching the gospel of discontent. Their harangues were, as a rule, as much political as religious, and the ground tone of them all was the social or economic misery of the time, and the urgency of immediate action to bring about a change. As in the literature, so in the discourses, Biblical phrases designed to give force to the new teaching abounded. The more thorough-going of these itinerant apostles openly aimed at nothing less than the establishment of a new Christian Commonwealth, or, as they termed it, "the Kingdom of God on Earth".

This vast agitation throughout Central Europe reached its climax in 1524, in the autumn and winter of which year definite preparations were in many places made for the general rebellion which was to break out in the following spring. In describing the course of the movement known as the Peasants War, since there is no concerted campaign throughout the whole of the districts affected, to be recorded, it is impossible to preserve complete chronological order. The several outbreaks, though the result of a common agitation working upon a common discontent, engendered by conditions everywhere essentially the same, had each of them its own local history and its own local colour. There was no general preconcerted plan of campaign, and this, as we shall see, was the main cause of the comparatively speedy and signally disastrous collapse of the movement. The outbreaks occurred for the most part simultaneously or within a few days of each other, but the immediate cause was often some local circumstance, and no sufficient communication was kept up, even between districts where this would not have been difficult, while any concerted action between the peasant forces of north and central, or of central and southern Germany, was scarcely even thought of. Like all other movements of the time, that of the peasants and small townsmen had a strong infusion of religious sentiment based on Christian theology. It was, it is true, primarily a social and economic agitation, but it had a strong religious colouring. The invocation of Christian doctrine and Biblical sentiments was no mere external flourish, but formed part of the essence of the movement. It must also be remembered that there was more than one side to the agitation; for example, the communism of Thomas Munzer, whose name is popularly most prominently associated with the social revolution of 1525, was confined to

one town, and it is doubtful whether it wa
really accepted by all the insurrectionary elements, even in Muhlhausen, not to speak of
the rest of Thuringia.   There was undoubtedly
—a sub-conscious communistic element underlying
the whole uprising, but for the most part it was
little more than a sentiment which took no
definite shape.   While partially successful in
impressing his teaching on the Thuringian
revolt, Münzer it seems had little success in
Franconia or in southern Germany.   Indeed,
the south Germans appear to have been actually
averse to any definite utopistic idealism such as
that of Thomas Münzer. and to have tended to
confine themselves strictly to the limits of the
celebrated "twelve articles".   It is, moreover, in
the latter document, which certainly comes from
a south German source, that we find formulated
the definite demands which constituted the
practical basis of the movement generally.   In
the "twelve articles" we have expressed undoubtedly the ideas and aspirations of the
average man throughout Germany who took
part in the movement.   What went beyond
these demands was mere vague sentiment, in
which possibly the average man shared but

which did not take definite shape in his mind. In this remarkable document, the precise author-ship of which is matter of conjecture only, we have unquestionably the best expression of the average public opinion of the "peasant" of Central Europe in the first half of the sixteenth century.

CHAPTER II.

THE OUTBREAK OF THE PEASANTS WAR.

HE growing discontent among the peasantry
had led to many an attempt to curtail the right
of assembly in the rural districts throughout
Germany. These attempts were specially aimed
at the popular merry-makings and festivals
which brought the inhabitants of different
parishes together. Weddings, pilgrimages,
church-ales (*kirchweihen*), guild-feasts, etc.,
were sought to be suppressed or curtailed in
many places. Even the ancient right of the
village assembly was entrenched upon, or, in
some cases, altogether withdrawn. But it was
all of no avail. The fermentation continued to
grow. From the spring of 1524 onwards,
sporadic disturbances took place on various
manors throughout the country. In many places
tithes [1] were refused.

---

[1] The tithe was of two kinds, the so-called great tithe
—d the little tithe. The great tithe consisted usually of

The first serious outbreak occurred in August, 1524, in the Rhine valley, in the Black Forest, at Stuhlingen, on the domains of the Count of Lupfen, and the immediate cause is said to have been trivial exactions on the part of the countess. She required her tenants on some church holiday to gather strawberries and to collect snail shells on which to wind her skeins after spinning.[1] This slight impost evoked a spark that speedily became a flame running through all the neighbouring manors, where the various forms of *corvée* and dues were simultaneously refused. A leader suddenly appeared in one Hans Müller, a former soldier of fortune, who was a native of the village of Bulgenbach, belonging to the monastery of St. Blasien. A flag of the imperial colours, black, red and yellow, was made, and on St. Bartholomew's Day, the 24th August, Hans Muller at the head of 1200 peasants marched

crops (of hay, corn, barley, etc.) ; the little tithe generally of a head of cattle. This latter appears to have been especially obnoxious to the peasantry.

[1] This story represents the uniform tradition ; but although not refuted, it is not authenticated, by any contemporary documentary evidence.

to Waldshut under cover of a church-ale which was, being held in that town.

Waldshut, which constituted the most eastern of the four so-called "forest towns"—the others being Laufenburg, Sakingen and Rheinfelden —was, at this moment, in strained relations with the Austrian authorities.

The peasants fraternised with the inhabitants of the little town, and the first "Evangelical Brotherhood" sprang into existence.[1] Every member of this organisation was required to contribute a small coin weekly to defray the expenses of the bearers of the secret despatches, which were to be distributed far and wide throughout Germany, inciting to amalgamation and a general rising. Throughout the districts of Baden in the Black Forest, throughout Elsass, the Rhein, the Mosel territories, as far as Thuringia, the message ran : no lord should there be but the emperor, to whom proper

---

[1] This is the view taken by Zimmermann, the great historian of the Peasants War, but it should be mentioned that Bezold and other later authorities are of the opinion that no formal association of this kind was constituted on this occasion, although they admit that an informal fraternisation took place, which was not without its results on the ensuing agitation.

tribute should be rendered, on the guarantee of their ancient rights. but all castles and monasteries should be destroyed together with their charters and their jurisdictions.

As soon as the news of the agitation reached the Swabian League, unsuccessful attempts at pacification were made. The Swabian League, it must be premised, was a federation of princes, barons and towns, whose function was keeping up an armed force for the main purpose of seeing that imperial decrees were carried out, and for preserving public tranquillity generally. It was really the only effective instrument of imperial power that existed. As we shall presently see, it was this Swabian League that chiefly contributed to crushing the peasant revolt throughout southern Germany. Meanwhile the forces of Hans Müller were growing, until by the middle of October well-nigh 5000 men were ranged under the black, red and gold banner. At the same time, the troops at the disposal of the nobility within the revolting area were altogether inadequate to cope with the situation. In the districts of the Black Forest and elsewhere, the Italian War of Charles V. had drained off the best and most numerous of the fighting men.

After marching through the neighbouring districts with his peasant army, whose weapons consisted largely of pitchforks, scythes and axes, proclaiming the principles and the objects of the revolt, Hans Muller withdrew into a safe retreat in the neighbourhood of the village of Rietheim on learning that a small force of about a thousand men had been got together against him. The winter was now fast approaching, and it did not appear to the aristocratic party desirable for the time being to pursue matters any further in the direction of open hostilities. Accordingly Hans von Friedingen, the Chancellor of the Bishop of Constanz, with three other gentlemen, proceeded to the camp of the peasants to attempt a negotiation. They succeeded in persuading the insurgents to disperse on the understanding that the lords specially inculpated should agree to consider proposals from their tenants, and that, failing an agreement on this basis, the matters in dispute should be referred to an independent tribunal, the district court of Stockach being suggested. A basis of agreement drawn up between the Count of Lupfen and his tenants contains some curious provisions ; while fishing was prohibited, a pregnant woman having a strong desire for a fish was to be supplied with one by the bailiff. Bears and wolves were declared free game, but the heads were to be reserved for the lord, and in the case of bears one of the paws as well. Meanwhile, the towns of northern Switzerland, in whose territories an agitation was also proceeding, began to get alarmed and to warn the Black Forest bands off their territories. Switzerland herself was at this time in the throes of the Reformation, and in the neighbouring lands of the St. Gallen Monastery a vehement agitation was going on. No attempt, however, was made by the German peasants to pass over into Swiss territory, although it seems to have been more than once threatened. Zurich, Schaffhausen, and other Swiss cantons, indeed, in the earlier phases of the Peasants War, endeavoured to effect a mediation between the peasants and their lords. They were partly afraid of the agitation taking dangerous form with their own peasants and partly regarded the movement as belonging to the religious reformation, which had now taken root in northern Switzerland.

The following articles were agreed upon as

the basis of negotiation by the united peasants of the Black Forest and the neighbouring lands of Southern Swabia, which were also now involved in the movement :—

1. The obligation to hunt or fish for the lord was to be abolished, and all game, likewise fishing, was to be declared free.

2. They should no longer be compelled to hang bells on their dogs' necks.

3. They should be free to carry weapons.

4. They should not be liable to punishment from huntsmen and forest rangers.

5. They should no longer carry dung for their lord.

6. They should have neither to mow, reap, hew wood, nor carry trusses of hay nor firewood for the uses of the castle.

7. They were to be free of the heavy market tolls and handicraft taxes.

8. No one should be cast into the lord's dungeon or otherwise imprisoned who could give guarantees for his appearance at the judicial bar.

9. They should no longer pay any tax, due, or charge whatsoever the right to which had not been judicially established.

10. No tithe of growing corn should be exacted, nor any agricultural *corvée*.

11. Neither man nor woman should be any longer punished for marrying without the permission of his or her lord.

12. The goods of suicides should no longer revert to the lord.

13. The lord should no longer inherit where relations of the deceased were living.

14. All bailiff rights should be abolished.

15 He who had wine in his house should be at liberty to serve it to whomsoever he pleased.

16. If a lord or his bailiff arrested any one on account of a transgression which he was unable to prove with good witnesses, the accused should be set at liberty.

Such were the very moderate demands put forward by the peasants of the Black Forest districts, of the *Klettgau*, of the *Hegau*, and of the other manors associated with them. But the object of the feudal lords, as appears from the documents[1] which have subsequently come to light, was not peace on the basis of a fair

---

[1] *Cf. Archives of the Swabian League* and the *Weingarten Archives* in the Schmidt collection, the substance of which given in Zimmermann.

understanding, but simply to hoodwink their
tenants with the pretence of negotiations, until
such time as they should have got together
sufficient men to crush the rising and compel
them to unconditional submission. The Archduke Ferdinand writes expressly as regards
George Truchsess, Count of Waldburg, the
chief commander of the forces of the Swabian
League at this time, that he should "amicably
treat with the peasants till he had collected his
military forces together". But it was not easy
to obtain fighting men at this time. The struggle
between the Emperor and Francis I., which was
being fought out in Italy, was reaching its most
critical stage, and nobles and soldiers of fortune
alike were being drafted off south. By the end
of 1524 Germany was almost denuded of the
usual supply of men-at-arms at the disposal
of constituted authority, and there seemed no
immediate prospect of their returning.

Meanwhile, the movement in the country
districts and the small towns was growing and
spreading on all sides. The leader of the Black
Forest peasants, Hans Müller of Bulgenbach,
in his red hat and mantle, was everywhere
active. He succeeded in collecting together

another force of some 6000 men under his flag, most of whom, however, shortly afterwards dispersed, leaving him with only a small residue of their number and some free-lances. The latter attacked and destroyed the castle of the Count of Lupfen, where the outbreak in August had originated. Other bands formed also in neighbouring territories. Truchsess, the generalissimo of the Swabian League, was not inactive. With the comparatively small force he had collected, he kept the peasants under observation, alternately negotiating with and threatening them. But as winter was near, comparatively little was done on either side. The peasant bands sacked a few monasteries; and the Austrian authorities at Ensisheim, between Colmar and Mühlhausen in Elsass—the official seat of the hereditary Hapsburg power in the west—succeeded in gathering a small force, with which they attacked a body of the insurgents, burning some homesteads and seizing cattle. The day originally fixed for the opening of the arbitration between the lords and their tenants was the day of St. John the Evangelist, the 27th of December. When, however, the peasant delegates found that the court was

composed entirely of noblemen, they entered a
protest, and the proceedings had to be adjourned
until 6th January, 1525 ("Three Kings' Day").
But the matter continued to grow more serious
for the nobility, many of whom withdrew from
their castles to Radolfzell and to other towns
whose loyalty and means of defence offered
sufficient guarantees of personal security. As
many as three hundred clergy, some of them
disguised as *Landsknechte*, and most of them
with the tonsure covered, fled to Ueberlingen,
on the Lake of Constanz.

The 6th of January came, and with it the
delegations, not only of the peasants, but also,
as had been agreed upon, of various towns
lying within the disaffected districts; but neither
the lords nor the representative of the Bishop
of Constanz appeared; consequently no court
could be held, and matters remained *in statu
quo*. Finally, on the 20th of January, what
seems to have been a kind of informal meeting
took place between Truchsess and some other
representatives of the Austrian power on the
one side and delegates from a section of the disaffected population on the other. Truchsess, by
fair words and promises, succeeded in inducing

a portion of those present to capitulate, but with the rest, notably with the inhabitants of the district called the *Hegau*, neither his promises nor his threats availed to make them consent to lay down their arms and disperse. They insisted upon their sixteen Articles, of which they refused to abate a single one. But he ruling classes now saw some prospect of acquiring an army sufficient to quell the threatened insurrection. The archduke had negotiated a loan from the Welsers of Augsburg, by means of which he was enabled to scour the country in the search for men-at-arms who might be willing to join the League's forces under Truchsess. This was now being done with partial success, and there seemed a prospect of the League being able to take the field against the insurgent populations, if necessary, within a few weeks. On the 15th of February, Truchsess sent the Hegau bands an insolent and impossible ultimatum, with the threat to pursue them without mercy on their failing to accept his conditions. In a few days the whole neighbouring country was up in arms. But the instructions from Innsbruck, from the archduke, who after all was timid and did not know how to act, considerably impeded the operations of Truchsess.

An accidental circumstance at this time caused a diversion favourable to the threatening insurrection. Duke Ulrich of Würtemberg was a fugitive from his ancestral domains under the ban of the Empire. Compelled to leave Würtemberg in 1519, on the grounds of a family quarrel, which had been decided against him by the imperial authorities, he had in vain sought help from the Swiss Confederation to re-establish himself, and was now constrained to turn to the very peasants whom he had driven out of his territories on the suppression of the rising known as that of "the poor Conrad" in 1514 (*cf. German Society*, pp. 75-77). As he himself expressed it, he was determined to come to his rights, "if not by the aid of the spur, by that of the shoe," by which was meant, of course, that on the failure of the negotiations he was making with the knights and nobles of various districts, extending even to Bohemia, he was prepared to enter into a league with the rebellious peasants. In fact, he now adopted the affectation of signing himself "Utz Bur" ("Utz the Peasant")—Utz being the short for Ulrich—instead of " Ulrich, Duke ". He had now established himself in his stronghold of Hohentwiel in Wurtemberg, on the frontier of Switzerland. Negotiations with the disaffected had certainly been carried on over a wide extent of territory ; and the imperial chancellor was emphatic in accusing Ulrich of fomenting the disorders.

Wurtemberg, whose inhabitants, for the most part, detested the house of Austria, and, in spite of exactions and oppression, retained a certain feudal-patriotic affection for their hereditary overlord, was favourably disposed to his return. The opportunity seemed now to have arrived for a successful invasion of his patrimonial territory. His negotiations with the peasant bands were not wholly successful, since he was largely mistrusted by them. However, an arrangement was come to with Hans Müller of Bulgenbach, who arrived with a body of Black Forest and Hegau peasants to his assist- ance. In addition, he had engaged a large number of mercenaries from the northern Swiss cantons and elsewhere, so that by the end of February he was enabled to start on his cam- paign with an army of some 6000 foot and 200

horse, besides a few pieces of artillery. But
the Swabian League was beforehand with
Duke Ulrich. At the instance of its commander George Truchsess, Count von Helfenstein seized Stuttgart, leaving a garrison within
the walls, while the duke was slowly advancing.
Truchsess rightly saw that, as capital of the
duchy, Stuttgart was the key of the situation.
The fact was that Ulrich had allowed his men
to carouse too long on the way at the little
town of Sindelfingen. Had he proceeded on
to Stuttgart at once without stopping, he would
probably have succeeded in entering his capital
before Helfenstein. As it was, all he could do
was to lay siege to the town. To make matters
worse for him, the news of the issue of the
battle of Pavia, which was fought on the 24th
of February, arrived. The signal victory obtained by the imperial forces decided the
struggle between Charles V. and Francis I.,
which had until then been hanging in the
balance. All whose interests, from whatever
cause, were contrary to that of the emperor,
Ulrich amongst the number, had naturally
placed their hopes on the French king. These
were now, of course, shattered. What was of

more immediate importance was that the Archduke Ferdinand, as representing the victorious
house of Austria and imperial power, had just
seized the opportunity of insisting that the
Swiss cantons should immediately order the
return of their men, who were serving with the
duke, on pain of outlawry and confiscation of
goods. The cantons at this juncture did not
dare to refuse the demand, and accordingly
the order was issued ; the Swiss free-lances,
whose pay was in arrears, on its announcement, accompanied, it is said, by Austrian gold,
promptly deserted and hurried back to their
fatherland.

Ulrich with his remaining forces was unable
to continue the siege ; indeed, he was glad
enough in his turn to hurry back to his stronghold—his Hohentwiel—as quickly as possible.
The Würtemberg peasants had not risen to his
aid with the enthusiasm he had anticipated.
Little as they might care for the Austrian
regency in Würtemberg, the memory of "the
poor Conrad," and of their friends and relations
who had been driven from house and home on
the suppression of that movement eleven years
before, was too recent for them to be especially

eager to sacrifice themselves to reinstate the
man primarily responsible for their troubles.
Thus ended this attempt of Duke Ulrich to
recover his territory by the aid of peasants and
mercenaries. The whole episode from first to
last occupied little more than three weeks, but
during this time it served to divert the attention
of the Swabian League.

The Swabian peasants, as already mentioned,
had begun to stir in the autumn of 1524, at
about the same time as those of the Black
Forest and the Lake of Constanz districts. In
Swabia, the first overt signs of disaffection
showed themselves in the lands of the abbey
of Kempten, and the immediate occasion of
them appears to have been the imprisonment
and harsh treatment by the abbot of an old
man, a tenant of the abbey, on the ground
of a disrespectful expression he had let fall
concerning him during the haymaking. The
abbot's despotic government of the manor had
everywhere incensed the peasantry. The prince
prelate, after having promised to consider the
grievances in conjunction with other high per-
sonages on a given day, appeared indeed, and
listened to the complaints laid before him, but

it was only to give a categorical refusal to make
any concession whatever. The result of his
action was that those immediately concerned
decided to call an assembly representing all the
subjects of the extensive abbey territory, to lay
the matter before them, and to consider what
further course should be taken. On the 21st
of January, a numerous assembly met together —
accordingly at a given place on the bank of
the little stream called the Luibas, to take
counsel as to further action. The little town of
Kempten was in a ferment, part of the burghers
sympathising with the peasants and part with
the abbey.

The meeting, at which in addition to representatives of the whole countryside, some
members of the town council (*Rath*) attended,
kept its proceedings within the bounds of the
strictest moderation, repudiating any hostile
intentions with regard to the foundation, and
finally decided to lay the dispute before a
competent tribunal, all present pledging themselves and their respective villages to contribute
to the cost of carrying it through. Three days
later, the representatives met in Kempten
itself, and chose a committee of their number

to take steps in the matter. This committee immediately drew up a formal protest against the wrongs suffered from the abbot, which was forwarded to the council of the Swabian League and to the emperor. In this document was expressed the readiness of the villeins of the abbey to furnish all dues and all service to which the prince-prelate could establish his right by charter. On the other hand, it energetically protested against new and unjustifiable exactions and arbitrary oppressions, and prayed that the case might be laid before the supreme court of the district. The league, meanwhile, undertook to prevent their lord, the abbot, from taking any hostile steps against them pending the decision. The latter, however, immediately answered this protest by a letter addressed to the Swabian League, in which he accused his subjects of having entered into a conspiracy against the foundation and demanded armed intervention in his favour. The Councillors of the League, who were sitting in permanence at the imperial town of Ulm, temporised, promising to consider the grievances of the peasantry, and, should it prove impossible to effect an informal compromise, to see that the matter was legally decided by a competent authority.

By this time, the whole country north and south of Ulm was in a state of nascent insurrection. From Kempten northwards to the latter city, ecclesiastical foundations pressed hard on one another. Their tenants were everywhere desperately angry. In the district known from its swampy character as the *Ried*, a blacksmith named Schmidt constituted himself leader of the rising. In all the village inns thereabouts bodies of peasants daily came together to take counsel. On the 9th of February, a camp of some 2000 peasants was formed at a place called Leipheim. Another contingent was started which soon rose to nearly 13,000 men. Armed bodies of peasants were now forming themselves into camps throughout Southern Germany. The insurgents were divided into three main bodies —those of the *Ried*, of the Lake of Constanz districts, and of the Black Forest. In the course of the month, these divisions amalgamated into the so-called " Christian brotherhood ". The leaders of the movement assembled at the small town of Memmingen, where the " Peasants

"Parliament" was held at the beginning of March, where in all probability the celebrated "Twelve Articles" were drawn up, and where they were certainly adopted. Here also the most studied moderation was observed in the demands made and in the proceedings generally. The decisions arrived at at this conference of Memmingen were sworn to by all the camps throughout the country. The restoration of ancient privileges, where these had been abrogated, was demanded, such as the ancient right to carry arms, together with that of free assembly.

On the same day on which the order of federation was adopted, the representatives at Memmingen addressed a formal letter to the Swabian League explaining that the action taken was in accordance with the Gospel and with Divine Justice. The Christian Brotherhood was to form the bond of organisation for the whole country. A president and four councillors were to be chosen from every camp or organised body of peasants. These should have plenary powers to enter into agreements with other similar camps or bodies, as well as in certain cases to negotiate with constituted authorities.

No one was to enter into an agreement with his feudal lord without the consent of the whole countryside, and even where such consent was granted the tenants in question should nevertheless continue to belong to the Christian Brotherhood and to be subject to its decisions. Any who from any cause had to leave their native place should first swear before the headman of the district to do nothing to the hurt of the Christian Brotherhood, but to assist it by word and deed wherever necessary. The existing judicial functions should continue in exercise as before. Unbecoming pastimes, blasphemy and drunkenness should be forbidden, and all such offences duly punished. Lastly, no one should, from any cause whatever, undertake any action against his lord, or commit any trespass on his lands or goods, until a further decision had been taken. There was now, therefore, it will be seen, a definite organisation of the peasantry throughout the whole of the South German territories—an organisation prepared for action at any moment.

The Black Forest, the Duchy of Würtemberg, and Eastern or Upper Swabia were already organised. In the course of this month of

March, the Episcopal territories of Bamberg, of Würtzburg, the Franconian districts generally, Bavaria, Tyrol, and the Arch-episcopal territories of Salzburg, rose—from Thuringia in the north to the Alpine lands in the south, from Elsass and Lorraine in the west to the Austrian hereditary dominions in the east, the whole of Central Europe was astir. The "common man" was everywhere in evidence. By the beginning of April, as though it had been concerted, the Peasants War had broken out throughout Germany.

Before giving a sketch of the chief incidents connected with the rising, we will cast a glance at the formulated demands represented in the "Twelve Articles," at the different currents embodied in the movement, and at the men who were its intellectual heads—Weigand, Hipler, Karlstadt, Gaismayr, Hubmayer, reserving Münzer and Pfeiffer for a subsequent chapter.

CHAPTER III.

DEMANDS, IDEALS AND APOSTLES OF THE MOVEMENT.

ASTROLOGY and mystical prophesyings appeared
in the times shortly preceding the great social
upheaval, foretelling strange things which were
to happen in the years 1524 and 1525.

One of the principal of these indicated a
Noachic deluge for the summer of 1524. This
vaticination was based on an alleged combination
of sixteen conjunctures in the sign of Aquarius.
So seriously was the prophesy believed in that
extensive preparations were made, in view of
the approaching catastrophe. Many, however,
explained the presage as indicating a social
inundation—the levelling of social distinctions
by the "common man". Portents were alleged
to have appeared; strange monsters to have
been born. Illustrated broadsheets and pamphlets were in circulation, on the title pages of
which might be seen portrayed pope, emperor,
cardinals and prince-prelates trembling before

the approach of a band of peasants armed with the implements of husbandry and led on by the planet Saturn.　All these things testified to the excited state of the public mind and the direction in which popular thought was turned.　Meanwhile, the thinkers of the movement were preparing to give definite form to the vague aspirations of the multitude.

In the uprising known as the "Peasants War," as already stated, there is more than one strain to be observed, though all turns on the central ideas of equality, economic reform and political reorganisation.　First of all, we have the immediate and practical side of the agrarian movement, on the lines of which the actual outbreak originated, and the special representatives of which were the peasants of South-Eastern Germany.　This side of the movement is, of course, most prominently present everywhere, but in other parts of the country, notably in Franconia and Thuringia, it is accompanied by ideas of a more far-reaching kind as regards social reconstruction, albeit clothed in a mystical religious garb.　Then again we have certain definite schemes of extensive political reform. Behind these things lay the distinction

between town and country, a distinction recently
become so important. / It need scarcely be said
that most of those wider aspirations that entered
into the movement had their origin in the new
life of the towns, and, as regards their expression, in the more educated elements to be found
within their walls./ We will first cast a glance
at the mainstay of the whole movement, the
celebrated "Twelve Articles".

In the last chapter we have already seen a
specimen of the immediate demands put forward
by the peasants of the Black Forest. In these
there is no mention of religion. They aptly
indicate the position of the cultivator of the
soil, robbed often of his common pasture, of the
right of hunting and fishing on his own account ;
compelled to perform all sorts of services for
his lord at any time, were it haymaking, harvest,
or vintage, even though it meant to him the loss
of his crop ; made to furnish dues of every
description payable in kind and now often in
money ; prohibited from catching, destroying,
or driving away animals of the chase, even
though they might be doing irreparable damage
to agricultural produce ; compelled to permit
the lord's hunting dogs to devour his poultry

at pleasure ; obliged to offer his live stock first
of all to the castle before selling it elsewhere ;
forced to furnish the castle with firewood and
timber and (a significant item) *wood for the
stake on the occasion of executions.* And what
was the penalty for the neglect of these things?
Imprisonment in the lord's dungeon ; the
piercing out of eyes ; or, in some cases, death
itself. At first the remedying of such grievances
was demanded in a different form on different
manors, sometimes in a greater, sometimes in
a lesser number of " Articles ". Thus, in one
case we find sixteen, in another thirty-four, in
another sixty-two " points " in these several
agrarian charters. In the month of March, 1525,
however, they were all condensed into twelve
main claims in a document entitled " The
fundamental and just chief articles of all the
peasantry and villeins of spiritual and temporal
lordships by which they deem themselves
opprest ". This document was accepted practically throughout Germany as the basis of the
revolution. Owing to its importance, we give
this charter of the German peasantry in full.
It reads as follows :—

INTRODUCTION.

" To the Christian reader, peace and the grace of God through Christ! There are many anti-Christians who now seek occasion to despise the Gospel on account of the assembled peasantry, in that they say : these be the fruits of the new Gospel : to obey none ; to resist in all places ; to band together with great power of arms to the end to reform, to root out, ay and maybe to slay spiritual and temporal authority. All such godless and wicked judgments are answered in the articles here written down as well that they remove this shame from the Word of God as also that they may excuse in a Christian manner this disobedience, yea, this rebellion of all peasants.

" For the first time, the Gospel is not a cause of rebellion or uproar, since it is the word of Christ, the promised Messiah, whose word and life teaches naught save love, peace, patience and unity (Rom. xi.). Therefore, that all who believe in this Christ may be loving, peaceful, patient and united, such is the ground of all Articles of the peasants, and as may be clearly seen they are designed to the intent that men should have the Gospel and should live according thereto. How shall the anti-Christians then call the Gospel a cause of rebellion and of disobedience? But that certain anti-Christians /and enemies of the Gospel should rise up \ | against such requirements, of this is not the | \Gospel the cause, but the devil, the most / hurtful enemy of the Gospel, who exciteth such by unbelief, in his own, that the Word of God which teacheth love, peace and unity may be trodden down and taken away.

" For the rest, it followeth clearly and mani-festly that the peasants who in their Articles require such Gospel as doctrine and as precept may not be called disobedient and rebellious. But should God hear those peasants who anxiously call upon Him that they may live according to His word ; who shall gainsay the will of God? (Rom. xi.). Who shall impeach His judgment? (Isa. xl.). Yea, who shall resist His Majesty? (Rom. viii.). Hath he heard the children of Israel and delivered them out of the hand of Pharoah, and shall He not to-day also save His own? Yea, He shall save them, and that speedily (Exod. iii. 14 ; Luke xviii. 8). Therefore, Christian reader, read hereunder with care and thereafter judge.

First Article.

"For the first, it is our humble prayer and desire, also the will and opinion of us all that henceforth the power to choose and elect a pastor shall lie with the whole community (1 Tim. iii.),[1] that it shall also have the power to displace such an one, if he behaveth unseemly. The pastor that is chosen shall preach the Gospel plainly and manifestly, without any addition of man or the doctrine or ordinance of men (Acts xiv.). For that the true Faith is preached to us giveth us a cause to pray God for His grace that He implant within us the same living Faith and confirm us therein (Deut. xviii. ; Exod. xxxi.). For if His grace be not implanted within us we remain flesh and blood which profiteth not (Deut. x. ; John vi.). How plainly is it written in the Scripture that we can alone through the true Faith come to God and that alone through His mercy shall we be saved (Gal. i.). Therefore is such an ensample

[1] *Gemeinde* in the original. This means, of course, the "rural community" of the village or district. It might be translated "commune," or in some cases even loosely as "parish," though the old English "hundred" probably answers most nearly to it.

and pastor of need to us and in suchwise founded on the Scripture.

SECOND ARTICLE.

" Furthermore, notwithstanding that the just tithe was imposed in the Old Testament, and in the New was fulfilled, yet are we nothing loth to furnish the just tithe of corn, but only such as is meet, accordingly shall we give it to God and His servants (Heb. ; also Ps. cix.). If it be the due of a pastor who clearly proclaimeth the Word of God, then it is our will that our church-overseers, such as are appointed by the community, shall collect and receive this tithe, and thereof shall give to the pastor who shall be chosen from a whole community suitable sufficient subsistence for him and his, as the whole community may deem just ; and what remaineth over shall be furnished to the poor and the needy of the same village, according to the circumstance of the case and the judgment of the community (Deut. xxv. ; 1 Tim. v. ; Matt. x. ; Cor. ix.). What further remaineth over shall be reserved for the event that the land being pressed, it should needs make war,

and so that no general tax should be laid upon
the poor, it shall be furnished from this surplusage. Should it be found that there were
one or more villages that had sold the tithe
itself because of need, he who can show respecting the same that he hath it in the form of
a whole village shall not want for it but we will,
as it beseemeth us, make an agreement with
him, as the matter requireth (Luke vi. ; Matt. v.)
to the end that we may absolve the same in
due manner and time. But to him who hath
bought such from no village, and whose fore-
fathers have usurped it for themselves, we will
not, and we ought not to give him anything,
and we owe no man further save as aforesaid
that we maintain our elected pastors, that we
absolve our just debts, or relieve the needy, as
is ordained by the Holy Scripture. The small
tithe will we not give, be it either to spiritual
or to temporal lord; for the God the Lord
hath created the beast freely for the use of
man (Gen. i.). For we esteem this tithe for
an unseemly tithe of man's devising. Therefore will we no longer give it.

THIRD ARTICLE.

" Thirdly, the custom hath hitherto been that we have been held for villeins ; which is to be deplored, since Christ hath purchased and redeemed us all with His precious blood (Isa. liii. ; 1 Peter i. ; 1 Cor. vii. ; Rom. xiii.), the poor hind as well as the highest, none excepted. Therefore do we find in the Scripture that we are free; and we will be free (Eccles. vi. ; 1 Peter ii.). Not that we would be wholly free as having no authority over us, for this God doth not teach us. We shall live in obedience and not in the freedom of our fleshly pride (Deut. vi. ; St. Matt. v.) ; shall love God as our Lord ; shall esteem our neighbours as brothers ; and do to them as we would have them do to us, as God hath commanded at the Last Supper (Luke iv. 6 ; Matt. v. ; John xiii.). Therefore shall we live according to His ordinance. This ordinance in no wise sheweth us that we should not obey authority. Not alone should we humble ourselves before authority, but before every man (Rom. xiii.) as we also are gladly obedient in all just and Christian matters to such authority as is elected

and set over us, so it be by God set over us
(Acts v.). We are also in no doubt but that
ye will as true and just Christians relieve us
from villeinage, or will show us, out of the
Gospel, that we are villeins.

Fourth Article.

" Fourthly, was it hitherto a custom that no
poor man hath the right to capture ground
game, fowls or fish in flowing water, which
to us seemeth unbecoming and unbrotherly,
churlish and not according to the Word of
God. Moreover, in some places the authority
letteth the game grow up to our despite and to
our mighty undoing, since we must suffer that
our own which God hath caused to grow for
the use of man should be unavailingly devoured
by beasts without reason, and that we should
hold our peace concerning this, which is against
God and our neighbours. For when God the
Lord created man, He gave him power over
all creatures, over the fowl in the air, and over
the fish in the water (Gen. i. ; Acts xix. ;
i Tim. iv. ; Cor. x. ; Coloss. xi.). Therefore
it is our desire when one possess a water that
he may prove it with sufficient writing as

unwittingly purchased. We do not desire to take such by force, but we must needs have a Christian understanding in the matter, because of brotherly love. But he who cannot bring sufficient proof thereof shall give it back to the community as beseemeth.

Fifth Article.

"Fifthly, we are troubled concerning the woods; for our lords have taken unto themselves all the woods, and if the poor man requireth aught he must buy it with double money. Our opinion is as touching the woods, be they possessed by spiritual or temporal lords, whichsoever they be that have them and that have not purchased them, they shall again to the whole community, and that each one from out the community shall be free as is fitting to take therefrom into his house so much as he may need. Even for carpentering, if he require it, shall he take wood for nothing ; yet with the knowledge of them who are chosen by the community to this end, whereby the destruction of the wood may be hindered ; but where there is no wood but such as hath been honestly purchased, a brotherly and Christian agreement with the buyers shall be come to. But when one hath first of all taken to himself the land and hath afterwards sold it, then shall an agreement be entered into with the buyers according to the circumstance of the matter and with regard to brotherly love and Holy Writ.

Sixth Article.

" Sixthly, our grievous complaint is as concerning the services which are heaped up from day to day and daily increased. We desire that these should be earnestly considered, and that we be not so heavily burdened withal ; but that we should be mercifully dealt with herein ; that we may serve as our fathers have served and only according to the Word of God (Rom. x.).

Seventh Article.

" Seventhly, will we henceforth no longer be opprest by a lordship, but in such wise as a lordship hath granted the land, so shall it be held according to the agreement between the lord and the peasant. The lord shall no longer compel him and press him, nor require of him

new services or aught else for naught (Luke
iii. ; Thess. vi.).   Thus shall the peasant enjoy
and use such land in peace, and undisturbed.
But when the lord hath need of the peasant's
services, the peasant shall be willing and
obedient to him before others ; but it shall be
at the hour and the time when it shall not be
to the hurt of the peasant, who shall do his
lord service for a befitting price.

Eighth Article.

" Eighthly, there are many among us who are
opprest in that they hold lands and in that
these lands will not bear the price on them, so
that the peasants must sacrifice that which
belongeth to them, to their undoing.   We desire
that the lordship will let such lands be seen by
honourable men, and will fix a price as may be
just in such wise that the peasant may not have
his labour in vain, for every labourer is worthy
of his hire (Matt. x.).

Ninth Article.

" Ninthly, do we suffer greatly concerning
misdemeanours in that new punishments are laid
upon us.   They punish us not according to

the circumstance of the matter, but sometimes from great envy, from the unrighteous favouring of others. We would be punished according to ancient written law, and according to the thing transgressed, and not according to respect of persons (Isa. x.; Eph. vi.; Luke iii.; Jer. xvi.).

Tenth Article.

" Tenthly, we suffer in that some have taken to themselves meadows and arable land, which belong to a community. We will take the same once more into the hands of our communities wheresoever it hath not been honestly purchased. But hath it been purchased in an unjust manner, then shall the case be agreed upon in peace and brotherly love according to the circumstance of the matter.

Eleventh Article. .

"Eleventhly, would we have the custom called the death-due utterly abolished, and will never suffer or permit that widows and orphans shall be shamefacedly robbed of their own, contrary to God and honour, as happeneth in many places and in divers manners. They have cut us

short of what we possessed and should protect,
and they have taken all. God will no longer
suffer this, but it must be wholly ended. No
man shall, henceforth, be compelled to give
aught, be it little or much, as death-due (Deut.
xiii. ; Matt. viii. ; Isa. x. 23).

TWELFTH ARTICLE.

" Twelfthly, it is our conclusion and final
opinion, if one or more of the Articles here set
up be not according to the Word of God, we
will, where the same articles are proved as
against the Word of God, withdraw therefrom,
so soon as this is declared to us by reason and
Scripture ; yea, even though certain Articles
were now granted to us, and it should hereafter
be found that they were unjust, they shall be
deemed from that hour null and void and of
none effect. The same shall happen if there
should be with truth found in the Scripture yet
more Articles which were against God and a
stumbling-block to our neighbour, even though
we should have determined to preserve such
for ourselves, and we practice and use ourselves
in all Christian doctrine, to which end we pray
God the Lord who can vouchsafe us the same

and none other. The peace of Christ be with us all."

Such are the celebrated "Twelve Articles". Such was the form in which they made the round of the countryside throughout Germany. They are moderate enough in all conscience, it must be admitted. It will be noticed that they embody the main demands of the Black — Forest peasants, already quoted. The same may be said of other formulations of peasant requirements. As I have said, they are supposed to have been drawn up, with all the Biblical phraseology and references as here given, at the small imperial town of Memmingen, in March, 1525, and it is further supposed, though this is somewhat uncertain, that they are at least mainly from the pen of the Swiss pastor, Schappeler, who is known to have been present at the conference at Memmingen, and who was one of the most prominent advocates of the peasant cause in south Germany. But although this was the usual form and content of the "Twelve Articles," and a form which seems to have been everywhere the most popular, it may be mentioned that it was supplemented, and perhaps in one or two cases superseded, in certain districts by other versions. As among the most important of these variations we may note the twelve demands formulated by the peasants of Elsass-Lothringen. They have the merit of being short and to the point, and divested of all sermonising, and are as follows :—

1. Gospel shall be preached according to the true faith.

2. No tithes shall be given—neither great nor small.

3. There shall be no longer interest and no longer dues, more than one gulden in twenty [five per cent.].

4. All waters shall be free.

5. All woods and forests shall be free.

6. All game shall be free.

7. None shall any longer be in a state of villeinage.

8. None shall obey any longer any prince or lord, but such as pleaseth him, and that shall be the emperor.

9. Justice and right shall be as of old time.

10. Should there be one having authority who displeaseth us, we would have the power to set up in his place another as it pleaseth us.

11. There shall be no more death-dues.

12. The common lands which the lords have taken to themselves *shall again become common lands.*

The idea of there being no lord but the emperor, at the time very popular amongst constitutional reformers, here finds direct expression. The articles, it will be noticed, are also more drastic than those given in the classical version.

The movement was frequently inaugurated in a village by the reading of the " Twelve Articles " in the ale-house or wine-room, or it might be in the open air. They were everywhere received with acclamation, and the ablebodied among the villagers usually formed themselves straightway into a fighting contingent of the " Evangelical Brotherhood ".

The " Twelve Articles " proper, as will be seen, were exclusively agrarian in character; they dealt with the grievances of the peasant against his lor , lay or ecclesiastic, but had nothing to say on the social problems and the ideas of political reconstruction agitating the mind of the landless proletarian or the impoverished handicraftsman within the walls of the towns. The many small, and, according

to our notions, even diminutive, townships
spread over central and southern Germany
had, it is true, many points of contact with the
agrarian revolution, but they none the less had
their own special point of view, which was also
in the main that of the larger towns. As we
already know, every town had its *Ehrbarkeit*
or patriciate, which often monopolised the seats
of the council (*Rath*) and all the higher
municipal offices. Many towns, even among
the small ones above referred to, had a discontented section of poor guildsmen, and
most had a proportionately larger or smaller
contingent of precariously employed proletarians,
who had either no municipal status at all, or
who had at best to content themselves with
that form of bare citizenship which conferred
on them and theirs no more than the mere right
of residence. The fact of living within fortified
town walls, however small the area they
enclosed, seemed itself to have the effect of
creating a distinction between the townsman
and the dweller in the open country, who in
time of war had at best to secure his family and
possessions in the fortified churchyard of his
village. Hence, in spite of the strong bond of

sympathy and common interest between the poor townsman and the peasant—a sympathy which as soon as the agrarian movement had begun to make headway showed solid fruits— it is clear that a programme that might suffice for the latter would not for the former. No sooner, therefore, did the towns begin to play a serious part in the revolutionary movement that the peasantry had inaugurated, than we find entering into it the new elements of a political, and, in some cases, of a religious-utopian character, elements which we fail to observe in the great peasant charter, the "Twelve Articles" itself, and only sporadically in the other subsidiary and local agrarian programmes.

Among the projects of political revolution to which the year 1525 gave birth, the foremost place is occupied by the "Evangelical Divine Reformation" of the empire, sketched out by two men, both of them townsmen of position and education, by name Wendel Hipler and Friedrich Weigand. These men embodied in their scheme, in definite form, the average aspirations of the revolutionary classes of the towns. As we have seen, the idea of centrali-

sation and of an equality based on a bureaucratic constitution was present in the spurious
reformation of Friedrich III., as in all the
new political tendencies of the time. As was
only to be expected, it entered into the general
revolutionary scheme drawn up by the two men
above named and designed to be laid before the
projected congress of peasant and town delegates to be held at Heilbronn. They both of
them had held office at feudal courts. Wendel
Hipler had been chancellor and secretary to
the Count of Hohenlohe and chief clerk to the
Palatinate. Friedrich Weigand had been a prominent court functionary of the Archbishop of
Mainz They both threw themselves energetically into the new movement. Their marked
intellectual superiority and practical knowledge
of tactics is shown by their endeavours to effect
a union on the basis of a definite plan of action
between the various peasant encampments, as
also in their conceptions of the proper position
to take up towards their princely and ecclesiastical adversaries. The aim of Hipler and
Weigand, as of most contemporary political
reformers, was to strengthen the power of the
emperor at the expense of the feudal estates.

Weigand, whilst supporting the general view of compelling princes and lords to humble themselves to becoming simple members of the Evangelical League, conceived the idea of specially enlisting the lower nobility and the towns against the princes. It is probable enough that this project was debated in the standing committee of the movement, which sat during the greater part of its course at the imperial town of Heilbronn, and of which Hipler and Weigand were members, but respecting the proceedings of which we have little information. Weigand appears also to have broached the idea of an agreement being arrived at by a remodelled *Reichsregiment*, manned by representatives of the lower nobility, of the towns, and of the peasantry.

The actual scheme of reconstruction drawn up by these two men was based upon the "Reformation of Kaiser Friedrich III." The language in which it is couched is studiously moderate, but the Biblical and pietistic phraseology of the "Twelve Articles" is almost entirely wanting. Whilst it embraces the agrarian demands of the peasants, these are merely incorporated as an element in the general

scheme of reform. The stress is laid on the
litical side of things—on the notions ſ
equality before the law, of reformed administration, and of national or imperial unity. The
secularisation of the empire is insisted on ;
the ecclesiastical property is to be confiscated
to the benefit of all needy men and of the
common good. Priests or pastors are to be
chosen by the community. They are to receive
a seemly stipend, but are to be excluded from
all political or juridical functions. Princes and
lords are to be reformed in the sense that the
poor man should be no longer oppressed by
them. At the same time, a distinction between
the estates was not to be entirely abolished.
In this case, as in that of the " Twelve Articles,"
the moderation or opportunism of the official
document is noteworthy when contrasted with
the more sweeping and radical measures which
were demanded in definite form by certain of
the men and sections of the revolutionary
party, and which, especially in northern and
central Germany, seemed at times to animate
the whole movement. In the Wendel Hipler
project, indeed, a fourfold social division of the
empire is proposed, consisting of ((1)) princes,

counts and barons; (2) knights and squires; (3) townships; ((4)) rural communities. Equal justice is to be meted out to all. But princes and barons, while retaining their nominal rank, shall cease to possess independent power and shall hold their positions merely as functionaries and servants of the emperor, the mediæval representative of German unity. As a necessary consequence, all rights of treaty, of jurisdiction, of coinage, or of levying tolls, appertaining to the separate estates, as such, shall cease to exist. An imperial coinage is to be established, with separate mints in different parts of the empire, bearing, in all cases, on the obverse the imperial eagle, and only on the reverse the armorial bearings of the prince or town within whose territory the particular mint happens to be situated. Customs dues, passage dues, direct and indirect taxes of every description are to cease. The emperor alone shall every ten years have the right of taxation. Justice is to be thoroughly reformed throughout the empire. Below the supreme court of the empire, the *Kammergericht*, are to be four subordinate courts; below these, four territorial courts; below these again four so-called "free courts, the administrative basis of the whole being the courts or open tribunals of the township and of the village-community. Whilst the higher judicial functions are allowed to be retained by the nobility and their assessors, every tribunal, from the highest to the lowest, is to be manned by sixteen persons, judges and jurors. Doctors of the Roman law are to be rigidly excluded from judicial functions and restricted to lecturing on their science at the universities. A thorough reform, in a democratic sense, of township and communal government is postulated. All mortgages on land are to be redeemable on payment down, of a sum amounting to twenty years' interest.

Such are the leading features of the reform project drawn up by Wendel Hipler and Friedrich Weigand for the consideration of the delegates from the townships and villages which should have come together in the month of June at Heilbronn. The congress in question was destined never to take place. The whole movement was, at the time it should have been held, in a state of imminent collapse, even in those districts where it had not already been crushed.

More agrarian and far more drastic in its revolutionary character was the plan of reform put forward by Michael Gaismayr, the intellectual leader of the revolt in Tyrol, in the Archbishopric of Salzburg, and in the Austrian hereditary territories generally. Michael Gaismayr, who was the son of a squire of Sterzing, had been secretary to the Bishop of Brixen. As soon as matters began to stir in the regions of the Eastern Alps, Gaismayr threw himself into the movement and ultimately became its chief. But it is noteworthy that, radical as were the demands he put forward, neither his activity nor his scheme of reform extended far outside the Tyrol and the neighbouring territories. This being the case, it is only natural that his revolutionary plans should be mainly of an agrarian type. All castles and all town-walls and fortifications were to be levelled with the ground, and henceforth there were to be no more towns, but only villages, to the end that no man should think himself better than his neighbour. A strong central government was to administer public affairs. There was to be one university at the seat of government, which was to devote itself exclusively to Biblical studies. The calling of the merchant was to be forbidden, so that none might besmirch themselves with the sin of usury. On the other hand, cattle-breeding, husbandry, vine-culture, the draining of marshes, and the reclaiming of waste lands were to be encouraged ; nay, were to constitute the exclusive occupations of the inhabitants of the countries concerned. All this is to a large extent an outcome of the general tendency of mediæval communistic thought, with its Biblical colouring, and would-be resuscitation of primitive Christian conditions, or what were believed to have been such. It is the true development of the tradition of the English Lollards, and still more directly of the Bohemian Taborites.

The classical expression, however, of the religious-utopian side of the Peasants War, and, indeed, of the closing period of the Middle Ages generally, is to be found in the doctrines and social theory of Thomas Münzer, which played so great a part in the Thuringian revolt, especially in the town of Mühlhausen, and which subsequently formed the theoretical basis of the anabaptist rising, as exemplified in the " Kingdom of God " in Münster. Since, how-

ever, we shall devote a special chapter to the
Thuringian episode of the Peasants War, with
particular reference to Thomas Münzer and his
career, it is unnecessary to deal at length with
it here. It is sufficient to say that if in the
political plan of constitution formulated by
Hipler and Weigand we have more especially
the revolution as it presented itself to the mind
of the townsman—just as in the *Twelve Articles*
we have its formulation from the moderate
peasant point of view, and in the scheme
of Gaismayr the more radical expression of
peasant aspirations as voiced by a man of
education and intellectual capacity—so in the
doctrines of Münzer we have both sides of the
movement fused and presented in the guise of
a religious utopia, on the traditional lines of
mediæval communism, but of a more thorough-
going and systematic character, the elaboration
of which, however, was reserved for Münzer's
anabaptist successors.

In the town-movement. as exemplified in the
Hipler-Weigand scheme, the stress of which
was political, the main ideas are on the lines of
the then trend of historic evolution—*i.e.,* towards
centralisation and bureaucratic administration,

equality before the law, etc. On the other hand, the distinctively peasant programme, as Lasalle has pointed out, was in the main reactionary, harking back as it did to the old village community with its primitive communistic basis, an institution which was destined to pass away in the natural course of economic development. The old group-holding of land, with communal property generally, was necessarily doomed to be gradually superseded by those individualistic rights of property that form the essential condition of the modern capitalist world.

In addition to the men who may be considered as the intellectual chiefs of the social revolt, we must not ignore the influence of those who were primarily religious reformers or sectaries, but who, notwithstanding, took sides with the social movement and formed a powerful stimulus throughout its course. The influence of the new religious doctrines, and of many of their preachers on the current of affairs is unmistakable to the most casual student of the period. As prominent types of this class of agitator, two names may be taken—that of Andreas Bodenstein, better known from his birthplace as Karlstadt, and that of Balthasar

Hubmayer. The first-named was born at Karlstadt, Franconia, about 1483, was educated in Rome and became a Professor of Theology at Wittenberg. Drawn into the vortex of the Lutheran movement at an early age, he soon developed into a partisan of the extreme sects, and of the social doctrines which almost invariably accompanied them. Karlstadt, who was somewhat older than Luther, was twice rector of his university, besides being canon and archdeacon of the celebrated *Stifskirche* at Wittenberg. He it was who in his official capacity conferred the degree of doctor upon Luther. Karlstadt enjoyed general esteem in the university. Though at first he was closely identified with Luther, the objects of the two men were probably different even at the outset. Luther was only concerned with the freeing of the soul; the theological interest with him outweighed every other. Karlstadt, on the contrary, though primarily a theologian, was still more concerned for the bodily welfare of his fellow Christians and for the establishment of a system of righteousness in this world. Luther had always regarded the authorities as his mainstay; Karlstadt appealed to the people.

In theology and ecclesiastical matters as in social views, Karlstadt was essentially revolutionary, while Luther was the mere reformer. Finally, the tendency of Luther was to become more conservative or opportunist with years, while, on the contrary, Karlstadt became more revolutionary. As Luther placed the Bible above Church tradition, Karlstadt placed the inner light of the soul above the Bible. Indeed, in his utterances respecting the latter, he anticipated many of the points of modern criticism.

While Luther was in the Wartburg, the mystics of Zwickau, the friends of Thomas Münzer came to Wittenberg. This was the turning-point with Karlstadt. Carried away by these enthusiasts, a new world seemed to open up before him. Theology lost its importance; life and political action became all in all. He now rejected all human learning as worthless and injurious; in the dress of a peasant or handicraftsman he went now among the people. That man should throw off all learning, all human authority, and should return to natural conditions, became henceforth his central teaching. In fact, his was the Rousseauite doctrine before its time. In fanatical iconoclasm he had scarcely an equal.

At length he was compelled to leave Wittenberg. He repaired to the farm of his father-in-law and worked as a labourer. The life of the husbandman and the handicraftsman he proclaimed as the only worthy one. He demanded that all ecclesiastical goods should be confiscated for the benefit of the poor. This new departure naturally offended Luther, and the inevitable rupture between the two men occurred on Luther's return to Wittenberg. Eventually, Karlstadt betook himself first to Orlamunda and then to Rothenburg on the Tauber, just as the revolutionary movement was beginning there, into which he energetically threw himself. He was subsequently compelled to conceal himself in the houses of friends in the town, escaping the hot pursuit of the reaction by letting himself down by a rope at night from the city wall.

Balthasar Hubmayer, born in the Bavarian town of Friedberg, near Augsburg, in the last quarter of the fifteenth century, began life as a learned theologian, and after teaching at the University of Friedberg became prorector of the University of Ingolstadt. He was then made chief preacher of the cathedral at Regensburg, where he initiated an anti-Jewish campaign, which resulted in the invasion of the Jewish quarter of the town and the total demolition of the synagogue. On the site of the latter a chapel was built in honour of the "fair Mary," the image contained in which had the reputation of effecting miraculous cures. Popular excitement caused by this led to a scandal (see *German Society*, pp. 268-271). This was in the year 1516. Shortly after the outbreak of the Reformation, being attracted by the latter, he left his post at Regensburg and became preacher in the little town of Waldshut on the borders of the Black Forest. About the same time, he made the acquaintance of Zwingli and the Swiss reformers, and soon assumed the character of an energetic apostle of the new doctrines. The citizens of Waldshut, together with the clergy of the town and surrounding districts, acclaimed him with enthusiasm. He became the hero and prophet of Waldshut. Such was his success in his new capacity that the Austrian authorities at Ensisheim, the seat of the Austrian Government in south-west Germany, became alarmed, and demanded the extradition of the popular preacher as a dangerous agitator. This was refused by the town. Hubmayer, however, insisted upon leaving "to the end that no man may be prejudiced or injured on my account, and that ye may preserve rest and peace". Accordingly, on the 17th of August, 1524, accompanied by the blessings and plaudits of the townsfolk, he rode out of the eastern gate. A small body of armed men were in readiness to receive him from the hands of the Waldshuters, and to conduct him to the Swiss town of Schaffhausen, where he found safety and a favourable reception.

Meanwhile, as we have seen, Hans Müller von Bulgenbach, with his peasant bands, had fraternised with the people of Waldshut, and the Peasants War began to threaten. The result of the situation was that, notwithstanding hostile preparations, the Austrian Government found it prudent for a while to let Waldshut alone, more especially as the Swiss cantons of Schaffhausen and Zurich showed signs of moving in its favour. Emboldened by immunity, the Waldshuters recalled their favourite

preacher. He was received, as an official
document of the time states, " with drums, pipes
and horns, and with such pomp as though
he were the emperor himself". A great feast
was given him in the guildhall, and general
rejoicing followed. About this time either
Thomas Münzer himself or some of his followers
who were agitating in the Black Forest districts,
appear to have visited Waldshut. Hubmayer
now became an enthusiastic partisan and apostle
of the new social doctrines of the realisation of
the Kingdom of God upon earth, in the shape
of a Christian commonwealth based on equality
of status and community of goods. Hubmayer
threw himself with renewed zeal into the
agitation for the cause to which he had been
won over by Münzer or his disciples.

The clergy more especially showed themselves
receptive for the new doctrines. In fact, we have
taken Karlstadt and Hubmayer as the most
eminent types of a class of reforming priest—
reforming in a social and political no less than
in a theological sense—which at the time of
which we write had numerous representatives
throughout Germany. All developments of the
social movement found their advocates among

the revolted priesthood—the moderate and immediate demands of the peasants as expressed
in the official *Twelve Articles*, the political and
administrative reformation of the empire upon
which the Hipler-Weigand scheme lays so
much stress, and, perhaps more than all, the
religious-economic utopianism of which Thomas
Münzer was the leading exponent.

CHAPTER IV.

THE MOVEMENT IN SOUTH GERMANY.

THE heads of the Swabian League sitting in the imperial town of Ulm were glad enough to keep up the farce of negotiations with the peasants, in accordance with the principle already laid down by the Archduke of Austria, namely, that of quieting them with promises and vague hopes until preparations for taking the field should be completed. Truchsess, the head of the military forces of the league, was meanwhile straining every nerve to get fighting men to join his standard. As a contemporary manuscript expressly has it, "they kept the peasants at bay with words so long as they could, and armed meanwhile to attack them". But the *landesknechte* [1] employed by Truchsess were inclined to be mutinous. Their pay was in arrears, and they were especially indisposed to

---

[1] *Landesknechte* or *lanzknechte* I shall in future throughout this work translate by its nearest English equivalent— *free-lances.*

take the field against the peasants, the class from which most of them sprang, and whose grievances they well appreciated. Still, by dint of threats, promises and money, Truchsess at length succeeded in getting together a force of 8000 foot and 3000 horse. By the ،end of March the peasants, on their side, began to weary of the interminable negotiations with the league at Ulm, whose object was now only too apparent, and determined to begin active operations. Truchsess, fearing lest the body encamped in the district known as the *Ried*, and called from its place of origin the "Baltringer contingent," might cut off his retreat to his own castle and domains and possibly invade them, determined to attack this section first. His relations with his own tenants seem to have been on the whole fairly good, and he appears to have left his family at the Waldsee.

As we have already seen, the Baltringer or *Ried* contingent formed one of the three sections of the " Evangelical Peasant Brotherhood," the other two being the Black Forest and the Lake contingents. But in the marshy district where the Baltringer division was encamped, Truchsess could not transport his heavy guns easily nor manœuvre his cavalry with effect. All he could do, therefore, was to send a detachment of foot under Frowen Von Hutten to attack them. The peasants retired to a favourable position in the hope of inducing Truchsess to risk his whole force on the treacherous ground. He remained, however, where he was, contenting himself with sending out a foraging party which plundered a few villages, but which was eventually cut off by a body of peasants and its members either killed or driven back into their camp. The object the leader of the Swabian army had in view was to draw the main peasant force into firm open country and compel them to engage in a pitched battle, knowing that under such circumstances they would be at a hopeless disadvantage. To this end he sent sundry spies in the form of messengers into the peasant camp, but the insurgents, though they answered peaceably, proceeded to entrench themselves still more securely behind a wood. The peasants further endeavoured to induce Truchsess's free-lances to desert to their camp by means of secret negotiations. They were, they said, their sons and brothers, and this, in

fact, was the case. Most of the foot-soldiery
of the time was recruited out of poor town
proletarians or impoverished peasants' sons, who,
in many cases as a last resort, had taken to the
trade of arms and were prepared to serve any
master for a few hellers a day and the hope of
booty. But, although this was their only chance
of victory—to induce experienced fighting men
to enter their ranks—many of their number
were averse to being led by, or even to having
in their company, any free-lances. The peasant
leaders were partly jealous of the latter's
superiority in war to themselves, while many
of the rank and file dreaded their dissolute
habits, for which they had an evil notoriety.
Wendel Hipler and the far-seeing heads of
the movement strove in vain to effect an
understanding between the free-lances and the
peasants. Their ways of life were different,
and, though both belonged to the people, a
certain mutual distrust could not be surmounted.

Finally, after a short and indecisive passage
of arms with the main Baltringer contingent,
Truchsess withdrew his forces in the direction
of the little town of Leipheim, in the neighbourhood of which an important detachment of

insurgents was commanded by the preacher Jakob_Wehe. Wehe was an enthusiastic up-holder of the peasant claims, and a prudent and energetic leader in action. He had already constituted a war-chest and a reserve fund. A train of sixty waggons, containing provisions and material of war, followed his detachment, which, in spite of the admonitions of their leader, showed itself not averse to excesses. The worthy priest had as his goal to unite with two other bodies encamped not far distant, to march on Ulm, and to seize that important imperial city, the seat of the heads of the Swabian League, whose patrician council had, moreover, shown itself so unsympathetic to the popular cause. His immediate objective, however, was the town of Weissenhorn. In Weissenhorn, as in all the towns, the wealthier guildsmen and the patriciate were on the side of the Swabian League. A garrison of 340 horsemen had been hastily thrown into the town by the Count Palatine. The gates were remorselessly shut against the peasants, the utmost concession made being the passing of bread and wine over the wall. Hearing of the near approach of Truchsess, and aware of the hopelessness of attempting to withstand his cavalry charge in the open field, Wehe decided to retreat on Leipheim, where he had entrench-ments.

On the following day a detachment stormed the castle of Roggenburg, making them-selves drunk on the contents of the wine-cellars. In this condition they destroyed the church, with its organ and costly plate, making bands for their hose out of the church banners and vestments. One of their number donned the chasuble and biretta of the Abbot of Roggenburg, and, seated on the altar, made his comrades do him homage. This besotted jesting went on the whole day. Another detachment, also on plunder bent, was cut off by some horsemen of the league and partly destroyed and partly taken prisoners to Ulm.

Jakob Wehe, anxious to gain time, sent by a trusty messenger the following letter to the council of the league at Ulm :—·

"As warriors of understanding and experi-ence, ye will easily see that the assembly of peasants waxeth ever greater with time, and that such a multitude may not readily be compelled. That which hath happened that

is unmete doth with truth grieve us and our
brethren in other places, who have been
innocently moved thereto, but to the end that
further mischief may be prevented, we entreat
that the league shall be a true furtherer of
God's glory and of peace. We will also ourselves, so far as in us lies, zealously do our
utmost with other assemblies that complaints
should be heard by God-fearing and understanding men, who hate time-serving and love
the common weal, and that all grievances shall be
made straight in peace and by judicial decisions."

The above letter had scarcely reached Ulm
before "Herr George" with his army was
already within sight of Leipheim. Here the
peasants were entrenched 3000 strong. The
town was already in their possession. The
camp was some distance outside and had on its
right the river, on its left the wood. Its front
was covered by a marsh, and behind it was a
barricade of waggons. A vanguard of horsemen was kept at bay, but, as soon as the
peasants saw Truchsess with his whole army
advancing on them, they decided to retreat
within the walls to await reinforcements. The
retreat was only partially successful. The

peasants carried indeed their dead and wounded with them and buried the former in a ditch by the roadside. About 2000 succeeded in reaching Leipheim, whilst about 1000 were either driven into the Danube and drowned or cut down in the field. Truchsess now made direct for Leipheim, which he decided to storm. The inhabitants, however, lost courage, sending an old man and some women to beg for mercy. The general of the league forces answered that they must surrender themselves at discretion, and first of all hand over to him their pastor and captain, Jakob Wehe, terms which were agreed to. No sooner did Wehe see the turn things had taken than, gathering together some 200 florins, he bethought himself of escape. His parsonage was built against the town wall, whence a secret subterranean passage led under the wall down to the Danube. Of this he availed himself in the company of a friend and succeeded in reaching a cave known to him in a rock on the banks of the river, where he remained in hiding. The town was entered, but under conditions causing great discontent to a portion of Truchsess's men, for the free-lances were not allowed to plunder as they had been promised in the event of the town being taken by storm. On Wednesday, the 5th of April, the neighbouring town of Günzburg, which had also gone with the peasants, capitulated to the league, having to pay in all a ransom amounting to 1000 gold gulden. Three of the leaders taken prisoners at Leipheim and four at Günzburg were condemned to death.

Meanwhile, search was made everywhere for Jakob Wehe in vain, until his whereabouts were disclosed to some free-lances by the barking of a dog outside his retreat. The offer of the 200 florins he had with him proved of no avail to free him. His captors took him bound on a hurdle to their master at Bubesheim, where he was condemned to share the fate of the seven other captives spoken of above. On the 5th of April towards evening, they were taken to a flowery meadow lying between Leipheim and Bubesheim to be executed. As Master Jakob was led forward to the block, Truchsess turned to him with the words : " Sir pastor, it had been well for thee and us hadst thou preached God's word, as it beseemeth, and not rebellion ". " Noble sir," answered the preacher, "ye do me wrong. I have not preached rebellion, but God's word." "I am otherwise informed," observed Truchsess, as his chaplain stepped forward to receive the confession of the condemned man. Wehe turned to those around, stating that he had already confessed to his Maker and commended his soul to Him. To his fellow-sufferers he observed : " Be of good cheer, brethren, we shall yet meet each other to-day in Paradise, for when our eyes seem to close, they are really first opening ". After having prayed aloud, concluding with the words : " Father, forgive them, for they know not what they do," he laid himself on the block, and in another moment his head fell in the long grass.

The preacher of Günzburg, who had also taken part in the movement, and an old soldier of fortune, who had joined the rebels, were brought forward in their turn to submit to the same fate, when the old soldier, turning to Truchsess, observed : " Doth it not seem to thee a little late in the day, noble lord, for one to lose one's head ? " This humorous observation saved the lives of himself and the preacher. The latter was carried about with the troops in a cage, until he had bought his freedom with eighty gulden. He lost, however, the right of preaching and of riding on horseback!

Meanwhile, the free-lances of "Herr George" were becoming more mutinous every day. They had not made the booty they expected, and their pay was long outstanding. The danger to the commander's own castles—notably the Waldburg or Waldsee, where his wife and child resided—was imminent. Still the free-lances would not budge. Some of his noble colleagues and neighbours took the matter in hand and occupied his territories. It was, however, too late. The Waldsee had capitulated to the Baltringer and bought itself off for 4000 gulden. The attacking party did not know that the countess and her child were located within, or it would probably have gone badly with them. In the course of a few days, the League having undertaken to pay the month's arrears of wages, the matter with the free-lances was arranged.

The peasants, however, were by no means disheartened by the check that their cause had received at Leipheim. Truchsess, with a force

of double their number, including cavalry, and
well-equipped with artillery, might succeed in
crushing one body, but, with his eight or nine
thousand men, he could not be everywhere at
the same time. A few days after, Truchsess
eagerly seized an opportunity of negotiating a
truce with the so-called Lake contingent and the
Hegauers, which relieved him for the moment
and of which we shall have occasion to speak
later on. Just at this juncture the movement
was rapidly reaching its height. It was
computed that no fewer than 300,000 peasants,
besides necessitous townsfolk, were armed and
in open rebellion. On the side of the nobles,
no adequate force was ready to meet the
emergency. In every direction were to be seen
flaming castles and monasteries. On all sides
were bodies of armed country-folk, organised
in military fashion, dictating their will to the
countryside and the small towns, whilst disaffection was beginning to show itself in a threatening
manner among the popular elements of not a
few important cities. The victory of the league
at Leipheim had done nothing to improve the
situation from the point of view of the governing
powers. In Easter week, 1525, it looked indeed

as if the "Twelve Articles," at least, would
become realised, if not the Christian Commonwealth dreamed of by the religious sectaries
established throughout the length and breadth
of Germany. Princes, lords and ecclesiastical
dignitaries were being compelled far and wide
to save their lives, after their property was
probably already confiscated, by swearing allegiance to the Christian League or Brotherhood
of the peasants and by countersigning the
Twelve Articles and other demands of their
refractory villeins and serfs. So threatening
was the situation that the Archduke Ferdinand
began himself to yield in so far as to enter into
negotiations with the insurgents. These were
mostly carried on through the intermediary of
a certain Walther Bach, one of the peasant
leaders in the Allgäu and an ex-soldier in the
Austrian service. The only result, however,
was that Walther Bach fell under the suspicion
of his followers and was shortly afterwards
deposed from his position by them.

In brilliancy of get-up, none equalled Hans
Muller from Bulgenbach and his two colleagues,
Hans Eitel and Johann Zügelmuller, and their
followings. We read of purple mantles and scarlet

birettas with ostrich plumes as the costume of the
leaders, of a suite of men in scarlet dress, of a
vanguard of ten heralds gorgeously attired. This
combined contingent of the Black Forest and
surrounding districts went from one success to
another, taking castle after castle, including as
before mentioned that of Lupfen, the seat of
the Countess Helena of "snail-shell" notoriety,
who was the alleged proximate cause of the
insurrection. After leaving peasant garrisons
in all the places captured, Hans Müller bethought himself of attacking Radolfzell, where,
as we have seen, a considerable number of
nobles and clergy had taken refuge. He
does not seem, however, to have immediately
attempted any formal siege of the town, but
simply to have cut off all communications and
laid waste the surrounding country. Indeed,
as is truly observed by Lamprecht (*Deutsche
Geschichte*, vol. v., p. 343), "the peasant revolts
were, in general, less of the nature of campaigns,
or even of an uninterrupted series of minor
military operations, than of a slow process of
mobilisation, interrupted and accompanied by
continual negotiations with the lords and princes
—a mobilisation which was rendered possible

by the standing right of assembly and of carrying arms possessed by the peasants ".

The duchy of Würtemberg, the home of the " poor Conrad," was, as we have seen, ripe for insurrection at the time of Duke Ulrich's abortive attempt to regain possession of his coronet. While Truchsess was operating about Leipheim and holding the Baltringer contingent at bay, the Würtemberg authorities, spiritual and temporal, found themselves face to face with a threatening peasant population, everywhere gathering under arms. The assembly of the estates of the duchy had been called together at Stuttgart to deliberate on the matter. The result was the immediate despatch of an embassy to Ulm to represent their case to the council of the Swabian League. The latter replied sympathetically, but observed that the regency of the archduke and the estates themselves were largely to blame for the position of affairs, pointing out that, while every member of the league was by the terms of its oath obliged to keep its most important castles and towns in a state of thorough defensive repair, in Würtemberg there was not a single castle which was capable of holding out, and that the frontiers especially were entirely exposed. All that they could promise was that, as soon as Truchsess had settled affairs in Upper Swabia, he should come to their assistance. The allegations were quite true ; the duchy was absolutely denuded of fighting men through the Italian war, the archduke having taken no care or having been unable to replace those he had sent to his brother with any other sufficient force. The finances of the country, bad as they had been before, were now almost entirely exhausted by the resistance to Duke Ulrich's invasion. Turning from the league to the archduke, the estates were similarly met by promises, but no assistance was forthcoming.

Meanwhile, the small towns were everywhere opening their gates without resistance to the peasants, between whom and the poorer inhabitants an understanding usually existed. Here as elsewhere, defenceless castles were falling into the hands of the insurgents, who waxed fat with plunder, and in many cases drank themselves senseless with the contents of rich monastic wine-cellars. In the valley of the Neckar an innkeeper, named Matern Feuerbacher, was chosen as captain of the popular forces. Feuerbacher was compelled to accept the leadership of the insurgents against his will. The nobles in the vicinity of the small town of Bottwar, where Feuerbacher had his inn, knew him well as an honest good-natured person, with whom they even at times conversed, as they sat in his wine-room, and they were by no means averse to the choice the insurgents had made. The innkeeper at first hid himself on the approach of the peasant delegates, who threatened his wife that if her husband did not, on their next demand, consent to place himself at their head, they would plant the ominous stake denoting his outlawry before his door.

Just at this time an event occurred at the little town of Weinsberg, of "faithful wife" fame, near the free imperial city of Heilbronn to the north of the duchy, which constitutes a landmark in the history of the peasant rising. The town-proletariat of Heilbronn had been stirring from February onwards, and by the end of March a good understanding had been arrived at between them and the peasantry of the surrounding country. The leader of the movement here was one Jakob Rohrbach, commonly called by the nick-name of " Jacklein Rohrbach," or sometimes simply " Jacklein ". He kept an inn in a village called Bockingen, a short distance from Heilbronn. He is described as young, well-built, and strong, of burgher descent, and intelligent withal. His reputation as a boon companion was immense, and as he was of a generous nature and treated freely, his popularity, especially with the young people of the district, was enormous. Always of a rebellious disposition, he had had many a tussle with constituted authority. The most serious appears to have been in 1519, when he was accused of stabbing the head man of his village, against whom he had a grievance. For this he was to be arrested and tried, but threatened the constable and the judges that, if they dared to lay hands upon him, the whole place should be burnt to the ground. Knowing that all the countrymen of the neighbourhood were on his side and would very probably put this threat into execution, or, at best, avenge themselves in some other unpleasant way, the local authorities found it prudent to let the matter drop. Jacklein Rohrbach, in short, was the terror of all respectable persons.

8

His chief companions were the sons of the peasantry, whom he saw oppressed on all sides. A village girl, with whom he was in love, was seized by the forest ranger of a neighbouring lord for gathering wild strawberries, maltreated and subsequently ravished. This may have given a deeper colour to his hatred of the aristocrat. In any case, by the end of 1524, Jacklein found his money spent and himself in an apparently hopeless condition economically. At the same time, his hatred of the existing order of society knew no bounds. An ecclesiastic had sought to obtain payment of a debt from Jacklein. The latter had assembled his peasants at Bockingen, and had, in addition, called out some of the town proletarians from Heilbronn in order to prevent the hearing of the case. On the demand of the priest, the council of Heilbronn sent one of their number to Bockingen, who speedily returned with the news that the village was full of armed men at the service of Rohrbach. The council, thereupon, advised the clergyman to let his plaint fall for the time being, as his pursuing it would only lead to a disturbance, which for the moment there was no means of quelling.

This was at the end of March. On the 2nd of April, Rohrbach, who had the previous day repaired with his following to the village of Flein, also in the Heilbronn territory, raised the standard of revolt, and soon had 300 more supporters from the neighbouring villages around him. He had been long in communication with Wendel Hipler and George Metzler, a leader of the Odenwald insurgents, of whom we shall speak presently. Jacklein was now strong enough to compel by threats, or otherwise, the neighbouring places to supply him with men to serve under his standard. As soon as he had gathered together 1500 partisans, he proceeded to join the main body of insurgents in the Schonthal, under the leadership of Metzler. The body was known as the " *Heller Haufen* " which may be translated as the "United Contingent". In the meantime, the bold Jacklein had seized the head-man of Bockingen, thrown him into prison, and set up a new one of his own choosing. As a taste of the good things in store for them, he had also allowed his men to fish out a small lake belonging to a patrician councillor of Heilbronn.

George Metzler, the commander of the

"United Contingent," had been from the beginning of the movement a zealous agitator
and organiser. He was an innkeeper in the
town of Balenberg, and his wine-room was the
resort of all the discontented and insurrectionary
elements of the neighbouring districts.   As
soon as the Swabians had begun to move,
Metzler bound a peasant's shoe (the *Bundschuh*)
to a pole and carried it about the country,
preceded by a man beating a drum. In a
short time he had 2000 men around his
"shoe". This body, which steadily increased,
was given a form of military organisation by
Wendel Hipler (the peasants chancellor), who
now appeared upon the scene, and Metzler was
definitely appointed its commander. Thus,
while some of the other contingents were little
better than hordes, the *Heller Haufen* assumed
more the character of an army. It had its
grades and its judiciary power, and in front of
it was carried the "Twelve Articles," which
all were required to swear to and to sign.
Princes, bishops and nobles had the alternative
offered them of loss of property or life, or of
entrance into the Evangelical Brotherhood.
The two Counts of Hohenlohe, the most

considerable feudal potentates of the neighbourhood, received the challenge in question in the
name of the "United Contingent". On their
scornfully replying that they were ignorant to
what order of animal the "United Contingent"
might belong, Hipler is reported to have given
the following rejoinder : "It is an animal that
usually feedeth on roots and wild herbs,
but which when driven by hunger sometimes
consumeth priests, bishops and fat citizens. It
is very old, but very strange it is that the older
it becometh, by so much doth it wax in strength,
even as with wine. The beast doth ail at times,
but it never dieth. At times, too, it forsaketh
the land of its birth for foreign parts, but early
or late it returneth home again." "Tell my
lords, the counts," added Hipler, it is said, to
the envoys who brought him the message, "that
it is even now come again into Germany, and
that at this hour it pastureth in the Schupfer
valley." On the foregoing message being
returned to them, the counts seem to have
given way. The two brothers, Albrecht and
George, met the delegates of the "United
Contingent," now 8000 strong, in the open air,
and after some negotiations, during which they

endeavoured to persuade the peasants to submit
their grievances to a judicial tribunal, they
re compelled to swear to the " Twelve
Articles ".   This they were required to do
with uplifted hands and to remove their gloves,
whilst the peasants, on the contrary, retained
theirs (probably assumed for the occasion).   By
this oath, the counts were admitted into the
Evangelical Brotherhood.

But these things did not create that profound
impression which constituted the landmark in the
Peasants War before spoken of.   It was the
celebrated " blood-vengeance " of the peasants
in the township of Weinsberg, near Heilbronn.
that did so.   Weinsberg, with its castle, had
been occupied, by the orders of the Archduke,
by Count Ludwig von Helfenstein, whose wife
was the illegitimate daughter of the Emperor
Maximillian and therefore half-sister to the
Emperor Charles and to his brother Ferdinand.
This Helfenstein, who was a young man of
twenty-seven, had seen fifteen years' service in
war and had recently shown himself very active
in killing peasants, wherever he found them
isolated or in small bands.   His recent journey
to Weinsberg had been signalised by several

acts of this description. A number of the citizens of the little town were inclined to open the gates to "the enemy". As a body of peasants appeared before the town demanding admission, Helfenstein without any parley made a sortie with his knights and men-at-arms and massacred them in cold blood. As he heard this, Jacklein Rohrbach is said to have exclaimed : "Death and hell! We shall know how to avenge ourselves on Count Helfenstein for his mode of warfare!" It must be admitted, indeed, that for this act alone Helfenstein richly deserved the fate which afterwards befel him.

On the same day, news arrived in the camp of the "United Contingent" that the brothers, the Counts of Hohenlohe, had refused to supply the force with the pieces of artillery for which it had applied to them and which it so urgently needed. This, coming immediately after the report of Jakob Wehe's execution at Leipheim, excited the indignation of the insurgents against the nobles to fever pitch. The counts had solemnly sworn to maintain and further the peasant cause, and this refusal of theirs to supply the ordnance required was seen in the light of an act of treachery. Jacklein Rohrbach

moved that a sufficient force be sent to storm
and enter "that nest of nobles," Weinsberg.
The proposition was carried, as against that
of going back to punish the Counts Hohenlohe,
as some would have wished. Accordingly, a
large body proceeded in the direction of Weinsberg by way of Neckarsal, which surrendered
to them.   After having pitched its camp, the
" United Contingent " sent an ultimatum to the
former town demanding unconditional surrender.
Helfenstein returned a contemptuous answer.
Shortly after, the wife of a citizen came out
to the peasants, urging them to the attack, and
stating that half the inhabitants were with them
and would open the gates.   Another citizen
offered to show them the weak points in the
town-walls and in the castle.

On the 16th of April, the count and all the
nobles at that time in Weinsberg were placed
by the peasants under a ban.   Helfenstein does
not seem to have believed in a serious attack.
He could not think that mere peasants would
be so daring.   He was awaiting the arrival of
reinforcements from Stuttgart and from the
Palatinate.   Meanwhile, he employed his men
in strengthening the weak parts of the forti-

fications. At break of day, the peasants moved forward from their encampment and established themselves on an eminence overlooking the town. For the last time, heralds were sent. They carried a hat upon a pole. " Open the gates," they cried, " open the town to the ' United Christian Band ' ! If not, remove wife and child, for all that remains in the town must be put to the sword ! " The only answer received was a shot from the walls, which wounded one of the heralds. He had just sufficient strength to crawl back into camp, and, fainting from loss of blood, to cry for vengeance. Within the walls of the township, the knights saddled their horses, and the free-lances made themselves ready. Only five men could be afforded for the defence of the castle, which contained Helfenstein's wife, child and valuables. The rest, not more than seventy or eighty all told, were necessary to defend the walls and gates. The count, with his knights and men-at-arms, appeared in the market-place and exhorted the assembled citizens to remain loyal to him, assuring them that help would come in the course of the day. Knights, citizens and men-at-arms thereupon repaired to the church

—it being Easter Sunday—to hear mass and take the sacrament.

At nine o'clock, before the service was ended, the cry arose that the peasants were advancing on the town. The first to attack was the great 'ranconian hero of the Peasants War, the :night Florian Geyer—of whom we shall hear more presently—with his "black troop," who had come down from the north and effected a juncture with Metzler and the "United Contingent". The point of attack was the castle. Before the defenders had time to set themselves in readiness, a shout was heard from above, and two of Florian Geyer's banners waved from the battlements of the castle, which had been taken by storm. At the same moment, two of the town gates fell before the attack of Jacklein Rohrbach and his comrades. Many of the inhabitants assisted the storming party from within. In a moment, seeing the situation hopeless, Helfenstein sent a monk on to the wall who cried : "Peace, peace!" The only answer returned was : "Death and vengeance!" On hearing these cries, the count bethought himself of flight, but was surrounded by a body of citizens, cursing and threatening him for attempting to leave them in the lurch.

At this moment Jacklein's storming party, mad with fury, dashed up the main street toward the market-place, shouting to the citizens to keep to their houses for that all nobles and men-at-arms were about to be put to death. The knights and men-at-arms had by this time fled into the church for protection, the count with eighteen nobles of his following escaping by a secret staircase into the church-tower. Jacklein's comrades now burst into the church-yard, striking down lords and fighting men right and left. In a few minutes as many as forty had fallen. Finally, they discovered the secret staircase.

" Here we have them altogether," cried Jacklein ; " strike them all dead ! " The knight Dietrich von Weiler stepped forward on the gallery of the church tower, as the peasants burst in upon the fugitives, offering 30,000 gold gulden as ransom.

" An' ye would offer us a tun-full of gold, yet should ye all die ! " shouted the peasants with one consent. " Vengeance for the blood of our fallen brethren ! "

At the next instant a musket shot laid him on the ground. A peasant then beat his brains out with a club. Others were compelled to spring from the top of the church tower, whence they were received on the spears of the peasants below. At last the main body of the " United Contingent " appeared upon the scene, under the command of George Metzler himself, who forthwith gave strict orders that the killing should discontinue, and that only prisoners should be taken. Helfenstein, with his wife and son, were seized, the child receiving a wound from a peasant as he was crossing the churchyard with his captors.

Jacklein begged his leader to allow him and his troop the custody of his prisoners. This was accorded him. The order was now given that all who concealed a nobleman or a free-lance should be put to death. The result was that all were surrendered, with the exception of three, one of whom escaped in woman's clothes, whilst another concealed himself in a stove, and the third, a handsome young fellow, was hidden in a hayloft by a girl. Curiously enough, Jacklein and some of his friends passed the night in this very hayloft, discussing the way in which they would bring about the slaughter of the prisoners taken.

The rank and file now demanded the right to plunder the town, but this was not conceded by Metzler and Hipler, who insisted upon only permitting the plunder of churches and monasteries and castles. In most cases, even where plundering was the order of the day, it was easy to hoodwink these naïve children of the soil. Having, for instance, found a trunk full of gold in the Bürgermeister's house, the innocent countrymen were induced not to lay hands on it by a story that it was a chest the contents of which were destined for almsgiving purposes.

But to booty, drink and women the former boon companion, roisterer and spendthrift, Jacklein Rohrbach, for the moment appeared indifferent. His whole soul seemed possessed by one idea—hatred and vengeance—vengeance on the privileged classes of the existing society. With this object always in view, he imprisoned his captives in a mill near the town wall, resolved to evade Metzler's orders and slay them, if possible, at break of day. Having ascertained that Metzler and the main body of the " United

Contingent" were still sleeping after their heavy drinking bout of the previous evening, Jacklein led his prisoners from the mill to a meadow outside the walls, hard by. They were eighteen in all, mostly knights, with a few free-lances and pages, foremost among them being of course the Count and Countess von Helfenstein and their two-year-old son. The men were all placed shoulder to shoulder in a semi-circle, and sentence of death was passed upon them by Jacklein. It was decided that they should be compelled to "run the gauntlet". This was regarded as a degrading punishment, which was only applied to common soldiers of fortune guilty of some grave criminal offence against military honour. Accordingly, on a signal given by Jacklein, a double row of spears was formed. Jacklein then cried out : " Count Helfenstein, it is your turn to open the dance!" "Mercy!" exclaimed the countess, as with child in her arms she threw herself at Jacklein's feet. " Thou pray'st for mercy for thy husband," cried he ; "it may not be!" Thereupon, he seized the countess by the arm, and throwing her back on the ground, knelt on her bosom, exclaiming : " Behold, brethren, Jacklein Rohrbach kneels

on the emperor's daughter!" "Vengeance!"
shouted the assembled peasants.

"Countess Helfenstein," cried one of their
number, "thy horsemen, thy dogs and thy
huntsmen have trodden down my fields. My
boys opposed you. They were gagged and
carried forth, as though they had been dogs
themselves," and, uttering a cry of "Vengeance," he flung a knife at the countess. It
struck the child in the arm, the blood spurting
into its mother's face. "Mercy, mercy!" the
woman continued to cry, as she rolled on the
ground.

"Count Helfenstein," shouted another peasant, "thou hast thrust my brother into thy
dungeon because, forsooth, he did not bare his
head as thou passedst by! Thou shalt perish!"
"Thou hast harnessed us like oxen to the
yoke! Thou hast caused the hands of my father
to be smitten off, for that he killed a hare on
his own field," shouted another. "Thou hast
wrung the last *heller* out of us," exclaimed
several.

These and other accusations of a like kind,
even if they may not all have been deserved
strictly by Helfenstein himself, certainly were

so by the feudal lords in general whose representative he on this occasion was. At last, the count himself was driven to beg for mercy at the hands of the peasant leader. He offered him his whole fortune and 60,000 gulden in addition, for which he was prepared to pledge the emperor's credit. He swore it on the head of his wife and son. It was now about half an hour before sunrise. "Not for 60,000 tuns of pearls," replied Jacklein. "Kneel down and confess, for thou shalt never again behold the sun!"

"Only wait," cried Melchior Nonnenmacher, a discharged piper of the count's, whose function it had been to play for him at his ancestral castle in Swabia during meals, but who now formed one of Jacklein's bodyguard. "Long enough have I made table music for thee. I know thy favourite tune and have kept it for this thy last dance!" The piper thereupon proceeded to tune his instrument, whilst his former master confessed to a priest. As soon as he had finished the piper seized the count's hat and donned it himself, and, dancing before him, whilst playing his favourite air, led the way to the double file of spears, through which he was condemned to pass. The countess was held upright by two men that she might see her husband fall.

Standing by and taking an active part in the scene was a woman known as the " black Hoffmann," a reputed witch, and one of the most striking dramatic figures of the Peasants War. She was, in respect of deep-seated, savage hatred of prince, noble and prelate, the female counterpart of Jacklein, though her lust of vengeance was, if anything, of a deeper hue, and she seems to have lacked Jacklein's original light-hearted generosity of disposition. Her dark skin and jet-black hair probably gave her her name. She was the cast-off child of a wandering gipsy woman. Her mother had deserted her in Bockingen, in the native village, that is, of Jacklein himself. Here she gained her living by tending cattle, a calling she subsequently abandoned for fortune-telling and kindred arts. She is described as the Egeria of Jacklein, whose purpose she was continuously sharpening. She was usually clad in a black cloak and hood, with a red girdle or sash, the ends of which fluttered in the wind. As soon as Jacklein had formed his band, she joined them as a kind of prophetess who presaged

9

them victory, blessed their weapons, and urged them on to the fight. During the storming of Weinsberg, she had stood upon a neighbouring hill and with outstretched arms had ceaselessly shouted : " Down with the dogs ; strike them all dead ! Fear nothing ! I bless your weapons ! I, the black Hoffmann ! Only strike ! God wills it ! "

The hour of vengeance had now come. As the Count von Helfenstein fell beneath the peasants' spears, seizing a knife from her girdle this strange unsexed fury plunged it into his body, and proceeded to smear the shoes and lances of the peasants with the " fat ". In half an hour the last of the knights and men-at-arms had fallen. As the sun rose, the countess and her young son alone remained.

After Jacklein and his partisans had dis- tributed the clothes of the dead nobles amongst themselves, Jacklein, who had himself assumed the garments of the count, addressed the countess and said : " In a golden chariot camest thou hither ; in a dungcart shalt thou depart hence ! Tell thine emperor this, and greet him from me ! " To this she replied : " I have sinned much and deserved my lot. Christ, our Saviour, also entered Jerusalem amid the shouts of the people, yet soon He went forth bearing His cross, mocked and derided by that very people. That is my consolation. I am a poor sinner and forgive you gladly." She was then stripped and dressed in the rags of a beggar woman, and in this condition, clutching her wounded child to her breast, was thrown on to a dungcart and conveyed to Heilbronn. We may here mention that her son was brought up to the Church, and she herself ended her days in a convent.

The sun having now risen, the peasants' camp within the walls of Weinsberg suddenly awoke to a knowledge of what had happened. A general outcry arose against the execution. A council of war was held, but of what actually passed therein little is known. It would seem, however, that at this time a division arose between the leaders. A "moderate" party, to which Metzler and Hipler belonged, definitely formed itself and appears to have got the upper hand. This party wished to give the knight Gotz von Berlichingen "with the iron hand" the command of all the insurgent bands. Florian Geyer, on the other hand, seems to have been strongly opposed to this step, though whether he was prepared to pursue the policy of Jacklein Rohrbach or approved of his recent action it is not easy to say. Certain is it that, from this moment, he and his "black troop" severed themselves from Metzler, Hipler and the "United Contingent," and returned into the Franconian country. The action of Rohrbach may well have had more behind it than the mere thirst for vengeance, however great the part this motive may have played therein. Rohrbach was an extremist who wished to carry the revolution through to its uttermost end. Respecting this end, his ideas may have been somewhat vague, but there is no doubt that he conceived it as involving the total destruction of the feudal orders, as against any mere partial concessions on their part. He may well, therefore, have wished to force the hand of the peasant council by making them feel that they had "burnt their boats". And, certainly, nothing was more calculated to incense the nobles and cut off the possibility of any compromise being arrived at than his "blood-vengeance" on their order at Weinsberg. As a matter of fact, the immediate effect on the authorities was that of a demoralising terror. The Counts Hohenlohe did not hesitate any longer, but immediately sent the two pieces of ordnance and the ammunition which the " United Contingent" had demanded.

Leaving a detachment in Weinsberg, the latter proceeded to Heilbronn, which city they regarded as already as good as won. They were accompanied by two prisoners, the Counts of Lowenstein, clad in peasant's costume, and bearing white staves in their hands, looking, a contemporary notice states, " as frightened as if they were dead ". The events at Weinsberg had naturally not been without their effect at Heilbronn.· The power of the aristocratic burgher party was completely broken, and the peasants' army entered the gates, after a short parley, almost without resistance. The city council took the oath of allegiance to the " Evangelical Brotherhood," or the " Christian Peasants League" as it was variously termed, and expressed their willingness to negotiate measures with the insurgents and to act as intermediaries towards an understanding with the feudal powers.

Hans Flux, a wealthy baker, a brother-in-law

of George Metzler, was the chief go-between
in the negotiations.   He belonged distinctly to
the moderate party, and he found it not difficult
to persuade the " United Contingent " to adopt
a conciliatory attitude, if only to show their
innocence of the Weinsberg affair.   It was thus
that the understanding was arrived at, the city
council promising to pay a subsidy and to furnish
500 men to the peasant army.   The " Twelve
Articles " were, as a matter of course, to be
sworn to.   Furthermore, it was agreed that the
town should be given into the hands of the
peasants on the condition that no house should
be plundered, save that of the Teutonic knights.
The patricians of the town council, who had
no intention of keeping their oath where it was
possible to break it, no sooner concluded the
bargain than they refused to furnish the force
promised.   Hans Flux, however, who had been
the medium of the negotiations, armed the men
at his own expense.   The situation generally
displeased a number of the peasant army.
Cries of treachery against Flux began to be
heard, especially when it leaked out that he
was negotiating with Hipler and Metzler for
a modification of the " Twelve Articles ".   The

"black Hoffmann" made an attempt one night to assassinate Flux, as he rode from the peasant camp back into the city, but his horse saved him.

An uncertain tradition relates that the last deed of this extraordinary female was the murder of the crier who proclaimed the annulling of the " Twelve Articles " at Bockingen, a month later, after the reaction had gained the day there. Respecting her death nothing definite is known.

According to the terms of the agreement entered into, the Carmelite monastery was to pay a ransom of 3000 gulden and the Clara convent 5000 gulden. Other smaller religious houses were to furnish sums in proportion. The great establishment of the " Knights of the Teutonic Order" was reserved for plunder. The heads of the order and most of the inmates made good their escape. In Heilbronn, as in other towns, the wealthy Teutonic knights were a special object of the hatred of the " common man ". The ferment among the poor citizens, town proletarians and impoverished guildsmen, was immense, as may be imagined. They had long held secret converse

with the peasants and now openly fraternised
with them.[1]

✓ The sacking of the wealthy establishment of
the knights took place under the ægis of the
city council, who sent to see that the place
was not set on fire and that the plundering did
not extend beyond its precincts. A motley
crew of peasants, consisting largely of tenants
of the lands belonging to the order, entered
the house, armed with weapons of destruction.
All documents were torn up and thrown into
the moat. Wine, silver and furniture of all
sorts were dragged out into the courtyard and
sold at an extemporised auction, over which
Jacklein Rohrbach presided. Women carried
away acolytes' garments and priests' vestments,
and cut them up for clothes for themselves and
their children. As soon as the business of
plunder and the sale of the booty was duly

---

[1] On the poverty of some of the proletarians of Heilbronn, an inventory subsequently taken throws some light.
The possessions of one were found to be limited to a bed,
an old wooden bedstead and two pillows, on which six
children were lying. Another with four children had only
a table and a small bed. A third, also with four children,
could only boast an old bedstead, a can, and a piece of
armour.

ended, a feast was spread in the refectory of the house, at which those few of the knights of the order who had remained were compelled to stand by and serve with their hats in their hands.

One peasant, who was sitting at table, remarked to a knight standing behind him: " How now, noble sir? To-day, we are the masters of the Teutonic Order," at the same time giving him a back-handed blow on the paunch, which caused him to stagger back against the wall with a cry. In addition to the furniture, a considerable sum of money was found in the house, of which the tenants of the order claimed the larger share, as having contributed most to the funds. As a matter of fact, a rich booty, sufficient for all, was obtained.

One citizen alone who had been active in the undertaking carried off a chest containing 1400 gulden to his house.

Meanwhile, the negotiations of the moderate party, which centred in the handing over of the command of the " United Contingent " to Gotz von Berlichingen went on apace. Gotz, the hero of Goethe's well-known drama, who was noted for his artificial iron hand (he having lost

his own hand in battle), had been a zealous
partisan of the knights' revolt under Sickingen.
His deeds as a warrior generally were famous,
and he was animated by a special hostility to
the clerical order.   But, unlike Florian Geyer,
he had no real sympathy with the peasants, for
whom at heart he entertained much the same
feelings as any other noble.   Gotz had recently
appealed to the Franconian knighthood to form
a league against the priesthood, and he may
have seen in the peasant revolt a possible
shoeing-horn to his plans.   His immediate
reasons, however, for connecting himself with
the movement were undoubtedly partly compulsion and partly fear.   Nearly all his knightly
colleagues had, from dread of the " common
man,"entered the service of the Swabian League.
Gotz also offered his services to the league
before suffering himself to be nominated to
the commandership on the other side.   According to his own account, which he gives in
his autobiography, it was only through a mis-
understanding that this came to pass at all.
It is true that his statements require to be
taken with some reserve, since the desire, for
obvious reasons, to dissociate himself from any

sympathy with the peasants and their lost cause
is only too apparent throughout the aforesaid
work, which, so far as this episode is concerned,
is couched in an apologetic tone. It is probable
notwithstanding, from all we know of the man,
that the account he gives is substantially true.
On finding his appeal to the Franconian knighthood unsuccessful, he had, it appears, offered
his services to the Count Palatine, his feudal
superior. Immediately after the capture of
Weinsberg, Gotz alleges that he took steps to
save his property and family archives, by having them deposited in a town for safety. As,
however, no town would accept the responsibility in the event of its being sacked, he
abandoned his plan. At the same time he
sent a messenger to the " United Contingent "
to know what he was to expect. The chief
men, as we have seen, were already discussing
among themselves the question of offering him
the leadership. Finding his messenger's return
delayed, he communicated with the marshal of
the Count Palatine, Wilhelm von Habern, asking
him to protect his castle. Gotz's wife, however,
and her sister seem to have mistrusted the
strength of the authorities to cope with the

insurrection. Everywhere around them they saw castles and monasteries falling into the hands of the peasants, so when a letter arrived from the Count Palatine himself, gladly accepting Gotz's offer of service and promising the desired protection, the two women concealed the letter and carefully kept the fact of its arrival from the knight's knowledge. In fact, according to Gotz's own account, his wife categorically denied having received any reply from the count. " Thereupon," he writes, " I feared me much in that I knew not how I should hold myself, the more so in that the story went that the count would make a compact with the peasants."

The upshot was, according to Gotz, that, thinking the proposals he had made to the marshal were rejected by the count and fearing for the safety of himself and his castle, he had, like so many other nobles, consented to join the " Evangelical Brotherhood," and was subsequently *compelled* to take over its command. This was effected almost entirely by the leaders Hipler, Metzler, Berlin (a member of the Heilbronn Council), Flux, and one or two others, amid strong protests from the bulk of the rank and file. With Gotz himself, it was a case of *aut Cæsar, aut nullus.* Non-acceptance, he felt, meant his ruin. The pact between Gotz and the peasant leaders was signed and sealed in an inn at the village of Gundelsheim, whither the contingent had retired after leaving Heilbronn. Gotz narrates in his autobiography how he rode from one company of the peasant army to another, offering to negotiate peace with the authorities, until he came to that consisting of the tenants of the Counts Hohenlohe. " Here I beheld myself," he says, " suddenly encompassed with muskets, spears and halberds, pointed at me. They cried that I should be their captain, an whether I would or no. They compelled me to be their fool and leader, and to the end that I might save my body and my life I must forsooth do as they willed."

Had Gotz been sincere in taking up the cause of the rebellion, there is no doubt that, experienced warrior as he was, he would have been a valuable acquisition. Even as it was, some of his suggestions respecting the maintenance of discipline were in the right direction, but the fact remained that he was acting under compulsion in a cause with which he had no

sympathy, and that his one concern was to
get rid of his responsibility at the first possible
moment, if not actually to betray his trust.

The appointment of Gotz von Berlichingen
was a victory for the moderate party, which had
suddenly acquired prominence owing to the
action of Rohrbach and his followers at Weinsberg. In addition to this, George Metzler,
the trusted leader of the " United Contingent,"
had been influenced in the direction of moderation by the machinations of his wife, as it would
seem, and by the persuasions of her brother,
the wealthy master-baker of Heilbronn. There
is, however, no reason to think that Metzler was
actually a traitor or consciously moved to the
course he took by unworthy motives.

The result soon showed itself in a modification
of the " Twelve Articles". On this Gotz insisted.
With Hans Berlin and Wendel Hipler, and
possibly others, the matter was discussed in a
sort of committee. Certain of the " Articles "
were declared suspended until the imperial
reform which Weigand, Hipler and the Heilbronn permanent committee were sketching out
for the consideration of a general congress
should be decided upon. Most of the old

feudal rights and dues were to be provisionally upheld. There was to be no more plundering. Obedience was provisionally to be paid to constituted authorities, and no new insurrectionary bands were to be formed—in short, with few exceptions, everything was to remain *in statu quo* until the adoption or introduction of the aforesaid imperial reform.

These modifications were carried by a narrow majority in the council of the "United Contingent," but naturally not without fresh murmuring among the rank and file. Jacklein Rohrbach and his company had separated at once from the main body on the first symptoms of the new turn that things were taking. Other sections followed later, and the "United Contingent" of the Evangelical Peasant Brotherhood began to acquire an unenviable reputation throughout the movement for "trimming". Certain practical proposals respecting military reorganisation which Hipler at this time put forward, notably the very sensible one to enrol free-lances in the service of the contingent, were incontinently rejected by the peasants, partly from mistrust and partly from an unwillingness to divide the spoil with these experienced booty-hunters.

For it must not be supposed that the "United Contingent" observed the rules laid down by Gotz and his moderate colleagues anent plundering. They burnt and plundered as much as ever. In fact, in one case on Gotz remonstrating with his supposed followers (over whom his actual authority was the very smallest) for destroying a castle which he had given express orders should be spared, he narrowly escaped with his life. He was only saved, indeed, by the prompt appearance of his henchmen, Berlin and Hipler.

On the other hand, however anxious he might be to protect the property of his own immediate order, when the possessions of the Church, which he hated perhaps more than the peasants themselves, were in question, he was perfectly willing to let the contingent have its way to the full. Thus, on the 30th of April, the various bodies comprising the contingent, with Gotz and Metzler at their head, appeared before the Benedictine Abbey of Amorbach, in order, as they declared, "as Christian brethren to make a reformation". The inmates were summoned to surrender all their money and treasures on pain of death. But while the negotiations were going on, a body of peasants burst into the house, and the same scene took place as had been enacted in scores of other ecclesiastical buildings for more than a month past. Vestments, chalices, books richly bound, with silver, gold and precious stones, furniture, the contents of the cellars and the granaries, the cattle, in short, all things that were of any value at all, were dragged out and divided amongst the assailants, or destroyed. Gotz himself took his share, including the costly vestments of the abbot, who had to go away in a smock which one of the peasants had given him out of com-passion. The immediate plan of operations was to proceed to the assistance of the insurgents in the Archbishopric of Mainz and the Bishopric of Wurzburg, and then by way of Frankfurt to invade the Archbishoprics of Trier and of Cologne. It was a favourite scheme of Gotz to divide up ecclesiastical property amongst the knightly order. Hipler and Metzler may well have been persuaded that leniency towards the lower nobility and its possessions, combined with the prospect of obtaining a share of those of the Church, would induce the former, if not to actively support the peasants cause, at

least to waver in their fidelity to the imperial
authorities.

In Mainz, the cardinal-archbishop was
seriously considering the question of secular-
ising his territories, and had been, in fact, in
correspondence with Luther on the subject, a
plan which he abandoned, owing, it is said, to
the influence of his mistress.   On the approach
of the peasants, the envoys, not of the archbishop, who had fled, but of the Bishop of
Strasburg, whom he had left in charge of his
affairs, hastened to sign the modified " Twelve
Articles," and to pay a ransom of 15,000
gulden.   In the whole territory of the archbishopric, including the towns of Mainz and
Aschaffenburg, the insurrection was now in
full swing.

It had even reached the neighbouring free
imperial city of Frankfurt-on-the-Main, where
the leaders of the city-proletariat had extorted
from the council a charter of rights and privileges containing forty-five "articles".   An
insurrectionary committee, mainly composed
of small craftsmen, under the leadership of
a shoemaker, had been formed in the town
and was in perpetual session, having relations

with the peasants of the surrounding territories and with the small towns of the neighbour-hood.

The " United Contingent," under Gotz and Metzler, after reducing Aschaffenburg to sub-mission, now decided to make straight for Würzburg, where the main body of the Fran-conian insurgents was encamped, their efforts being directed towards the capture of the important fortress on the Frauenberg which commanded the city.

Amongst the free imperial towns now threat-ened by the insurrection, none were more hardly pressed than Schwabisch Hall, lying on the borderland between Swabia and Franconia. Like other imperial cities, Hall had an exten-sive territory outside its walls, cultivated by a numerous peasantry, to which it and its council stood in the feudal relation of overlord. The peasants of this countryside and of those adjoining it had risen in the usual way. They formed themselves into companies with leaders, and arranged a plan of campaign for capturing the city, but it seems that these particular peas-ants were exceptionally well-to-do and accus-tomed to good living, and their fighting capacity

seems to have been in inverse proportion to
their boon companionship. They possessed,
indeed, muskets and ordnance, but as a general
rule they contented themselves with the ordinary
dagger as their weapon. Instead of making
straight for their objective, this contingent,
which was over 3000 strong "turned in" at
every village on the way, making free with the
wine-cellars of the priests, the Bürgermeisters
and the monks, whom they compelled to carouse
with them. When, finally, they came within
striking distance of the city, all they could do
was to encamp and fall asleep. The town of
Hall was, of course, in trepidation, having, like
the rest, within its walls its own discontented
population, which was well disposed to the
cause of the peasants, and the authorities were
not in a position to withstand the force of the
movement from within and from without. Some
of the country people had made so sure of
coming into possession of the town that they had
actually fixed upon the houses they were going
to appropriate. The well-beliquored peasants
were, however, awakened at break of day by a
shot from the neighbouring height. This was
followed by a second and a third. The peasant

camp was in confusion. Many in their still nebulous condition believed themselves struck and fell down accordingly. The rest scattered precipitately. The fact was that a small party had started from the town to reconnoitre, bringing with them a few hand-guns, but, as it happened, without shot. Seeing the state of affairs in the camp below them, they had fired more in jest than for any other reason. The upshot was that the peasants of the imperial city of Hall were glad to be allowed to return to their homesteads on renewing their oath of fidelity to the city, and thus the rebellion of the Hall peasants ignominiously collapsed.

The movement in Wurtemberg, meanwhile, went on apace ; but it was moderated by the influence of Matern Feuerbacher, the well-to-do innkeeper of Bottwar, who was anxious to remain on good terms with all sides, and, as we have seen, only placed himself at the head of the peasant force under compulsion and to a certain extent with the consent of some of his noble patrons. By their advice, he made it a special stipulation that he would have nothing to do with the " Weinsbergers," understanding thereby the party of Jacklein Rohrbach, who had been the agents in the slaughter of the knights. In Stuttgart the excitement was so great that the members of the regency, representing the Austrian Government, had fled, together with some of the patrician members of the city council. The chief pastor of the city, Dr. Johannes Mantel, was a zealous patron of the new doctrines, for which he had suffered imprisonment, being liberated by the peasants. After some negotiations, the peasants were admitted into the town, but they only remained within the walls for two days. The ransom money exacted for religious establishments and from the town itself was comparatively moderate. After two days, the contingent left the city for the valley of the Rems, in order to drive back an extraneous body of peasants, who were now accused of plundering ; for Matern Feuerbacher and the other leaders of the Würtemberg movement had pledged themselves not to allow foreign elements to intrude into the duchy. Here, as elsewhere, the Weinsberg affairs had strongly influenced the trend of sentiment, both within and without the movement, within by strengthening moderate counsels, and without by first of all terrorising and afterwards exacerbating the princes and nobles against the peasants and their demands. It is only one instance of the policy pursued by all governing classes in exploiting the conscience of mankind. Of the causes of the insurrection itself, of the infamous oppression of the feudal orders, no notice, of course, is taken. Of the slaughter by knights, well-armed and equipped, and experienced in the fighting art, of unarmed or badly-armed peasants, sometimes even of countryfolk who were not in rebellion, of the atrocities of this nature committed by that very Helfenstein, whose death was only the just penalty of his crimes, similarly nothing is said. Hundreds of peasants foully massacred count for nothing ; the important event, the "great crime," calculated to produce in all men a "thrill of horror," is that eighteen knights, the authors and abettors of these things, are slain by an act of justice, or, if you will, vengeance.

It was the same in the contest between the workmen of Paris and the reactionaries of Versailles, in the spring of 1871. The governing classes and all those who took their cue from them (either through interested motives, want of knowledge of the facts, or indifference), were, or pretended to be, dissolved in horror at the execution of seventy-two persons belonging to these classes. They had not one word to say in condemnation of the systematic butchery for two months previously in cold blood of insurgent prisoners of war, culminating perhaps in the vastest massacre on record, by the authorities representing those governing classes. Yet it was this that led up to the act of vengeance against which they pretend such an overflowing indignation.

Once more, the torturing and doing to death of nine working men, after a mock trial, by order of the late Spanish Minister, Canovas, is a trifle ; but no sooner is their death avenged on Canovas himself by a self-sacrificing fanatic than the governing classes and their organs talk with duly impressive fervour of the "sanctity of human life" and of the exceeding infamy of violating it. The power of position and wealth to create a public conscience agreeable to its interests, and to suit its purposes, is indeed convenient and wonderful.

The German peasants of 1525, as did the

Commune of Paris, and as is the wont of successful insurgents generally, signalised their success as a rule by their studied moderation and good-nature, as contrasted with the ferocious cruelty of their enemies, the con-stituted authorities.

CHAPTER V.

THE PEASANTS WAR IN FRANCONIA.

The starting point and centre of the insurrectionary movement in the Franconian districts
of middle Germany was the free imperial city
of Rothenburg-on-the-Tauber, a town situated
on a plateau of table-land in the valley watered
by the little river Tauber (*cf. German Society,*
pp. 208, 209). As we have before seen, the
rival of Martin Luther, Andreas Bodenstein,
better known as Dr. Karlstadt, betook himself
here, after having been compelled to leave Wittenberg. Another preacher, Joahann Deuschlin,
had already discoursed on the new doctrines in
the town for a year or two previously. Deuschlin's career, like his doctrines, bore a striking
resemblance to that of Hubmeyer. He also had
undertaken an anti-Jewish campaign and had
been instrumental in the destruction of Jewish
quarters and synagogues before his conversion
to the new revolutionary principles, political

and religious. One of his most zealous disciples and co-operators was Hans Schmidt, a blind monk. The Teutonic Order in Rothenburg, as in other towns, possessed an establishment, but in this case the preacher Deuschlin succeeded in gaining over certain of their number to the Reformation, and indeed Melchior, one of the heads of the order, had even ventured to marry publicly with the usual festivities, and as fate had it, to marry the sister of Hans Schmidt, the blind monk. The two preachers had severely attacked the Commenthur, or supreme head of the order, and had so far carried their point as to get him deposed and another Commenthur, Christen, established in his place. These things, of course, did not go on without friction with the Episcopal authorities at Würzburg. but for the moment the revolutionary party remained victorious.

By the end of March, the peasant population in the territory belonging to Rothenburg had begun to assemble with a view to revolutionary action, whilst inside the town the ex-Bürgermeister, Ehrenfried Kumpf, the Church reformer, had inaugurated an iconoclastic campaign, in the course of which priests and

choristers were driven from the cathedral, the
mass-book was hurled from the altar, images
and pictures were mutilated and destroyed,
and the chapel of the immaculate virgin was
levelled with the ground. Karlstadt followed
in the same strain. A richly ornamented and
endowed church, just outside the walls, was
plundered by the members of the miller's
guild, and costly pictures, images and plate
were thrown into the Tauber. But while
Kumpf remained a mere anti-popish fanatic,
Karlstadt went forward on the lines of the
political movement. The party of the people
within the walls had now become strong and,
as usual, sympathised with the peasants without.
The latter, on the 26th of March, presented their
grievances to the city council in the form of
"articles," which in this, as in so many other
cases, had been drawn up by ex-priests. The
part that the recalcitrant clergy played in the
political and social, no less than the religious
movement of the time, we have more than
once had occasion to remark. These "articles"
were of the usual character, alleging the
weight of feudal dues—many of them of recent
imposition. The appeal to the religious senti-

ment in them is also strong. The negotiations, however, which ensued did not result in any definite agreement.

Karlstadt, who had fled from Orlamunde to Rothenburg, was received on his arrival with acclamation by the town populace. The Markgraf Casimir set a price upon his head, but Karlstadt, notwithstanding that, once within the walls of Rothenburg, felt himself comparatively secure and did not hesitate to preach openly even in the streets. The inner council, manned as usual by the patrician class, eventually forbade him the right of preaching and at the same time withdrew from him permission to reside in the town. The council in this matter, there is no doubt, acted partly in obedience to strong pressure from outside. In consequence, the learned agitator found it necessary to disappear for a time. It was given out by his friends that he had repaired to Strassburg. The truth was that he was in hiding within the city in the houses of the preacher Deuschlin, the new Commenthur of the Teutonic Order, Christen, the ex-Bürgermeister and iconoclast Kumpf, and especially in that of the master-tailor Phillip. During his concealment and supposed absence, tracts and brochures from the pen of Karlstadt found a mysterious circulation in the town, his friends having seen to the printing of them, whilst there were plenty of willing hands to attend to their sale or distribution.

One of the most active leaders in the revolt was Stephan Menzingen, a Swabian knight of an old family and a partisan of Duke Ulrich, who had married the daughter of one of the city councillors and had been admitted to the citizenship. From this, in consequence of a quarrel with the council on a question of taxation, he had subsequently withdrawn, and had taken up his abode in northern Switzerland, whence he suddenly returned to Rothenburg early in the year 1525, in time to take part in the new religious and political movement. He was instrumental in procuring the formation of a citizen's committee, to which all prominent members of the people's party belonged and which served as a sort of counterpoise to the aristocratic council. It was this committee that brought the peasants' demands before the council. By the end of March, Menzingen had carried the matter so far that the great

council of the town dissolved itself, many of its
members joining the new citizens' committee,
which now formally constituted itself the governing power of the town, while the small or
executive council was allowed to continue on
its good behaviour, after having sworn to carry
out the will of the citizens or to abdicate.
The victory was now practically won for the
new gospel of "evangelical brotherly love,"
according to which all things should be in
common, and the authority of *status* should
cease. As reported by a contemporary writer,
"the common people did will that one should
have as much as another and no more, that it
should be the duty of one to lend to another,
but that none should require of another that
he should give back and repay" (Thomas
Zweifel ap. Baumann, *Quellen aus Rothenburg*). The alliance with the peasants, the
tenants of the city lands without the gates, was
now concluded.

Karlstadt now came out of his hiding-place,
Kumpf openly admitting that he had given him
shelter. On being remonstrated with by his
old colleagues of the council, Kumpf replied
that he had acted in the service of God and

for the good of the town, always believing
Karlstadt to be the man to negotiate between
the town and the peasants.   No little wonder,
as may be imagined, was excited by the sudden
reappearance of a man believed to be at the
time in another part of Germany.   The Roth-
– enburg peasants now began to adopt the same
tactics as those of other parts.   Whoever
refused to join their " brotherhood " had his
house sacked, if not also burnt down.   A " high
time " moreover was had with clerical wine-
cellars, whilst in the town itself the clergy were
compelled to supply gratuitously the poorer
citizens, who quartered themselves upon them.
The peasant-army already numbered from four
to five thousand men, and the leaders, amongst
whom were some impoverished knights, better
understood the art of war and military organisation than those of some of the other contingents.

A part of their force remained encamped
near the town, while the rest swept along the
valley of the Tauber.   Chief among the
military heads of the Franconian peasant forces
was the knight Florian Geyer, to whom we
had occasion to refer in the last chapter.

Little is known of his antecedents, save that he was the lord of the old castle of Giebelstadt, near Würzburg. He suddenly appeared on the scene in the Tauber valley at the end of March, 1525, with a small company of free-lances that he had engaged, and shortly after he took over the command of the Rothenburg *Landwehr,* a body whose members were enrolled for the defence of the Rothenburg territory, on the initiation of the revolution. Out of these two elements he formed his famous "Black Troop," a company distinguished among the peasant forces for its bravery, cohesion and organisation. Florian Geyer, though himself a noble, threw himself heart and soul into the peasant cause, championing the most radical demands of the popular party, notably advising the destruction of all castles, and the reduction of their lords to the status of simple citizens or tillers of the soil. The fame of his "Black Troop" soon spread far and wide, and its co-operation was eagerly sought by other bands.

The Franconian insurrection had now spread to the immediate territory of the Bishop of Würzburg. Early in April, the whole diocese was in motion, in the towns no less

than on the country-side. On the 5th of the
month, Fritz Lobel. another Franconian knight.
led a body of peasants to the sack of the
wealthy Carthusian monastery of Zackelhausen.
The chapter at Würzburg became alarmed, and
sent three canons to secure the allegiance, amid
the general collapse of authority, of the town
of Ochsenfurt, but they were received with
closed gates and had to remain outside all
night. Eventually, the town consented to a
pact with the Episcopal authorities on the basis
of certain substantial concessions, which the
latter were compelled with a heavy heart to
grant by charter.

In the Würzburg territories the insurrection
was carried on largely through an association
founded here again by two preachers, and bearing the name of the "infinites" or "eternals"
("*Die Unendlichen*"). One township after
another was won. Everywhere the alarm-bell
clanged forth, calling to arms all within the
walls. In the north of the diocese, the drum
of insurrection first made itself heard on the
9th of April. The matter followed its usual
course. In a few days the original small band
had increased to formidable dimensions and had

been joined by other bands. Monasteries of various orders were entered and plundered. Within the walls of the townships, as usual, the Teutonic Order fared worst of all.

The Bishop of Würzburg and Duke of Franconia, Konrad von Thungen, became now seriously alarmed, especially on hearing that the peasants of the Rothenburg *Landwehr*, led by Florian Geyer, meditated making a descent upon Würzburg. In vain he sought help from the surrounding districts. In vain he applied to the Bishop of Bamberg, whose hands were full with his own rebellious subjects ; in vain to the Swabian League, which offered to pay for three hundred horsemen for a month, if they could be obtained, but sent neither man nor horse. The duke-bishop assembled his vassals, his "noble counsellors," to consult what measures should be adopted. Opinions were divided. Some thought that active steps should be taken against the recalcitrant country people, and that the wives and children of those who had banded themselves together should be driven from their homesteads and villages, and the latter set on fire. Others feared to take immediate repressive measures,

more especially as the neighbouring princes
had hitherto held their hands, arguing the
meagreness of the bishop's resources and con-
tending for a policy of delay until an arrangement could be come to with the adjacent
potentates. This view was finally adopted.
The peasants, as a result, pursued their course
unopposed. "Where they came, or where they
lay," writes Lorenz Fries, the Prince-Bishop's
private secretary, "they fell upon the monasteries, the priests' houses, the chests and the
cellars of the authority, consuming in gluttony
and in drunkenness that which they found. And
it did exceedingly please this new brotherhood
that they might consume by devouring and
drinking their fill, and had not to pay withal.
More drunken, more full-bellied, more helpless
folk, one had hardly seen together than during
the time of this rebellion. So that I know not
whether the peasants' device and conduct, had
they but abstained from fire and bloodshed,
should rather be called a carnival's jest or a
war . . . and whether a peasants-war, and not
rather a wine-war."

So much from a hostile source. It must,
however, be admitted by the best friends of the

peasants and their cause that gluttony and wine-bibbing contributed as potently as any other influence to the politically unproductive character of the peasant successes and to that lack of cohesion and discipline which led the way to the final catastrophe and soaked the German soil with the blood of its tillers.

All authority throughout the bishopric of Würzburg was now paralysed. Even the Count Henneberg, whose territory lay on its northern frontier, the most powerful feudatory of the bishop, showed no signs of furnishing his overlord with men or money, but, on the contrary, as it soon appeared, was entering into negotiations with a view to adoption into the "Christian Brotherhood"—an event which shortly after happened. The count was required, at the same time, to furnish his tenants with a charter of emancipation and to swear to act in accordance with the Word of God and with the precepts of the Gospel.

Würzburg itself, the seat of government and residence of the bishop and his chapter, soon showed signs of disaffection. The town had been captured a century before by the then duke-bishop by force of arms, and deprived of its ancient municipal rights. This had never been forgotten. So, one fine day, a body of the poorer citizens were to be seen gathered together in earnest discussion near the gate of St. Stephen. A prebendary of the cathedral, who was passing by at the time, and who fancied he heard himself unfavourably criticised by some of the crowd, began to call them names, and to threaten to have their heads struck off on the market-place. The news of the abuse and the threat flew through the poorer townsfolk like lightning. An uproar was the result, the populace marching with arms and in extemporised battle array to the sound of pipe and drum before the residences of the cathedral authorities. The disturbance was only partially and for the moment quelled by the gift of a tun of wine to the people by one of the canons. In a day or two, affairs had come to such a pass that the bishop betook himself to the overhanging fortress on the Frauenberghill, the Marienburg, as it was called, after having provided the stronghold with victuals to sustain a siege, and having given orders that all available men-at-arms and loyal subjects capable of such service, from the town and country round, should be brought in to garrison the place.

Those among the patrician councillors of the city, who had fled to the stronghold of authority, escaped with their bishop, and, after having conferred with the latter, sent Sebastian von Rotenhan and two others of their number down into the town to discuss with the citizens, and to seek by threats or cajolery to bring them to obedience. They were to secure the punishment of the ringleaders and if possible the expulsion of unruly and dangerous elements from within the walls, and further to see that the town was placed in a proper state of defence against peasant bands from outside.

Rotenhan and his companions rode pompously through the streets, and, calling together the heads of the different wards, handed over to them his instructions. Thinking to frighten the Würzburgers, he at the same time announced that a body of horsemen was on its way and had orders to quarter itself in the town. This threat, which Rotenhan had no instructions to make, had as its only result to precipitate matters. The leaders of the movement were at once aroused, urging the citizens to close the gates

against any force the bishop might send. The
citizens, they said, or at least the "common
man" of the town—in the language familiar
now everywhere to the dwellers within walls,
when the man from the open country knocked
at their gates—had no cause of quarrel with
the peasant, who was his brother. So, far from
fighting against him or refusing him admittance,
they should both join hands in a common
brotherhood against the oppressor, be he prince
or prelate, noble or city-magnate. The peasants were only fighting for the Gospel, said
they. A dissolute priesthood had already
seduced enough burghers' wives and daughters.
Would they march out to fight the peasants
leaving their women a prey to such? Already
it was alleged that ordnance was being placed
in position by the bishop's orders to attack the
town, should it refuse him obedience.

Excitement manifested itself on all hands.
In response to the exhortations of the agitators,
towers and gates were soon garrisoned by sturdy
burghers. The warden of the fishers' guild
saw that the approaches to the river—the
Main—were duly secured by heavy chains; he
also took in charge defensive operations as

regards the paths leading up the Frauenberg.
Up these paths Rotenhan and his two colleagues now wended their sorrowful way back
to the castle with the tidings that their mission
had proved a failure. Further intercourse
between the castle and town was now rendered
well-nigh impossible by the defensive obstruc-
tions alone, apart from the fact that the vintners'
guild had organised itself into a company of
sharp-shooters, to " pot," from behind the vines
which covered the slopes of the Frauenberg,
any knight, patrician or prelate, who might be
seeking his way to the town from the heights
above. The cooks' and the carpenters' guilds
alike refused to obey the mandate calling upon
them to furnish certain of their number for
service in the Marienburg. It fared now badly
with the ecclesiastical foundations and residences
within the town. Wine-cellars and larders, as
may be imagined, were not spared more in
Würzburg than elsewhere.

But negotiations were not yet entirely broken
off between the bishop and the city. On the
13th of April, a delegation went up to the castle
to negotiate. with the result that the bishop
was compelled to call a Landtag for the 30th of

the month, consisting of representatives of the
knighthood and the towns, at which all grievances were to be discussed and considered.

At the same time that these things were
passing in Würzburg, the five different bodies
of insurgents, which had formed in the northern
part of the Duchy of Franconia, united themselves into a single contingent with a commander
and military organisation.   On the 15th of April,
amidst the flames of castles and monasteries
fallen an easy prey to the peasant bands, a great
council of war was held at which it was decided
to at once advance on Würzburg.   The negotiations with Count Henneberg, however, which
were not concluded till some days later, delayed
matters for a time.

On the 2nd of May the bishop with certain
of his councillors descended, under a promise
of safe conduct, into the town to open the
Landtag agreed on.   This was against the
advice of many of his following, who thought
the proceeding dangerous and would have
liked the Landtag to have been called on the
Frauenberg, or, indeed, anywhere else rather
than in the now openly-rebellious town of
Würzburg.   However, as a large number of

representatives had already assembled, no other course seemed possible. Before the proceedings had fairly begun, loud complaints reached the bishop's ears of the oppression of the " common man " by his prelates, contrary to the Word of God, and of how the Word of God, which had only a few years ago been again brought to light, was being smothered and its preachers persecuted. Many of the town representatives demanded that the peasants should be called upon to send their own delegates to confer in the deliberations. With this demand the bishop was, much against his will, compelled to comply. The response, however, was not satisfactory. The peasantry of the Tauber valley answered the bishop's messengers that at the moment it was not the time for deliberating at diets, but that they would reserve anything they had to say till they arrived in force at Würzburg, which would be before long. The same with other districts. All saw now that things had gone too far to be settled in the way proposed. The result was the collapse of the Landtag, which was hastily closed, every man riding away to his own town or castle.

There was now a formal understanding between the town of Würzburg and the insurgents in the open country. The bishop on his side took his measures, collecting the garrisons, such as they were, from neighbouring castles to reinforce the Frauenberg. The united insurgent contingent from the north was now encamped before the gates, where it was joined in a day or two by Florian Geyer and his black troop from the Tauber valley, and almost immediately after, as before related, by the famous " United Contingent " of George Metzler and Wendel Hipler. In this extremity, the bishop was advised as a last resort, to apply personally to the Elector Palatine for assistance. On the 5th of May, accordingly, with a heavy heart, he rode down, accompanied by a few followers, from the Frauenberg, his last remaining stronghold, into the plain, and struck out westward towards Heidelberg, where he arrived two days later.

The castle of the Marienburg on the Frauenberg was now garrisoned by 244 men-at-arms, besides ecclesiastics, nobles and servants. The Markgraf Friedrich of Brandenburg was left as commander, while Rotenhan undertook the victualling. Florian Geyer and his black troop were soon followed by the whole of the Tauber-valley contingent, which recruited itself, during a victorious march, with hundreds of new followers. The course of the " Franconian Army," as the Tauber-valley contingent now called itself, was characterised, needless to say, by the usual plunder and destruction, an especially rich booty being furnished by the wealthy Cistercian foundation at Ebrich. Flocks and herds were slaughtered or driven away, larders and cellars emptied of their contents, precious stones and gold torn out of the settings ; vestments, chalices and ornaments appropriated, and the building finally given over to the flames.

With the advent of the Tauber-valley peasantry on Würzburg there was united, in and around the town, the greatest force of the peasant army at that moment to be found at any one point throughout Germany. Most of the ablest leaders from a military point of view were also present—Metzler, Hipler, not to mention Götz von Berlichingen, and, above all, Florian Geyer. But, as the event turned out, this almost solitary instance of co-operation on a great scale between different sections of the insurgents proved not only a failure in itself, but a source of weakness to the whole movement. The peasants of middle Germany placed too heavy stakes on this one event, the capture of the Frauenberg. Now the Frauenberg itself was a strong natural strategic position, and the Marienburg, the object of attack, was an exceptionally well-built and well-appointed mediæval fortress. It had been thoroughly victualled, so that it would take some time to reduce by famine, and it was well-garrisoned with experienced fighting-men, with no lack of weapons, ordnance and ammunition. The result was as might have been expected; valuable as the acquisition of the Frauenberg would have been to the peasant cause, yet the chance of capturing it was not worth the price paid. For what was the price? Nothing less than the locking up at one point of a force constituting the main strength of the insurrection—a force comprising the only reliable military nucleus in the whole movement. Had a plan of campaign been worked out, according to which by means of rapid marches this force or portions of it should have undertaken the task of supporting the movement generally at places where it needed support, in conjunction with the local insurgent bands, the contest would undoubtedly have been prolonged, and though complete success may not have been possible. owing to the political and economical trend of the time, the completeness of the catastrophe, which nearly everywhere overtook the movement, would almost certainly have been averted.

The peasants, in accordance with the pact made with the town, had free ingress and egress. The sympathetic citizens, of course, fraternised with them, though possibly they may have winced somewhat at the free and easy behaviour of their guests at times and at the outspokenness of the communistic sentiments expressed.

According to a contemporary, the peasants " were always full (drunken); showed much ill-behaviour in word and deed, and neither in the afternoon nor the morning would they be ruled by any ". The language was openly heard that, since they were brethren, it was only fair that all things should be equal, and that the rich should divide with the poor,

especially they who had acquired their wealth
through trade or otherwise gained it from the
poor man.   The improved discipline sought to
be introduced by the leaders of the " United
Contingent " proved as impossible to carry out
in the camp and in the city as it had been on
the march.   The orders issued in this sense
remained for the most part unobeyed.   Even
the gallows erected on the market-place proved
no adequate deterrent.   In fact, in most of the
companies, a tendency to insubordination was,
as might be expected, increased by the life of
idleness and dissipation, which the camp and
Würzburg afforded them.   In vain the leaders
endeavoured to drive home to their following
the fable of the " head and the members ".
In vain they descanted on the impossibility of
a "civil brotherly constitution" without the
maintenance of an organised administration.
The reply was that they were brothers, and
would be equal.

Even after the departure of the bishop, negotiations with the Marienburg were not finally
broken off.   On the 9th of May, the dean of
the cathedral with some canons and knights
descended into the town, and met the leaders,

Gotz, Metzler, Geyer, and others, in the inn, whose sign was the "Green Tree". They pleaded their willingness and that of the bishop to make concessions as regarded the "Twelve Articles". Gotz and Metzler seem to have been anxious to accept the terms offered, which included a truce until some of their number could go to and from Heidelberg to obtain the bishop's consent ; but Florian Geyer was strongly opposed to any compromise, believing in the possibility of compelling the castle to an unconditional surrender within a few days. When the matter was brought before a general council of the peasants, Florian, with his accustomed fire, observed : "The time is come ; the axe is laid to the root of the tree ; the dance has now begun, and before the door of every prince shall it be piped. Will we hold back the axe? Will we, of ourselves, turn aside?" Others followed in the same strain, with the result that the terms proposed by the dean and his colleagues were rejected and the siege continued.

A few days later, another attempt at negotiation was made. Gotz and Metzler were now more emphatic than ever in their advice to come to terms. Gotz reasonably urged the imprudence of lying idle with their immense force for weeks, awaiting the surrender of the impregnable Frauenberg, and pointed out very justly that there was more important work to do, even going so far as to propose as an alternative an attempt to capture the imperial city of Nürnberg. In this advice, Gotz undoubtedly bore himself and his order more in mind than the peasants. In his capacity of knight, he despised and hated the burgher as much as he did the priest. But it was all of no avail. Either from a false view of the situation or, as is more probable, from an unwillingness to exchange the ease and good living afforded them by the bishop's capital for the dangers and hardships of a serious campaign, none of the contingents would consent to abandon the Frauenberg.

On May 14-15, the castle was stormed. With much shouting and beating of drums, several companies, foremost among them the "Black Troop," swarmed up the Frauenberg. The light stockade was swept away, the moat was crossed, the assailants reached to the very walls. But it was only to be received by a

rain of bullets, missiles of burning pitch, huge
stones from windows and battlements, followed
by the thunder of all the ordnance with which
the castle was provided. Twice the attacking
party was driven back with enormous loss.
Hundreds of peasants lay dead and dying in
the moats. Seen from the town, the whole
castle appeared brilliantly illuminated. It was
clear that so long as provisions and powder
and shot remained in the castle, the Frauenberg
was not to be captured. The idea of taking
the fortress by storm before a breach had been
made in the walls was in itself chimerical. As
ill-luck would have it, moreover, the peasantry's
greatest military genius, Florian Geyer, was
absent when the storming was decided upon,
having gone to Rothenburg to demand ordnance of a larger calibre than any in the peasant
camp, and to negotiate for the formal adoption
of that town into the " Evangelical Brotherhood ". Even Wendel Hipler was not there,
having left for Heilbronn to attend the permanent official committee there sitting, to elaborate, in conjunction with Friedrich Weigand
and the rest, the scheme of imperial reform
already spoken of. Discouraged at the result

of their unsuccessful attempts at taking the
fortress by storm, the peasants continued the
siege in the hope of starving it into surrender.
But this took longer than they imagined.

Meanwhile, the popular cause scored another
success by the formal entry of the city of
Rothenburg into the " Evangelical Brotherhood ". On the appeal of the peasant-contin-
gents being handed in to the council by Florian
Geyer and his colleagues, the whole body of
the poorer citizens threatened to march out
with all the ordnance and join the peasants
against the town if a favourable response were
not given. Even the free-lances in the service
of the city threatened to desert to the enemy
as soon as it should appear before the gates.
The fortunes of Rothenburg were now completely in the hands of the populace. A
resolution had been carried for the communisa-
tion of ecclesiastical goods. The stores of corn
and wine were also to be divided in equal
shares between the citizens. Jewels and
chalices were to be sold, and with the proceeds
of the sale the citizens were to be armed and
maintained. A fine frolic went on within the
walls. According to contemporary accounts,

"old and young did drink and became drunken. Many lay in the streets who could go no further, especially young children who had made themselves overful with wine."

Rothenburg formally entered the " Evangelical Brotherhood " on the 14th of May, under the following pledges : Firstly, shall the general assembly of burghers set up the Evangelical doctrine, the Holy Word of God, and shall see that the same be preached in pure simplicity without superaddition of human teaching. And what the Holy Gospel doth set up, shall be set up ; what it layeth low, shall be laid low, and shall so remain. And, in the meanwhile, no interest due or aught such thing shall be given to any lord until by those most learned in the Holy, Divine, and true Scripture shall a Reformation have been appointed. Injurious castles, water-houses and fortresses, whence hitherto a dreadful oppression have been practised upon the "common man," shall be broken up or consumed by fire. Yet what is therein of goods that can be borne shall go to them who would be brethren, and who have committed naught against the general assembly. Such ordnance as may be found in these houses shall belong to the general assembly. Clergy and lay-men, nobles and commons, shall henceforth hold to the right of the plain citizen and the peasant, and shall be no more than the "common man". The nobles shall surrender to the assembly all goods of clergy or others, especially of them of their own class, who have done aught against the brotherhood, on pain of loss of life and goods. And, in fine, every man, be he church-man or lay-man, shall henceforth hold in all obedience that which is ordained in the reformation and order concluded by them who are learned in the Holy Scripture.

The city thus entered the " Evangelical Brotherhood" for the formal term of 101 years. The best and heaviest pieces of ordnance in its possession were, with the requisite powder and balls, handed over to the peasants. The late Burgermeister, Ehrenfried Kumpf, the zealous church-reformer and iconoclast, clad in full armour, rode back with the peasant delegates to the camp of Würzburg. Six hundred Rothenburg peasants, fully armed and equipped, followed with the two guns and the powder-waggon. By the aid of the new artillery, the assailants succeeded in making some impression on the walls of the Marienburg, but, even now, no serious damage appears to have been done. News now came of the successful advance of Truchsess and the army of the Swabian League in the south. The leaders all saw the urgent necessity of making an end of this Würzburg business at the earliest possible date. On the 20th of May, they, through a public crier, offered the entire booty to be found in the castle, including gold, silver, jewels and furniture, together with the assurance of a high rate of continuous pay to any company that should first carry the castle by storm. They, indeed, endeavoured to form a special company for the purpose, keeping a list of volunteers before them in the "Green Tree," where they sat as an executive council ; but it all came to nothing.

In the neighbouring Bishopric of Bamberg, the insurrection had also broken out about the same time as in the Wurzburg territories. The chief preacher of the new doctrines here was one Johann Schwanhäuser. Like his colleagues elsewhere, he attacked in the first instance the clergy and then proceeded to descant on general social inequalities. The clergy were hypocrites and godless men, "they do thrust Christ out of the vineyard," said Schwanhauser, "and do set up themselves in His stead. They call themselves the vicegerents of Christ, and the true ambassadors are persecuted by them. They let the poor sit without houses, perish with cold and starve, yet to dead saints do they build great stone houses and bear to them gold, silver and precious stones. Were we true Christians," he added, "we should sell monstrances, chalices, church and mass vestments, and live as the twelve apostles, giving all our surplusage to the poor."

The sermons of Schwanhauser worked in Bamberg, as similar discourses had worked elsewhere, like a spark, firing the inflammable material furnished in such quantity both within and without walls at this epoch. On the 11th of April, the tocsin rang out from the belfry of the town, and Bamberg proclaimed itself in insurrection. The town populace formed itself into companies, chose leaders, closed the gates, and compelled members of the town patriciate and the clergy to assist. They sent messengers throughout all the country round, urging the villages to join them. On the bishop's refusal to surrender the church property, his castle above the town, which was practically unde-fended, was taken by assault, pillaged and burnt. For three days the usual scenes of plunder took place in and around Bamberg.

On the 15th of April, however, a compromise was arrived at with the bishop, by which he was recognised as the sole responsible authority in the land, the chapter losing all its separate rights. The bishop on his side promised to call a Landtag for the discussion and removal of all grievances. This treaty, although publicly proclaimed in the streets, does not seem to have been of much effect. The destruction of castles and monasteries throughout the episcopal territories went on apace. As many as seventy castles, besides religious houses, fell a prey to rapine and flames. Crowds from the country-side flocked into the capital. An old chronicle informs us that "no one was certain of his life and goods, after the multitude had bedrunk themselves in the wine-cellars of the churchmen, as continually came to pass. So evil and so unruly did it become in Bamberg, that not alone the old pious burghers were grieved thereat, but also the others, even they who had, at first, had right good pleasure in the tumult."

By the middle of April the movement was everywhere reaching its height, and was not to be quelled by promises or even by written concessions any more than by threats. The insurrection was going from one success to another.

CHAPTER VI.

THE MOVEMENT IN THE EAST AND WEST.

WE have now to follow the rise and progress of the movement in the eastern Austrian territories of Tyrol and Salzburg. We s'a l then briefly trace its fortunes in the western dependencies of Austria, in the Breisgau and Upper Elsass, and along the Rhine.

In the first rank of the prince-ecclesiastics of the extensive hereditary domains of the house of Austria stood the Archbishop of Salzburg. Amongst the numerous well-hated prince-prelates of the age, Archbishop Matthaus Lang by no means took a back place. The town of Salzburg had long been at cross purposes with the arch-episcopal castle overhanging it. History tells how the predecessor of Lang, Leonhard by name, had invited the burger-meister and some distinguished members of the city-council to a banquet. As soon as they sat down to table, he caused the castle ban-queting-hall to fill with armed men, to whom he gave orders for his guests to be seized, fettered and carried off to a distant portion of his territories to be executed. The reason of this act of treachery was a report that had reached his ears of the intention of the council to apply to the emperor for a charter constituting Salzburg a free city. This act, however, seems to have excited less indignation amongst the body of the burghers, owing to the class hatred entertained for the wealthy town patricians whom it immediately concerned.

As for the peasants in the Salzburg lands, they, like other peasantries on ecclesiastical domains, had a standing quarrel with their lord, and had more than once risen against what they deemed unjust exactions during the latter half of the preceding century. It was natural, therefore, that the great popular wave of 1525 should not have passed over the town and country of Salzburg without leaving its impression.

The then Archbishop Matthaus Lang came to his see in 1519. He had sprung from a patrician family of the town of Augsburg, and by cunning and diplomacy had attained to one of the wealthiest and most powerful sees in the empire. His character may be judged from the statement of one of his own privy councillors that " it were well known with what roguery and knavery he had come into the benefice, how his whole life long he had naught that was good in his thought, was full of malice, a knave, and his disposition never good towards his countryfolk". That the foregoing estimate is in nowise too severe his public acts amply testify.

On the opening of the Lutheran Reformation, it is not surprising that the Salzburgers showed themselves eminently favourable to the new doctrines. Here, as elsewhere, were to be found enthusiastic reformers amongst the clergy. With these must be included the confessor of the archbishop himself. No sooner did the latter become aware of the fact than he threw the priest, whose name was Kastenbauer, into prison, and gave orders for all those acknowledging the Lutheran heresy, were they clerical or lay, to be pursued with heavy pains and penalties. But the cunning prelate had a plan in view for making the spread of the Lutheran movement a shoeing-horn to an ambitious scheme of his own for doing away with all ancient rights and privileges in the town and the country alike, and for reducing the whole territory beneath his absolute sway. Under pretence of repressing heresy, and protecting the see against disaffection, it was his aim, namely, to collect a body of mercenaries from outside, to fall upon his own subjects, and by a display of severity to reduce them to an abject submission. "The burghers," he is reported to have said, "must be the first that I shall undo; then those of the country must follow."

In Tyrol, accordingly, whither he journeyed to do homage to his feudal superior, the Archduke Ferdinand, who was at Innsbruck, he engaged six companies of free-lances, alleging to the archduke as his excuse the necessity of being prepared against a possible Lutheran rising in his dominions. The citizens of Salzburg were horrified at the return of their liege lord with a small army at his back. Their alarm was increased on observing signs at the castle of the planting of ordnance in a position to threaten the town. So great was the panic that, on the peremptory demand of the cardinal-archbishop, the city surrendered at once unconditionally, and the prince-prelate rode in in triumph, followed by his retinue, to the guildhall on the bread market.

This entry lacked none of the pomp and magnificence characteristic of the age. The archbishop, clad in full armour, was mounted on a white charger, surrounded by his pages and courtiers, and followed by two companies of free-lances. A humble address delivered to the archbishop by the bürgermeister was answered by his chancellor in haughty and almost insulting language. All imperial charters, granting privileges to the town, were ordered to be surrendered, as well as those given by himself or by his predecessors. A formal document was then required to be drawn up and signed by the burgermeister and principal councillors, pledging the town to submit in all things to the will of its feudal superior. Salzburg thus, unlike most of the other important towns of Germany, which had long ago settled accounts with their feudal overlords, was still in the throes of a struggle which, in not a few other cases, had been left two centuries behind. As a natural consequence, the class-antagonism within the walls, although

unmistakably existing, was somewhat overshadowed. There was at least a solidarity of
all classes against the feudal oppressor. A
similar despotic policy was pursued throughout
the whole territory of the archbishopric.

Severe persecutions of the preachers of the
new gospel now followed. The recalcitrant
priest, Matthaus, who had been amongst the
most active of its propagandists, was sentenced
to perpetual imprisonment. He was bound on
a horse with an iron chain and was to be conveyed to a distant castle. On the way thither,
however, his conductors turned into a friendly
inn to refresh, leaving their prisoner alone
outside. Finding a few peasants around him,
attracted by curiosity, the preacher appealed to
them to release him. In a short time a considerable crowd had gathered, and, a young
peasant constituting himself leader, the preacher
was released and went his way. The leader
and another peasant engaged in this affair were
afterwards secretly executed at Salzburg within
the castle. As soon as this was known, however, it acted as a powerful stimulus to the
prevailing disaffection. The friends of the
victims and of the new doctrines went about

from valley to valley, secretly urging the country-folk to defend the gospel and avenge innocent blood.

The measureless exactions of the Cardinal-Archbishop all helped in the same direction. Not only was the peasantry taxed up to the hilt, but heavy subsidies were demanded from the wealthy burghers of the town of Salzburg. Insults, oppressions, exactions, continued throughout the winter of 1524-1525. But, at the same time, here as elsewhere, the opposition, which was to break out in the spring in the form of open rebellion, was organising itself. This first took definite shape in the valley of Gastein. Fourteen "articles" were formulated by this peasant population, whom the celebrated " Twelve Articles " of Upper Swabia appear not yet to have reached. First and foremost, the free preaching of the gospel without human additions was demanded. The free election of preachers was also insisted upon. Furthermore, various imposts were to be done away with, notably the *merchet* (or due payable on the marriage of a son or daughter), the death due, the so-called small tithe, and many other things of a like nature. A righteous administration of justice—and especially that the judges should be independent of the lord and his bailiffs—was also amongst the demands. A further curious item was that the cost of the execution of criminals should not fall upon the rural community. Finally, the maintenance of public roads for the facility of trade and intercourse was required.

On the basis of these articles, a " Christian Brotherhood" was formed here also. Messengers were sent into all the neighbouring valleys to secure adhesion. Soon the whole of the Alpine archbishopric was in motion, and by the end of April the insurrection had reached Styria, Carinthia and Upper Austria. The " Christian Brotherhood" was now well-established in all the Austrian lands.

The Archduke Ferdinand, who held court at Innsbruck, at this time called together the assembly of the Estates of the five Austrian Duchies to consider what action should be taken. The local assemblies of the territories also met. It was generally admitted on all sides that the revolt was brought about by highhanded and oppressive action on the part of the territorial magnates. Here, indeed, even the lower nobility, when offering the archduke their aid in quelling the insurrection, made the redress of certain specified wrongs, under which the "common man" was suffering, a necessary condition. The archduke himself had to agree. His real views and inclinations as regards the situation were probably better expressed by a rescript previously issued by himself and the court-council at Vienna to the effect that "the crime must be chastised with a rod of iron, to the end that the evil and wanton device of the peasants should be punished, so that others may take warning thereby, also that those who are elsewhere already rebellious may be stilled and brought into submission. It is therefore our counsel and good opinion that ye all do proceed against all chiefs and leaders, wheresoever they may arise, or show themselves, with spearing, flaying, quartering, and every cruel punishment."

In Styria, Sigmund von Dietrichstein, who ten years before had mercilessly suppressed a peasant insurrection in the duchy (*cf. German Society*, pp. 82-86) held still the chief authority in the land. He was, however, without men. Even the mercenaries sent him from Vienna

refused to march against the peasantry, a
section of them actually deserting to the latter.
He would have been absolutely powerless, had
not a contingent of three hundred Bohemian
men-at-arms arrived upon the scene. An
attempt, nevertheless, to attack a peasant
encampment at Goysen resulted in the repulse
and flight of his whole force. In his retreat
through a narrow defile, the sides of which
were occupied by parties of insurgents, Dietrichstein suffered almost more than in the open
field. He himself was wounded, and confessed
to a loss of over a hundred men killed, though
this was undoubtedly far below the true number.
To make matters worse, his remaining men now
mutinied, and it was only with difficulty, and
with the expenditure of a large sum of money,
that he could induce them to remain with him.
Two companies of free-lances and some three
hundred horsemen were, however, on their way
from Carinthia to his assistance. With the aid
of these he was able to maintain his position,
though he did not dare to attack the main body
of rebels, consisting of some six thousand
peasants, under the leadership of one Reustl.
His attempts at negotiations, though they first

of all failed owing to the opposition of Reustl, were eventually successful, the majority of the contingent deserting their leader and accepting the terms offered. Reustl, with a band of faithful followers, mostly workers in the salt mines, made good his retreat, and succeeded in reaching the main Salzburg contingent, which he joined.

By this time, things were getting hotter than ever in the archbishopric. The main body of the insurgent peasants were encamped in a village a few miles from Salzburg. They were armed with the most motley weapons, clubs, pitchforks and sickles, with only here and there a rusty sword or spear or a worn-out piece of armour. In this way they streamed forth from their valleys and mountain pastures. The episcopal functionaries were taken by surprise. They had omitted to occupy the leading pass. In vain the archbishop altered his tone; in vain he became mild, persuasive and even fatherly. The peasants were not so boorish as not to know the worth of his assurances. The townspeople of Salzburg were in full sympathy with them. So threatening did matters become that Matthaus Lang felt himself no longer safe in his palace on the market-place, and made good his retreat to his castle immediately above. A steep and narrow path led from the city to this impregnable fortress, which boasted a double wall, in part hewn out of the natural rock. The south side rested on a sheer precipice of 440 feet. Here the archbishop was safe enough as regards his person, but the position was not favourable for conducting negotiations with the town, in which his whole force consisted of one of the companies afore-mentioned, under the command of two knights named Schenk and Thurn. As in the case of the Frauenberg, members of his council were active in riding to and fro between the castle and the town, with the object of establishing a pact with the citizens.

The peasants kept in close touch with the Salzburgers. The chief intermediary of the latter with their overlord was a municipal functionary of the name of Gold. He was, however, suspected of treachery. One day, as the archbishop's military commanders, Hans Schenk and Sigmund von Thurn, were endeavouring to appease a tumultuous general assembly of the citizens on the market-place, Hans Gold was seen on horseback in the neighbourhood. Believing him to be acting the spy, or swayed by motives of personal vengeance, a butcher, against whom Gold had given an unfair decision in his judicial capacity, dragged him off his horse by the hook of his halberd. He was only prevented from running him through by the intervention of a brewer named Pickler. The incident was, nevertheless, a signal for the assembly to become openly insurrectionary ; so much so that Schenk and Thurn themselves, fearing that their force was insufficient for the emergency, made a dash for the castle. Gold himself was not so fortunate, being seized and thrown into one of the towers, where he was put to the torture and had to confess matters concerning the archbishop's policy not calculated to conciliate the popular feeling. Finding that their official leaders had abandoned them, the company of free-lances were nothing loth to allow themselves to be enrolled in the service of the citizens.

The peasants now drew nearer the town, and on Whit Monday the brother of one of the peasants whom Lang had had secretly executed in his castle, entered the gates and rushed through the streets, affixing notices on the houses of the canons and councillors of the archbishop with the words: "This house is mine until the innocent blood of my brother be avenged". The same evening the main body of the peasants entered the city, the gates of which were thrown open to them. The usual scenes ensued on the following day; the palace of the prince-prelate on the market-place was entered; charters, documents and registers were destroyed, so that, as it was stated, one might wade knee-deep in the fragments; kitchens, cellars and dwelling-rooms were sacked, the retainers being turned out. By evening the building was empty, and became a place from the windows of which women hung their washing. In a few days, reinforcements arrived from the mining districts, well-armed and disciplined. Finding this to be the case, a large number of the original ill-armed contingent withdrew to their fields and villages, undertaking to maintain their newly-arrived comrades.

The insurgent city now set about laying siege in earnest to the archbishop and his nobles in the castle, the Hohen-Salzburg, as it

was called. Every possible means of egress
was occupied by them. They were, however,
too late to prevent one of the prelatical councillors from riding off to solicit aid from the
courts of Bavaria and Austria. The Archduke
was himself already too much pressed to afford
any assistance, for in addition to his troubles
previously spoken of in the so-called "five
duchies," the movement had now reached Tyrol.
As for the Duke of Bavaria, so far from being
anxious to assist his brother potentate, he was
disposed to treat secretly with the insurgents,
with the view of obtaining possession of the
Salzburg territories, and was only with difficulty
prevented from carrying out this policy by the
advice of his chancellor, Leonhard von Eck.

The Tyrolese movement is remarkable as
being the only one of which it can be said
that it obtained ultimate success of a modified
kind. With the rest, rapid and complete as
seemed their success at first, as rapidly and
completely were they crushed in a few weeks.
The Tyrolese, on the other hand, not only succeeded in prolonging the struggle far into the
summer of 1526, but, although the far-reaching

aspirations of those engaged in the conflict were
doomed to disappointment, the peasantry as a
whole did not go out altogether empty-handed.
They obtained certain distinct concessions of
a permanent nature. This was partly due, no
doubt, to the intrepid character of the inhabitants, accustomed as they were from the earliest
ages to a life of comparative freedom and in-
dependence ; partly also to the formation of
the country, in many parts inaccessible to any
but natives, and everywhere easily capable of
defence by small bands, and, last but not least,
to the remarkable man who was not only the
intellectual head of the movement, but who
was as eminent as an organiser and diplomatist
as he was bold and logical as a thinker—I refer
to Michael Gaismayr.)

On the Tyrolese insurrection, it may be
worth while to quote here a report of a hostile
contemporary witness, George Kirchmair (*apud*
Jansen, vol. ii., pp. 492-494) : " There arose,"
writes Kirchmair, "a cruel, fearful, inhuman
insurrection of the common peasant-folk in this
land, at which I was at hand and beheld many
wonders. Certain noisy, base people did
adventure with violence to free from the judge

a condemned rebel who had done mischief and
who justly had been ordained to the penalty.
After that they had done this thing on a Wednesday, did the peasants run together out of all
mountains and valleys on Whit Sunday, young
and old, albeit they knew not what they would
do. As then a great concourse was come
together in the Muklander Au within the
Eisack valley, their conclusion was to free
themselves from their oppression. A noble
gentleman, Sigmund Brandisser, bailiff at
Rodenegg, went straightway to the assembled
peasants and showed to them all the danger,
vanity, mischief, trouble and care. Notwithstanding that they promised him not to go
forward to deeds, but to bring their complaint
before their rightful prince, who was then in
Innsbruck, yet did they not keep their promise,
but on Whit Sunday at night made assault
to Brixen, plundering and robbing in defiance
of God and right, all priests, canons and
chaplains. Thereafter did they assemble before the bishop's court and drave thence his
councillors and his servants, with much violence, and in such inhuman manner that one
may not write thereof. They of Brixen had

as soon forgotten their duty toward Bishop
Sebastian as the peasants of the new foundation toward their lord, the Prior Augustin.
In fine, was there no duty, faith, vow, or other
thing whatsoever bethought. The Brixeners
and the peasants were of one mind. Every
part had its chief men. These chiefs did
without any cause or any renunciation (of
allegiance) move with five thousand men against
the monastery of the new foundation, and
overran the priory on Friday, the 12th of May,
1525. Of the wantonness which they there
wrought, a man might write a whole book.
Prior Augustin, a pious man, was driven out
and pursued, and the priests in such wise
despised, mocked and tormented, that they
must forsooth be made ashamed of the priestly
sign and name. More than twenty-five thousand
florins of loss in houses, silver, treasure, fur-
nishings and eating vessels, charters and books,
did the peasants bring about. No man may
say with how much pride, drunkenness, blas-
pheming and sacrilege the priory was at this
time offended. It had also been burned, had
not God willed it otherwise. On Saturday, the
13th of May, they chose a captain, a fair-spoken

yet cunning man, named Michael Gaismayr, son of a squire of Sterzing, an evil, a rebellious, but a cunning man. So soon as he was chosen their captain, the plundering of priests went on in the whole land. There was no priest so poor in the land but that he must lose all that was his own. Thereafter fell they upon divers nobles and did destroy so many that no man could or would arm himself to resist them ; nay, even the Archduke Ferdinand and his most excellent wife held themselves nowhere saved. For in this whole land, in the valley of the Inn and of the Etsch, there was in the towns and amongst the peasants such a concourse, cry, and tumult, that hardly might a good man walk in the streets. Robbing, plundering and stealing did become so common that even not a few pious men were tempted thereto, who afterwards bitterly repented. And I speak the truth when I say that through this robbing, plundering and stealing, did no man wax rich."

A spy of the Archbishop of Trier reports to his master that emissaries from the Tyrolese insurgents were to be found in southern Germany and in Elsass, seeking to establish communications and an understanding between the two movements. He cautions his master at the same time, probably with the fear of Michael Gaismayr's constitutional reforms before his eyes, not to be deceived by the comparatively harmless "articles" of the peasants, for that something quite different lay behind these.

The Tyrolese peasantry had been stirring already, a few years before the great outbreak. They complained of much having been promised, but little carried out, by their lords and rulers. One of their great grievances was the prohibition of the killing of game. This prohibition, at last, they openly disregarded, and so impossible did it become to rehabilitate it that the Austrian Government at Innsbruck formally conceded the right of every peasant to hunt and shoot game on his own land. But, here as elsewhere, the embitterment of the people against nobles and clergy had gone too far to be appeased by partial concessions. In the mining districts, especially those belonging to the Fugger family at Schwatz, where the capitalistic wage-system was apparently first introduced, wages are said to have been in arrear at this time to the extent of forty thousand gulden. Add to this that the imperial council had recently put on an additional tax.

The new religious doctrines had soon obtained adherents in the Tyrol, especially amongst the miners. Foremost of the preachers were Johannes Strauss and Urbanus Regius. The evil life of princes and great ones was, of course, denounced. The rights proclaimed by the new jurists were likewise attacked as heathenish, and as not binding on Christian men. The year of jubilee was declared to be an institution still in force. Many other doctrines of a like nature were promulgated. A friar left his cell and engaged himself as a workman in the Fugger mines, in order to follow out the scriptural injunction to earn bread by the sweat of his brow. Here he had a taste of the newly-introduced wages-system for profit.

Followers of Thomas Munzer, or at least persons holding similar views, appeared also about this time in the valleys in question. Finally, these mining and peasant communities assembled together in the usual manner and drew up nineteen "articles" of reform. Most

of these " articles " deal with the right of
preaching the Gospel and other rights iden-
tical with those demanded elsewhere.   The
novel points were protests against the constant
passage of armed men through the country and
the quartering of alien troops in the frontier
villages.   One of the complaints was directed
against the free exportation of the wines of
Trient ; another against the reckless riding of
lords over cultivated fields ; another against
the new lawyer class ; yet another against the
keeping of wine-rooms by the judges and
clerks of tribunals.   Most noteworthy of all was
a remonstrance against the Fugger family and
against other privileged companies of merchants,
which through their agents produced such a
great increase in the cost of provisions that
many articles had risen in price from eighteen
kreutzers to a gulden.   The assembled country
people gave also, as one of the immediate
causes of their action in coming together, the
attempted removal by the authorities of certain
ordnance and ammunition, which removal, however, it would appear, they had been successful
in preventing.   Zimmermann conjectures that
they feared that the war-material in question

was to be used against their brethren who had risen in the neighbouring provinces.

The concessions of the archduke had their effect for the moment. Most of the rural communities consented to await the Landtag which was to consider their grievances. This applies to the Tyrol itself, but not to the Vorarlberg. In and around Bregenz the insurrection gathered, until it soon numbered forty thousand men, who insultingly replied to the emissaries from the archducal court at Innsbruck that they would come in a few days and bring the answer themselves to the proposals made.

In the south also, the movement showed no signs of abating. As we have seen, the source and centre of the Tyrolese rising was the neighbourhood of the town of Brixen, many public functionaries there joining the cause. Michael Gaismayr himself had been the bishop's secretary and the keeper of the customs at Klausen. From the proceeds of the sacking of the wealthy house of the Teutonic Order at Bozen, Gaismayr, now elected captain of the local contingent, formed the nucleus of a war-chest. It was augmented by numerous other spoliations of ecclesiastical possessions.   Gaismayr, further, at once opened up a correspondence with the view of gathering into his hand the threads of agitation in the surrounding territories.   In his manifestoes he knew how to combine in the cleverest way the immediate aspirations and the popular demands of those with whom he was dealing, whilst hinting at the more far-reaching projects of the Christian commonwealth that formed his ultimate goal.   For example, he knew how to exploit patriotic sentiment by pointing out the evils resulting from the occupation of important posts by aliens, notably by Spaniards, whose promotion Charles V. and his brother had naturally favoured.

Under Gaismayr the insurrection rapidly spread, in spite of the archduke's blandishments and the temporary character of the peasants' success in certain interior districts of the Tyrol itself.   From the lake of Garda and Trient in the south, the whole country soon broke out into open and organised revolt.   One peasant camp was formed outside the city of Trient itself. Other contingents swept the valleys of the Brixen territories and of the Etsch, plundering monasteries and castles, and occupying the smaller towns or laying them under contribution. Gaismayr's headquarters were at Meran. With him were the delegates of the towns and of the various jurisdictions of the Tyrol province, endeavouring with difficulty to reconcile local demands with one another and with the general object of the movement. Loyalty to the feudal chiefs of the province, the house of Austria, seems to have been deeply ingrained in the hearts of the countryfolk, and, in spite of his own ultimate end, Gaismayr was careful not to openly collide with, or even disregard, this feeling. Although the local nobility and clergy were everywhere regarded as fair game for plunder and rapine, the agrarians were particularly concerned to spare the archduke's castles.

Meanwhile, the archduke himself continued to adopt a conciliatory and even friendly tone in his messages. It is said that he had really an affection for his patrimonial province, but in any case he had no force of fighting men at hand with which to quell the revolted populations. That this latter motive was chiefly responsible for his mildness is evidenced by the fact that he gave orders to the Innsbruck council to negotiate a loan by the pledging of certain lands and jewellery for the purpose of raising the force he wanted. At the same time he sought to hurry on the promised Landtag.

Gaismayr, on his side, had called a Landtag, which, however, was forbidden by the archduke by special messengers with signed and sealed despatches. On the despatches being read, the majority of the peasant council at Meran accepted the armistice and abandoned the projected Landtag, which was to have been held at that place. But difficulties arose when it was found that the Austrian Government did not interpret the armistice as implying any duty on its part to abstain from further armaments. In a special rescript to the imperial authorities, written about this date by the archduke, the latter lets his mask of mildness fall, complaining that the machinations of the evil-minded populations were such that they would allow no foreign mercenaries to enter the country, that he himself was practically a prisoner in his own land, and that from day to day there was no certainty that the capital, Innsbruck itself, would not be attacked.

The insurrection was master throughout the duchy. On the calling of the Landtag at Innsbruck, a hundred and six "articles," formulated by the standing council at Meran, probably under Gaismayr's direction, were submitted, and the archduke was compelled to concede a number of points that must have proved very sour to him. These were finally brought together in the form of a new constitution for the province, containing strong and democratic provisions. But further demands were made in many quarters, and the insurrection, everywhere smouldering, burst out into renewed activity in several districts.

We must now, for the present, leave the fortunes of the Tyrolese, in order to turn to those of the movement in west Austrian lands and in the Alsatian and Rhenish districts abutting on them. It is impossible to separate, either topographically or historically, the hither Austrian dominion of Breisgau from the Margravate of Baden and the adjoining districts. The Black Forest contingent, under Hans Müller von Bulgenbach, moved westward early in May for the purpose of combining with contingents which had formed, in the latter part of April, in the Austrian territory and in the Margravate, and of making a combined attack upon the important city of Freiburg, one of the best defended and most noteworthy towns of south-west Germany. Breisgau and Baden had been in a state of fermentation for a year past. Local disturbances and a threatened general rising are recorded from the early summer of 1524 onwards. By the end of that year, large numbers of nobles and clerics, apprehending a new "*Bundschuh*" had fled into Freiburg for security, amongst them the Markgraf Ernst, with his wife and children. Freiburg had, therefore, become a nest of the privileged classes and a repository of vast treasures.

The chief of the Margravate contingent was one Hans Hammerstein. In dread of an attack by Hammerstein upon his castle of Rotelen, the Markgraf had taken to flight. Rotelen, however, did not share the fate of so many other strongholds of Baden, and was reserved for destruction in the second half of the seventeenth century during the wars of Louis XIV. Arrived at Freiburg, the Markgraf sent conciliatory letters, accompanied by offers of mediation on the part of the Freiburg authorities. But, unlike his brother Philip, a man of exceptional humanity for that age, and immensely popular with his subjects, Ernst was mistrusted, and could not succeed in making any impression with his overtures. After discussing the matter in conclave, the peasants returned answer that if he would unreservedly countersign the " Twelve Articles," and regard himself henceforward as no more than the trustee and vicegerent of the emperor, he might retain his castle and his lands. If, on the other hand, he refused to consider himself as *primus inter pares* of themselves, it would go badly with him, since they were determined to have done with nobles, to have nobody in authority over them save peasants like themselves, and to acknowledge no lord but the emperor. These proposals obviously did not suit this wealthy territorial magnate, who, finding himself in security for the time being, was content to let matters drift.

The practical refusal of the Markgraf to concede anything resulted in a rising of the whole land. All the important castles, including Rotelen, were occupied. A camp of peasant contingents was formed at Heidersheim. The wealthy monastery of Thennenbach was stripped, suffering damage, as was alleged, to the amount of thirty thousand gulden, whilst the small town of Kenzingen was taken and garrisoned, and the arrival was awaited of Hans Müller with his contingent before Freiburg.

Freiburg was at its wits' end, and was well-nigh denuded of fighting men, having a few weeks previously sent some bodies of free-lances in its service to the assistance of other towns more immediately threatened than itself. The Schlossberg, the great stronghold commanding the town, was manned by no more than a hundred and twenty-four men. All available persons, however, who were in the town, made ready to assist in its defence, and all flaws in the fortifications were repaired. The authorities then sent out to know the meaning of the presence of Hans Müller and the Black Forest contingent in the Breisgau territory. The reply was an expression of regret that Freiburg should be on the side of the oppressors of the "common man," and of hope that the city would enter the " Evangelical Brotherhood ". To this the city answered that its oath to the House of Austria prevented its undertaking such obligations as those suggested, but professed its willingness to mediate where special grievances could be shown, and concluded with hoping that the Black Forest peasants, mindful of how divine and blessed it was to live in peace, would withdraw themselves from the neighbourhood of Breisgau. Hans Müller, thereupon, declared that his Black Forest men were not acting without the concurrence of their brethren, the Breisgau peasants. He then moved his camp into the city's immediate proximity.

By the 17th of May, the local contingents also arrived before Freiburg, from the battlements of which the banners of twenty companies were to be counted. Accordingly, the forces being now joined, an ultimatum was sent on this day requiring the formal alliance of Freiburg with the " Evangelical Brotherhood ". No answer was returned, and the siege began by the close investment of the city. Aqueducts were constructed to draw off the water. The block-house on the Schlossberg was taken by surprise a day or two later, and, as some nobles were sitting on a fine May evening drinking their wine before a hostelry in the cathedral close, five hundred shots fell around them. The fighting power of the town was forthwith drawn up in readiness on the fish-market. The citizens were divided into twelve companies corresponding to the twelve guilds, each of which had to defend its own gate, tower and section of the wall. Even the University supplied its company, consisting of some forty students under the leadership of the rector and two professors. Help from without was nowhere forthcoming. The civic authorities thus expressed themselves in a report made later on : " No man did come to our help. From Hegau to Strasburg, and thence from Würtemberg to the Welsh [French] country we had no friends. All townships, hamlets and villages were against us."

On the evening of the 21st, a further ultimatum from the peasants was sent into the town. They only wished well to the country, but demanded "a goodly Christian order and the freeing of the common man from excessive and unjust burdens". Meanwhile, within the town,

ominous voices made themselves heard in the
guildrooms. Freiburg was not in a position to
sustain a long siege, and the idea of its being
taken by assault was not palatable to the
wealthy citizens. Moreover, sympathy with
the peasant cause, though not so widely spread
as in some other towns, was not wanting, and -
there were many poor citizens who had friendly
relations with the besiegers without the walls.
The upshot was that on the 24th of May, a
week after the siege had been begun, Freiburg
capitulated and agreed to enter the "Evangelical
Brotherhood ".

Both sides pledged themselves to do their
utmost to further a general peace, and the
removal of the burdens of the " common man,"
and also to cherish the true principles of the
Gospel. The relations of the town to its feudal
overlord were not to be compromised, nor
its liberty in any way curtailed. It was to pay
to the assembled contingents the sum of three
thousand gulden as earnest of its good intentions. This sum was afterwards increased, and
further pecuniary demands were made. Freiburg appears also to have supplied the peasants
with some artillery, for in an exculpatory

report, subsequently made to the Austrian Government, we read : " We have indeed loaned the peasants four falconets, the which had no great worth, but yet for no other end than that they might hold the Rhine at Limburg against the Welsh [the foreigners]. For we have given the commandment to the twain to whom we delivered them that they should destroy this ordnance so soon as there were danger against any other person soever." Thus ended the peasant siege of Freiburg.

The attention of the peasant bodies was at this time drawn off from Freiburg and Breisgau generally to the disasters that were befalling their cause in the neighbouring Elsass. Even the strongly-fortified town of Breisach they were content to leave, after having threatened it for some days, on a pledge being given that no foreign troops should be permitted to cross the river at any point within the defensive capacity of the town.

The attack on the town of Villingen was repulsed, the garrison making sorties and razing the peasant homesteads near by. Rudolfzell, which, as we have seen, had received into its walls numbers of fugitive nobles, who con-

stituted its main armed force, had also compelled the Black Foresters to retire. A body
of knights, in fact, in making a sortie, distinguished themselves by burning the neighbouring villages and throwing women and children
into the flames. An agreement was ultimately
made through the mediation of the popular and
amiable Markgraf Philip of Baden, who also
acted on behalf of his brother Ernst. It consisted of the following two articles : (1) that the
great tithe should be rendered as of wont, but,
until the judgment of the matter, should be laid
by in a neutral place, while the small tithe
should not be rendered until this judgment, and
that *corvées* should also cease meanwhile ; (2)
that all the ordnance of the Markgraf and all
other that might be in the hands of the peasant
bodies should be brought into the town of Neuen-
burg, should be there preserved until the issue
of the matter, and should be by neither side
used against the other.

About this time—the middle of June—further
understandings as regards an armistice were
entered into between the various contingents
and Freiburg, Breisach, Offenburg, and other
towns of Breisgau and Baden.

We now turn to the contiguous, and in many respects allied, movement in Elsass. Here the insurrection began, as elsewhere, early in April. It spread like wild-fire from town to town and from village to village. A contemporary, writing from Strasburg at the end of April, says: " The peasants have everywhere assembled themselves in companies. They hold the most towns and divers castles. The Papists are in a fear such as is not to be believed. The rich are filled with alarm for their treasure, and even we in our strong town live not wholly without dread."

Iconoclasm was the order of the day in Strasburg. Churches were ransacked; monks and nuns were driven out of cloister and convent. The city, in fact, was at one time in imminent danger of falling into the hands of the rebels. The council, however, appears to have got wind of a conspiracy to introduce the armed peasants into the town, and sixteen worthy burghers were in consequence arrested, some of them paying for their temerity with their lives. Unfortunately, throughout Elsass many priceless works of mediæval art were destroyed in the pillaging ; pictures, wood carvings, and the contents of monastic libraries being often used for the lighting of fires.

On the 28th of April the " United Contingent of Elsass," as it was called, which numbered 20,000 men, commanded by one Erasmus Gerber, marched along a mountain ridge constituted by a spur of the Vosges, to attack the town of Zabern, the residence of the Bishop of Strasburg. Zabern, although comparatively small, was well fortified, and was calculated to form a most valuable base and storehouse for the insurgent forces. Their first objective was the wealthy abbey of Mauersmunster, between two and three miles from Zabern. The foundation was completely sacked from cellar to roof. An establishment of the Teutonic Order was also sacked, and a valuable booty was obtained. In fact, the insurgent camp glittered with chalices, salvers, church utensils, and decorations of all sorts. Zabern was then challenged to open its gates and join the Peasant League. The canons and the patrician councillors wished to send for help to Duke Antoine of Lorraine, who on the first symptoms of danger had offered to throw a garrison into the town. The bulk of the citizens, however, declared that they would rather open their gates to the peasants than to these Frenchmen. They refused to receive any aliens at all. Finally, after some negotiations, the gates were opened, and the peasant army entered Zabern on the 13th of May, occupying the fortifications with a strong force, and also entrenching themselves immediately outside the walls.

Far-reaching plans seem to have been talked of at this time of the invasion of France and of the humiliation of the French *seigneur* like the German *adelige*. The impression seems to have prevailed that the whole strength of the French *noblesse* had been exhausted at the battle of Pavia. The importance of the capture of Zabern was hardly to be exaggerated, and Duke Antoine hurried on his preparations for crushing the rebels. Weissenburg was from the very first entirely in their hands, even the bürgermeister and the majority of the council being on the insurgent side, together with the powerful vintners' guild, to which most of the councillors belonged.

The formula of the peasants was to demand, "in the name of Jesus Christ our Lord," that every town, hamlet and village should furnish their fourth man to the contingent. As we have seen in a former chapter, the demands put forward in Elsass were considerably more drastic than the celebrated " Twelve Articles ". An agent of the Archbishop of Trier reports to his master that the " common man " of the towns was far more violent even than the peasant. " With one accord," he writes, " cry they : ' we will not alone win monasteries and castles. but will have our hands busy in the towns, and there also will we be as gentlemen '." He alleges that they had definite relations with the Breisgau and Black Forest contingents.

The movement did not leave the town of Colmar untouched. The discontented here formulated fourteen " articles," which they laid before the council. The matter was quieted for a time, but in the second week of April renewed disturbances took place. The insurrection, however, did not succeed in making any headway within the walls, and in spite of repeated threats the gates remained closed to the peasants. Colmar in fact at this time, like many other towns that had successfully resisted invasion, was full of fugitives glad to

save the wreck of their property. Jews were
especially in evidence.

From Elsass, the movement spread along the
Rhine. On the 23rd of April, in a village in
the neighbourhood of Landau, on the occasion
of a *kirchweih* (church-ale), a peasant band
formed itself, which subsequently developed into
the so-called Geilweiler contingent. Emissaries
from the band went round all the neighbouring villages, visited the peasants in their
houses, and even fetched them out of their
beds, persuading or compelling them to join
the ranks. The band almost immediately
began the pillaging of monasteries and other
ecclesiastical foundations. They took therefrom
" corn, wine, cattle and victuals, and lived in
wantonness," says a contemporary chronicler.
The neighbouring castles shared the same fate.
Such an enormous amount of spoil was collected,
that the half of it had to be left behind in a
village through which the contingent passed.
Day by day their numbers swelled. Feeling
themselves strong enough now to proceed to
greater things, they summoned, on Sunday, the
13th of April, the little, well-fortified town of
Neustadt to surrender. The Rhenish Elector

in vain admonished the citizens to hold no
converse with " the wanton, lawless band ".
The Bishop of Speyer, who counted a large
number of his own *villeins* in the contingent,
also interposed without effect.

At the beginning of May another body formed
near Lauterburg, the captain being the burgermeister of that place. The bishop was forced
to concede to them the entry into one or two
strongholds, on their professing to have no
disloyal sentiments towards himself, but only
to wish to defend the territory against the
foreigner. In Lauterburg, high festival was
held. The overhanging castle was broken
into, and, according to a contemporary account,
" the women from the villages hard by did
come into the castles and did drink themselves
so full of wine that they might no more walk ".
Meanwhile the town of Landau itself had become the prey of the Geilweiler contingent, and
had to hand over all the corn and wine in its
possession, most of which had been entrusted
to its care by various neighbouring monasteries.
Two peasant delegates from each company
were sent into the town to see that there was
no cheating in this transaction.

A band now formed in the neighbourhood of Worms which swept the country round, receiving the adhesion of all the villages through which it passed. On learning of the approach of the Marshal of the Palatinate, Wilhelm von Habern, with a force of three hundred horse and five hundred foot, they established themselves in a strong position in a vine-clad hill above the little town of Westhofen. The marshal was prevented by the favourable position of the peasants from making a direct attack, but he had no sooner fired three shots into their camp than they fled into the village below—a flight that cost the lives of sixty of them at the hands of the marshal's men. During the night they retreated to Neustadt, where they united with the Geilweiler contingent.

The Elector Ludwig, besides being unable for want of men to suppress the rising by force, showed signs of his being sincerely desirous of an amicable arrangement with his subjects. Through the mediation of the town of Neustadt, an interview was arranged between the elector and the peasant leaders in a field outside the village of Forst. It was stipulated, however, that the elector should be accompanied by no more than thirty horsemen as his retinue. As soon as the parties were met, the whole of the peasant forces appeared on the brow of an elevation a little way off.

This was evidently a device of the leaders to overawe the elector. After protracted negotiations, it was agreed that the towns, castles and villages taken should be surrendered to their lawful lords and masters, that no further hostile acts should be committed, and that the peasant bands, which here numbered some 8000 men, should disperse to their homes. On his side, the Elector Ludwig promised the peasants a complete amnesty, and, in addition, the calling at an early date of a Landtag, at which their grievances should be considered and remedied.

Thereupon the elector retired for the night to Neustadt. The following day, on representatives of the peasants announcing themselves with a view of obtaining a definite promise as to the date of the Landtag in question, the elector not only satisfied their demands, but invited them to his table. " There," in the words of Harer, a contemporary historian of the war, " one saw *villeins* and their lord sit together, and eat and drink together. He had, so it seemed, one heart to them and they to him."

The Landtag was then convened for the week after Whitsuntide. Its decisions were to be binding throughout the whole country, that is to say, on both sides of the Rhine. The seemingly mild, and even generous conduct of the elector did not, however, entirely quell the insurrection. General excitement and the temptation of plunder were too great. Bands of peasants throughout the Palatinate continued the old course of pillage and destruction. It was not until the common suppression of the movement that these bands dispersed, and the Palatinate settled down to its wonted state. Similarly, in the adjacent bishopric of Speyer, in spite of agreements, it was not until the advance of Truchsess and the forces of the Swabian League that all hostilities on the side of the peasants came to an end.

CHAPTER VII.

THE THURINGIAN REVOLT AND THOMAS MÜNZER.

WE come now to speak of the figure most prominently associated by tradition and the popular mind with the Peasants War. In the view of most persons, the whole movement that we are describing centres in the figure of the schoolmaster and preacher who came from Stolberg in the Hartz Mountains. For weal or for woe, history seems to have indelibly stamped the last great peasant revolt of the Middle Ages with the name of Thomas Münzer. Yet it may be fairly doubted whether the stupendous influence on the events of the year 1525 attributed by historical tradition to the personality in question has not been very much exaggerated.

That Münzer, in the winter of 1524-5, made a tour of agitation through central and southern Germany, including those districts where the revolt earliest broke out, is undoubtedly

, but we find, if we analyse the accounts, that the reception of his preaching was by no means everywhere encouraging. Thus Melancthon, in his pamphlet *Historie Thoma Müntzers*, etc., expressly states that the Franconians, who, as we have seen, played such a zealous and important part in the movement, would have none of Münzer or his doctrine. It is, of course, perfectly true that the object of the malignant toady Melancthon in writing this political manifesto, was to curry favour with the victorious princes and to defame Münzer's character. But, seeing that the whole trend of the work in question is to display Münzer in the *role* of a powerful and dangerous demagogue, as, in fact, a kind of arch-fiend of rebellion, Melancthon can have had no conceivable object in making the above statement. Moreover, a statement of this kind, not referring to an obscure episode in a man's life, but to his public activity of a few months before, if untrue, must have been so notoriously untrue as not to have been worth the stating. Hence, in the absence of rebutting evidence which does not seem forthcoming, we can hardly do otherwise than accept it. Other accounts, which speak of Münzer's influence in south Germany, especially in the *Klettgau* and the *Hegau*, leave it uncertain how far they refer to Münzer himself and how far to those preaching similar doctrines—doctrines unquestionably in the air at the time, and not exclusively ascribable to any single man.

Turning from Münzer as agitator to Münzer as thinker, the same tendency to exaggeration with otherwise accurate and sober-minded historians is often to be found. Münzer is represented as an embodiment not only of the practical movement of the time but also of its idealistic side. That he energetically championed the chiliastic notion of a Christian Commonwealth, tnen so generally prevalent amongst the thinking heads of the revolt, is true enough. But, on the other hand, we fail to discover in his extant writings anything more than vague aspirations towards it ; there is certainly nothing approaching the originality of handling, and the elaboration of the idea, exhibited by Michael Gaismayr. We find this even in the pamphlet where the social views of Münzer are most prominent, his " Emphatic Exposure of the False Belief of the Faithless

World " ("*Aussgetruckte emplossung des falschen Glaubens der ungetrewen Welt*"), published at Mühlhausen late in 1524.   Here also all we have is a vague expression of belief in the necessity of the establishment of a communistic society and in its approaching advent.

Münzer strikes us as before everything a theologian.   This is noticeable in his pamphlets down to the very eve of the Peasants War. In the one on the ordering of the German mass at Allstatt, in another on the book of Daniel, and in an exposition of the nineteenth Psalm—the last published in 1525—we see him most concerned to justify his ecclesiastical innovations and his theories respecting infant baptism, the Eucharist, and other edifying theological topics.   He speaks, indeed, at times bitterly enough of the oppression of prince, noble and prelate, and of the right of the " common man " to rebel, but, we repeat, there is no evidence of any constructive theory beyond the most casual expressions.   Of course, in saying this, we by no means forget that his main strength lay in his fervid oratory, and that his influence from this point of view was considerable.   All we contend is that, as in so many historical cases, chance has played kindly with his fame, and has obtained for him credit for an influence, theoretical and practical, over the general movement of 1525 which the cold light of research hardly seems to justify.

Thomas Munzer appears to have been born in the last decade of the fifteenth century. An uncertain tradition states that his father was hanged by the Count of Stolberg. The first we hear of him with certainty is as teacher in the Latin school at Aschersleben and afterwards at Halle. Where he studied is doubtful, but by this time he had already graduated as doctor. In Halle he is alleged to have started an abortive conspiracy against the Archbishop of Madgeburg. In 1515 we find him as confessor in a nunnery and afterwards as teacher in a foundation school at Brunswick. Finally, in 1520, he became preacher at the *Marienkirche* at Zwickau, and here his public activity in the wider sense really began. The democratic tendencies previously displayed by him broke all bounds. He thundered against those who devoured widows' houses and made long prayers and who at death-beds were concerned not with the faith of the dying but with the gratification of their measureless greed.

At this time Münzer was still a follower of Luther, but it was not long before he found him a lukewarm church-reformer. Luther's bibliolatry, as opposed to his own belief in the continuous inspiration of certain chosen men by the Divine spirit, excited his opposition. He criticised still more severely as an unpardonable inconsistency Luther's retention of certain dogmas of the old Church whilst rejecting others. He now began to study with enthusiasm the works of the old German mystics, Meister Eck and Johannes Tauler, and more than all those of Joachim Florus, the Italian enthusiast of the twelfth century. A general conviction soon became uppermost in his mind of the necessity of a thorough revolution alike of Church and State.

His mystical tendencies were strengthened by contact with a sect which had recently sprung up amongst the clothworkers of Zwickau, and of which one Nicholas Storch, a master clothworker, was corypheus. The sect in question lived in a constant belief in the approach of a millennium to be brought about by the efforts of the " elect ". Visions and ecstasies were the

order of the day amongst these good people.
This remarkable sect influenced various prominent persons at this time. Karlstadt was
completely fascinated by them. Melancthon
was carried away ; and even Luther admits
having had some doubts whether they had not
a Divine mission. The worthy Elector Friedrich
himself would take no measures against them,
in spite of the dangerous nature of their teaching
from the point of view of political stability. He
was afraid, as he said, " lest perchance he should
be found fighting against God ".

It was not long before Munzer allied himself with these " enthusiasts," or " prophets
of Zwickau," as they were called. When
the patrician council at Zwickau forbade the
cloth-workers to preach, Munzer denounced
the ordinance and encouraged them to disobey
it. New prohibitions followed, culminating in
prosecutions and imprisonments. The result
was that, by the end of 1521, the cloth-working
town had become too hot to hold the new
reformers. Some fled to Wittenberg, and
others, including Munzer himself, into Bohemia.
Arrived in Prague, Munzer posted up an
announcement in Latin and German that he

would "like that excellent warrior of Christ, Johann Huss, fill the trumpets with a new song". He proceeded in his addresses to denounce the clergy, and to prophesy the approaching vengeance of heaven upon their order. He here also preached against the "dead letter," as he called it, of the Bible, expounding his favourite theory of the necessity of believing in the supplemental inspiration of all elect persons. But the soil of Bohemia proved not a grateful one. It had been exhausted by over a century of religious fanaticism and utopistic dreams of social regeneration.

The next we hear of Münzer is as preacher at Alstatt in Thuringia. Allstatt was the scene of his great Church reformation, in defence of which he published a pamphlet. The whole service was conducted in the German language. All the books of the Bible were read and expounded in their order, instead of the isolated passages used in the Roman ritual. His success here was immense. Crowds streamed to hear him from the neighbouring towns and villages. He soon counted not a few theologians and other learned persons amongst his adherents.

Great was the rush from all sides to listen to the popular preacher. As Munzer himself has it, "the poor thirsty folk did so yearn for the truth that all the streets were full of people come to hear it".

He was still, up to the spring of 1523, almost ⎞
entirely a drastic Church reformer rather than ⊢
a political or social revolutionist. He wrote ⎠
repeatedly to the Elector Friedrich of Saxony and to his brother, Duke Johann, exhorting them as his "dearest, most beloved rulers," and warning them not to be deceived by hypocritical priests, but to boldly take their stand on the Gospel. Finding that his admonitions to those in authority produced no immediate effect, he turned with increasing zeal to the "common man". Although the religious side of Munzer's character probably remained the most prominent to the end, the political side now came distinctly ⊣
to the fore. He founded a secret society at /
Allstatt pledged by a solemn oath to labour /
unceasingly for the promotion of the new king-dom of God on earth, a kingdom to be based on the model of the primitive Christian Church as he supposed it to have been. Freedom and equality must reign here. The princes and the

great ones of the earth refused to espouse the
cause of the new Gospel. Hence, they must
be overthrown, and the "common man," who
was prepared to embrace the Gospel, must be
raised up in their place. He who would not
become a citizen of the kingdom of God must
be banished or killed. The great barrier to
the awakening of the inward light was the
riches of this world. Hence, in the kingdom
of God, private wealth should cease to be, and
all things should be in common.

Münzer now began to send out missionaries
to different parts of Germany, and soon after
established a special printing press in Allstatt
for the publication of the pamphlets he was
issuing. Whilst at this town he also, like
Luther, married an escaped nun. As a result
of his preaching against the worship of images,
a chapel, a well-known place of pilgrimages
near Allstatt, was burned to the ground. Called
to account for this by Duke Johann, those
responsible, Münzer at their head, refused to
appear to answer for their action, justifying
themselves by texts out of the Old Testament.

Finally, Elector Friedrich and Duke Johann

came in person to the castle at Allstatt, where
they summoned Münzer to preach before them
and expound the doctrines that seemed so
subversive of "social order". Münzer, obeying
the summons, delivered an impassioned sermon,
well stocked with Biblical quotations. In this
discourse he vehemently demanded the death
of all priests and monks who perverted the
people and who stigmatised the Gospel preached
by him as heresy. The godless, he said, had
no right to live. If the princes refused themselves to exterminate the godless, God would
take the sword from them and accomplish the
work through others. He then proceeded to
attack such social evils of the times as usury,
oppression by princes and lords, and the appro-
priation by them of what of right belonged to
the "common man," the fish in the water, the
fowls of the air, the produce of the soil. While
professing to protect the commandments of
God, one of which said "Thou shalt not steal,"
they themselves robbed without mercy the poor
husbandman and the poor craftsman. If the
latter in their turn committed aught, be it never
so little, against the property of their lords, they
must forsooth hang for it. To all this iniquity,

said he, your Doctor Liar — his favourite
sobriquet for Luther — saith Amen.

The effect on his princely hearers may be
imagined, an effect that was enhanced when
Münzer immediately caused his discourse to
be printed and circulated amongst their liege
subjects.   It does not appear that even now
the mild and benevolent-minded prince-elector
took any action, but Duke Johann at once ordered the printer to quit the territory.   Münzer,
in a document dated the 13th of July, 1524,
protests against the attempt to prevent his freely
expounding the doctrines with which the Divine
Spirit had inspired him.   He refused the in-
vitation of Luther to debate with him at Wittenberg, alleging the undue influence of Luther's
party in that town.   He would not, he said,
preach in a corner, but only before the people.

The new doctrines were now gall and worm-
wood to Luther, who had hurried back from
the Wartburg in the spring of 1523, on learning
of the turn things were taking in Wittenberg
owing to the doctrines of the Zwickau enthusiasts.   In imminent fear of the Reformation
getting beyond his control, he had succeeded
by his strong personality and authority in

stemming the tide, but only after he had made
some outward concessions, at least, to the new
tendencies. Thus, the German mass, the total
abolition of images, and other innovations introduced by Karlstadt and his friends were
reluctantly adopted by Luther. But the new
political and social doctrines, represented by
Münzer, Luther could not away with. In a
letter to his patron, the prince-elector, against
the rebellious spirit abroad, Luther entreats the
princes to banish these unruly prophets. " Let
them keep their hands still," said he, "or
straightway be cast out of the land. Thus
should be the speech of princes to the prophets.
For Satan worketh through these misguided
spirits." Münzer, not without reason, retorted
on Luther that he (Luther) wished to hand
over the Church he had torn from the Pope to
the secular princes, and that he himself would
fain be the new Pope. Luther's little dog,
Melancthon, wrote to his friend Spalatin in
tones of unctuous horror that the new preachers
would make worldly politics of the Gospel.
Territorial lords forbade their villeins to attend
Münzer's preaching.

A false disciple at this time betrayed Münzer's

secret propagandist organisation to the authorities. The result was the citation of Münzer to the castle at Weimar once more to give an account of himself before the princes, this time on a direct accusation of incitement to rebellion. He went alone and ably defended himself when confronted with passages from his published tracts. The prince-elector still maintained his unwillingness to take active measures against the new doctrines, preferring, as he expressed it, to take his staff in hand and quit for ever his ancestral territories rather than risk doing aught against the will of God. Certainly, Prince Friedrich of Saxony is one of the very few potentates in history of whose complete sincerity and single-mindedness we can have no reasonable doubt. His brother, however, Duke Johann, and the councillors, threatened Münzer with peremptory expulsion from the land should he continue his present course. Münzer was then dismissed. As he descended from the castle he met one of his friends who was in the princely service. " How hath it gone with thee ? " asked the latter. " It hath so gone with me," replied Münzer, " that I must needs seek another principality."

Münzer hurried back to Allstatt, but only to find that the sworn enemy of the Reformation, the aggressively Catholic Duke George of Saxony, had interposed, demanding of the elector his deliverance into his hands, and threatening to interfere by force of arms if he were longer allowed to remain at Allstatt. At last the elector gave way to the extent of issuing an order to the town council of Allstatt to direct Münzer to leave that place. Münzer immediately quitted Allstatt for the neighbouring imperial city of Mühlhausen. This city, like the other Thuringian towns, notably Erfurt, had been profoundly excited by the events of the Reformation. Münzer here encountered the man who was destined to be his colleague in the noteworthy historical events that followed. This was Heinrich Pfeiffer, who was originally a monk in a neighbouring monastery, and had Luther-wise cast his cowl. He preached the new doctrines, first of all, in the territory of the Archbishop of Mainz. Driven thence he returned to his native town. Here he further carried on the work of a popular preacher and agitator.

One Sunday, as the public crier summoned

the burghers to partake of beer and wine, he stood upon the stone when the crier quitted it, shouting : " Hear me, ye citizens ; I will offer you another drink ". He proceeded abusing the clergy, monks and nuns in the usual church reformer's manner. His discourse exciting attention, he promised to preach again from the same place next day. The city council in vain summoned him before them, he replying that he would first keep his word and deliver the promised speech. At its close, he deigned to appear at the *Rathhaus*, but accompanied by such a formidable crowd of sympathisers that the council (*Rath*) feared to take immediate steps against him.

Pfeiffer continued to preach at Mühlhausen, and his adherents increased every day. He now boldly demanded a guard of honour from the council, to ensure his safety from the enemies of the Gospel. This being naturally refused, he again ascended the stone of the public crier, and challenged the immense crowd assembled to indicate by holding up their hands their determination to stand by him and the Gospel. A forest of hands appeared in response. The matter now shaped itself as a conflict between the town population, zealous supporters of Pfeiffer, and the patrician council, as zealous upholders of the old order in Church and State.

Pfeiffer soon became convinced of the need for a radical reformation of the council. What happened in other towns happened also in Mühlhausen. A non-official council or committee of the citizens was formed to oppose the *Rath*. Pfeiffer's chief claim was that the churches should cease to be the exclusive appanage of members of the " Teutonic Order," but should be occupied by competent preachers of the new doctrines. The *Rath* finally took the step of driving Pfeiffer from the town. A short time afterwards, however, he seems to have returned. The iconoclastic zeal of the citizens now took the form of the destruction of pictures and ornaments in the churches, but Pfeiffer appears to have taken little part in this action. His chief interest henceforth was the reform of the town government.

On the 24th of August, 1524, he was again driven from Mühlhausen. He now turned to the environs and the peasants. A document containing twelve "articles" was drawn up by

him and presented to the *Rath*.   The articles
were probably the same as those which Munzer
laid before his own contingent, claiming the
confiscation of all the landed property of the
Church, the abolition of *corvées*, the annulment
of feudal dues that could not show a prescription
of two hundred years, and the freedom of the
chase and of fishing.   Reform of the criminal
law was also demanded, with what amounted to
the abolition of the arbitrary jurisdiction of the
territorial feudal lords.   Finally, the election of
the city council by the body of the citizens was
claimed, with the power of revoking mandates.
Eligibility should not be confined to members
of the *Geschlechter* or old patrician families ; at
least a certain number of the council were to
be ordinary guildsmen.

Munzer now arrived in Muhlhausen and
constituted himself the leader of the town
proletariat, just as Pfeiffer was already the
successful champion of the guildsmen or main
body of the citizens against the patrician *Rath*.
The diversity of interests between the two
classes and between the ultimate aims of the
two men caused a certain amount of friction in
the popular movement.   Pfeiffer, as a represen-

tative of the small middle class, desired the destruction of feudalism for middle class purposes, but does not appear to have had any communistic sympathies. Münzer, on the contrary, as we have already seen, was now nothing if not a prophet of the Christian Commonwealth, or Kingdom of God on earth, of which communism, as understood in the Middle Ages, was an essential element. Hence the patrician party was able to force the assent of the requisite number of the body of the citizens to Münzer's expulsion. But that of Pfeiffer followed hard upon it, the guildsmen having apparently become frightened at the intrusion of the extramural proletarians and the peasantry of the city territory into the movement. For it must not be forgotten that the two men, despite divergencies of ultimate purpose, worked hand in hand for the attainment of their immediate objects, Pfeiffer using the eloquence and energy of Münzer to increase the adherents of the revolutionary movement, and Münzer not unwillingly allowing himself to be guided by Pfeiffer's sagacity in matters of organisation, tactics, and the present ends to be striven for.

The expulsion occurred in September, 1524,

and was accompanied by the exodus of many adherents of the movement. Münzer now entered upon a period of several weeks' travel, staying a short time in Nürnberg and then passing the winter in some part of south Germany. This tour, it has been, without doubt rightly, assumed, was of a propagandist character. Münzer certainly traversed various districts, possibly returning by way of Franconia. Pfeiffer, it it said, was back in Mühl-hausen early in December, but it was certainly not before February, 1525, that Münzer again entered the gates of the imperial city. The powerful guild-following of Pfeiffer succeeded in effecting the latter's recall. This success led the adherents of Münzer in and around the town to agitate on behalf also of their leader. Foremost amongst these was an enthusiastic master of the skinners' guild, named Rothe, who, during his leader's absence, kept together the poor journeymen and city proletarians constituting the bulk of Münzer's following. On hearing the call of his disciples, Münzer hurried back to Thuringia. He was arrested on his way in the Fulda territory, but not being identified was released after a few days.

On his return, Münzer naturally found a strong opposition in the patrician party to his being allowed to preach, but his friends, who had secured his re-admission to the city, reinforced by Pfeiffer's party, proved strong enough to overcome it. Münzer now began a vigorous agitation in the suburbs and the open country round the town. Presently, crowds flocked through the gates from the adjacent districts.

The council, alarmed, suddenly ordered the gates to be shut, but it was too late. The partisans of Münzer paraded the town at night, raising seditious cries and even demanding in menacing terms the death of certain prominent representatives of the old families and members of the council. The next day saw a most numerous exodus of the town patriciate.

Both Pfeiffer and Münzer had already established their position in the town, the one having taken possession of the Church of St. Nicholas and the other that of St. Mary. As town preachers they had insisted on the right of being present at all council meetings—a claim that the affrighted councillors durst not gainsay. A few of the patrician party, from either fear or conviction, now joined the popular government.

An armed assembly of the citizens was called for the purpose of taking a muster roll. The opportunity was seized by Pfeiffer and Münzer to persuade the people to overthrow the existing council altogether. By an overwhelming majority the council was deposed.

The new council was nominated, with the consent of those assembled, by the burgher committee already spoken of, which Pfeiffer had instituted some months previously. It received the name of the " Eternal Council," a designation explained as implying that it should not, like its predecessor, be subject to a periodic renewal of a fourth of its members, but should continue to govern in its entirety until its mandate was formally revoked by the general assembly of the citizens. This explanation of the name is probably correct, but as the archives containing the constitution of this "Eternal Council" were destroyed in the events which followed, it is impossible now to determine its character precisely. The foregoing decisive stage in the Mühlhausen revolution was reached on the 17th of March, 1525. Pfeiffer and Münzer were henceforth practically dictators in their respective spheres, although they both remained in name merely the leading preachers of the two chief churches of the town. They attended all meetings of the new council, and important or doubtful points were, as a rule, referred to them to decide from the standpoint of the new religious doctrines. Pfeiffer probably exercised the greater influence within the town itself, whilst Münzer had the surrounding districts under his sway. Münzer endeavoured, moreover, it would seem, to keep in touch with the movements in other parts of Germany with which he had become acquainted in the course of his recent travels. His efforts in this direction were not crowned with any practical success, save in so far as Thuringia and the adjacent Hesse and Saxony were concerned.

Münzer now proceeded to put his communistic principles into practice on a small scale. The Johanniterhof, the foundation of the monks of St. John, was selected by him as a residence for himself and his chief disciples. The monks were turned out and the place reorganised on principles dictated by Münzer. Here the new religionists seemed to have lived in a manner after all not essentially different from that of a

monastic order,—so true it is that the new,
when it appears on the arena of history, almost
uniformly adopts the garb of the old to which
it opposes itself! Thus Christianity started
first of all as a Jewish sect, and this it remained
as long as its conscious opposition lay in Judaism.
Later on, after it had spread throughout the
Roman Empire, and after this opposition had
been shifted to Paganism, it absorbed pagan
doctrines, practices and rites wholesale, until
in the final stage of the conflict in the fourth
century there was little outwardly to distinguish
the two.

To compare great things with small we find
a similar phenomenon in the movement of English sectarian freethought, known as Secularism,
which became popular some generations ago
with some of the more intelligent of the lower
middle and upper fringe of the working classes.
This was supposed to be a protest against
"church and chapel". Yet the moment it began
to organise itself positively as a cult, it uncon-
sciously had to adopt the forms of Nonconformist
services. Turning to things economic, we find
similarly the rising middle class holding fast
to guild regulations and to various other relics

of feudal times long after its opposition to the feudal classes had been emphasised by more than one violent crisis. So it will probably be in the future. When new socialistic conditions of society take the place of present conditions, it will doubtless be found that for a time production and distribution of social wealth will be carried on upon lines little more than a development of the most advanced economic forms of modern capitalism.

There are in all new movements a Scylla and a Charybdis ; the one consists in the mistaking the swaddling-clothes derived from the old as part of the essential garb of the new, and the other consists in the premature and too drastic attempt to rid the new of these very swaddling-clothes. This applies to all changes, be they primarily religious, political, intellectual, æsthetic or economic. Thus the original Judaic Christianity was in time sloughed off as a heresy—the Ebionite heresy. On the opposite, the pagan side, the same thing happened with Gnosticism and Montanism. In modern Socialism again, we have the state-socialistic tendency known in this country as Fabianism, which hugs old bureaucratic forms, and, on the other hand, we have the anarchistic tendency, which would abruptly abolish all existing administrative organisations.

Of course, it may be objected that Münzer's ideas were not new, that all mediæval communistic theories issued in the long run in a species of monkery. This is true as far as the positive side of his teaching and action were concerned, but it must not be forgotten that the movements with which we are dealing, although on the positive side reactionary, as Lassalle justly pointed out, were on the negative side sufficiently in accord with the contemporary trend of social evolution. In fact, their failure definitely to break up the old feudal organisation contributed in a great measure to the backwardness of Germany for well-nigh three centuries, as compared with other countries of western Europe. Münzer's communism was still-born, but his antagonism to feudal and ecclesiastical privileges became common-places of the democratic thought of a later age. Again, his insistence on the paramount nature of the "inner light" was simply a mystical way of asserting the right of private judgment against tradition, and also the rights of the individual within his

own sphere against external authority—ideas
that have likewise become the theoretical corner-
stones of post-mediæval progressive movements.
Outside the Johanniterhof, Münzer's communism at most extended itself to a distribution
of corn and possibly other food-stuffs, and of
pieces of cloth for the making of garments.

The new state of things attracted thousands
of the country-folk into the town, where they
were now gladly received. Münzer preached
assiduously in the Marienkirche, and his sermons
were followed by anthems sung by a choir of
youths and maidens organised by himself, the
words being taken from Old Testament exhortations and promises to the children of Israel.

The agitation, under Münzer's auspices, soon
spread from Muhlhausen to the neighbouring
territories, as far as Erfurt, Coburg, and even
into the Hesse Duchy and the neighbourhood
of Brunswick. At the beginning of April, the
country was everywhere aflame. The archiepiscopal city of Erfurt itself was at one time
besieged by bands of peasants some three or
four thousand strong. They were induced
to disperse by a harangue from the popular
preacher Eberlin. Here, as elsewhere, noble-

17

men were compelled to enter the peasant brotherhood, amongst them the Counts von Hohenstein. One of them narrowly escaped being lynched for a veiled threat uttered in response to an observation by one of the peasant leaders.

All this time Münzer remained in Mühlhausen, although he was in constant communication with his agents, notably with certain of them in the mining districts of the Mansfeld territories. He issued an address to the miners, exhorting them to hold together in the common cause, which was now everywhere in the ascendant. His activity within the city showed itself in the casting of cannon of heavy calibre, and in the holding of the forces together. Pfeiffer, on his side, occupied himself with organising and drilling his partisans.

It is a mistake to suppose that during the two months' *régime* of Münzer in Mühlhausen the whole town was animated by communistic sentiments. On the contrary, as Karl Kautsky has pointed out, Münzer's sect formed at most a tolerated *imperium in imperio*, the fighting strength of which, judging by the number of those who went out with Münzer to the final battle, amounted to not more than some three hundred men. The close union with Pfeiffer and his movement was caused by the exigencies of the situation and the necessity for the complete overthrow of the patrician party in the town. Pfeiffer was almost exclusively interested in the success of the local revolt. Münzer, on the other hand, with his visions of a universal social revolution, was one of the few leaders in the Peasants War who attempted to bring unity, at least so far as Germany was concerned, into the insurrection, by establishing organised communication between the different centres. That he failed was due to the conditions already alluded to under which the movement arose, and not, as far as we can see, to any fault on his part. The whole movement was essentially local, and the materials for an effective centralisation were nowhere at hand.

Meanwhile, the princes, the Landgraf of Hesse and Duke George Henry of Brunswick, with other minor potentates, had collected their resources with a determination to make a definite end of the Thuringian revolt. The followers of Pfeiffer and Münzer within the walls of Mühlhausen seem to have got restive and to have

forced the hands of their chiefs. That Münzer's
hands were forced, if not Pfeiffer's, admits of no
doubt. He seems to have been well aware that
matters were not yet ripe, and that the artisans
and peasants at the disposal of the insurrection
were inadequate to meet the army of trained
fighting men that the princes were preparing to
hurl against them. Finally, Pfeiffer, either
unable to keep his men in hand, or having
become otherwise convinced of the necessity
for action, compelled Münzer to join him in a
sortie. In this sortie the usual booty was
obtained, but no permanent results were
achieved.

A few days later, Pfeiffer, on his part,
remained inactive at Mühlhausen, when the
situation urgently demanded an expedition for
the relief of the main camp at Frankenhausen
some miles away. The position of this camp
was itself unwise. The correct policy would
obviously have been for the whole available
insurgent strength, to have entrenched itself in
the well-fortified imperial city and to have used
this as a base. Münzer in vain endeavoured to
effectually arouse the Mansfelders, notwithstanding that Frankenhausen was in close

proximity to the Mansfeld mines. The encamped peasants by the usual trickery were
lured into negotiations with Count Albrecht
until the arrival of the princes with their overwhelming force. Münzer joined the peasant
bodies outside Frankenhausen on the 12th of
May. Two days later, the Landgraf of Hesse
with the Duke of Brunswick came within
striking distance, and their strength was reinforced within twenty-four hours, by the arrival
of the Duke of Saxony with a large and well-
disciplined body of troops.

In point of numbers the two camps were now
nearly equal, being composed of about eight
thousand men each. But, in the one case, they
were finely-equipped men-at-arms, well-supported
by artillery, while, in the other case, they were
inexperienced, badly-armed rustics and poor
citizens, with only one or two pieces of ordnance
in their midst. The insurgents were entrenched
on an elevation a short distance from the town
behind a stockade of waggons.

For information respecting the course of the
battle, which took place on the 15th of May,
the usual source is the highly-coloured and
partisan narrative of Melancthon in his well-

known pamphlet on Münzer and the Thuringian revolt. Melancthon puts a speech into the mouth of Münzer, in which he bids his followers to have no fear, for that God would deliver their enemies into their hands, and guarantees that the bullets should not hurt them, for that he himself would catch them in the sleeve of his mantle. This speech was followed, according to the same account, with one from the Landgraf Philip to his men, in the course of which he deprecated the aspersions cast by the insurgent leaders upon princes, nobles and the authorities generally. On the attack being thereupon made by the Landgraf's followers, it is stated that the peasants stood still singing the chorale, *Nun bitten wir den Heiligen Geist* (Now beseech we the Holy Ghost).

Another pamphlet, published the same year, 1525, implies that the princes and barons had given the insurgents a three hours' truce to consider their terms of surrender, but that having gained over the Count von Stolberg and some other nobles, who had hitherto been forced into siding with the peasants, they proceeded at once to the attack, thereby taking their adversaries by surprise. The latter account is unquestionably the more reliable of the two, since it coincides with the general treatment of the revolted peasants by their treacherous oppressors.

The following account of the battle is based upon Zimmermann (iii., pp. 776-781), who had opportunities of consulting the Mühlhausen archives and other manuscript sources.

Münzer marched with his men to the elevation above Frankenhausen, called to this day the Schlachtberg. The negotiations entered into by the princes had had a demoralising effect upon the peasant army. A full amnesty was promised if they would only hand over their leaders, among whom Münzer was specially singled out. The noblemen who had been forced to join the peasants were naturally the most zealous advocates of surrender. On seeing themselves surrounded by the hostile ordnance, the peasant army sent the three Counts, von Stolberg, von Rixleben, and von Wertern, into the princely camp. This was the occasion of the three hours' truce already spoken of. Unconditional submission, with the surrender of Münzer, were the terms insisted upon. Two of the counts remained in the princely camp, and one returned to tell the tale. The party of surrender redoubled their efforts, a nobleman and a priest signalising themselves specially in their opposition to Münzer. The latter, still with his devoted bodyguard intact, and with a strong party amongst the other combatants, was able to cause the nobleman and priest to be beheaded. He then endeavoured to raise the enthusiasm of the camp by a discourse, denouncing the godless tyrants with more than his accustomed vehemence and adding allusions to Gideon, David, and other Biblical heroes, who with a small force of the chosen people had conquered hosts. This is the "bullet-catching" speech reported by Melancthon. He wound up, according to the same source, by pointing to a suddenly-appearing rainbow as a sign from heaven of their predestined triumph.

Whether the speech in question was genuine or was fabricated by Melancthon, the episode of the rainbow need not be doubted. In any case, Münzer succeeded in rousing his hearers to a momentary enthusiasm. They rejected the terms offered, and began to sing their hymn, the time of the truce not having yet expired. Suddenly the cannon of the princes thundered into the camp. Many looked upwards, says a contemporary manuscript quoted by Zimmermann, to behold whether help would not come from heaven. But before the legions of angels descended, the waggon-stockade was broken through, and "they were shot, pierced and miserably slain". In a few minutes the peasant army was dispersed and in full flight in various directions. A small body held its own for a short time in a stone quarry, only to be ultimately overpowered.

The bulk of the fugitives made for the town of Frankenhausen, hotly pursued by a detachment of the Landgraf's men-at-arms. Within the walls, the massacre was frightful, extending to churches, houses and monasteries, where refuge had been sought. The stream running through the chief street seemed turned to blood. More than five thousand peasants perished within a few hours, but, not yet satisfied, the princes had three hundred prisoners brought into the square before the Rathhaus to be beheaded, among them an old priest and his young assistant. The women of Frankenhausen begged for mercy for their husbands and brothers. This was accorded them on condition that they slew these two priests with their own hands.

According to the manuscript chronicle of Erfurt, "the Landgraf and Duke George delivered to the women a preacher and his assistant. They must perforce strike them dead with clubs, to the end that their husbands might remain in life. Therefore did the women in such wise beat them that their heads were like unto a rotten cabbage and the brains did cling unto the clubs. Thereupon were their husbands given unto them. The princes themselves did behold how this thing came to pass." The singling out of the clericals as scapegoats was obviously dictated by the feeling that they were in a special sense traitors to the cause of the governing classes.

Münzer, upon whose head a price had been set, and who was amongst the fugitives who reached Frankenhausen, fled into a deserted house hard by the gate. Concealing himself here in a loft, he threw off some of his clothes, and, binding his head with the hope of rendering himself unrecognisable lay down on a bed. A knight's servant, one of the pursuers, shortly

afterwards entered the same house and discovered him in the loft. Münzer, whom he
did not identify, pretended that he was ill of a
fever, but the fellow's plundering instincts led
him to search the knapsack lying near. He
found therein correspondence that revealed the
identity of the apparently sick man, and he
straightway apprised his master of his valuable
discovery.

Münzer was seized and brought before the
princes, who asked him why he had misled the
poor people. He had done what he had done,
he replied, because the princes persecuted the
Gospel and sacrificed all to their avarice and'
lusts. The young Landgraf then admonished
him with the well-known quotations from
Holy Writ as to the duty of obeying authority,
to which admonitions Münzer made no reply.
Thereupon he was handed over to the executioner to be tortured. In the midst of his
suffering, on being once more reproached with
having led his followers to destruction, he said
with a grim smile, "They would not have it
otherwise," apparently referring to the premature action of the insurgents.

He was subsequently sent to his arch-enemy,

Count Ernst von Mansfeld, who immured him
in a dungeon in the tower at Heldrungen.
Here he dictated his celebrated letter to the
inhabitants of Muhlhausen, in which he certainly "backs down". So much must be said in
spite of the attempt of Zimmermann and other
admirers of Münzer to give the letter a more
favourable interpretation. He not merely de-
precates any further attempts at insurrection,
advice that might be dictated by the hopelessness of the situation, but confesses to having
"seductively and rebelliously preached many
opinions, delusions and errors concerning the
Holy Sacrament . . . as also against the ordi-
nances of the universal Christian Church".
Further, he confesses himself as dying as "a
once again reconciled member of the Holy
Christian Church," praying God to forgive
him his former conduct. The only redeeming
passage is one that pleads for his wife and
child, that they might not be deprived of his
worldly goods.

The doubts suggested by Kautsky as to the
genuineness of this letter are hardly tenable.
It may have been to the interest of the princes
that such a letter should have been written, and

they may have terrorised him into writing it, in the same way as prison authorities may from time to time have terrorised innocent persons condemned to death into " confessing " and " acknowledging the justice of their sentence ". But when Kautsky endeavours to impugn its having issued from Münzer by asking why he dictated it instead of writing it, the answer is sufficiently clear. A man who had so recently suffered the last extremities of the thumbscrew would hardly be able to write autograph letters.

The scandalous lack of solidarity among the peasants is particularly illustrated in this Thuringian revolt. Two important armed bodies which might well have turned the scale, heavy weighted as it was on the side of the nobles, were carousing not many miles away, when they ought to have been hastening to the assistance of their brethren at Frankenhausen.

Pfeiffer's party in Mühlhausen. on the 19th of May, wrote a despairing letter to the Franconian insurgents, apprising them of the destruction of the Frankenhausen force and imploring them to come to their assistance. But it was of no avail. They had their own dissensions and

their own local objects, with but little feeling
for the general movement.

Meanwhile Münzer was taken from the tower
at Heldrungen and brought for execution into
the camp of the princes, which now lay before
Mühlhausen itself. The imperial city was surrounded on three sides. Pfeiffer, who com
manded in the town, was, in face of the imminent danger, beginning to lose his popularity.
The demand for the unconditional surrender
of the ringleaders, and especially of Pfeiffer,
became increasingly favoured by the citizens.
As breaches were made in the walls and the
position seemed more and more hopeless, notwithstanding the heroic defence of Pfeiffer's
twelve hundred faithful followers, the public
sentiment in favour of capitulation quickly
gained the upper hand. Finally, on the 24th
of May, seeing that all was lost, Pfeiffer escaped
from the town with four hundred adherents,
with the object of joining the Franconian
insurgents.

The next day twelve hundred Mühlhausen
women, with tattered clothes, bare feet and
dishevelled hair, and five hundred virgins with
mourning wreaths, streamed out of the gate

leading to the princes' camp, where they presented themselves to implore mercy for their
native city. They were given bread and
cheese, but were informed that the men themselves of the town must put in an appearance. This was done. A number of prominent
citizens came, bareheaded and barefooted, with
white staves in their hands, and kneeling three
times before the assembled princes handed
over the keys of the town. After the com
bined army had made its entry the citizens
were compelled to deliver up their arms. The
" Eternal Council " set up by Pfeiffer and
Münzer was deposed, and the old patrician
council reinstated. Executions followed, that
of the bürgermeister amongst them. The chief
fortifications were levelled with the ground.
The imperial city was deprived of its freedom,
and reduced to the status of a tribute-paying
town. Weapons, treasure, horses were seized,
and it was only spared a wholesale sacking
by a ransom of 40,000 gulden.

On learning of Pfeiffer's flight, the princes
sent a body of horsemen in pursuit. They
came up with his party near Eisenach, where,
after a desperate resistance, Pfeiffer was taken

with ninety-two of his men and brought back
bound into the camp.   They were all, or nearly
all, instantly condemned to death and executed
together, Pfeiffer scorning confession and sacrament, and dying without sign of fear or wavering.
These facts regarding Pfeiffer are admitted even
by his enemies.

Münzer, on the other hand, is accused by the
same chroniclers of having shown up to the last
a spirit of faltering and pusillanimity which,
it must be admitted, accords with the tone of
his Heldrungen letter.   The badgering of their
victim by the princes was significant.   The
Catholic Duke George of Saxony admonished
him to repent of having forsaken his order and
of having taken a wife.   The young Lutheran
Landgraf of Hesse told him that he had no
need to repent of these things, but that what he
had to repent of was his having led the people
into rebellion.   Münzer, in his turn, admitted
that he had attempted matters beyond his
powers, but urgently entreated the princes
and nobles to deal more mercifully with their
subjects, and to read diligently the Holy
Scriptures, especially the books of Samuel
and the Kings, and to take to heart the lesson,

as there related, as to the miserable end of tyrants.

After this speech he said no more, as he was awaiting the stroke of the executioner. He did not even break his silence on being challenged to recite the " Credo," owing, as his enemies allege, to the extremity of his fear, or, as his friends suggest, to his contempt of the conventional usage. His head was struck off, and was fixed upon a long pole, as also was that of Pfeiffer, and his body was impaled.

After the defeat at Frankenhausen, and the surrender of Mühlhausen, the suppression of the revolt throughout the rest of Thuringia offered no great difficulty, and was largely effected by the individual princes and lords, each in his own territory. The plunder and devastation by the insurgents had not been less in Thuringia than elsewhere. As many as forty-six castles and monasteries lay in ruins. In the chief places the usual bloodthirsty executions followed. In Erfurt the old council was restored to office, and proceeded with merciless severity against all connected with the recent risings.

The battle of Frankenhausen is a landmark

in the history of the Peasants War, and was synchronous within a few days with crushing defeats of the insurgents in other parts of Germany. The insurrection, which up to the beginning of May had, speaking generally, carried all before it, by that time had reached the turning-point, and its fortunes henceforward as steadily receded. In our next chapter we shall follow the disasters and the final extinction of the various movements, the rise and temporary success of which we have been describing.

CHAPTER VIII.

THE SUPPRESSION OF THE INSURRECTION THROUGHOUT GERMANY.

It is now time to consider the attitude of Luther throughout the crisis. His action was mainly embodied in two documents, of which the first was issued about the middle of April, and the second a month later. The difference in tone between them is sufficiently striking. In the first, which bore the title, "An Exhortation to Peace on the Twelve Articles of the Peasantry in Swabia," Luther sits on the fence, admonishing both parties of what he deemed their shortcomings. He was naturally pleased with those articles that demanded the free preaching of the Gospel and abused the Catholic clergy, and was not indisposed to assent to many of the economic demands. In fact, the document strikes one as distinctly more favourable to the insurgents than to their opponents.

"We have," he wrote, "no one to thank for this mischief and sedition, save ye princes and lords, in especial ye blind bishops and mad priests and monks, who up to this day remain obstinate and do not cease to rage and rave against the holy Gospel, albeit ye know that it is righteous, and that ye may not gainsay it. Moreover, in your worldly regiment, ye do naught otherwise than flay and extort tribute, that ye may satisfy your pomp and vanity, till the poor, common man cannot, and may not, bear with it longer. The sword is on your neck. Ye think ye sit so strongly in your seats, that none may cast you from them. Such presumption and obstinate pride will twist your necks, as ye will see." And again : "God hath made it thus that they cannot, and will not longer bear with your raging. If ye do it not of your free will, so shall ye be made to do it by way of violence and undoing." Once more : " It is not peasants, my dear lords, who have set themselves up against you. God Himself it is who setteth Himself against you to chastise your evil-doing."

He counsels the princes and lords to make 'peace with their peasants, observing with reference to the Twelve Articles, that some of them are so just and righteous, that before God and the world their worthiness is manifested, making good the words of the psalm that they heap contempt upon the heads of the princes. Whilst he warns the peasants against sedition and rebellion, and criticises some of the Articles as going beyond the justification of Holy Writ, and whilst he makes side-hits at " the prophets of murder and the spirits of confusion which had found their way among them," the general impression given by the pamphlet is, as already said, one of unmistakable friendliness to the peasants and hostility to the lords.

The manifesto may be summed up in the following terms : Both sides are, strictly speaking, in the wrong, but the princes and lords have provoked the " common man " by their unjust exactions and oppressions ; the peasants, on their side, have gone too far in many of their demands, notably in the refusal to pay tithes, and most of all in the notion of abolishing villeinage, which Luther declares to be "straightway contrary to the Gospel and thievish ". The great sin of the princes remains, however, that of having thrown stumbling-blocks in the way of the Gospel—*bien entendu* the Gospel according to Luther—and the main virtue of the peasants was their claim to have this Gospel preached. It can scarcely be doubted that the ambiguous tone of Luther's rescript was interpreted by the rebellious peasants to their advantage and served to stimulate, rather than to check, the insurrection.

Meanwhile, the movement rose higher and higher, and reached Thuringia, the district with which Luther personally was most associated. His patron, and what is more, the only friend of toleration in high places, the noble-minded Elector Friedrich of Saxony, fell ill and died on the 5th of May, and was succeeded by his younger brother Johann, the same who afterwards assisted in the suppression of the Thuringian revolt. Almost immediately thereupon, Luther, who had been visiting his native town of Eisleben, travelled through the revolted districts on his way back to Wittenberg. He everywhere encountered black looks and jeers. When he preached, the Münzerites would drown his voice by the ringing of bells. The signs of rebellion greeted him on all sides. The "Twelve Articles" were constantly thrown at his head. As the reports of violence towards the property and persons of some of his own noble friends reached him, his rage broke all bounds. He seems, however, to have prudently waited a few days, until the cause of the peasants was obviously hopeless, before publicly taking his stand on the side of the authorities.

On his arrival in Wittenberg, he wrote a second pronouncement on the contemporary events, in which no uncertainty was left as to his attitude. It is entitled, "Against the Murderous and Thievish Bands of Peasants".[1] Here he lets himself loose on the side of the oppressors with a bestial ferocity. "Crush them [the peasants]," he writes, "strangle them and pierce them, in secret places and in sight of men, he who can, even as one would strike dead a mad dog." All having authority who hesitated to extirpate the insurgents to the uttermost were committing a sin against God. "Findest thou thy death therein," he writes, addressing the reader,

[1] Amongst the curiosities of literature may be included the translation of the title of this manifesto by Prof. T. M. Lindsay, D.D., in the *Encyclopædia Britannica*, 9th Edition (Article, "Luther"). The German title is "Wider die morderischen und rauberischen Rotten der Bauern". Prof. Lindsay's translation is "*Against the murdering, robbing Rats [sic] of Peasants*"!

" happy art thou ; a more blessed death can never overtake thee, for thou diest in obedience to the Divine word and the command of Romans xiii. 1, and in the service of love, to save thy neighbour from the bonds of hell and the devil." Never had there been such an infamous exhortation to the most dastardly murder on a wholesale scale since the Albigensian crusade with its " Strike them all ; God will know His own ".—a sentiment indeed that Luther almost literally reproduces in one passage.

Many efforts have been made by Protestant historians to palliate this crime of Luther's, more especially to shield him against the charge of time-serving and cowardice in adopting an attitude of benevolent neutrality to the peasants' cause at a time when it bade fair to be successful, whilst hounding on its executioners to hideous barbarities when its prospects were obviously desperate. One of the more recent of these Protestant writers, Egelhaaf (*Deutsche Geschichte im sechszehnten Jahrhundert*, vol. i., p. 614), endeavours to establish the probability that Luther issued this pamphlet a day or two before the catastrophe at Frankenhausen, or at least before he could have known of the

peasants' overthrow in Würtemberg. Even if
this were true, which is hardly probable, it
would not help Luther's character, for, from his
immediate personal knowledge of the situation
in Thuringia, he must have seen, at least from
the beginning of the second week in May, that
the forces of the combined princes, with their
trained men-at-arms and adequate supply of
artillery, were destined to win against bands of
peasants and handicraftsmen, ill-armed, unused
to fighting, and insufficiently munitioned. As
for the other districts, a report could hardly
have failed to reach him concerning the de-
moralisation of the peasant armies and the
reinforcement of the Swabian League's strength
with knights and free-lances returned from the
Italian campaign. Altogether, this second manifesto remains an ineffaceable stigma upon the
powerful personality of the "rebellious monk"
of Wittenberg.

We turn now again to the fortunes of
Truchsess and the overthrow of the movement
in south Germany. The force of the Swabian
League, under Truchsess, by the armistice or
treaty at Weingarten, made with the three

combined contingents of the Swabian insurgents, known respectively as the Ried, the
Lake, and the Algau contingents, was saved,
as Zimmermann has pointed out, from imminent
disaster—since the insurgents not only considerably outnumbered the troops of imperial order,
but were well supplied with ordnance captured
from sundry castles, and occupied a strong
position. The utter fecklessness of the counsels
of the insurrection was never more exemplified than in the feeble surrender of all these
advantages to the blandishments of Truchsess.
At this time, Truchsess was practically hemmed
in, but, on the dispersal of the greater part of
the country-folk arrayed against him, he was at
once extricated from a difficult situation, and
had his hands left free to move southwards,
destroying or scattering bodies of peasants
on the way.

He took this direction with a view of attacking the Black Forest contingent. which was now
making itself very active, especially in the
siege of Radolfzell with its refugee nobles. On
the 25th of April, he was met by a deputation
of the Hegau and Black Forest insurgents for
the purpose of negotiations. A similar arrange-

ment to the one mentioned was attempted but failed. On the emissaries returning to their respective contingents, Truchsess continued his march to Stockach, and finally pitched his camp a short distance from the important fortress of Duke Ulrich, the Hohentwiel. His further movements in this neighbourhood were stopped by the peremptory order from the Council of the Swabian League at Ulm that he was to proceed straight to the relief of Würtemberg. Unwillingly giving up his plans in the south, he returned by forced marches to his old camp on the Neckar.

Meanwhile, on the 7th of May, some cavalry of the Markgraf Kasimir von Anspach, strengthened by a force sent by the Count Palatine from the Upper Palatinate, attacked a large body of peasants, who had just captured the small town of Wettingen. They had come from plundering a neighbouring monastery, and were marching in great disorder, intent in the main apparently upon carrying off their heavily-laden waggons of booty. The onslaught was sudden and unexpected, and resulted in the slaughter, almost without resistance, of over a thousand peasants. This was the first serious check inflicted by the princely power upon the movement in south Germany since the Leipheim affair; but the decisive battle was fought on May 12th, when the united forces under Truchsess, consisting of 6000 free-lances and 1200 horse, met the main body of the peasant army of Würtemberg, 12,000 strong, between the towns of Boblingen and Sindelfingen. Ritter Bernhardt von Winterstetten was the commander of this section, Matern Feuerbacher, owing to his moderate tendencies and general indecision, having been deposed.

Truchsess succeeded, by the aid of treachery on the part of some of the leading citizens of Boblingen, who opened their gates to his men, in throwing a detachment into the castle above the town. From this point of vantage he opened fire upon the insurgents, who were entrenched in a strong position behind some marshy ground, compelling them ultimately to gain the open. No sooner was this the case than the horse of the Palatinate and of the Austrians attacked them in front, whilst four companies of foot opened fire on their flank. The battle, which began at ten in the morning, lasted four hours. By two o'clock the flight was general. The fugitives were hotly pursued, and for seven or eight miles the way was strewed with the corpses of peasants cut down by the horsemen of the princes' army. The accounts of the numbers slain vary between two thousand and six thousand. The whole of the peasants' ordnance, thirty-three pieces, fell into the hands of the League.

Amongst the prisoners captured after the battle was Melchior Nonnenmacher, Helfenstein's former piper, who, it will be remembered, had taken so prominent a part in the execution of his master and the other knights outside the walls of Weinsberg. With savage ferocity, Truchsess, the same evening, had him bound by chains to an apple-tree, his tether allowing him a run of two paces, and then, faggots having been heaped up in a circle round, they were set alight and the wretched piper was slowly roasted to death.

The victorious League and its allies swept through the villages and small towns of Würtemberg, plundering, burning and slaying. At every halt made executions took place, hangings or beheadings. Neckarsulm and

Oehringen were bombarded and surrendered. Weinsberg was reserved for a heavy vengeance; its few remaining inhabitants were driven out, with the exception of one or two who refused to go, and who therefore perished, and the town itself with all it contained was burned to the ground. By order of Truchsess, in the name of the League, it was forbidden to be rebuilt, and it remained for some years a witness of princely vindictiveness. Poor Jacklein Rohrbach, endeavouring in vain to rally a few defenders of the people's cause, was recognised as he was passing through a village, and delivered over to Truchsess. He met a similar fate to that of Nonnenmacher, being, it is stated, chained to an elm-tree and roasted alive, whilst the assembled princes and nobles gloated over his agony.

Meanwhile the Count Palatine had taken the town of Bruchsal and hewn off nine heads there. Truchsess proceeded against Wimpfen, sending a messenger to demand the surrender of the leaders of the movement in that town. The council, with some unwillingness, consented to the arrest of certain persons. The Counts of Hohenlohe, who, it will be remembered, had

had to make a pact with the peasants, were visited by Truchsess, and compelled to swear never again to have aught to do with the malcontents. One of the Weinsberg rebels was caught in the town of Oehringen and hanged on a tree.

Würtemberg was thus effectively subdued. The property of Hans Flux in Heilbronn was made over by Truchsess to the executioner who accompanied him throughout his campaign, and whose truculence was even a little too much for the not too sensitive councillors of the Swabian League at Ulm. This ruffian, however, was safe in the sunshine of the favour and protection of his master, who called him his " dear Berthold ".

The peasant council in Heilbronn, of which Wendel Hipler was the presiding genius, hastily dispersed and fled before the approach of Truchsess. Hipler himself hurried back to the camp at Würzburg. At the end of May Truchsess combined his forces with those of the Count Palatine Ludwig, by which step the League's strength was increased by two thousand foot, twelve hundred horse and fourteen large pieces of ordnance. The Archbishop of Trier and the Bishop of Würzburg, with other territorial magnates, subsequently joined hands with Truchsess, with the ultimate object of relieving the Frauenberg and the town of Würzburg, where, as we have already seen, the main army of the insurrection in central Germany was massed.

Although the backbone of the movement in Würtemberg was broken by the recent victories of the League and its allies, the insurrection elsewhere, as, for instance, in the Black Forest and in Breisgau, not to speak of the hereditary Austrian dominions, was still maintaining itself with unabated vigour. Hans Müller von Bulgenbach was threatening all who did not join his Christian Brotherhood with the worldly ban, in modern phraseology a universal "boycott," which forbade men to eat or drink with them, to work in their company, to offer them food, drink, salt, or wood, and to buy or sell with them. Freiburg, Breisach and Waldkirch were with difficulty holding out against the bodies of peasants by which they were being pressed. The town of Villingen was especially in a bad way. But the destruction of the great Franconian peasant army at Würzburg, and above all the relief of the Frauenberg, which it was feared would have to surrender in a few days, were undoubtedly of first importance at the moment to the League and its allies. The capture of the strong fortress that commanded the episcopal city would have given the insurrection a *point d'appui* in the very heart of Germany, and although, as already remarked, the possible gain was certainly not worth the locking up of such an enormous mass of the peasant forces in one place, its significance for the popular movement cannot be denied.

The successes of the princely power in Würtemberg had the effect of strengthening the Würzburg camp, which had thus become a rallying point whither fragments of dispersed contingents and companies of peasants hurriedly took their way. It will be remembered that on the 15th of May, the same day, that is, as that on which the defeat at Frankenhausen took place, and only three days after the overthrow at Boblingen, the besiegers had unsuccessfully stormed the aforesaid Würzburg castle of the Marienburg. This failure, as we know, led to recriminations between the army and its leaders, Gotz being specially singled out for suspicion of

treachery. In the end, however, a council of
war was held, and Gotz was sent with a detachment of eight thousand men to endeavour to
prevent the union of the Palatinate force with
that of the League under Truchsess, of which
project news had already arrived. All along,
according to his own account, Gotz had been
acting from compulsion, and under present circumstances we may well believe that he wished
nothing better than to shake off his responsibilities at the earliest opportunity. Thus it
happened that one dark night he disappeared,
afterwards salving his conscience for this seeming treachery with the excuse that the four
weeks for which he had pledged himself to
act as peasant commander had expired.

On his escape becoming known, about a
fourth part of his men deserted to their homes.
The remainder moved onwards in a body to
Konigshofen on the Tauber. Here, some six
thousand in number, they solemnly swore to be
avenged upon Truchsess, the League, and the
Princes. On the 2nd of June the combined
forces of the nobles reached Konigshofen,
passing over the Tauber at a place feebly
defended by the peasants. The camp was

attacked, and soon the whole contingent was in confused flight, leaving its stockade of waggons and its ordnance a prey to the enemy, who soon held complete possession of the elevation on which the camp had stood. Only about one thousand succeeded in rallying and entrenching themselves in a neighbouring wooc where, quickly improvising a stockade of trees and bushes, they succeeded in holding out for a short time. Their stockade, however, was ultimately broken through, and five hundred were speared on the spot, shot from trees, or trampled down by the horsemen. More than two thousand had already fallen in the original encounter. Most of the leaders are stated to have escaped on the backs of the horses taken from the munition waggons. Truchsess was wounded in the hip by a lance.

The defeat at Konigshofen was for the peasants little less serious than those at Boblingen and Frankenhausen. The main force, it is true, was still at Würzburg. Other divisions, however, had detached themselves with the view of checking the League's advance. At this moment some of Truchsess's mercenaries demanded their battle-pay, notwithstanding that they had not been among those actively engaged in the encounter. A serious mutiny seemed inevitable, and thus a gleam of hope showed itself for the peasants. Enough men, however, including the military leaders, remained to save the situation for the League.

Florian Geyer, with his " Black Troop," to which were joined several other peasant companies, now broke from the camp at Würzburg with the intention of intercepting the princely forces on the road to that city. He and his men, furious at the reports that reached them of burning villages and of peasants strung up on every tree, the traces left of the victorious march of Truchsess and his allies, avowed that they would hang every knight and cut the throat of every free-lance. Meanwhile, the bulk of Truchsess's mutinous mercenaries had caught him up and returned to their allegiance. Truchsess, who would gladly have punished them, was nevertheless compelled by the exigencies of the situation to pardon and reinstate them.

Florian Geyer, with his troop, appears to have had no certain information respecting the

battle of Konigshofen and still believed that
the camp of his friends lay between himself
and the allied princes. Accompanied by a few
horsemen, Florian was riding in front, below
the castle of Ingolstatt, when the advancing
body of peasants found themselves suddenly
surrounded and attacked by the whole force of
the enemy. Taken unawares, they had scarcely
time to get their ordnance into position or to
bring their train of waggons properly into a
stockade. With the presence of mind of a
trained fighting man, however, Florian at once
rallied all his companies into some sort of battle
array, improvising a rough stockade and immediately beginning a fire from such artillery
as he had. But in a few minutes it was only
too evident that his force was outmatched.
The attack of the free-lances was supported by
the entire body of horsemen, but the signal
for flight seems to have been given by the
sudden and simultaneous thunder of all the
enemy's heavy ordnance, which had just been
brought to the other side of the stockade. The
panic was immediate and general. Dispersed
in their mad flight, the insurgents were ridden
down, run down, or clubbed to death. For

miles around the slaughter extended. Sixty who were taken alive, from whom some of the free-lances wished to extract ransom-money, were ordered by Truchsess to be butchered in a heap.

A remnant of the "Black Troop" alone held together, and with Florian at their head, some six hundred in number, succeeded in reaching the village of Ingolstatt. Having entrenched themselves behind a hedge stockade, they awaited the onslaught of the Count Palatine Ludwig, who advanced against them at the head of twelve hundred knights. Two hundred of the troopers occupied the churchyard and the church, whilst more than three hundred seized upon the castle above the village. Here a continuous fire was kept up, to which was added the hurling down of tiles and pieces of the wall. The attacking party flung fire brands into the church, which after some time blazed up, all the defenders being destroyed.

The last defence was the castle, already partly in ruins from an attack of the peasants some weeks previously. Florian himself commanded the brave band within. They barricaded the gates and breaches so effectively

that the stormers were held in check for a long
while, besides being repeatedly driven back
by the hail of bullets that rained from every
opening. Soon the whole army of the enemy,
which had meanwhile come up, was engaged
exclusively in the attack on this stronghold,
but the thick wall of the old feudal fortress did
not yield until all the strength of Truchsess's
cannon had been brought to bear upon it.
Dismounting, knights and barons struggled
together with the free-lances for an entrance
at the breach made. More than a hundred of
the storming contingent lay killed and wounded
in the *fosse* below, and still the attack seemed
no nearer success. Finally, a last effort was
about to be made, when suddenly the firing
from within ceased ; the defenders had exhausted their ammunition. Resistance was
still kept up with tiles and stones. Even on
an entrance being effected, a hand-to-hand
fight ensued. The besieged neither asked nor
obtained quarter. At last, fifty of them withdrew fighting into the deep cellars, whilst from
amid the mass of dead surrounding them,
about two hundred of the " Black Troop," led by
Florian, succeeded in escaping under cover of

the approaching darkness, just as the allied forces poured into the heap of ruins, which was now all that was left above ground of the ancient castle of Ingolstatt.

The two hundred entrenched themselves in a wood hard by, whence at intervals they made sorties. With daylight, the men of Truchsess burst into the wood, slaughtering all who remained there. But even now the valiant knight was not amongst the dead. With a few who were prepared to follow him to the death, he had towards morning struck out into the open country. All the neighbouring villages were set on fire by Truchsess's men, and all the inhabitants who were not consumed were put to the sword. Amongst these villages was Giebelstatt, the castle above which was Florian's hereditary home. His ultimate aim was, probably, to reach Würzburg. In the neighbouring territories far and wide all the companies, including the great Gailsdorf con-/tingent, seven thousand strong, which had as yet suffered no great losses, were dispersed. Alarmed by the accounts of the disasters of Konigshofen and Ingolstatt, their members had fled into the woods or had returned to their homes and again done homage to their feudal lords.

It is doubtful whether Florian Geyer ever again saw Würzburg. After a few days' wandering in company with a handful of followers, during which days he had reached, as the old account alleges, the Hall territory far to the south, he and his men are said to have been surprised by a detachment of horsemen led by the brother of his betrothed, Wilhelm von Grumbach. A fierce, desperate struggle ensued, in the course of which the chivalrous hero of the people's cause fell fighting.[1] Recent researches have pointed to the

[1] The above is the traditional account accepted by Zimmermann and other authorities. Wilhelm Blos and some recent investigators have, however, unearthed statements in contemporary documents which place the matter in a different light. An old chronicle of the time states : " On the 9th of June, Florian Geyer was stabbed on the field near Rimpar ". It is suggested that the theory that he fell near Schwabisch-Hall was caused by a badly-written manuscript. Florian, it is said, fled to the castle near Rimpar of the knight Grumbach, to whose sister, Barbara, he was betrothed. This Grumbach is alleged to have caused Florian to be treacherously murdered by one of his servants in a wood as he rode away from the castle. The story is expressly confirmed in a pamphlet issued by the Bishop of Würzburg against Grumbach, when some years later he was at feud with him : " It is the certain truth that

probability that family disputes, or jealousies, played their part in the death of Geyer. His name has ever since been cherished in Germany by the lovers of freedom, and his personality has always been surrounded by the nimbus of popular fancy, as that of the ideal hero of revolt against oppression. For centuries after, legend related how the figure of his bride was to be seen flitting through the moonlit glades in the neighbourhood of her ancestral castle.

After these bloody conflicts, Truchsess had to make a roll-call of the forces of the Swabian League under his command. His losses had been considerable, a fourth of the men having perished in several companies. The losses of his allies can hardly have been less. The march on Würzburg could now be undertaken without danger of serious resistance. On the evening of Whit Monday, the 5th of June, the outlying

Grumbach, a man of evil fame, did cause in the Peasants War a nobleman named Florian Geyer, who had lodged with him in his house, to be pierced through by one of his servants by his command in a wood, called the Gramschatz Wood. And, albeit that this murder be now somewhat forgotten of the younger people, yet are there many old and worthy persons to whom it is not hidden, but who are much mindful thereof."

township of Heidingsfeld was reached, and here the princely army pitched its camp, the ordnance being pointed against the city. There were still, however, from five to six thousand peasants and burghers under arms, determined on defence, within the walls.

Meanwhile the bürgermeister and the members of the old city council placed themselves in negotiation with Truchsess with a view of betraying the city together with the insurgent leaders. They came to a secret understanding with Truchsess and the Count Palatine, by which the town was to pay a heavy ransom to the latter and to the bishop. The citizens were to be disarmed. Allegiance to the bishop was to be resworn under the old conditions, and last, but not least, the chiefs of the peasant army still within the town were to be surrendered. At the same time the bürgermeister and council pretended to the defenders that all they had done had been to negotiate favourable terms with the conquering host now before the walls, further resistance being represented by them as hopeless. The deception did its work, and on the morning of the 8th of June, Truchsess and the princes entered Würzburg in triumph, followed by fifteen hundred men-at-arms. The citizens were ordered to present themselves on the market-place. Those from the smaller country towns in the neighbourhood and the peasants were to appear at two other points respectively. All three places were afterwards surrounded by armed men. Truchsess then appeared on horseback, accompanied by four executioners with drawn swords. After admonishing the crowd on their crime of disobedience and declaring their lives all forfeit, while the assembled citizens with bared heads knelt before him, he retired with the princes into the Rathhaus and deliberated for more than an hour. On returning, sentences were delivered and the executions began. The heads of the principal leaders of the town-democracy fell.

Truchsess and his executioners then betook themselves to the open space where the companies furnished by the neighbouring small towns were assembled. Their leaders, to the number of twenty-four, were beheaded. The conquerors then went to the ditch whither the peasants had been summoned. Thirty-seven of the latter were singled out for death, to gratify the blood-lust of their baronial enemies.

Altogether, eighty-one executions took place within the town on this day. Amongst them was that of a peasant who had not been called, but who had pushed his way to the front to see how it fared with his comrades. He was seized by the executioner and beheaded with the others. As for the rank and file, their arms and armour had been already surrendered. Staves were now placed in their hands and they were driven from the town. Of these, many were slain on their way home by the brutal free-lances, who were prowling about. The town had to pay 8000 gulden to the Swabian League, whilst the bishop with his clergy, together with the nobles who had held fiefs of him, subsequently received more than 200,000 gulden.

With the capture of the town of Würzburg was involved the relief of its citadel, the Marienburg, on the Frauenberg. When the conquerors entered it, the extent of the damage done to this powerful fortress by the peasant attack seems to have created surprise. Hans Lutz, the herald of Truchsess, observes in his diary : " Afterwards beheld I the castle at Würzburg, which was altogether shot through, together with the outer wall, which had a breach in it six klafters wide, and the peasants had made two ditches on the hill such as no man might believe. Moreover, had they brought up on the hill more than an hundred ladders and had made a ditch above the church called that of Saint Burckhardt, the which I have measured and did number an hundred and eighteen steps from the beginning of the ditch." He further adds the detail that " the peasants in this same church had smote off the heads of all the saints and of our Lord also ".

The idea of the peasants seems to have been to blow up the castle, and to this end trains were apparently laid from the *fosse* in question. The besieged, whose provisions and ammunition were running low, had been apprised by Truchsess by certain signs, probably by beacon fires, of his approach. In consequence they did not spare powder and shot, but at once opened a heavy fire upon the town. It is probable that this, combined with the intelligence of the victories in the proximity, of the army of the allied princes, had its psychological effect in cowing the inhabitants of the town, including the peasant contingents, and in inducing them to consent to surrender rather than to insist on holding out to the last.

For eight days the "terror" in the surrounding districts lasted. Amongst the plundering and murdering princes and barons, the Markgraf Kasimir specially signalised himself. Promises of mercy were treacherously and wantonly broken. Executions took place everywhere, whilst those who did not suffer by the headsman, or the hangman, had their hands or their fingers hacked off, or their eyes pierced out. To the latter victims the Markgraf observed: " Ye swore ye would not see me again, and I will look to it that ye shall not break your oath ". It was forbidden under severe penalties to shelter, to lead, or to heal them. Many died, and others were seen long afterwards wandering as beggars on the highway. For miles around the free-lances continued to plunder and burn the villages. Heavy ransoms were laid upon all districts. In the country they were usually reckoned at so much per hearth, whilst the towns paid as a rule *en bloc.* In Nordlingen, and other places which had not collectively taken an active part in the rebellion, only suspect citizens had to pay ransom money.

The Markgraf Kasimir alone extracted 200,000 gulden within the next two years from his own subjects.

The free imperial town of Rothenburg was taken by Kasimir on the 28th of June. The populace had quite lost head and heart. A few of the leaders in this case, however, succeeded in escaping. Karlstadt was let down one night by a rope from a window in a house on the town wall, and ended his days as a respectable professor of theology in the Basel University. The Commenthur Christen also managed to flee to a safe place, as did Ehrenfried Kumpf, the old iconoclastic burgermeister. On the other hand, Menzinger, Deuschlin, and the blind monk Schmidt, with other preachers of the new doctrine and popular leaders, met their deaths at the hands of Kasimir and the vengeful patricians now again in office. The latter indeed continued, after Kasimir and his men had left, to wreak vengeance upon their victims, slaying, branding and scourging without mercy, levelling houses to the ground and confiscating goods.

In the northern part of the Duchy of Franconia, the prince-bishop of Würzburg, the prince-

coadjutor of Fulda and the old Count Henneberg, who, it will be remembered, had been
forced some weeks previously to join the
peasant brotherhood, raged from end to end of
the district, revoking charters, taking ransoms,
beheading for the pleasure of it, and enjoying the spectacle with their boon companions
over their cups. The bishopric of Bamberg
had been subdued without any difficulty by
Truchsess after he left Würzburg. The usual
executions followed. Here also houses were
destroyed, and the ransom of 170,000 gulden
was exacted for the bishop and his noble
feudatories.

In the towns of the Rhenish district the
revolt collapsed almost of itself. Mainz again
did homage. Speyer made up its account with
its bishop. Worms returned to its allegiance.
Frankfurt-on-the-Main, however, whither many
fugitives of the people's cause had come for
refuge, was not visited by the soldiery of the
princes, the council having succeeded by bribes
in getting the town spared. Meanwhile the
guilds and the popular party here, alarmed
by the events occurring outside, had made
terms with the council, or, rather, had dropped

their original demands. Truchsess had turned
his steps in the direction of Upper Swabia,
where the insurrection had, as yet, not been
crushed. Here also the peasants were destined
to undergo a similar fate to that of their
brethren in other parts of Germany.

Memmingen, the town where the peasants'
parliament had been held in the early days of
the revolt, and where the "Twelve Articles"
were first adopted and probably drawn up, fell,
as others had done, through treachery. The
party of the *Ehrbarkeit* and certain councillors
held secret communications with the Swabian
League. On the Friday of Whitsun week the
watchman announced to the council that a vast
force of soldiery was bearing down upon the
town. The citizens were instantly aroused,
and the market-place glittered with armour and
halberds. But on the leaders of the approaching force reaching the town. they merely asked
with fair words for quarters for one hundred
horsemen, the rest of their following to remain
outside. This was eventually agreed to, and the
citizens, imagining all danger over, laid down
their arms and went home. No sooner were
they out of the way than the League's men

suddenly forced open the gates, and admitted their fellows from outside the walls to the number of two hundred horse and two thousand foot. Several citizens compromised in the recent rising immediately fled, among them the supposed author of the " Twelve Articles," the preacher Schappeler, who succeeded in reaching his native town of St. Gallen in safety. Five who remained were beheaded on the marketplace.

The Archduke Friedrich, who was anxious to get the territory of Upper Swabia as a fief of the House of Austria, and who had been negotiating to this end with the Algau insurgents, wished to prevent Truchsess, at all events for the moment, from carrying hostilities into this region, and wrote to Truchsess to this effect. The latter communicated with Ulm on the matter, but was told by the council of the League that he was acting in their service and not in that of the Archduke Friedrich, and that he was to proceed without delay. He obeyed, but seems to have been rather nettled by the peremptory language, since a short time afterwards, on the council's remonstrating with him for his wholesale burning of villages and homesteads, he sent back a reply that if they were going to teach him how to carry on war they had better come out and take the command themselves, and he would sit quiet at Kempten.

A portion of the Algau peasant army, on the approach of Truchsess, withdrew after a short skirmish to the other side of the river Luibas, and took up their position on a steep elevation, first destroying the ford. Here messengers were sent to call up the whole of the Algau forces. They had good and sufficient ordnance. The Algau peasants enjoyed the reputation, which seems to have been well founded, of being the best and most practised fighting men amongst the country population. Many of them had already served as free-lances, and a considerable body of men-at-arms, recently back from the Italian war, had joined them. Walter Bach, before spoken of, who had once been in the Austrian service, and Kaspar Schneider, who had served in Italy under the well-known Georg von Frundsberg, were amongst their leaders. In a few days their number had risen to 23,000, one of the largest masses the peasants ever succeeded in bringing together to any one place.

The insurgents never had a more favourable opportunity. Had they succeeded in crushing Truchsess, as they could easily have done, the cause of the rebellion might still, even now, have been saved. But where mischance or superior fighting strength did not destroy the peasants, treachery came in to do the work. Walter Bach opened negotiations with the head of the League's forces, under whom at an earlier period he had served. Truchsess was awaiting the advent of Georg von Frundsberg, who was on his way to reinforce him with three thousand free-lances. These had all fought under him at the battle of Pavia.

It was on the evening of the 21st of July that Frundsberg arrived with his following. On his side, Frundsberg knew Schneider and other of the peasant leaders, and he and Truchsess agreed to effect their purpose, if possible, through the treachery of these men. The subordinate leaders were won over by Walter Bach, and a secret meeting was arranged at which a large sum of money was handed to the traitors. A signal having been agreed upon, they returned to the insurgent camp and persuaded the peasants to leave their strong position on the pretext that it was impossible to attack the combined forces from it! Truchsess immediately opened a heavy cannonade against the peasant position, which gave Bach the opportunity of setting fire, without being suspected, to the kegs containing the store of powder.

There were now three contingents massed on the Luibas, on the opposite side to Truchsess's camp. Two of these were commanded respectively by Schneider and Bach, and the third was under Knopf von Luibas, who was not in the conspiracy. The two traitors had bribed the keepers of the ordnance to leave it behind, whilst they marched out with their following. This occurred at midnight. No sooner had they reached open ground than the whole forces of the League were heard approaching. The unexpected move caused a sudden panic. Companies got into confusion and began to disperse in all directions, the peasants seeking cover in the neighbouring valleys and woods. Meanwhile, the guilty leaders had fled, and gained Swiss territory within a few days. The whole ordnance fell into the hands of the League's forces.

But the victory was not quite complete, since the contingent led by Knopf von Luibas, unaware of what was taking place, held together. When, at daybreak, it was perceived treachery had been at work and that the two contingents had melted away, Knopf and his men hurriedly withdrew and managed to safely reach a good position on a hill above the town of Kempten. Truchsess, who could not attack them there, adopted the tactics of surrounding the hill with a sea of fire, caused by the conflagration of more than two hundred villages and homesteads. Numbers of women and children and old people perished in these fires. At the same time, the horsemen of the League occupied all outlets. As the result, the peasants were on the point of being starved out.

Finally they were compelled to surrender, and descended into the hostile camp with the usual white staves in their hands. The conditions exacted were a fresh oath of allegiance, a tribute of six gulden from every hearth, and a further indemnity to their lords, the amount to be decided by the Swabian League, which should also be the arbiter in all disputes between them and their lords. Truchsess immediately had eighteen leaders executed, besides others later on—in all some thirty persons. Knopf himself, with some other leaders, escaped. He was seized later on, however, in Bregenz, and, with a comrade named Kunzwirth, hanged after a long imprisonment.

Truchsess now threw strong garrisons into the towns of Kempten and Kaufbeuren, to overawe the country-folk. Thus ended the peasant revolt in the districts of Upper Swabia.

In the meantime, Duke Antoine of Lorraine had arrived with a large force of local men-at-arms, together with German and Italian mercenaries and others, intent on suppressing the peasant insurrection in Elsass. With these troops he pressed through the Vosges and appeared before Zabern, where Erasmus Gerber had fixed his camp. On the 17th of May, a body of peasants that had come to the relief of the main force in Zabern was defeated and driven back into the village of Lipstein, which was surrounded and burnt. This was not effected without some hard fighting. There was a desperate struggle for the position. Several times the attack was renewed, until the ducal army was finally successful in penetrating through the peasant stockade into the village. The church now became the citadel of the defenders. Flames then burst out on all sides, eventually reaching the defenders them selves. The latter, seeing their case to be hopeless, begged for grace, but it was too late. They rushed from the flames only to be mercilessly run through in the streets and lanes of the village. The accounts of the numbers slain vary between 2000 and 6000.

Amongst the mercenaries employed by the duke were Albanians, Stratiots, and possibly others from eastern Europe. These contributed an element of cold-blooded butchery which was not to be found amongst the Germans even of that age. Children of eight, ten and twelve were ruthlessly killed. Women and girls were dragged through the corn, ravished, and butchered. News of these things caused a panic throughout all the surrounding territory, and thirty waggons containing women and children from the neighbouring villages presented themselves the same evening at the gates of Kochersberg, a town belonging to Strasburg.

The occurrence naturally had its effect upon
Zabern itself which surrendered. Next morning
the peasants opened the gates, and under the
solemn promise of mercy from the duke they
streamed out without their arms but with the
necessary tokens of submission—the white staves
—in their hands. The account of what followed
is here quoted from Hardtfelder (*Geschichte des
Bauernkriegs in Südwest-Deutschland*, p. 130
sqq). "The free-lances of the duke accompanied the exodus of the peasants. Suddenly
there arose a quarrel between a free-lance and
a peasant, the latter defending himself because,
as the report says, he feared to be robbed
of his money. Vollcyr also relates that the
peasants had irritated the soldiers by the cry
of 'Long live Luther!' Suddenly the shout
was heard 'Strike! It is allowed us!' Thereupon began a frightful massacre. The free-
lances struck down the defenceless peasants,
who sought to reach the town by precipitate
flight. The majority, however, were despatched
before they got there; the free-lances simultaneously with the fugitives pressed into the
town, although Count Salm with his horsemen
tried to prevent this. The slaughter was here

continued, not only the peasants who were in the town being murdered, but the greater portion of the citizens sharing their fate. Those peasants who had sought to flee from the town in other directions fell into the hands of the Lorrainers and were killed. Still worse would have happened, if the princes had not at this time hurried up and stopped further mischief. The Geldrian mercenaries, who had plundered Zabern, would have set fire to the whole town had they not been prevented. Even the wounded had now to be spared, and the inhabitants also escaped if they fastened on themselves the cross of Lorraine."

So great was the number of the slain that the roads leading to the town were strewn with corpses, and it was hardly possible to enter the gates for the heaps of dead that lay there. From sixteen to twenty thousand peasants were slain on this occasion.

The brutal Bavarian chancellor, Leonhard von Eck, reports on the 27th of May, that the duke had destroyed 20,000 peasants, and adds that so many peasants lay unburied that " to write with modesty, the self-same dead have so stunk that many women who fled from the country did leave their children untended, the which, therefore, did perish of hunger ". He continues : " The said duke hath on Saturday slain a band of four thousand peasants, and now turneth against other bands who in the same place are rebellious, so that it bethinketh me that he will make a wilderness of the length of the whole Rhine ".

The Duke Antoine treated the campaign as a kind of religious crusade against the new Lutheran doctrines. There is some doubt as to his guilt as regards the treacherous massacre of Zabern. Whether it was carried out by his positive orders or not, it is sufficiently clear that no adequate measures were taken to prevent the heterogeneous elements of his army from getting beyond control.

The ducal forces raged, slaughtering and plundering, throughout Elsass. Heavy ransoms and tributes were everywhere exacted from the towns and villages that had taken part in the insurrection. Everywhere feudal homage had to be made anew. The peasants were again forced under the old yokes, the original dues and *corvées* being exacted from them. In many places they were forbidden the right of assembly and of bearing any arms except the short dagger. Indemnity was insisted upon for the religious houses plundered. Oftentimes they had to hand over any charters or written concessions they might have previously obtained from their feudal superiors.

In Baden, the Austrian Government at Ensisheim showed itself merciless in the punishment of all who had taken any prominent share in the rebellion. So numerous were the executions that, playing on the name of the town, people were wont to say that it was indeed "the home of the sword".—Ensis-heim. Curiously enough the peasants, when the insurrection was at its height, do not seem to have made any serious attempt to capture this small township, the seat of the Hapsburg power in the country, although they without doubt threatened it on more than one occasion. This is the more remarkable seeing that Ensisheim is situated on a plain, and hence is easy of access, and that the walls, the ruins of which I have carefully examined, were exceptionally thin and could hardly have sustained themselves long, even against the rough and imperfect ordnance at the disposal of the peasant forces.

It is interesting to note that on the manor of
Stühlingen, the territory of Count Georg von
Lupfen, where the movement, according to
tradition, first began, in the autumn of 1524,
the peasants succumbed and were brought
again under the yoke early in July. The only
concession they seem to have obtained was the
curious one of freedom of the chase of bears
and wolves, which would seem to indicate that
these animals were common at that time in the
district. All other objects of the chase were
prohibited to the peasants. The new religious
doctrines were forbidden to be preached. A
ransom of six gulden per hearth was enforced.
The tocsins or alarm-bells on the church
towers, which in so many places had given
the signal for the rising, were ordered to be
removed. Every form of combination was
suppressed.

At the same time the movements along the
lake of Constance collapsed. The peasants of
the Hegau, as it was called, after Truchsess's
retreat into Würtemberg, before the battle of
Boblingen, had carried on a bitter conflict with
the garrisons of the towns Stockach and Zell.
The latter set several villages on fire, and

committed such atrocities as the burning of women and children.

Count Felix von Werdenberg, who had returned from Italy at the same time as Frundsberg with a force of mercenaries and others, attacked the peasants on the 16th of July at Hilzingen, the place where the great " church-ale" was held in October, 1524, at which the movement of the district was consolidated. Here, too, the peasants were totally defeated, and the revolt perished in slaughter and flight. Radolfzell was relieved, and the besieging force was scattered. The greatest of the peasant leaders in south-western Germany, Hans Müller von Bulgenbach, was seized and beheaded.

Later on, one of his colleagues, Conrad Jehle, was captured and hanged upon the nearest oak tree without form of trial. This took place on the lands of the Abbey of St. Blasien in the Black Forest, which he had spared when it was in the power of his followers. One morning the right hand of his corpse was found nailed to the great gate of the abbey, with the words " This hand will avenge itself" scrawled underneath, evidently the writing of one of Jehle's faithful adherents. A short time afterwards the buildings of the wealthy foundation burst into flame one night, and in a few hours the massive pile was a heap of ruins. The cause of the fire was never ascertained.

The Archduke Ferdinand would like to have punished with the usual brutality those bands of the Breisgau district which had forced the town of Freiburg into their brotherhood. But the peasants of the Sundgau and the Klettgau, who had also assisted in the matter, had appealed to the Swiss to take them into their hands. The Baselers did not seem unwilling to listen to their proposal, and offered them at all events their friendly offices as mediators. They appear to have threatened both sides that they would interfere with the recalcitrant party if a compromise were rejected. The military repute of the Swiss, which, in spite of the defeat of Marignano ten years before, was still sufficiently great to make even the archduke pause before driving matters to extremities.

egotiations were entered into with the insurgents, which were concluded on the 18th of September by the treaty of Offenburg, by which the peasants agreed to accept provisions rein-

stating their lords in their old rights as to dues
and services, and fixing a sum as indemnity for
damage done and a fine of six gulden for every
hearth. But, although compelled by the force
of circumstances to accept these terms, the
Breisgau and Sundgau peasants were by no
means cowed. "*Erzwungener Eid ist Gott
leid*" or, as we may translate it, "Forced oaths
God loathes," said they. They made no secret
of their intention to rebel again as soon as the
archduke's men-at-arms should have left the
land. So threatening did they become that
the town of Freiburg had to demand of the
Austrian authorities a standing force of three
hundred men to overawe the countryside
throughout the ensuing winter.

The most favourable conditions of all were
obtained by the peasants on the lands of the
humane Markgraf Philip of Baden, who
granted some notable ameliorations in their
condition. He had done his best to obtain
favourable conditions for those on his brother's
and others' territories.

The town of Waldshut, one of the earliest
centres of the rebellion, held out against its
Austrian masters long after the surrounding

country had been completely subdued. But on
the 12th of December it, too, was taken and
suffered the usual pains and penalties. A short
time before, Balthaser Hubmayer, the revolutionary preacher, whom the citizens had
welcomed with such transports in the spring
of the year, succeeded in escaping, but it was
only to meet a death at the stake, in Vienna,
four years later, as an Anabaptist.

Let us now cast a retrospective glance at the
course of the Civil War. We have seen that
the rebellion, which had carried all before it
with a few noteworthy exceptions, from its
beginning up to the second week in May,
thenceforward underwent defeat after defeat.
The first of these irreparable disasters, the
battle of Boblingen, took place on the 12th of
May. This meant practically the end of the
movement in Wurtemberg. Three days afterwards occurred the overthrow of the revolt
in Thuringia and the neighbouring countries,
effected by the fatal blow dealt the peasant
forces at Frankenhausen. The capture and
massacre of Zabern, which followed two days
later, was the decisive event in Duke Antoine's
campaign against the peasants of the far-off

lands of the extreme south-west. Then came
the battle of Konigshofen on the 2nd of June, a
disaster which delivered the Franconian movement into the hands of the Swabian League and
its allies. It was not before the end of July
that treachery dissolved the powerful contingents massed on the Luibas in Upper Swabia.
But by this time the movement throughout
those countries which in the present day constitute the new German Empire was to all
intents and purposes crushed. " Military operations," as the modern phrase goes, were continued
in special districts throughout August, and it
was not indeed before the middle of September
that the last sparks of the active revolt were
trodden out.

The fact is, that as long as the German
territories were denuded of fighting men, and
as long as the only resistance the peasant bands
met with was the small force under Truchsess,
which was all the Swabian League could then
muster, and which could obviously only be in
one place at one time, the insurrection naturally
had things all its own way. The case was very
different when large bodies of knights, mercenaries, and men-at-arms of all descriptions began

to troop back from Italy on the termination of
the Italian campaign after the imperial victory
at Pavia.   The inability of raw peasant levies
to successfully encounter trained fighting men—
their superiors alike in experience, organisation and equipment, was immediately apparent.
The demoralising influence of drink, gluttony
and general laxness, which was so much in
evidence amongst the peasant bands, was, of
course, a contributory cause of the rapid extinction of the movement, but even apart from this,
as we have elsewhere pointed out, the case was
hopeless.

Hangings, beheadings and slaughter were
at last too much even for the palate of the
governing classes, and at the Reichstag held
at the end of August, a rescript was issued
urging mercy and forbearance upon the lords
of the soil, deprecating fresh impositions or
undue exactions, and even going so far as
to threaten that those lords who acted in a
contrary sense might find themselves refused
imperial assistance when in need.   For in
spite of the discomfiture he had suffered, the
" common man " had by no means even yet
lost all hope.   A belief in the possibility of

speedily renewing the rising was active amongst the peasantry throughout the winter of 1525 and the spring of 1526, and this hope did not at the time seem altogether groundless. There was, indeed, amidst the general wilderness of disaster, one oasis in which the peasant was still holding his own, and was even scoring some relatively lasting successes. In the arch-bishopric of Salzburg the insurgents were still practically the masters of the situation. In Tyrol, under the chief leadership of the most able, and many-sided genius of the whole insurrection, Michael Gaismayr, the peasants had extorted noteworthy concessions from their feudal lord, the arch-duke, at the Landtag opened by him at Innsbruck on the 15th of June. In the neighbouring territories, more-over, the rebels were still active. With events in these Austrian lands we shall deal in the following chapter.

CHAPTER IX.

THE ALPINE GLOW IN THE AUSTRIAN TERRITORIES.

THE revolt in Styria (Steuermarck) which Sigismund Dietrichstein had partially suppressed, broke out again later on. Encouraged from Vienna, Dietrichstein glutted himself with the most monstrous exactions and cruelties. All the districts where the revolt had sprung up were condemned to ruinous tribute and ransom money. In addition to this, impaling, flaying and quartering constituted the order of the day with him. His mercenaries amused themselves with cutting off the breasts of the peasant women and ripping open the abdomens of those about to become mothers. So at last the cup was filled to overflowing. The town of Schladming, on the border of the Salzburg territory, had yielded to Dietrichstein. Seeing the situation, the united contingent of the Styrian and Salzburg peasants sent a demand to the town to enter the " Christian Brotherhood ". Dietrichstein, on being informed of this, proceeded to the township with a force which he disposed partly inside the walls and partly before them outside. He then proceeded to enter into negotiations with the peasants, being, of course, on treachery intent. Suddenly, on the morning of the 3rd of July, the alarm was given that the enemy was approaching. On showing himself at the window of the inn where he was lodging, he was struck by a missile. He succeeded, however, in rushing downstairs and mounting his horse, and with two hundred followers he gained the place where fighting was going on. His horse was stabbed under him, and he himself received a blow on the head. By his side other knights fell. But now most of the men he had about him deserted to the peasants. The rest of the knights fled and entrenched themselves in the church, Dietrichstein himself surrendering to his own mutinous free-lances. By a surprise, a body of about four thousand peasants had overpowered the camp outside the town, and had become possessed of its ordnance and ammunition. The horsemen had fled in a panic. Of the Bohemian mercenaries, some escaped and some were made prisoners. Numbers were killed or driven into the stream. The town opened its gates after three thousand of Dietrichstein's force were killed, amongst them a large number of Carinthian and Styrian nobles. Eighteen knights were taken in the church alone.

The prisoners of rank were brought into the peasant camp, Dietrichstein amongst them. A ring was formed, and the whole body of peasants was called together to give judgment. The captain of the baronial forces was brought forward, and a formal accusation of all his crimes was entered against him. A demand was made that he should be impaled. On the matter being put to the vote, the whole four thousand hands were held up in favour of the execution. Dietrichstein pleaded the promise of knightly treatment he had obtained from the free-lances. Thereupon a dissension arose between the latter and the peasants, and eventually the matter was referred to the peasant council sitting at Salzburg. Here again, dissension seems to have arisen between the council and the main body of the insurgents assembled in the town. The council wrote recommending honourable captivity for the noble prisoners. The general assembly, on the contrary, sent a letter demanding their execution.

A compromise is stated to have been effected in the camp outside Schladming, by which the Bohemian and other foreigners, noble and otherwise, were beheaded in the market-place of the town. The German nobles, on the other hand, including Dietrichstein, were spared, but had to suffer every imaginable contumely from their captors. They were stripped of their knightly raiment and dressed in peasant clothes. Peasant hats were put upon their heads, and they were led away on waggon-horses to the castle of Werfen, already occupied by the insurgents. The peasants found in the town all the money which Dietrichstein had amassed through his impositions, besides considerable property belonging to the imprisoned nobles.

After these events the Schladming contingent proceeded to take steps to renew the insurrection throughout Styria. In Carinthia and the Austrian hereditary dominions an agreement had been come to between the peasants and their lords. The smaller nobles and the townships in fact, in many cases, had themselves urged a general reduction of the burdens of the "common man". They were lenient as regarded ransom-money, in spite of the representations of the archduke. The leaders fled into the Salzburg territory.

In the Landtag at Innsbruck the archduke had succeeded in pacifying the greater part of his own Duchy of Tyrol. He had abolished many grievances, and had fixed the next Landtag to be held at Bozen. The concessions which Ferdinand accorded the Tyrolese were in fact sufficiently remarkable to lend colour to the supposition that he had a sentimental affection for his patrimonial province. Amongst other things, a complete amnesty was granted. Gaismayr, however, does not seem to have been at all satisfied with the result. As we have already seen, he looked farther than the mere alleviation of the feudal yoke. He had meanwhile resigned the leadership, but his followers were not inactive. Two of them were zealously preaching at Meran and Sterzing, and inveighing against the decisions of the Landtag. Several of the rural communities refused to give their assent, and organised themselves anew, notably in the Brixen territories. Having appointed leaders, they formed themselves into a contingent and marched upon Trient, which town they bombarded.

About sixteen thousand men were got together to suppress the revolt. By the end of September it was completely crushed, several of the leaders being executed, and the rest fleeing, mostly into Venetian territory, which at this time furnished a refuge for numbers of the archduke's rebellious subjects. In Trient and the surrounding district the repression was frightful. The current forms of torture were ruthlessly applied—mutilation, quartering, impaling and roasting alive. Some, according to the contemporary chronicle, had their hearts cut out and suspended round their necks. Every prisoner was branded on the forehead before being dismissed. Numbers, however, succeeded in escaping into Italy.

Gaismayr was meanwhile arrested and brought to Innsbruck. He was at first liberated on parole, but, finding that the authorities neglected to carry out the accepted decisions of the Landtag and were everywhere shedding the blood of the peasants, he probably thought himself absolved from his oath, and accordingly, at the end of September, he sought refuge in flight. He threatened that, should he be molested, he had eighteen townships and villages sworn to defend him.

Meanwhile the movement in Salzburg went on apace. As we have seen, Duke Wilhelm of Bavaria was not displeased at the uncomfortable position of his feudal neighbour, the Archbishop of Salzburg. Indeed, he let the insurgents clearly understand that his emissaries were sent merely to mediate and not to intimidate. The Bavarian chancellor, the stern old aristocrat Leonhard von Eck, opposed this policy of his master, which threatened at one time to bring about a serious conflict between the Bavarian Wittelsbachs and the Austrian Hapsburgs, but which in the long run came to nothing. When, towards the end of June, the Swabian League, in response to the urgent representations of the archbishop, claimed Bavarian assistance for the suppression of the Salzburg rebels, the duke succeeded in postponing the day of decision. It was thus not until the end of August that the terms of peace were arranged, by which the old dues and *corvées* were to be re-established, indemnification made for loss sustained by the rebellion, and a fine of 14,000 gulden paid to the Swabian League. An amnesty was granted, and the Swabian League was to decide the villeins' claims against their lords. But ominous threatenings were still heard that "so soon as the bushes should be green they would be rid of nobles and gentlemen". The Duke of Bavaria had thus to be satisfied with effecting what proved little more than an armistice. In fact, the peasants had shown themselves more than a match for the League's troops sent against them under Frundsberg in conjunction with the reluctant assistance of the Bavarian duke.

As a result of the treaty, the nobles detained in the castle of Werfen were released, and the archbishop, who for months had been besieged in his fortress above Salzburg, was, of course, once more free. But the remembrance of the defeat at Schladming still rankled in the breasts of the Archduke Ferdinand and the nobles. The peasants were indeed magnanimous enough in their treatment of their captives, notably of Dietrichstein, from whom they had suffered so much.[1] But this did not satisfy the authorities

[1] Indeed, if we may believe a recent authority, the story of the executions by the peasants on Schladming market-place is a historical fable [*Krones apud Janssen*, vol. ii., p. 571, *note*].

and territorial lords, who thought that they
ought to have a monopoly of killing. Accordingly, in the midst of the peace, Count Salm
with a company of free-lances swept down
upon the town and fired it on all sides. The
wretched inhabitants rushing out were hurled
back into the flames, without regard to age
or sex. Large numbers of peasants in the
neighbourhood of Schladming were hanged
from the trees. The town itself was reduced
to a heap of ashes. This dastardly and bloodthirsty act of treachery excited the peasants
anew. Finally, about the middle of October,
the countrymen once more met together near
the town of Radstadt, and drew up a remonstrance against the archbishop's multitudinous
breaches of the treaty, and against the atrocities
committed by the imperial troops, presumably
at the instance of the archduke.

Similar assemblies were held in other places,
and communications were entered into with
the Brixen district of Tyrol, special use being
made of the great "church-ale" of the town
of Brixen itself. But the inhabitants were dis-
inclined for the moment to break the treaty
they had entered into with their bishop, and

in fact the revolt did not burst into renewed activity until early in the following year.

Meanwhile Michael Gaismayr had escaped into Switzerland, visiting Zurich, Luzern, and parts of Graubunden, and entering into relations with the numerous refugees from South Germany and elsewhere then in the Swiss cantons. In Chur he was seen, it was alleged, in company with an emissary of the French court. Francis I. was at this time in league with Venice to secretly further the rebellion in the Alpine districts, with a view of harassing his enemy Charles V. He was now, it is true, a prisoner in the hands of the latter, but his policy was, of course, being carried on by his representatives. Towards the end of the winter, Gaismayr took up his abode at Taufers, on the Tyrolese frontier of Appenzell, whence he endeavoured to stir up a revolt in order to seize some of the Bishop of Chur's ordnance in the neighbourhood. This plan, however, miscarried.

In the beginning of January, 1526, he issued a manifesto containing the objects for which the Tyrolese were to rise. The first demand was the destruction of all the godless, who persecuted the true word of God and oppressed the "common man". Pictures, masses and shrines were to be abolished. The walls and towers of the towns, together with all castles and strongholds, were to be levelled with the ground. Henceforth, there were to be only villages, to the end that complete equality might obtain. Each year magistrates were to be chosen by the popular voice, who were to hold court every Monday. All the judicial authorities were to be paid for out of the common treasury. A central government was to be chosen by the whole country and a university established at Brixen, three members of which were to be appointed as permanent assessors to the government. Dues and rents were to be done away with; the tithe was to be retained, but applied to the support of the Reformed Church and of the poor. The monasteries were to be turned into hospitals and schools. The breeding of cattle was to be improved and the land irrigated. Oil-trees, saffron, vines and corn were to be everywhere planted. There was to be a public inspection of wares to ensure their quality and reasonable price. Usury and debasement of the coinage

were to be punished. The mines were to become the property of the whole land. Passes,
roads, bridges and rivers were to be kept in
order by the public authority and suitable
measures taken for the defence of the country
against external foes.

Such is the main substance of the manifesto
which the messengers of Michael Gaismayr
now distributed in the valleys of western Tyrol.
The ink with which he had written it was
scarcely dry before news arrived of the resuscitation, in the archiepiscopal territories of
Salzburg, of the movement of the previous
autumn. In a few days, Gaismayr was on
his way to the seat of the struggle. Arrived
there, he soon became practically the head of
the movement, and later on its recognised
commander, whilst his friends, most of whom
he had brought with him, became his lieu-
tenants. The miners, however, remained quiet.
In fact, two companies, composed partly of
miners and partly of handicraftsmen, were
enrolled by the archbishop and induced to
march against their peasant brethren. They
were, however, defeated by the rebels.

Radstadt, a town on the frontier of Salzburg

22

and the Austrian hereditary lands, Styria and Carinthia, was besieged by Gaismayr on the 1st of May, 1526.   The capture of this town was important alike from its strategic position and from its possession of some of the best ordnance at the disposal of Archduke Ferdinand. The latter, on hearing of Gaismayr's operations, immediately sent reinforcements to relieve Radstadt.   The Swabian League also sent a small force.   Gaismayr, however, as a good strategist, had taken the precaution of blocking the main roads leading to the beleaguered town.   Amidst rain and sleet, the forces of the authorities with difficulty traversed the rough mountain roads, but before they were half-way to Radstadt they were fallen upon by a large body of peasants in a narrow defile, and out of a force of more than a thousand less than two hundred escaped.

On the 14th of June, Gaismayr's men defeated with heavy loss eight companies of the Swabian League's best fighting men.   They fled in confusion, and were pursued nearly to the gates of Salzburg.   Three days later, the remainder suffered as heavy a loss in a storm on a mountain pass.   But the League continued to send reinforcements, and on the 3rd of July they gained their first victory in these districts, which cost the peasants six hundred men.

Meanwhile, Gaismayr pressed closer and closer the siege of Radstadt. He stormed the town three times, but without result. At length, he found himself borne down upon from three sides by the forces of the League and of Count Salm. Accordingly, he was compelled to raise the siege, and retired hurriedly but in perfect order, with a considerable body of men, first to his former camp a little way from the town and then over a pass into the Pusterthal. But Frundsberg, with three thousand mercenaries of the League, followed close upon his heels, and eventually overtook him, and the insurgent leader's contingent was forced to make its way over the passes into Venetian territory. He himself with a following reached Venice, where he received a pension of four hundred ducats, and where, it is said, he lived like a cardinal for some time.

Thus ended the campaign which Michael Gaismayr had entered upon so full of hope. Indeed the genius of this remarkable man had given this last episode in the peasant rising—

this afterglow in the Alpine lands—a reasonable
probability of success which scarcely any previous enterprise of the "common man" had
possessed. He had, however, taken steps to
negotiate with the French and Venetians with
a view to military assistance, and, although his
allies failed him so far as active support was
concerned, the credit belongs to him of a more
far-sighted diplomacy than was exhibited by
any of the other leaders of the movement. His
plan was for a simultaneous rising in the Salzburg district, in Tyrol and in Upper Swabia,
and the failure of this plan was not due to any
want of energy on his part.

"The nobleman of Etschland," as Michael
was called, had a brother, Hans Gaismayr,
living in a good position at Sterzing, equally
enthusiastic and with unlimited confidence in
his relative. Unfortunately this brother, without having succeeded in raising the district,
was captured by the Austrian authorities at
Sterzing, and brought to Innsbruck on the 9th
of April, where he was cruelly tortured and
afterwards drawn and quartered as a traitor.
That this incident made Michael more un-
bending in his vow of destruction to all nobles

may well be imagined. Indeed, until his death his name was one of terror to the constituted authorities.

In Venice, Gaismayr continued to gather up the threads of his relations alike with the popular leaders and with the agents of the more powerful states, and the prospect, in spite of the heavy discomfiture of the " common man " throughout the German territories, seemed by no means hopeless. On the contrary, from many points of view the signs of success appeared more promising than in the period just passed through of the great spontaneous but ill-organised and badly-disciplined upheaval of the peasantry and poor townsmen. For the Protestant districts and principalities were now becoming alarmed at the turn things were taking. There was a growing feeling that an attempt would be made by the victorious feudal lords, still mainly Catholic and inspired by the archduke and the chief ecclesiastical princes, to crush Lutheranism itself. A commanding personality—a strong man in the Carlylean sense—had at last appeared in the person of Gaismayr. In addition, was there not " the Man of Twiel," Duke Ulrich, secure

in his powerful stronghold on the Swiss frontier
of Würtemberg? Was he not surrounded by
numbers of refugees, including many of the
local leaders of the late movement, who had
fled thither? Was he not simply waiting
his opportunity to march into his hereditary
dominions with a force sufficient to defy the
imperial power, and to re-establish himself as
Würtemberg's master at Stuttgart?

Meanwhile, on the collapse of the Tyrol
movement, consequent upon the retreat of
Gaismayr, the usual policy of ferocious and
bestial oppression combined with treachery was
pursued. An appearance of moderation was
affected in the treatment of the first batch of
insurgents who surrendered. They were merely
required to give up their arms and to pay a fine
of eight gulden per hearth. An appeal was
then made to those who had not yet given in
their submission to appear on a specified day at
Radstadt. The seeming clemency enticed large
numbers to offer themselves on the day in question. On the peasants having assembled at the
town gate, the nobles rode out at the head of a
body of horse and foot. One of their number
then addressed the unarmed people, descanting

on the sin of rebellion against their lords. This ended, a list of twenty-seven names was read out, and those who bore them were ordered to come forward. Four executioners at the same time appeared, and proceeded to strike off the heads of the designated twenty-seven leaders. The remainder of those present were compelled to take their old oath of allegiance and obedience before they were allowed to return home. The houses of those known to have taken a prominent part in the rebellion, who now either were executed or had fled, were pulled down, and painted posts were set up in their place. Small towns were degraded to the rank of villages, and the alarm-bells were torn down from the church towers.

The two towns of Radstadt and Zell, which had closed their gates and resolutely resisted the followers of Gaismayr, were, on the other hand, rewarded with special privileges. They were accorded the right of making, every Whit Monday, a procession round the high altar of the cathedral of St. Ruprecht at Salzburg during vespers and there singing the songs of their district. The same evening, they were to be entertained from the archbishop's cellar and

kitchen, the cathedral canons and the courtiers
taking part. On the Tuesday after St. Vitus's
Day, they might hang their flag from the
Rathhaus, and also received a gift of wine from
the archiepiscopal cellars, besides being allowed
to fish in the preserved streams of their feudal
overlord.

Throughout the year 1527, especially in the
early summer, the whole Catholic feudal world
was filled with dread at the return of Gaismayr
to revivify the suppressed movement, perhaps
with a French and Venetian understanding and
the co-operation or benevolent neutrality of
some at least of the Protestant states. The
peasants, the small townsmen, and the Protestant
sectaries generally were correspondingly hopeful.
The Alpine lands were looked toward on the
one side with fear and on the other with joyful
expectation as the hearth and refuge of popular
freedom. Through the whole of central and
southern Germany the name of the great
peasant leader from Tyrol became in every
village a household word. Free-lances back
from serving in the recent campaigns spoke in
terms of unconcealed admiration for the valiant
commander against whom they had been

fighting. In the public room of many a hostelry the deeds of Michael Gaismayr, and the chances of his return to head a larger movement than the one just defeated, were eagerly discussed.

Various were the reports as to his probable action. It was said at one time that he was about to proceed from Venetian territory to Trient, and thence by forced marches into the Tyrol valleys, to call the people to arms under the protection of the Venetian Republic and its allies, who would thereby secure a free hand against Charles V. in other directions. But time passed on and yet there was no invasion from the south. Finally, in the early spring of 1528, Gaismayr was reported to have been seen in Switzerland, particularly in Zurich. The rumour was confirmed, and it further became known that he had received the citizenship of this canton, and that he was regarded as plenipotentiary for the Venetian Republic, in which capacity he was negotiating with Count Ulrich of Wurtemberg, with the reformed Swiss cantons, and with other powerful Protestant interests in Germany. It was believed that he had, in short, in his hands the threads of

a strong combination against the emperor.
Certain it was that extensive recruitings in
various districts, especially in Graubunden,
were being made in his name.

By the middle of June. the matter had so far
taken definite shape that it was reported that
several thousand Swiss were already on the
march to join Gaismayr in the mountain passes
leading to Austria, and that the intention was
to invade his native Etschland. This last
report was not true, and it is difficult now to
say precisely how far the negotiations for an
anti-imperial league had proceeded, but that
there were such there is no doubt. We may
reasonably suppose that affairs were in train
by August, 1528, when news arrived of
Charles's victory at Naples on the 19th of
that month, and the parties concerned seemed
to have lost heart, the scheme coming to nothing
in a few weeks. Ferdinand and his councillors
had already set a price on Gaismayr's head.
One of his followers was bribed to murder him.
The man took the money, but omitted his part
of the bargain. The Bishop of Brixen now
also adopted the assassination policy, but still
no German-speaking man was forthcoming to

carry it out. At last, two wretched Spanish bravos expressed their readiness for a large sum in gold to undertake the crime. They repaired to Padua, in the Venetian territory, whither Gaismayr had returned, and one night, breaking into his apartment whilst he was asleep, they stabbed him to the heart, subsequently severing his head from his body. The head was then carefully preserved and brought by the assassins to the archduke at Innsbruck. Shortly afterwards, Gaismayr's chief lieutenant, a brave man named Passler, was murdered by one of his own followers, also bribed to the deed by the Austrian Court. The money was again in this case handed over on the receipt of the head at Innsbruck.

All prospects were now gone, for the time being, for the popular movement. The terror of the Catholic feudal estates and the hope of the "common man," Michael Gaismayr, was dead. The other leaders were dispersed in exile or killed or imprisoned, save for a few who remained with Duke Ulrich in the "Hohentwiel". The duke himself was to regain his patrimony of Würtemberg, but not as he at one time imagined by the aid of

the peasants ostensibly fighting for their own
rights.   In short, with Gaismayr's death the
afterglow of the Peasants War finally faded
away.   The revolt of the "common man" had
been extinguished.

CHAPTER X.

CONCLUSION.

In the foregoing pages we have followed the chief episodes in the last great agrarian uprising of the Middle Ages. Its result was, with some few exceptions, a rivetting of the peasant's chains and an increase of his burdens. More than a thousand castles and religious houses were destroyed in Germany alone during 1525. Many priceless works of mediæval art of all kinds perished. But we must not allow our regret at such vandalism to blind us in any way to the intrinsic righteousness of the popular demands.

Just as little should our judgment be influenced by the fact that we can now see that much of the peasant programme was out of the line of natural social progress, and that the war itself was carried on from the beginning in a manner that rendered success well-nigh impossible, if only from a military point of view. The revolt, as we have seen, was crushed piecemeal, just

(349)

as it had arisen piecemeal. Co-operation there was none. Thomas Munzer found it hopeless to connect effectively the movement in the countries of Thuringia and Franconia, allied as they were in many ways. In consequence of the movements being thus territorially limited, the forces of the authorities, such as that of the Swabian League, had little difficulty in defeating the several insurgent bodies one after the other.

Of the ruthless and cold-blooded butchery which usually followed we have seen enough. The blow was indeed a heavy one for the " common man " generally, and for the peasant more especially. As to the few exceptions where something was gained, one of the most noteworthy was the case of the subjects of Count Philip of Baden, who were granted some solid ameliorations.

The attitude of the official Lutheran party towards the poor country-folk continued as infamous after the war as it had been on the first sign that fortune was forsaking their cause. Like master, like man. Luther's jackal, the " gentle " Melancthon, specially signalised himself by urging on the feudal barons with

Scriptural arguments to the blood-sucking and oppression of their villeins. A humane and honourable nobleman, Heinrich von Einsiedel, was touched in conscience at the *corvées* and heavy dues to which he found himself entitled. He sent to Luther for advice upon the subject. Luther replied that the existing exactions which had been handed down to him from his parents need not trouble his conscience, adding that it would not be good for *corvées* to be given up, since the " common man " ought to have burdens imposed upon him, as otherwise he would become overbearing. He further remarked that a severe treatment in material things was pleasing to God, even though it might seem to be too harsh. Spalatin writes in a like strain that the burdens in Germany were, if anything, too light. Subjects, according to Melancthon, ought to know that they are serving God in the burdens they bear for their superiors, whether it were journeying, paying tribute, or otherwise, and as pleasing to God as though they raised the dead at God's own behest. Subjects should look up to their lords as wise and just men, and hence be thankful to them. However unjust, tyrannical and

| cruel the lord might be, there was never any justification for rebellion.

A friend and follower of Luther and Melancthon — Martin Butzer by name — went still further. According to this "reforming" worthy, a subject was to obey his lord in everything. This was all that concerned him. It was not for him to consider whether what was enjoined was, or was not, contrary to the will of God. That was a matter for his feudal superior and God to settle between them. Referring to the doctrines of the revolutionary sects, Butzer urges the authorities to extirpate all those professing a false religion. Such men, he says, deserve a heavier punishment than thieves, robbers and murderers. Even their wives and innocent children and cattle should be destroyed (*ap. Janssen*, vol. i., p. 595).

Luther himself quotes, in a sermon on "Genesis," the instances of Abraham and Abimelech and other Old Testament worthies, as justifying slavery and the treatment of a slave as a beast of burden. "Sheep, cattle, men-servants and maid-servants, they were all possessions," says Luther, "to be sold as it pleased them like other beasts. It were even a good thing were it still so. For else no man may compel nor tame the servile folk" (*Sämmtliche Werke*, xv., 276). In other discourses he enforces the same doctrine, observing that if the world is to last for any time, and is to be kept going, it will be necessary to restore the patriarchal condition. Capito, the Strassburg preacher, in a letter to a colleague, writes lamenting that the pamphlets and discourses of Luther had contributed not a little to give edge to the bloodthirsty vengeance of the princes and nobles after the insurrection.

The total number of the peasants and their allies who fell either in fighting or at the hands of the executioners is estimated by Anselm in his *Berner Chronik* at a hundred and thirty thousand. It was certainly not less than a hundred thousand. For months after, the executioner was active in many of the affected districts. Spalatin says: "Of hanging and beheading there is no end". Another writer has it: "It was all so that even a stone had been moved to pity, for the chastisement and vengeance of the conquering lords was great". The executions within the jurisdiction of the Swabian League alone are stated at ten thousand. Truchsess's provost boasted of having hanged or beheaded twelve hundred with his own hand. More than fifty thousand fugitives were recorded. These, according to a Swabian League order, were all outlawed in such wise that any one who found them might slay them without fear of consequences.

The sentences and executions were conducted with true mediæval levity. It is narrated in a contemporary chronicle that in one village in the Henneberg territory all the inhabitants had fled on the approach of the count and his men-at-arms save two tilers. The two were being led to execution when one appeared to weep bitterly, and his reply to interrogatories was that he bewailed the dwellings of the aristocracy thereabouts, for henceforth there would be no one to supply them with durable tiles. Thereupon his companion burst out laughing, because, said he, it had just occurred to him that he would not know where to place his hat after his head had been taken off. These mildly humorous remarks obtained for both of them a free pardon.

The aspect of those parts of the country where the war had most heavily raged was deplorable in the extreme. In addition to the many hundreds of castles and monasteries destroyed, almost as many villages and small towns had been levelled with the ground by one side or the other, especially by the Swabian League and the various princely forces. Many places were annihilated for having taken part with the peasants, even when they had been compelled by force to do so. Fields in these districts were everywhere laid waste or left uncultivated. Enormous sums were exacted as indemnity. In many of the villages peasants previously well - to - do were ruined. There seemed no limit to the bleeding of the " common man," under the pretence of compensation for damage done by the insurrection.

The condition of the families of the dead and of the fugitives was appalling. Numbers perished from starvation. The wives and children of the insurgents were in some cases forcibly driven from their homesteads and even from their native territory. In one of the pamphlets published in 1525 anent the events of that year, we read : " Houses are burned ; fields and vineyards lie fallow ; clothes and household goods are robbed or burned ; cattle and sheep are taken away; the same as to horses and trappings. The prince, the gentleman, or the nobleman will have his rent and due. Eternal God, whither shall the widows and poor children go forth to seek it?" Referring to the Lutheran campaign against friars and poor scholars, beggars and pilgrims, the writer observes: "Think ye now that because of God's anger for the sake of one beggar, ye must even for a season bear with twenty, thirty, nay still more?"

The courts of arbitration, which were established in various districts to adjudicate on the relations between lords and villeins, were naturally not given to favour the latter, whilst the fact that large numbers of deeds and charters had been burnt or otherwise destroyed in the course of the insurrection left open an extensive field for the imposition of fresh burdens. The record of the proceedings of one of the most important of these courts— that of the Swabian League's jurisdiction, which sat at Memmingen—in the dispute between the prince-abbot of Kempten and his villeins is given in full in Baumann's *Akten*, pp. 329-346. Here, however, the peasants did not come off so badly as in some other places. Meanwhile, all the other evils of the time, the monopolies of the merchant-princes of the cities and of the trading-syndicates, the dearness of living, the scarcity of money, etc., did not abate, but rather increased from year to year. The Catholic Church maintained itself especially in the south of Germany, and the official Reformation took on a definitely aristocratic character.

According to Baumann (*Akten, Vorwort*, v., vi.), the true soul of the movement of 1525 consisted in the notion of " Divine justice," the principle "that all relations, whether of political, social, or religious nature, have got to be ordered according to the directions of the 'Gospel' as the sole and exclusive source and standard of all justice". The same writer maintains that there are three phases in the development of this idea, according to which he would have the scheme of historical investigation sub-divided. In Upper Swabia, says he, " Divine justice" found expression in the well-known " Twelve Articles," but here the notion of a political reformation was as good as absent.

In the second phase, the " Divine justice"

idea began to be applied to political conditions. In Tyrol and the Austrian dominions, he observes, this political side manifested itself in local or, at best, territorial patriotism. It was only in Franconia that all territorial patriotism or "particularism" was shaken off, and the idea of the unity of the German peoples received as a political goal. The Franconian influence gained over the Würtembergers to a large extent, and the plan of reform elaborated by Weigand and Hipler for the Heilbron Parliament was the most complete expression of this second phase of the movement.

The third phase is represented by the rising in Thuringia, and especially in its intellectual head, Thomas Münzer. Here we have the doctrine of "Divine justice" taking the form of a thoroughgoing theocratic scheme, to be realised by the German people.

This division Baumann is led to make with a view to the formulation of a convenient scheme for a "codex" of documents relating to the Peasants War. It may be taken as, in the main, the best general division that can be put forward, although, as we have seen, there are places where, and times when, the practical demands of the movement seem to have asserted themselves directly and spontaneously apart from any theory whatever.

Of the fate of many of the most active leaders of the revolt, we know nothing. George Metzler disappeared, and was seen no more after the battle of Konigshofen. Several heads of the movement, according to a contemporary writer, wandered about for a long time in misery, some of them indeed seeking refuge with the Turks, who were still a standing menace to imperial Christendom. The popular preachers vanished also on the suppression of the movement. The disastrous result of the Peasants War was prejudicial even to Luther's cause in south Germany. The Catholic party reaped the advantage everywhere, evangelical preachers, even, where not insurrectionists, being persecuted. Little distinction, in fact, was made in most districts between an opponent of the Catholic Church from Luther's standpoint and one from Karlstadt's or Hubmayer's. Amongst seventy-one heretics arraigned before the Austrian court at Ensisheim, only one was acquitted. The others were broken on the wheel, burnt or drowned.

Amongst the non-clerical leaders of the popular party, Friedrich Weigand alone seems to have come off scot free. Hans Flux, of Heilbron, was denounced by his own fellow-citizens, and, for the time being, driven from his native town. It cost him a hundred gold gulden to be reinstated in the rights of citizenship. Some of the heads of the peasant companies found temporary refuge in ruined castles and other out-of-the-way places. Some even became chiefs of robber bands, and were at a later date killed in conflict with the authorities. Martin Feuerbacher was imprisoned in the imperial town of Esslingen and suffered the torture several times. Owing, however, to the good repute in which he stood with certain nobles of his neighbourhood, he was after some years reinstated in his property.

There were some who were arrested ten or fifteen years later on charges connected with the 1525 revolt. Treachery, of course, played a large part, as it has done in all defeated movements, in ensuring the fate of many of those who had been at all prominent. In fairness to Luther, who otherwise played such a villainous *role*, the fact should be recorded that he sheltered his old colleague, Karlstadt, for a short time in the Augustine monastery at Wittenberg, after the latter's escape from Rothenburg. Ehrenfried Kumpf, the iconoclast and ex-bürgermeister of Rothenburg, died of melancholy some little while after the suppression of the insurrection. The nobility of Gotz von Berlichingen and his treachery to the peasants' cause did not save him from the consequences of the part he had ostensibly played. He lay for some time an imperial prisoner in one of the towers on the town wall of Nurnberg. He was subsequently released on a solemn pledge not to quit his ancestral domains, and remained a captive on his own lands for years.

Wendel Hipler continued for some time at liberty, and might probably have escaped altogether had he not entered a process against the Counts of Hohenlohe for having seized a portion of his private fortune that lay within their power. The result of his action might have been foreseen. The counts, on hearing of it, revenged themselves by accusing him of having been a chief pillar of the rebellion. He had to flee immediately, and, after wandering about for some time in a disguise, one of the features of which is stated to have been a false nose, he was seized on his way to the Reichstag which was being held at Speier in 1526. Tenacious of his property to the last, he had hoped to obtain restitution of his rights from the assembled estates of the empire. Some months later he died in prison at Neustadt.

Of the victors, Truchsess and Frundsberg considered themselves badly treated by the authorities whom they had served so well, and Frundsberg even composed a lament on his neglect. This he loved to hear sung to the accompaniment of the harp as he swilled down his red wine. The cruel Markgraf Kasimir met a miserable death not long after from dysentery, whilst Cardinal Matthaus Lang, the Archbishop of Salzburg, ended his days insane.

Of the fate of other prominent men connected with the events described, we have spoken in the course of the narrative.

The castles and religious houses, which were destroyed, as already said, to the number of many hundreds, were in most cases not built up again. The ruins of not a few of them are indeed visible to this day. Their owners often spent the sums relentlessly wrung out of the "common man" as indemnity, in the extravagances of a gay life in the free towns or in dancing attendance at the courts of the princes and the higher nobles. The collapse of the revolt was indeed an important link in the particular chain of events that was so rapidly destroying the independent existence of the lower nobility as a separate status with a definite political position, and transforming the face of society generally. Life in the smaller castle, the knight's *burg* or tower, was already tending to become an anachronism. The court of the prince, lay or ecclesiastic, was attracting to itself all the elements of nobility below it in the social hierarchy. The revolt of 1525 gave a further edge to this development, the first act of which closed with the collapse of the knights' rebellion and death of Sickingen in 1523.

The knight was becoming superfluous in the economy of the body politic. The rise of capitalism, the sudden development of the world-market, the substitution of a money medium of exchange for direct barter—all these new factors were doing their work. Obviously the great gainers by the events of the momentous year were the representatives of the centralising principle. But the effective centralising principle was not represented by the emperor, for he stood for what was after all largely a sham centralism, because it was a centralism on a scale for which the Germanic world was not ripe. Princes and margraves were destined to be the bearers of the *territorial* centralisation, the only real one to which the German peoples were to attain for a long time to come. Accordingly, just as the provincial *grand seigneur* of France became the courtier of the French king at Paris or Versailles, so the previously quasi-independent German knight or baron became the courtier or hanger-on of the prince within or near whose territory his hereditary manor was situate.

The eventful year 1525 was truly a landmark in German history in many ways—the year of one of the most accredited exploits of Doctor Faustus, the last mythical hero the progressive races have created; the year in which Martin Luther, the ex-monk, capped his repudiation of Catholicism and all its ways by marrying an ex-nun; the year of the definite victory of Charles V. the German Emperor over Francis I. the French King, which meant the final assertion of the "Holy Roman Empire" as a national German institution; and last, but not least, the year of the greatest and the most widespread popular movement central Europe had yet seen, and the last of the mediæval peasant risings on a large scale. The movement of the eventful year did not, however, as many hoped and many feared, within any short time rise up again from its ashes, after discomfiture had overtaken it. In 1526, as we have seen, the genius of Gaismayr succeeded in resuscitating it, not without prospect of ultimate success, in Tyrol and other of the Austrian territories. In this year, moreover, in other outlying districts, even outside German-speaking populations, the movement flickered. Thus the traveller between the town of Bellinzona in the Swiss Canton of Ticino and the Bernardino pass in Canton Graubunden may see to-day an imposing ruin, situated on an eminence in the narrow valley just above the small Italian-speaking town of Misox. This was one of the ancestral strongholds of the family, well-known in Italian history, of the Trefuzios or Trevulzir, and was sacked by the inhabitants of Misox and the neighbouring peasants in the summer of 1526, contemporaneously with Gaismayr's rising in Tyrol. A connection between the two events would be difficult to trace, and the destruction of the castle of Misox, if not a purely spontaneous local effervescence, looks like an afterglow of the great movement, such as may well have happened in other secluded mountain valleys.

With the death of Gaismayr, however, the insurrectionary party lost its last hope for the time being. Matters gradually settled down, and the agitation took a somewhat different form. The elements of revolution now became absorbed by the Anabaptist movement, a continuation primarily in the religious sphere of the doctrines of the Zwickau enthusiasts and also in many respects of Thomas Münzer. At first northern Switzerland, especially the towns of Basel and Zurich, became the headquarters of the new sect, which, however, spread rapidly on all sides. Persecution of the direst description did not destroy it. On the contrary, it seemed only to have the effect of evoking those social and revolutionary elements latent within it which were at first overshadowed by more purely theological interests. As it was, the hopes and aspirations of the "common man" revived this time in a form indissolubly associated with the theocratic commonwealth, the most prominent representative of which during the earlier movement had been Thomas Münzer. The Anabaptist sect subsequently concentrated its main strength at Strasburg. Driven thence, Holland and north-west Germany became its chief seat, until events culminated in the drama enacted at Munster in Westphalia in 1534, with the prophet John Bockelson as its leading figure. But neither this serious attempt to realise the popular conception of the Kingdom of God on earth nor the fortunes of the Anabaptist sect in general fall within the scope of the present volume.

THE END.

Printed in Great Britain
by Amazon

28053073R00214

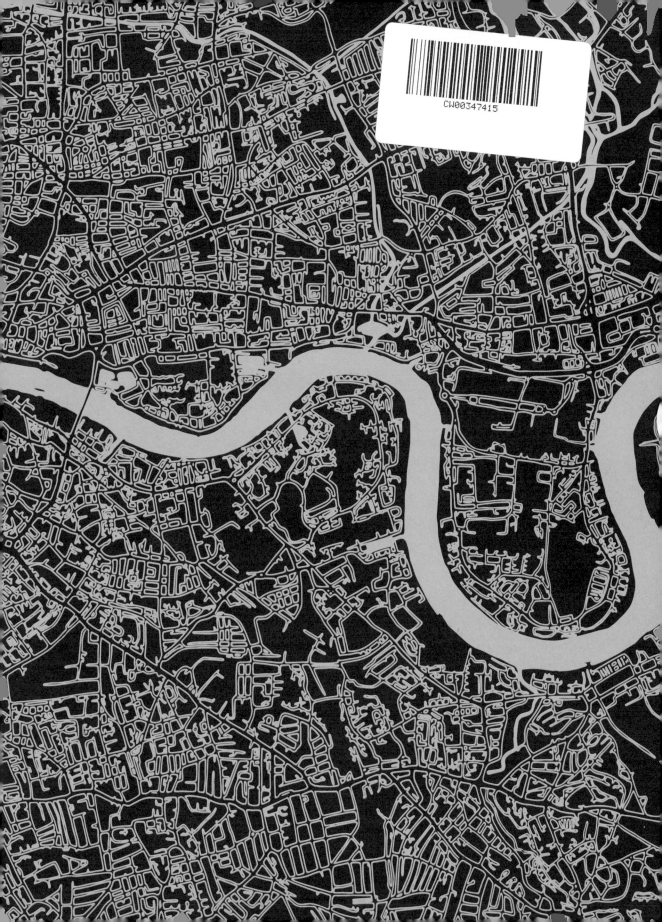

MADE IN LONDON

For Craig,
who washes everything up

MADE IN LONDON

THE COOKBOOK

Leah Hyslop

A.

FOOD AND DRINK RUNS THROUGH LONDON'S HISTORY LIKE THE THAMES.

INTRODUCTION 8

LON-DINNER 138

LATE-NIGHT LONDON 232

CAPITAL DRINKS 260

20 BREAKFAST & BRUNCH

58 STARTERS & SMALL PLATES

102 AFTERNOON TEA

196 PUDDING

296 BIBLIOGRAPHY & INDEX

INTRODUCTION

'THE MAN WHO CAN DOMINATE
A LONDON DINNER TABLE CAN
DOMINATE THE WORLD.'

OSCAR WILDE

London is a greedy city.

Take a walk through the bustling West End, in the heart of the capital, and a world of food swallows you up. The waft of vinegar and batter from fish and chip shops; the sizzle of burgers at a street food van; the cries of the hustling curry house owner, urging you to 'Come in, come in, best balti in town'. With more than 7,000 restaurants in the capital, Londoners could conceivably eat at a different place for every single meal for seven years, without ever having to make a repeat visit. Food is even written into the geography: a quick glance at a London A–Z reveals a feast of streets, from Bread Street and Saffron Hill to Fish Street and Honey Lane, all named for the foods once hawked on their cobbles.

I was born in London. One of my earliest memories is of sitting on the muddy foreshore of the Thames at Greenwich, covering my face with a Mr Whippy ice cream as boats sailed by. My family eventually moved to Kent, and when I returned to London as a young graduate, with few friends and even fewer pennies in my pocket, the city seemed vast and unnavigable. Food was how I found my feet. Hopping on the tube on a Saturday morning to visit Borough Market; pressing my nose up against the windows of iconic restaurants like The Ivy; detouring to famous bakeries on the way home from work to buy a loaf was how I learnt the map of the city, and how I came to feel at home here. I made new friends in old pubs, and filled my tiny kitchen with jams and cheeses from the brilliant London producers I discovered on every corner. My love affair with London's food coincided with a decade in which its reputation as a gourmand's paradise exploded. New Yorkers might disagree, but I truly believe that, right now, London is the world's leading culinary destination.

Unlike many capital cities, it's hard to identify a single food, or cuisine, that defines London. The map of Rome is one of pizza and pasta joints; in Paris, cassoulet or steak frites are as much a part of the city's foundations as the creepy catacombs. There are London institutions, to be sure: the old-fashioned pie and mash shops, or the swanky hotels offering afternoon tea. But London's huge, diverse immigrant population means the city has always cherry-picked its food from the best of world cuisine. Walk into a London restaurant and you might end up ordering beef reared on heathered English hills, but roasted with Middle Eastern spices, or a fillet of Scottish salmon, cooked just the way the Spanish chef's mother taught him. Like London's hodge-podge architecture, where timbered Tudor houses and Norman churches rub shoulders with shining skyscrapers, new traditions are layered on top of old. You never know quite what you'll get, which is what makes eating in the capital such a unique adventure.

What does unite London's sprawling food scene is creativity. The list of famous dishes invented in the city is endless, from Maids of Honour, dainty little cakes that were a favourite of King Henry VIII all the way back in the sixteenth century, to Omelette Arnold Bennett, dreamt up at the Savoy hotel in 1929. Modern classics, too, constantly make their debut. At Craft in Greenwich, chef Stevie Parle has a cult following for his roasted duck, cooked in a shell of pale clay and served on a bed of pine. And Middle Eastern restaurant Berber & Q's whole roasted cauliflower, slathered with spiced butter and sprinkled with rose petals, has been so influential you'll spot versions of it flowering all around the city.

IT'S HARD TO IDENTIFY A SINGLE FOOD, OR CUISINE, THAT DEFINES LONDON… WHAT DOES UNITE THE CITY'S SPRAWLING FOOD SCENE IS CREATIVITY.

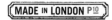

The Golden Boy of Pye Corner
(View Pictures/Getty Images)

Of course, the culinary map of London has not always been so enticing. For many years, its traditional, stodgy British dishes, with peculiar names such as 'spotted dick' and 'toad in the hole', horrified foreign visitors. 'The badness of London restaurants,' observed the American author Henry James in 1877, 'is literally fabulous.' But in the 1980s, a wave of innovative chefs and restaurants – Rose Gray and Ruth Roger's The River Café and Rowley Leigh's Kensington Place among them – surged over London, transforming it into a culinary mecca. The city's cuisine has gone from strength to strength ever since.

The story of London and food begins thousands of years ago. Around 50AD Romans built a city they called Londinium on the banks of the River Thames. Being fond of the finer things in life, the Italian newcomers used the river to ship in their favourite foods from all corners of the Roman empire. Excavations of Roman London have revealed the remnants of such exotic produce as cherries and plums, peas and walnuts, none of which had been tasted in Britain before. The Romans even introduced their beloved, explosively pungent fish sauce: an amphora dug up in Southwark in South London carries the advert: 'Luccius Tettius Aficanus supplies the finest fish sauce from Antipolis'. One can't help but wonder what the native Britons (used to a blander diet of salted meat and bread) thought of this new condiment.

Later waves of immigrants added yet more foods to the London larder, heightening the city's hunger for the new and exotic. In the seventeenth century, Jewish refugees from Portugal and Spain brought over the tradition of frying fish in flour. Before long, the crispy fish had been paired with another immigrant dish, the fried potatoes beloved of French and Belgian Huguenots, to create the now-classic British treat fish and chips. (There is fierce debate over which fish and chip shop was Britain's first, but the humble shop opened by a Jewish immigrant called Joseph Malin in the East End in 1860 has as good a claim as any.)

In the twentieth century, the colourful Caribbean markets and shops of Brixton in South London were founded by West Indian immigrants. The first arrivals came on a ship called the *Empire Windrush* in 1948, bringing with them the sunshine flavours of jerk chicken, fish fritters and plantain. A few decades later, in the 1970s and 80s, the Vietnamese 'boat people' – many of whom were fleeing persecution after the Vietnam War – introduced the city to the delights of lemongrass and ginger, often combined to miraculous effect in hot steaming bowls of noodle soup, or pho.

As the home of Britain's most powerful citizens, the Royal family, London was often the first place new foods were brought to – sometimes at the express demand of the monarch. In the sixteenth century, King Henry VIII's salad-loving Spanish queen, Catherine of Aragon, introduced the royal court to lettuce, which she had especially imported from Holland. A century later, Charles II's wife, Catherine of Braganza, popularised the drinking of tea,

The hustle and bustle of Covent Garden Market, 1864. (Photo by Museum of London/Heritage Images/Getty Images)

turning the exotic Chinese drink into the aristocracy's new favourite pastime. Every corner of the then-formidable British Empire was raided for the dinner table; pineapples from the Caribbean, spices from India and corn from the Americas were all shipped down the Thames for the upper classes to marvel at.

What began as upper-class crazes quickly filtered down. In the 1600s, Londoners developed an insatiable taste for turtle soup, made from imported West Indian green turtles, and often served in the turtles' own shell. By 1776, there was such high demand for the delicacy that the London Tavern built huge tanks to store its live turtles; not a far cry, I like to think, from the upmarket restaurants which today keep live lobsters for their customers. Eating well, and copiously, was considered the true mark of a Londoner – though some people feared the city's love of good food verged on the immoral. On Pye Corner, not far from St Paul's Cathedral, there is a curious statue of a plump, golden-skinned boy mounted on a wall. He marks the place where the Great Fire of London of 1666 was finally put out, and a stern inscription below reads: 'This boy is in memory put up for the late Fire of London, occasioned by the sin of gluttony'. Many people associate London with the statue of Nelson, standing haughtily on his plinth in Trafalgar Square, or Queen Victoria, keeping watch over Buckingham Palace from her seat on the fountain outside. For me, that round-bellied little boy, wearing the beatific smirk of the well fed, is the most quintessentially London monument of them all.

Restaurants are a crucial thread in the fabric of London life. For centuries, the city's poorest citizens had little access to working kitchens, so 'cookshops' or 'ordinaries' where, for a few pennies, they could bring a lump of meat to be cooked in the oven, thrived. In the eighteenth century, diners filled their bellies at 'chophouses' or 'beefhouses', such as Dolly's Chophouse in Paternoster Row, which was famous for its hot steaks, and attracted such well-known figures as *Robinson Crusoe* author Daniel Defoe, and Jonathan Swift, who wrote *Gulliver's Travels*. Chophouses were far from luxurious: Nathaniel Hawthorne, in his English Notebooks (1853–58) talks disparagingly of one, the Albert Dining Rooms, which offered only a 'filthy tablecloth, covered with other's people's crumbs; iron forks, leaden salt cellar, the commonest earthen plates; a little dark stall, to sit and eat in'. But just like London's pie and mash shops, they offered a convivial place for tired labourers to refuel and chat, with a pint of ale, for little more than sixpence.

There was also, of course, more high-end dining. In the nineteenth century, many of London's most iconic restaurants opened their doors. Among them were the Café Royal, favoured by King Edward VIII and Oscar Wilde, and the opulent The Criterion in Piccadilly, famously featured in Arthur Conan Doyle's Sherlock Holmes stories, as the place where Dr Watson first hears the name of the mysterious detective who will become his room-mate.

Today, London's restaurant scene is more vibrant than ever. Many of the country's top chefs operate here, from Gordon Ramsay to Heston Blumenthal, and new eateries bubble up every day; in 2015, an unprecedented 179 new venues opened. With seventy-two Michelin stars (and counting), fine dining is still a draw for tourists and locals alike. But one of the great delights of the past decade has been the flurry of top-quality, more casual eateries. At Polpo in Soho, guests sip wine from tumblers and tuck into the gorgeous Venetian-style tapas called cichetti without a white tablecloth or snooty sommelier in

THE STORY OF LONDON AND FOOD BEGINS THOUSANDS OF YEARS AGO.

sight. At pasta restaurant Padella, near London Bridge, office workers spend their lunch breaks queuing for a bowl of pappardelle with rich slow-cooked beef shin or tender ravioli of pumpkin and marjoram, for as little as £5 a plate. And perhaps most excitingly of all, there is street food.

Street food has been part of London life for centuries. In the Victorian period, the city's cobbled alleys and bustling thoroughfares heaved with hawkers selling every delicacy imaginable – fried fish and pea soup, baked potatoes and Chelsea buns, imported oranges and pickled whelks. Eels were a favourite, fished fresh from the Thames, often skinned alive in front of buyers, and served hot and steaming. In his book *London Labour and the London Poor*, the journalist Henry Mayhew painted a vivid picture of a crowded Saturday night market, 'where the working-classes generally purchase their Sunday's dinner'.

A fishmonger with pots of jellied eels, cockles and whelks in the 1950s.(Hulton-Deutsch Collection/Getty Images)

After pay-time on Saturday night, or early on Sunday morning, the crowd in the New-cut, and the Brill in particular, is almost impassable. Indeed, the scene in these parts has more of the character of a fair than a market… The pavement and the road are crowded with purchasers and street-sellers. The housewife in her thick shawl, with the market-basket on her arm, walks slowly on, stopping now to look at the stall of caps, and now to cheapen a bunch of greens. Little boys, holding three or four onions in their hand, creep between the people, wriggling their way through every interstice, and asking for custom in whining tones, as if seeking charity. Then the tumult of the thousand different cries of the eager dealers, all shouting at the top of their voices, at one and the same time, is almost bewildering. 'So-old again,' roars one. 'Chestnuts all 'to, a penny a score,' bawls another. 'An 'aypenny a skin, blacking,' squeaks a boy. 'Buy, buy, buy, buy, buy – bu-u-uy!' cries the butcher. 'Half-quire of paper for a penny,' bellows the street stationer. 'An 'aypenny a lot ing-uns.' 'Twopence a pound grapes.' 'Three a penny Yarmouth bloaters.' 'Who'll buy a bonnet for fourpence?' 'Pick 'em out cheap here! Three pair for a halfpenny, bootlaces.' 'Now's your time! beautiful whelks, a penny a lot.' 'Here's ha'p'orths,' shouts the perambulating confectioner. 'Come and look at 'em! Here's toasters!' bellows one with a Yarmouth bloater stuck on a toasting-fork. 'Penny a lot, fine russets,' calls the apple woman: and so the Babel goes on.

As time went by, London's vibrant street food scene dwindled. Ten years ago, the phrase evoked limp hot dogs or dry burgers from vans, probably eaten while drunk, and with a nasty bout of food poisoning afterwards. But today there is a new generation of passionate traders, serving mouthwatering

THE GRAPES . LIMEHOUSE

*The Grapes public house in Limehouse, a favourite of Dickens, as pictured
in the* Illustrated London News, *1887. (The Print Collector/Getty Images)*

food from all over the world. Peckish Londoners can choose between bao (soft Taiwanese steamed buns, often filled with gooey chunks of pork belly), Argentinian-style steaks smeared with vibrant jalapeño salsa, or Hawaiian poke: zingy, spicy bowls of marinated fresh fish, served with fluffy rice and a crunchy scattering of sesame seeds. Many of these stalls operate in dedicated street food markets, such as Dinerama in Dalston or Model Market in Lewisham, and give young, talented chefs – who don't have the money to set up their own restaurants, or perhaps want more freedom to experiment – a platform from which to share their food with their world. Many of London's best and most cutting-edge dishes are now to be found in a polystyrene box, eaten with a plastic fork, in front of a truck.

It would feel wrong to write a book about London's food without mentioning drink. The city has always had a thirst for alcohol. 'To see the number of taverns, alehouses etc, one would imagine Bacchus the only god that is worshipped here,' sniffed Thomas Brown in 1730. For centuries, beer and ale were the most popular drinks, especially with the lower classes; the deliciously dark style of beer known as porter was actually invented in London in the eighteenth century, and is so named because of its popularity with the 'porters' – the men who transferred goods up and down the city in the days before Amazon delivery trucks.

The preferred place to drink beer is, of course, the pub. London's watering holes are an institution, with the oldest buildings dating back to at least Tudor times. Sadly, just as in the rest of Britain, many pubs are dying, the sorrowful consequence of a maelstrom of factors including rising rents for landlords and the smoking ban. Thankfully, many beautiful old pubs, such as The Grapes in Limehouse (which features in Charles Dickens' *Our Mutual Friend*) and The Olde Cheshire Cheese in Fleet Street, a favourite haunt of journalists, are still open for business. And while the pubs might be struggling, bars – in particular, cocktail bars – are on the rise. Artesian, at the Langham Hotel, has been repeatedly named the world's best cocktail bar. All across the city, innovative mixologists are crafting astonishing drinks featuring homemade syrups, exotic spirits and clouds of scented smoke which billow from the glass.

Of course, not all of London's drinking history has been so jolly. One particular tipple, gin, became a demon which stalked the city for half a century. By the 1740s, the average Londoner was necking 10 litres of the spirit a year; it was, in the grave words of Sir John Fielding, a 'liquid fire by which men drink their hell'. The orgy of lethal drinking only ended when the price of grain, from which gin is distilled, rose. Gin is now undergoing a renaissance; several new distilleries, such as Sipsmith, have popped up in the city in recent years, and sales are soaring. Thankfully, the modern Londoner is more likely to sip a refreshing G&T in a fashionable gin bar than neck a bottle and have a lie-down in the gutter... unless we've had a really bad day at work.

Food and drink runs through London's history like the Thames. If New York is the city that never sleeps, London is the city that lives to eat. From gourmet cheese shops to old-fashioned butchers, street food vans to sleek Italian restaurants – whatever your heart (or stomach) desires in London, it is there. And while the tourists might come for Buckingham Palace, the Tower of London and the shiny red buses, you can bet your last Liquorice Allsort that some of their best memories will be of the food. To get up at 4am to visit the fish market at Billingsgate, where chefs bid for huge crates of glitteringly fresh fish, and hungry seals wait for scraps in the neighbouring dock, is an unforgettable experience. And what could be a better way of spending a Saturday night than touring the atmospheric cocktail bars of East London (followed, if you really want to be authentic, by a late-night kebab).

This book is a celebration of all the culinary joys that Britain's capital has to offer. Whether you're a long-time resident, a visitor, or someone far, far away who dreams of one day sipping a cup of tea in the shadow of Big Ben, I hope you enjoy it.

Shoppers browse stalls at Brixton, the heart of the West Indian community, in 1952. (Charles Hewitt/Getty Images)

A NOTE ON INGREDIENTS

SALT

The most important ingredient in your cupboard. Salt obviously adds, well, saltiness, but it also intensifies and unifies flavours. Most recipes in this book tell you to season according to taste, but in cases where I think it is crucial, I have specified a measurement, e.g. half a teaspoon. Always add a pinch to your baking – you won't taste it, but the flavour of the cakes and biscuits will be magically heightened.

DAIRY

Use whole milk when cooking, if you can; the taste and texture is much better. You'll notice crème fraîche popping up a lot in the book; it has all the richness of cream, but brings a lovely tanginess, too. I use crème fraîche frequently in savoury dishes, but also on the side of very sweet desserts. I find it a more balanced accompaniment than ice cream or cream.

BAKING

Eggs are always large, unless otherwise specified, and preferably free-range and organic. If you use smaller eggs, be aware it might affect the success of the recipe. Traditionally salted butter is used for savoury cooking and unsalted for baking, but I often lob salted butter into a cake if it's all I've got in the fridge … and nobody's turned down a slice yet. When baking, try and make sure the ingredients are room temperature before you start; the end result will be lighter and fluffier.

ENGLISH MUSTARD POWDER

A cook's secret weapon. Add a teaspoon or so of this primrose-coloured powder to creamy sauces, pastry, dumplings – anywhere you want a gentle kick of heat.

GOLDEN SYRUP AND TREACLE

No London kitchen is complete without tins of Tate & Lyle's golden syrup and treacle, usually welded to the bottom of the cupboard by the sticky rivulets running down the side. Invented during the Victorian era, these are both by-products of the sugar refining process and add a rich sweetness to classic British bakes such as flapjack and gingerbread. If you're not in the UK, maple syrup or corn syrup makes a reasonable substitute for golden syrup, while treacle can be swapped for light molasses, though the results won't be exactly the same.

EXOTIC INGREDIENTS

The London larder has expanded considerably in recent years, as immigration and globalisation introduce us to exciting new flavours. In these pages you will spot such new arrivals as gochujang (spicy Korean chilli paste) black rice (an East Asian staple) and sumac (a fragrant berry, widely used as a spice in Middle Eastern cuisine). All the more exotic ingredients I have used should be available in large supermarkets, and if you can't find them there, they can easily be bought online. Souschef.co.uk is my favourite website for ordering unusual foods.

BREAKFAST & BRUNCH

YOU CAN TELL A LOT ABOUT A CITY BY THE FOOD IT STARTS THE DAY WITH. PARISIANS NIBBLE ELEGANT CROISSANTS, AND NEW YORKERS WOLF DOWN BAGELS AS THEY RUN FOR THE SUBWAY.

THE CAPITAL OF A PROUD BREAKFASTING NATION, LONDON'S TRADITIONAL HEARTY STANDBYS INCLUDE THE FULL ENGLISH AND STEAMING BOWLS OF PORRIDGE. WHILE PLUMP SAUSAGES AND BAKED BEANS CAN STILL BE ENJOYED IN A LONDON CAFF OR 'GREASY SPOON', THAT CAFÉ IS NOW LIKELY TO BE FOUND ALONGSIDE A MIDDLE EASTERN BAKERY SELLING HONEY-DRENCHED PASTRIES, OR AN INDIAN RESTAURANT OFFERING ITS SPICY TAKE ON THE CLASSIC BACON SARNIE, A UNIQUE DISH YOU WON'T FIND ANYWHERE ELSE IN THE WORLD.

BUT WHEREVER LONDONERS BREAKFAST, YOU CAN BE SURE A MUG OF MILKY TEA OR STEAMING COFFEE IS NEVER FAR AWAY.

BURNT HONEY GRAPEFRUIT WITH CARDAMOM-GINGER YOGHURT

I feel the same way about The Wolseley, the grand café next to the Ritz hotel, as Holly Golightly did about Tiffany's: 'Nothing very bad could happen to you there.' There is something about its soaring arches and elegant black-and-gold colour scheme that immediately makes me take a deep breath and relax. My breakfast of choice is the grapefruit, where the segments are caramelised to glossy perfection, then piled triumphantly back into the shell. At home, I make a slightly more rustic breakfast of grapefruit coated in honey, served on a fragrant pillow of yoghurt. Burnt honey is a recent discovery of mine; you simply cook honey in a pan until it transforms into a dark, rich, caramel-like sauce.

SERVES 4

2 pink grapefruit
70ml runny honey
500ml thick, natural
    Greek-style yoghurt
seeds from 3 green cardamom
    pods, crushed
5 pieces of stem ginger from a jar
    (about 100g), finely chopped
80g pistachios, chopped (optional)

Using a sharp knife, cut down the side of each grapefruit to remove the skin and pith. Cut each one horizontally into about six round slices, around 0.5cm each in thickness.

Put the honey in a medium-sized saucepan over a medium heat. Within a minute or so it will start to bubble vigorously. Cook without stirring, occasionally swirling the pan, until the honey has gone a deep amber brown and smells rich and nutty. This shouldn't take more than 5 minutes or so, but watch the pan carefully – the honey can burn very quickly.

Take the pan off the heat and tumble in the grapefruit, along with any juices. Using tongs, swirl the slices so they are nicely coated in the honey, then tip the whole lot into a bowl. Leave to cool for about 10 minutes.

Mix the yoghurt with the crushed cardamom and ginger in a bowl. Divide between four plates, bowls or glasses, then arrange the grapefruit slices on top, along with a drizzle of any leftover honey. Sprinkle over the pistachios, if using.

FIG AND FETA PIDE

Honey and Co. is a restaurant so tiny that eating there feels as though you've accidentally wandered into somebody's home and plonked yourself at the dinner table. But husband-and-wife team Itamar Srulovich and Sarit Packer serve their vibrant Middle-Eastern-inspired food with such boundless charm and energy, it's hard not to love every cramped minute.

This is their recipe for pide, the boat-shaped flatbreads popular in Turkey. They are very easy to make, and if figs and feta don't float your pide, they can be customised with any flavours you like. I serve these for a late breakfast at the weekend, drizzled with honey and escorted by a strong coffee.

SERVES 6

For the dough
300g plain flour
7g sachet fast-action dried yeast
1 teaspoon caster sugar
1 teaspoon salt
½ teaspoon ground black pepper
1 tablespoon nigella seeds
pinch of cayenne pepper
1 teaspoon honey
150ml natural yoghurt
oil, for greasing

For the filling
5 tablespoons natural yoghurt
100g feta cheese, crumbled
½ teaspoon dried oregano
½ teaspoon sumac, or grated zest
  of 1 lemon

For the topping
100g baby spinach
6 figs, each cut into 4–5 slices
1 green chilli, thinly sliced
olive oil, for drizzling
pinch of dried oregano
salt and freshly ground black pepper

To make the dough, place the flour, yeast, sugar, salt, pepper, nigella seeds and cayenne pepper in a large mixing bowl. Dissolve the honey in 100ml of warm water, and add to the bowl along with the yoghurt. Use a wooden spoon to mix together into a dough, then knead for about 3 minutes by hand. The dough will be quite soft.

Put the dough in a lightly oiled bowl, covered with oiled cling film or a damp tea towel, making sure the cover doesn't touch the dough. Leave in a warm place for 1–1½ hours, until it has doubled in size.

Make the filling by mixing the yoghurt, crumbled feta, oregano, sumac or lemon zest in a bowl to create a paste.

Flour your hands, then divide the dough into six pieces and roughly stretch each one into a boat-like oval, around 18cm long and 10cm wide. Place onto a baking tray lined with baking parchment. Spread 1 tablespoon of the feta mix on to the centre of each one, leaving a 1cm border around the edge. Top with a handful of baby spinach, a few slices of fig and chilli, and a drizzle of oil. Season with salt and pepper, and sprinkle over the oregano.

Use your thumb and forefinger to pinch the sides of the dough so it stands up slightly, just as if you were crimping pastry, then pinch the two ends to create even more of a boat shape. Don't worry if they're messy. Cover with clingfilm or a tea towel, and leave for about 30 minutes.

Preheat the oven to 220°C/200°C Fan/Gas Mark 7. Bake for 12–15 minutes, until golden. Serve warm.

BLACK RICE AND COCONUT PORRIDGE

Few London chefs have been as influential as Yotam Ottolenghi. When the Israeli-born chef opened his first deli in Notting Hill in 1992, his bold palette of global flavours ran like an electric shock through the city and rewired our tastebuds forever. Now harissa paste and preserved lemons rub shoulders with the Marmite and Bisto gravy in our cupboards.

My favourite Ottolenghi-led discovery is black rice. I first tried this dish at his Soho restaurant Nopi, and it has been a staple breakfast in my house ever since. Inspired by a popular south-east Asian recipe, it's essentially a rice pudding, but don't expect it to taste like the pappy English version – the rice has a delicious nutty chewiness, while the coconut is delicate and sweet. You can eat this hot, but I also love it served cold, topped with a spoonful of yoghurt and whatever fruit needs using up in the fridge.

SERVES 4

300g black glutinous rice
250ml coconut cream
400ml coconut milk
70g caster sugar
pinch of salt
1 vanilla pod, or 1 teaspoon vanilla
   bean paste or extract

To serve (optional)
grated zest of 1 lime
palm sugar or soft light brown sugar
tropical fruits of your choice, chopped
   (I like pineapple, mango and kiwi)

If you have time, soak the rice in a bowl of cold water for a few hours (this will soften it slightly) and drain. If not, just rinse it a few times.

Put the rice in a pan with the coconut cream and milk, the sugar, a generous pinch of salt and 200ml of water. Halve the vanilla pod lengthways and scrape the seeds into the pan, or add the vanilla paste or extract. Bring to the boil, then reduce the heat and simmer vigorously for about an hour, stirring frequently, until soft, creamy and oozy (loosen the mixture with a little extra milk or water, if needed).

Divide the porridge between bowls and top with a sprinkling of lime zest, a smattering of sugar and some fruit, if using.

'NEWFANGLED, ABOMINABLE, HEATHENISH': HOW THE CAPITAL FELL IN LOVE WITH COFFEE

In 1674, a pamphlet appeared on the streets of London. Supposedly written on behalf of the city's women, it railed against a 'newfangled, abominable, heathenish' drink that had taken the city by storm. This 'puddlewater', the pamphlet's outraged authors declared, had transformed their hard-working husbands into lazy, gossiping, effeminate 'cocksparrows', who rolled into bed so stupefied at the end of the day that they weren't even capable of satisfying their wives. So what was this toxic brew? Not gin or beer, but something rather more exotic – coffee.

The first coffee house in London was opened by a Greek entrepreneur called Pasqua Roseé in 1652, after he developed a taste for the bitter drink in Turkey. By the turn of the eighteenth century, they were all over the city; as many as 2,000, according to contemporaries. The attraction of the coffee house was little to do with coffee itself. Thick and gritty and black as soot, it was a far cry from the silky cappuccinos and sweet vanilla lattes of today. Instead, these rough-and-ready cafés became the go-to place for discussion and debate. People from every walk of life went to read newspapers, fight over politics or transact killer deals, all fuelled by jitter-inducing levels of caffeine.

The popularity of the coffee houses was much noticed by foreign visitors. 'All English men are great newsmongers,' wrote the Swiss noble César de Saussure in 1726. 'Workmen habitually begin the day by going to coffee-rooms to read the latest news.' The coffee houses' role as a forum for political debate also unsettled those in power: in 1675, King Charles II issued a proclamation against them, though it was never upheld.

Each coffee house attracted a different flavour of clientele. Lawyers and scientists frequented The Grecian in Wapping; artists drank at Old Slaughter's; army men favoured The Little Devil. Some houses were rowdier than others. The Hoxton Square Coffeehouse had an unsavoury habit of putting people on mock trial. A suspected lunatic would be wheeled in for a 'jury' of coffee fiends to interrogate; if the poor soul was found guilty of madness, he would be carted off to the nearest asylum. There is even a story that Sir Isaac Newton and his chums from The Royal Society dissected a live dolphin on the table of The Grecian – though I imagine it's more likely they went to the coffee house to discuss the experiment, rather than getting out their knives midway through an Americano.

Despite such eccentricities, coffee houses really were a crucible of knowledge and enterprise. Lloyd's Coffee House was popular with sailors and shipowners, and became the go-to spot for marine insurers to meet. It eventually grew into the global insurance business Lloyd's of London. And when a broker called John Castaing started posting lists of stocks and commodity prices at Jonathan's Coffee House in Change Alley, he laid the foundations for the Stock Exchange. The historian Dr Matthew Green has a persuasive theory that such an outburst of economic initiative might have had

PEOPLE FROM EVERY WALK OF LIFE WENT TO COFFEE HOUSES TO READ NEWSPAPERS, FIGHT OVER POLITICS OR TRANSACT KILLER DEALS.

Algerian coffee stores, Soho. (Keith van-Loen/Alamy)

something to do with the fact Londoners were drinking coffee instead of booze: 'Until the mid-seventeenth century, most people in England were either slightly – or very – drunk all of the time. Drink London's fetid river water at your own peril; most people wisely favoured watered-down ale or beer. The arrival of coffee, then, triggered a dawn of sobriety that laid the foundations for truly spectacular economic growth … as people thought clearly for the first time.'

The coffee houses' reign didn't last for long. Well-heeled members' clubs lured some patrons away, while many gentlemen transferred their allegiance to a different fashionable drink, tea. It wasn't until the 1950s and 60s, when Italian culture became cool, that coffee shops returned in serious numbers to London. Sipping an espresso at Soho bars like Moka – the first place in Britain to have a Gaggia coffee machine – was

seen as the ultimate in sophistication by worldly young Londoners. 'Once our beer was frothy / But now it's frothy coffee,' sang Max Bygraves in his 1960 hit 'Fings ain't wot they used t'be'. These mini-skirted and hair-gelled rebels clutching their dinky Italian coffee cups might have been less enamoured if they'd realised they were actually taking part in a British tradition that stretched back centuries.

London's workers still run on coffee. Many get their fix from bland American chains like Starbucks; recently, however, there has been a pleasing explosion of independent shops, run by coffee buffs whose brews are made with passion and care. Although it's rather sad that the wild spirit of the original coffee houses has evaporated, at least you can enjoy your espresso without watching a live dissection.

Customers at Lloyd's coffee house, which gave birth to insurance company Lloyd's of London. (Bettmann/Getty Images)

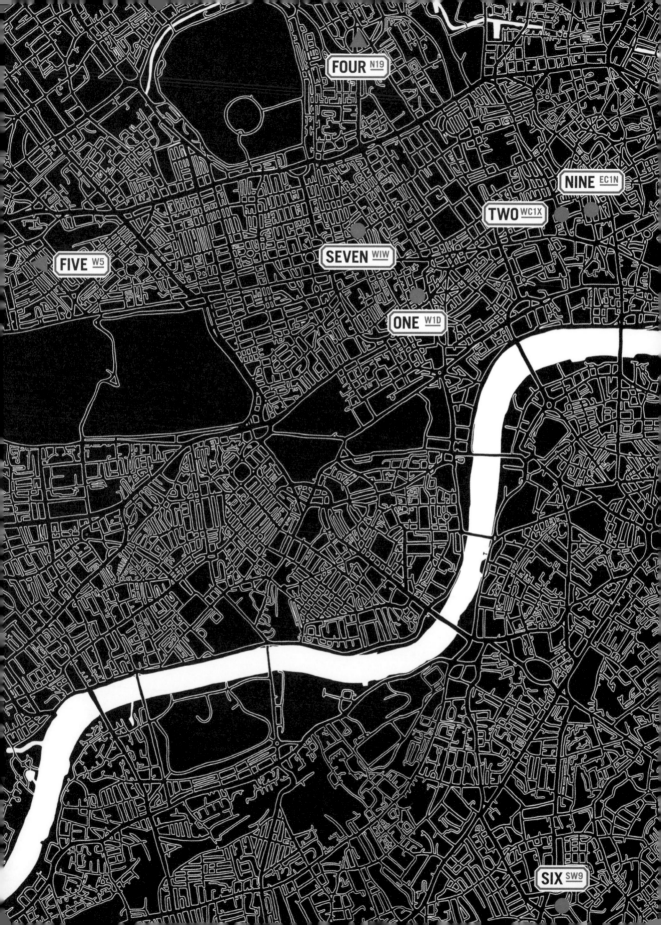

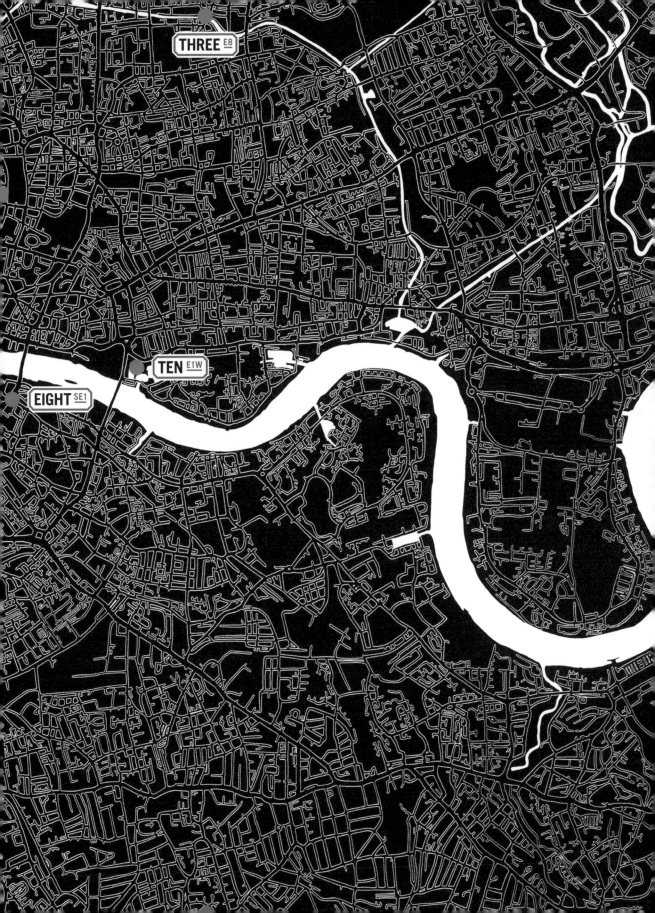

THREE E8

TEN E1W

EIGHT SE1

LONDON'S BEST COFFEE SHOPS

1. Algerian Coffee Stores

52 Old Compton St,
Soho, W1D 4PB
algcoffee.co.uk

A façade as scarlet as a telephone box welcomes visitors to this quaint timewarp of a shop, which has been plying Londoners with caffeine since 1887. The original wooden shelves are crammed with a huge range of coffee beans from all around the world, which staff will weigh out for you on antique brass scales (my favourite is the heavenly Five Spice, rich with cinnamon and cassia). There's nowhere to sit, but the takeaway coffee is the best value in central London – just £1 for an espresso, or £1.20 for a latte or cappuccino.

2. Catalyst

48 Grays Inn Rd,
WC1X 8LT
catalyst.cafe

A relative newbie on the coffee scene, only opening its doors in 2016, but home to some of London's most knowledgeable and friendly baristas. With its elegant white and gold decor, it's a very peaceful place to sip a coffee in the morning; you can even watch the beans being roasted downstairs, through a glass panel in the floor. As night falls, the café rolls out a cocktail menu, including a wickedly powerful espresso martini.

3. Climpson & Sons

67 Broadway Market,
E8 4PH
climpsonandsons.com

Yes, there's nearly always a queue. And yes, the staff are hipsters with silly moustaches who drawl things like 'You know you've got great vibes?' as you wait for your cappuccino. But those hipsters know their stuff. The beans are roasted just down the road, and the coffee is smooth and rich. Visit during the week, when the shop is less crowded and you can nab one of the comfy wooden seats outside.

4. Cricks Corner

80 Dartmouth Park Hill,
Highgate, N19 5HU
crickscorner.co.uk

Perched unassumingly in a quiet residential area of North London is this tiny neighbourhood café. Its curious name comes from a subscription library, which stood on the same site until the 1950s. Friendly owners Simon and Kelly serve top-notch coffee and quite possibly the best bacon bap in London.

5. Electric Coffee Company

40 Haven Green,
Ealing, W5 2NX
electriccoffee.co.uk

With its dangling lightbulbs and exposed brickwork, Electric feels as industrial as its name. But don't be fooled; this is an independent café fuelled by passion for good coffee. Husband and wife owners Simon and Oksana source their own beans and roast them in the Sussex countryside, then transform them into the best coffee in West London. I love the range of refreshing summer drinks, from a killer iced latte to espresso on the rocks.

The British might be a famous nation of tea-drinkers, but Londoners have long been seduced by tea's dark and powerful cousin, coffee. There's no excuse for visiting a chain coffee store – this city is awash with brilliant independent coffee shops, where the humble cup of Joe is elevated into an art form.

6. Federation Coffee

77–78 Brixton Village and Market Row, Coldharbour Ln, Brixton, SW9 8PS
federation.coffee

'Good tippers make better lovers' jokes the sign by the till at Federation, which sums up the friendly character of this pint-sized (or should that be espresso-sized?) café. Occupying a corner spot inside Brixton's covered market, its coveted outside tables are ideal for people-watching. Go for breakfast, and order a flat white with their heavenly homemade ricotta on toast.

7. Kaffeine

66 Great Titchfield St, W1W 7QJ
kaffeine.co.uk

Just a five-minute stroll from the hurly-burly of Oxford Street is this dreamy temple to coffee, inspired by the chilled-out vibes of Australian and New Zealand coffee shops. The coffee comes from East London roastery Square Mile, and the food is excellent; think onion and Cheddar rolls, fluffy Nutella cakes, and roasted cauliflower and pesto salad.

8. Monmouth Coffee Company

2 Park Street, The Borough, SE1 9AB
monmouthcoffee.co.uk

One of Britain's first independent coffee companies, Monmouth paved the way for the current boom of high-quality coffee houses when it opened in the 1970s. The flagship store on the edge of Borough Market is invariably rammed, but a cup of their rich, dark coffee will always perk up your daily grind.

9. Prufrock Coffee

23–25 Leather Ln, EC1N 7TE
prufrockcoffee.com

Leather Lane in Clerkenwell is crammed with high-quality cafés, but Prufrock is the coffee nerds' favourite. An airy space spread over two floors, its baristas love experimenting with new beans and brewing methods, though they are particularly proud of their filter coffee. The café also sells a vast range of coffee paraphernalia, from books to beautiful glass coffeemakers, and holds regular classes on subjects from latte art to 'advanced roasting techniques'.

10. White Mulberries

D3 Ivory House, St Katharine Docks, E1W 1AT
whitemulberries.com

Perch at the window bar of this small, brick-lined café in a historic warehouse on St Katharine Docks and enjoy the tranquil sight of boats bobbing up and down on the water. Coffee is served in pretty turquoise or espresso-black cups and comes from a variety of roasters, including London's Allpress and Nude Espresso.

COFFEE AND BANANA SMOOTHIE

London has been hooked on coffee since the 1650s, when a Greek immigrant named Pasqua Roseé opened the city's first coffee house. This smoothie is a good way to get both a caffeine hit and a few vitamins in the morning.

SERVES 1

2 teaspoons instant espresso powder
1 banana
200ml hazelnut or other nut milk
6 dates, stones removed
1 tablespoon hazelnuts (optional)
ice cubes

Put all the ingredients in a blender with a handful of ice, and blitz until smooth.

COCONUT BREAD WITH LEMON CURD CREAM CHEESE AND POACHED RHUBARB

London is a city of culinary magpies: we constantly steal tasty morsels from other cultures, remixing them with our own traditions. I had never heard of coconut bread before I stumbled across Caravan, a small group of restaurants with a relaxed Antipodean vibe. Chef Miles Kirby says this dish is a nod to the type of bread he enjoyed, growing up in New Zealand, but it's his addition of tangy British rhubarb, cream cheese and lemon curd that elevates it to greatness. If you prefer, you can swap the rhubarb for fresh strawberries.

SERVES 6

For the coconut bread

3 eggs
1½ teaspoons vanilla extract
60ml milk
240ml coconut milk
360g plain flour
1½ teaspoons baking powder
1½ teaspoons salt
180g caster sugar
135g desiccated coconut
butter, for frying

For the lemon curd cream cheese

60g butter
130g caster sugar
grated zest of 2 lemons and juice of 5 lemons
2 eggs, plus 2 egg yolks
100g cream cheese

For the poached rhubarb

400g rhubarb, chopped into 8cm sections
300g caster sugar
4 tablespoons lemon juice
1 vanilla pod, cut lengthways and seeds scraped out, or 1 teaspoon vanilla extract

First, make the bread. Preheat the oven to 190°C/170°C Fan/Gas Mark 5. Line a 900g loaf tin with baking parchment.

In a large mixing bowl, combine the eggs, vanilla extract, milk and coconut milk. Add the flour, baking powder, salt, sugar and coconut, and mix into a smooth batter.

Pour the batter into the lined loaf tin and bake for 45–50 minutes. You can check to see whether the loaf is cooked by piercing it with a wooden or metal skewer. If it comes out clean, the bread is cooked. Remove from the oven and allow to cool on a wire rack.

To make the lemon curd, heat the butter, sugar, lemon zest and juice together in a pan over a medium heat until melted.

In a small bowl, lightly whisk the eggs and yolks. Pour the eggs into the pan and heat gently, stirring regularly with a whisk, until thick and creamy. Be patient – this can take up to 10 minutes. Remove from the heat, pass through a sieve into a jug and leave to cool. Once cooled, whisk the cream cheese through the lemon curd and refrigerate until needed.

To make the poached rhubarb, put the rhubarb, sugar, lemon juice, vanilla pod and its seeds or extract and 300ml of water into a small pan on a medium heat and bring to the boil. As soon as it has come to the boil, turn off the heat and put a lid on the pan. Leave for 15 minutes, then transfer to a container and allow to cool.

To serve, slice the coconut bread into thick slices and melt a large knob of butter in a frying pan or griddle pan. Toast on one side for around 3 minutes, until golden brown, then flip and toast for another minute or so. Remove from the pan, put on a plate, spoon over the lemon curd cream cheese and top with a few rhubarb pieces.

CHELSEA BUNS

Our answer to the croissant or Danish pastry, Chelsea buns have adorned the London breakfast table for centuries. A sweet swirl of bread filled with richly spiced fruit, they were created by a West London bakery called the Old Chelsea Bun House around the start of the eighteenth century, and were so popular that people would queue in their hundreds to lay hands on one.

Even the Royal family were partial to a Chelsea bun: both King George II and George III were frequent visitors to the Bun House.

The bakery's most famous owner was Richard Hand, an eccentric ex-soldier with exotic taste in clothes who liked to be known as 'Captain Bun'. The Captain's bakery was demolished in 1839, but the buns are still a common sight in bakeries all across Britain.

MAKES 9

For the dough
270ml milk
60g butter
300g strong white flour
200g plain flour
3 tablespoons caster sugar
1 teaspoon salt
7g sachet fast-action dried yeast
1 egg, lightly beaten
1 teaspoon mixed spice
grated zest of 1 lemon
oil, for greasing

For the filling
30g butter, softened
60g soft light brown sugar
1 teaspoon ground cinnamon
1 teaspoon mixed spice
200g dried vine fruit of your
    choice – a mix of sultanas and
    currants work well

For the icing
100g icing sugar
2–3 tablespoons lemon juice or water

Put the milk and butter in a small pan over a low heat, until the butter is melted and the mixture is lukewarm, but not hot.

Put the flours, sugar and salt into a large mixing bowl. Make a well in the centre and add the yeast. Pour in the butter and milk mixture and the beaten egg, plus the mixed spice and lemon zest. Stir until combined into a soft dough.

Knead the dough for 5 minutes using a stand mixer fitted with a dough hook on a low speed, or for about 10 minutes by hand, until the dough is soft and elastic. Put the dough in a lightly oiled bowl and cover with cling film or a damp tea towel. Leave to rise in a warm place for an hour or so, until roughly doubled in size.

Give the dough a quick knead with your hands, then roll out onto a lightly floured surface into a large rectangle, about 30 × 20cm and about 4mm thick.

Spread the softened butter evenly over the dough. Scatter over the brown sugar and the spices, then the fruit. From the longest edge, roll the dough as tightly as possible to create a log shape, as if making a Swiss roll; use a dab of water on the long edge of the dough to seal the roll if needed. Using a sharp knife, cut the roll into 9 slices.

Arrange the rolls, spiral side facing upwards, in a baking tin or tray that measures about 35 × 25cm. Try and leave just a small gap between each one – the rolls traditionally squish together during baking so you can 'tear and share'. Cover the tray and leave to rise for 30 minutes.

Preheat the oven to 190°C/170°C Fan/Gas Mark 5. Bake the rolls for 20–30 minutes, until risen and golden (if the fruit looks like it is burning at any point, cover the rolls with kitchen foil).

Leave the buns to cool slightly while you make the icing. Simply combine the icing sugar with the lemon juice or water – it should be very thick. Move the buns onto a cooling rack and drizzle with the icing. Enjoy while still warm.

BACON NAAN WITH CHILLI TOMATO JAM

Ask a Londoner to name their favourite restaurant, and there's a good chance many of them will say Dishoom. This small chain of Indian restaurants, modelled on elegant Mumbai cafés of yesteryear, has a cult following for its bacon naan – an ingenious twist on that British classic, the bacon sandwich. A fluffy Indian bread is baked to order in the tandoor, stuffed with crispy bacon, dolloped with chilli tomato jam, then finished off with a slick of cream cheese and a scattering of coriander.

I became so obsessed with this dish that I had to come up with a way to make it at home. I use a simple no-yeast naan recipe, so you don't have to wait for hours for the dough to rise, and a hot pan instead of a tandoor. If you don't want to make the jam, a good-quality shop-bought jar will suffice.

SERVES 4

For the chilli tomato jam
400g cherry tomatoes, halved
1 small red onion, finely chopped
2 garlic cloves, grated
2 large red chillies, finely chopped
thumb-sized knob of ginger, grated
60g soft dark brown sugar
60g caster sugar
100ml red wine vinegar

For the naan breads
320g plain flour, plus extra for dusting
3 teaspoons caster sugar
½ teaspoon salt
1 teaspoon baking powder
½ teaspoon bicarbonate of soda
100ml milk
3 tablespoons natural yoghurt
3 tablespoons melted butter
oil, for greasing

To serve
12 slices of good-quality smoked
    streaky bacon
cream cheese
handful of fresh coriander, roughly
    chopped, optional

First, make the chilli tomato jam. Put the tomatoes, onion, garlic, chillies and ginger into a medium pan. Add the sugars and vinegar. Bring to the boil and allow to bubble vigorously, stirring occasionally, until the tomatoes have broken down and the jam is thick, dark and sticky, about 15–20 minutes. Set aside to cool. You can purée the jam in a food processor if you like, but I like it chunky.

To make the naan breads, sift the flour, sugar, salt, baking powder and bicarbonate of soda into a bowl. In another bowl, mix the milk, yoghurt, butter and 50ml of water.

Make a well in the centre of the flour mixture and pour in the liquid. Mix together with a knife, then, using your hands, make a soft ball of dough (add a splash more water if needed). Knead the dough for 4 minutes in a stand mixer fitted with a dough hook on a low speed, or for around 8 minutes by hand, then place into a lightly oiled bowl. Cover with a tea towel and leave in a warm place for 15 minutes.

Cook your bacon according to preference; I usually grill mine for a few minutes on each side until crunchy.

Now it's time to cook your naans. Heat a non-stick frying pan over a very high heat and put the oven on low (110°C/90°C Fan/Gas Mark ¼). Tip the dough onto a lightly floured surface and divide into 4 balls. Using your hands or a rolling pin, stretch or roll each ball out thinly, ideally into a teardrop shape.

Put a naan (or two if you can fit them) into the hot pan and cook for a few minutes, until bubbles appear on top and brown patches on the underside. Flip over and cook until patches appear on the other side. Repeat with the remaining breads, transferring the cooked breads onto a tray into the oven to keep warm.

To assemble, use a knife to spread the naans with cream cheese and a generous layer of the chilli tomato jam. Add 3 slices of bacon and a sprinkling of chopped coriander, if using, then fold over to make a sandwich. Serve with more jam on the side and devour, preferably to a Bollywood soundtrack.

POACHED EGGS WITH SPICY SAUSAGE, YOGHURT AND CHILLI BUTTER

Chef Peter Gordon first put Turkish-style poached eggs on the menu of his restaurant The Providores and Tapa Room in 2001, after tasting a similar dish in Istanbul. More than sixteen years later, the eggs are still the most popular breakfast at the Marylebone restaurant, with incarnations of his iconic dish now found in restaurants all over the capital. My version includes a few slices of spicy sausage, like the Turkish sujuk – I love the slight reddish hue it gives the chilli butter – but you can easily leave it out.

SERVES 2

150ml thick natural yoghurt
½ garlic clove, peeled and finely crushed (optional)
¼ teaspoon flaky sea salt
25ml extra virgin olive oil
25g butter
70g sujuk or other cured spicy sausage, such as chorizo, chopped into small chunks
½ teaspoon chilli flakes
4 eggs
100ml white wine vinegar
1 tablespoon chopped fresh flat-leaf parsley or dill
toasted bread, to serve

In a bowl, whisk the yoghurt, garlic (if using) and salt with half the oil for 15 seconds, then put to one side (it's best served at room temperature). Warm the bowls you'll serve it in.

In a small pan over a medium heat, melt the butter, then add the sausage and the chilli flakes and fry for about 3 minutes. Add the remaining oil and leave the mixture to one side, keeping it warm.

To poach the eggs, add the vinegar to 1.5 litres simmering water in a medium-sized deep pan. Create a whirlpool by stirring the water with a spoon, then carefully break the eggs, one at a time, into the pan. Simmer for 3–4 minutes, until the egg whites are set. Scoop the eggs out using a slotted spoon and leave to drain on kitchen paper.

To serve, divide three-quarters of the yoghurt mixture between the warmed bowls. Place a couple of poached eggs in each bowl, then divide the remaining yoghurt on top. Spoon over the sausage and chilli butter, sprinkle with the parsley or dill, and serve with the toasted bread.

SUGAR-CURED PRAWN OMELETTE WITH SMOKED CHILLI SAMBAL

The signature dish of Anna Hansen, chef at The Modern Pantry, and one of London's must-try breakfasts (though it also makes a fine dinner). Fragrant, sweet prawns work beautifully in an omelette, especially when topped with sambal, a fiery south-east Asian chilli sauce. The omelette takes a little effort – you'll need to start it the day before – but it is worth it. The recipe makes more sambal than you'll need, but you can keep it in a sterilised jar in the fridge for a few months. Dollop it on everything from curries to grilled fish.

SERVES 6

For the sugar-cured prawns
18 large raw prawns, peeled, cut in half and de-veined
1 lemongrass stalk, bashed gently with a rolling pin and chopped into 4 pieces
30g peeled fresh ginger, sliced
3 kaffir lime leaves, shredded
1 teaspoon chipotle chilli flakes
1 tablespoon soy sauce
1 tablespoon fish sauce
100g caster sugar
1 tablespoon flaky sea salt

For the smoked chilli sambal
vegetable or sunflower oil, for deep-frying (you will need at least 1 litre)
250g red peppers, sliced
250g onions, sliced
50g red chillies
250g cherry tomatoes
80g peeled fresh ginger, thinly sliced
100g garlic cloves, peeled and sliced
25g dried shrimp, ground in a spice grinder or pestle and mortar
1 tablespoon dried shrimp paste
1 large dried chipotle chilli, stalk removed, soaked until soft
2 teaspoons sweet smoked paprika
2 teaspoons hot smoked paprika
125ml tamarind paste
40ml fish sauce

For the omelette
12 eggs
butter, for frying
1 green chilli, sliced into super-fine rounds
1 bunch of spring onions, sliced
1 bunch of fresh coriander, leaves picked
salt

To cure the prawns, mix all the ingredients together in a bowl, and leave to marinate, covered, in the fridge for 24 hours. Rinse the prawns, pat dry with kitchen paper and refrigerate until ready to use.

To make the sambal, heat the oil in a medium saucepan to 180°C, or until a cube of bread dropped in to the oil goes crispy within 1 minute. Deep-fry the red peppers, onions, red chillies and cherry tomatoes separately in small batches until they are a rich golden brown – almost burnt-looking – draining them on kitchen paper and tipping them into a large bowl as you go. Fry the ginger and garlic, in separate batches also, until just golden brown, and add to the bowl.

In a small frying pan, heat a little oil and fry the ground shrimp until aromatic, then add to the bowl. Toast the dried shrimp paste in the pan for about a minute, then put in the bowl. Add the chipotle chilli, paprikas, tamarind paste and fish sauce, and mix everything together thoroughly.

Whizz the sambal in a food processor until almost smooth (you may need to do this in batches). Transfer to a container and refrigerate until needed.

For each omelette, whisk two eggs together in a small bowl with ½ teaspoon of the sambal and a small pinch of salt. Melt a knob of butter in an omelette pan over a medium heat, and when it begins to sizzle, add 6 prawn halves. Toss these in the pan until almost cooked, then pour in the eggs. Swirl the pan once or twice, then reduce the heat. Sprinkle over 3 green chilli rounds and a small handful of spring onions. When the eggs look almost cooked, use a flat heatproof spatula to fold the omelette in half. Slide onto a plate and keep somewhere warm while you repeat the process. To serve, garnish each omelette with coriander leaves and a spoonful of the sambal.

OMELETTE ARNOLD BENNETT

This rich, smoky omelette is a London icon. The story goes that it was invented at the Savoy hotel in 1929 for the author Arnold Bennett, who was staying there while he worked on a book. Bennett loved the omelette so much, he demanded it was made for him wherever he travelled. The Savoy has never taken it off the menu.

The original recipe calls for generous ladlefuls of hollandaise and béchamel sauce, but making these is a faff for those of us not lucky enough to have a team of obedient kitchen staff at our disposal – plus, the finished product is overwhelmingly rich. My version uses a simple white sauce, enlivened by the tang of crème fraîche and thickened with a splash of double cream. It's divine as an indulgent weekend breakfast, but I also commend it to you as a simple supper, served with good crusty bread and a crisp watercress salad.

SERVES 2

200ml milk
100ml double cream
50ml crème fraîche
200g smoked haddock
20g butter, plus extra for cooking
   the omelette
20g plain flour
30g Parmesan cheese
6 eggs
handful of chopped chives,
   to serve (optional)
lemon wedges, to serve
salt and freshly ground black pepper

Put the milk, cream and crème fraîche, plus a generous grinding of black pepper, in to a small pan and bring to a simmer over a medium-low heat. Add the smoked haddock and poach gently until cooked through, about 5 minutes. Remove the fish, retaining the cooking liquid, and flake into small pieces.

In a separate pan, melt the butter and stir in the flour. Cook for a few minutes, then slowly pour in the milk mixture you cooked the fish in. Give it a good whisk. Cook until you have a thick sauce, then remove from the heat and stir in the flaked fish and about a third of the Parmesan. Add salt and pepper to taste.

Preheat the grill to its highest setting. Whisk the eggs in a mug or small bowl, and season with a little salt and pepper.

Put a large, deep frying pan over a medium heat and add a knob of butter, swirling it around the pan as it melts. When the pan is hot, pour in the eggs and tilt the pan to make sure the eggs form an even layer. Cook the omelette until it is set, but still a little runny in the middle. Spoon the fish mixture over the top and sprinkle with the remaining Parmesan.

Transfer to the grill and cook until the omelette is golden and crunchy on top, about 3–4 minutes. Leave to rest for 5 minutes, then divide between serving plates. Sprinkle with the chopped chives, if using, and serve with the lemon wedges for squeezing.

A STEP BACK IN TIME

It's 2pm on a blisteringly hot day in June, and the entire population of East London seems to be packed into a tiny Italian caff. Every seat is taken, and the espresso machine is spluttering in protest. 'Sorry, signorina!' shouts one of the energetic owners, Nevio Jr, as he barges past me with a steaming plate of lasagne. His sister, Anna, runs to hug a smiling lady with greying hair as she steps through the narrow doorway. 'Iris!' she declares with a wink. 'I meant to check up on you this week, a lot of the oldies keel over when it's hot, don't they?'

E. Pellicci is a real family affair. The café was opened in Bethnal Green, then a run-down slum, by Nevio and Anna's Italian grandfather, Priamo Pellicci, in 1900. Anna and Nevio's mother, Maria, still cooks all the food in the cramped back kitchen, despite being seventy-seven years old – 'She puts in a longer day than any of us!' says Anna proudly – while cousin Tony also lends a hand. The family know everyone, and are as quick with the wisecracks as they are at handing out cappuccinos. 'I come here, get a bit of abuse and then I go on my way,' grins Dave, who's popped in for a quick break and a plate of pasta. 'Well, that's the appeal of it,' his friend replies.

Sixty years ago, there were hundreds of Italian cafés like E. Pellicci in London. Most have vanished, driven out by high rents and the rise of bland corporate coffee chains. E. Pellicci has survived – partly because anybody who tried to force out the exuberant Pellicci family would be decked with one of the Formica tables, and partly because of its beauty. The Art-Deco-style interior was created in 1946, and is a masterpiece of inlaid wooden panels. 'There used to be lots of carpenters in this area, and there was guy called Achille Capocci who was meant to be the bee's knees,' says Anna. 'My grandmother Elide didn't have the money to have the whole room done, so the story goes that he'd do a single panel, and she'd pay him, then he'd do the next, until it was finished. In the 1950s my dad wanted to rip it all out and do that trendy American chrome look, but thankfully Grandma put her foot down.' In 2009, English Heritage granted the building listed status, calling it a 'rare example' of a dying tradition.

The food at Pellicci's is simple and hearty: a mish-

The beautiful interiors of the iconic E Pellicci, Bethnal Green. (Alex Segre/Alamy)

mash of greasy spoon British and traditional Italian at bargain prices. There is Maria's famous lasagne, served swimming in white sauce; huge fry-ups; golden syrup sponge and bowls of ice cream drizzled with cheap strawberry sauce for the kids. 'There are some things on the menu that didn't used to be,' whispers Norman, who has eaten here for sixty-two years, clearly talking about that dastardly foreign interloper in the 'breakfast' section, the American pancakes. 'We have to change with the times!' shouts Nevio Jr from the other side of the room, somehow managing to eavesdrop even as he tosses a delightedly shrieking child into the air.

You can't sit long in E. Pellicci without seeing 'The

Book', a sticky, frayed black leather photo album filled with faded pictures and scrawled autographs of celebrities who have visited over the years. There's Jarvis Cocker (''Twas delicious, ta!') and Ronan Keating ('Best ham egg and chips!'), plus a slightly bemused-looking David Schwimmer ('Thanks'). No sign, though, of the infamous Kray twins, who used to live just round the corner and would pop in for a cuppa before a crime spree. Despite obvious pride in such starry visitors, it is serving the community that really matters to the Pelliccis. 'The demographics of this area are changing. It used to be the poorest of the poor, and now it's not,' says Anna. 'I don't mind that, but there's something missing.

People have such busy lives and nobody seems to have any time to talk to each other, but you can't get away from that here because it's so small. It's a real social hub.'

A few locals who are sitting nearby and listening nod in agreement. 'I have travelled the world, and there is nowhere like Pellicci's,' says one. 'It always lifts my spirits,' declares another. Anna grins mischievously and looks me straight in the eye. 'And that's nothing to do with the cocaine I've just put in their coffee cups,' she says.

332 Bethnal Green Road, London, E2 0AG

...GLISH

With the honourable exceptions of the steam train, the toothbrush and dry humour, the English breakfast is truly this country's greatest invention. Wars would not have been won or countries discovered without this hallowed dish of fat sausages, crispy bacon and runny-yolked eggs, all floating ecstatically in a sea of baked beans.

Every Londoner has a favourite neighbourhood café, or 'greasy spoon', where they can get their fry-up fix: mine is the slightly bonkers E. Pellicci. When I fancy a fry-up at home, however, all that shuffling about with different pots and pans – eggs in one, beans in another, bacon under the grill – puts me off. Hence this recipe. Everything is cooked in one pan, so you won't spend the rest of your morning washing up. Even better, it makes a star of what I firmly believe to be the most underrated part of the English breakfast: the beans.

SERVES 2, GENEROUSLY

1 tablespoon vegetable or sunflower oil
2 good-quality sausages
½ onion, chopped
4 rashers smoked streaky bacon, diced
1 garlic clove, grated
400g can white haricot beans, drained
400g can chopped tomatoes
1 tablespoon black treacle
2 tablespoons tomato purée
½ teaspoon English mustard powder
3 tablespoons red wine vinegar
2 tablespoons soft dark brown sugar
2 eggs
salt and freshly ground black pepper

Heat the oil in a medium frying pan and add the sausages. Fry, turning often, for about 10 minutes, until cooked through. Remove and leave to one side.

Add the onion and bacon to the pan. Cook for about 5 minutes, until the onion is soft and the bacon starts to crisp. Add the garlic clove and cook for a further minute, then add the beans, chopped tomatoes, treacle, tomato purée, mustard powder, vinegar and sugar. Season with salt and pepper, give everything a good stir, then bring to the boil and cook for 7–10 minutes, until slightly thickened and reduced. Turn the heat down to medium and return the sausages to one side of the pan.

Make two wells in the tomato-bean mix and crack in the eggs. Grind over plenty of fresh black pepper, cover the pan with a lid and simmer for 5–10 minutes, or until the egg whites are just set but the yolks still runny. Serve with buttered toast for dipping.

CHEESE AND MARMITE ROLLS

I work in Clerkenwell, and my entire office has fallen deeply for the cheese and Marmite rolls at Albion, a nearby bakery. Whenever someone is unwell, recovering from a break-up or struggling through a hangover, one of these bronze beauties appears, as if by magic, on their desk. After a short but intense harassment campaign, the kind people at Albion finally gave me the recipe.

MAKES 8 ENORMOUS ROLLS

600g white bread flour, plus extra
   for dusting
7g sachet fast-action dried yeast
2 teaspoons salt
1 teaspoon caster sugar
65g Marmite
400g mature Cheddar cheese, grated
oil, for greasing

Put the flour, yeast, salt and sugar into a large bowl, and make a well in the centre. Pour in 370ml of warm water and mix until a dough is formed (add a splash more water if needed). Knead by hand for 10 minutes until you have a neat, smooth ball of dough. Alternatively, you can put all the ingredients in a stand mixer fitted with a dough hook attachment, and mix on a low speed for about 10 minutes.

Put the dough in a lightly oiled bowl, covered with oiled cling film or a damp tea towel, making sure the cover doesn't touch the dough. Leave in a warm place for 60–90 minutes, until it has doubled in size.

Meanwhile, combine the Marmite with 20ml of boiling water in a bowl, and stir vigorously until you have a thick paste. Put to one side.

Once the dough is ready, roll it out on a lightly floured surface into a 4mm thick rectangle. With a palette knife, spread the Marmite paste all over the dough. Scatter over the grated Cheddar.

From the longest edge, roll the dough as tightly as possible to create a log shape, as if making a Swiss roll. Cut the large roll into eight smaller rolls and put on a large baking tray lined with baking parchment, cut side down. Cover and leave for about 1 hour, until they have almost doubled in size.

Preheat the oven to 220°C/200°C Fan/Gas Mark 7. Bake the rolls for about 20–25 minutes, or until a light golden colour. Scoff while still warm, with or without your colleagues.

EARL GREY PANCAKES WITH BLUEBERRY AND VANILLA COMPOTE

Earl Grey is a delicate black tea flavoured with the citrus fruit bergamot. It is thought to have been created for Charles Grey, prime minister in the 1830s, who popularised it in London society.

Two venerable London tea shops, Jacksons of Piccadilly and Twinings, both claim to have been the first to produce Earl Grey. I cannot vouch for either, but I will say with authority that the tea lends a lovely subtle fragrance to pancakes. Top them with a trickle of homemade blueberry compote and a dollop of crème fraîche, and eat with prime ministerial gravitas.

SERVES 4

300ml milk
4 Earl Grey tea bags
225g self-raising flour
2 tablespoons caster sugar
pinch of salt
2 large eggs
2 tablespoons butter, melted, plus
    extra for frying
1 large ripe banana, peeled and mashed

**For the blueberry and
    vanilla compote**
250g blueberries
3 tablespoons caster sugar
1 teaspoon vanilla extract

To make the compote, put the blueberries, sugar and vanilla extract along with 1 tablespoon of water in a saucepan over a medium heat. Cook until thick and jammy, but with some blueberries still holding their shape, about 8–10 minutes. Set aside to cool.

Heat the milk and tea bags in a separate saucepan over a medium heat, until just about simmering and a pale brown colour. Leave to cool for 5 minutes, then remove the teabags, squeezing them to extract every drop of flavour.

Mix the flour, sugar and salt together in a large bowl. In a separate bowl or jug, whisk together the eggs, melted butter and the tea-infused milk.

Pour the milk mixture into the bowl of dry ingredients and whisk together with a balloon whisk or an electric hand whisk. Add the mashed banana and whisk again until smooth; the mixture will be very thick.

Heat a knob of butter in a large non-stick frying pan until foaming, then add a scant ladleful of the batter, or two if your pan is big enough. Cook the pancake for about 2 minutes, or until small bubbles start to appear on the surface. Flip the pancakes over with a spatula and cook for a further minute or so until both sides are golden brown.

Repeat until all the batter is used up – you should get at least 10 pancakes. You can keep the pancakes warm in a low oven, or – this is a clever trick – pop them on a plate, cover them with a tea towel and put the plate over a bowl of just-boiled water. Serve with the compote.

STARTERS & SMALL PLATES

LONDON IS A BUSY PLACE.
DASHING TO CATCH A BUS
OR JOSTLING THROUGH THE
CROWDS OF SHOPPERS ON
OXFORD STREET CAN LEAVE
A VISITOR FEELING PECKISH.
THANKFULLY, FROM SCOTCH
EGGS TO PEA AND HAM SOUP,
THE CITY HAS PLENTY OF
LIGHT BITES TO TIDE YOU
OVER UNTIL DINNER.

TREACLE SODA BREAD

This dense, dark bread might be London's most beloved loaf. It comes from the chef Stephen Harris, who oversees the food at my favourite wine bar, Noble Rot. He, in turn, based it on a recipe by the Irish chef Richard Corrigan, who owns Bentley's Oyster Bar & Grill, so think of it as the culinary equivalent of a comfy, hand-me-down jumper. Soda bread is wonderfully easy to make – there's no need for yeast or kneading, and you can make a loaf from start to finish in less than an hour. Try it with crème fraîche, capers and a little smoked fish, or just lightly toasted with a thick layer of salted butter.

MAKES 1 LOAF

125g plain wholemeal flour, plus extra for dusting
65g self-raising flour
65g oats
30g wheat bran
15g wheatgerm (or use more bran)
1 teaspoon bicarbonate of soda
1 teaspoon salt
1 tablespoon black treacle
300ml buttermilk

Preheat the oven to 220°C/200°C Fan/Gas Mark 7.

Combine all of the dry ingredients in a bowl, then add the treacle and buttermilk. Mix together just until you have a sticky dough.

Turn out the dough onto a well-floured surface and use your hands to shape it into a round loaf, squashing it down slightly with the palm of your hand. Make three slashes across the top with a knife.

Put the loaf onto a floured tray and bake for 5 minutes, then turn down the temperature to 180°C/160°C Fan/Gas Mark 4. Bake for a further 30–35 minutes. The loaf is ready if it sounds hollow when you tap the underside, and when a skewer inserted into the centre comes out clean. Leave to cool on a wire rack.

...ASTED

The slippery eel is intertwined with London's history. A few hundred years ago, the Thames swarmed with them, and they were a staple food of the working classes, especially in the impoverished East End.

The traditional way to eat eels is 'jellied' – chopped and boiled in a stock which, when cooled, sets into a quivering, jelly-like substance. But I would urge you to try smoked eel. Rich, yet delicate in flavour, it is even more delicious than smoked salmon. Pair it with cheese in a toastie for the perfect lunch. It's also very good in a creamy pasta sauce, rippled with peas and a generous squeeze of lemon.

SERVES 1

2 thick slices of sourdough or white bread of your choice
1 scant teaspoon English mustard (optional)
50g smoked eel fillets
1 teaspoon capers
25g mozzarella cheese, thinly sliced
35g Emmental cheese, grated
15g butter, softened
salt and freshly ground black pepper

Lay a slice of the bread on a chopping board or plate, and spread with the mustard, if using.

Place the eel fillets on top, then sprinkle over the capers. Top with the mozzarella and Emmental, and season generously with salt and pepper.

Put the second slice of bread on top, and butter both sides of the sandwich. Gently press the sandwich down with your hand, or a spatula, so it flattens slightly.

Heat a griddle pan or non-stick frying pan over a medium–high heat. Add the sandwich to the pan and cook for 3–4 minutes each side, pressing down occasionally with the spatula, until the cheese has melted and the bread is gloriously golden and crisp. Enjoy with a beer.

SCOTCH EGGS WITH SPICY MUSTARD MAYONNAISE

A well-made Scotch egg, all rich, yielding yolk and delicately breadcrumbed sausagemeat, is a thing of beauty. And it has absolutely nothing to do with Scotland. Luxury department store Fortnum & Mason claims the Scotch egg was invented at its Piccadilly headquarters some time in the seventeenth century; apparently, aristocratic customers used to buy the eggs as snacks for the long coach journey to their country estate. Add a spiced mayonnaise for dipping and you have the best picnic food on earth.

MAKES 8

10 medium eggs
300g sausagemeat (alternatively, squeeze the meat out of about 8 sausages)
300g pork mince
2 tablespoons finely chopped fresh sage
1 tablespoon finely chopped fresh thyme
2 teaspoons English mustard powder
1 teaspoon black peppercorns, crushed
1 teaspoon salt
splash of milk
100g plain flour, seasoned with salt and freshly ground black pepper
200g breadcrumbs (I like panko)
vegetable or sunflower oil, for frying (you'll need about 2 litres)

For the spicy mustard mayonnaise
350g mayonnaise
1 heaped teaspoon curry powder
¼ teaspoon turmeric
squeeze of lemon juice
2 tablespoons Dijon mustard
salt and freshly ground black pepper

Heat a large pan of water until simmering rapidly, then add eight of the eggs and cook for 7 minutes. Remove the eggs from the pan and quickly plunge them into a bowl of iced water for a few minutes (this stops the cooking process), then peel carefully.

Mix the sausagemeat, mince, sage, thyme, mustard powder, crushed peppercorns and salt in a bowl. Divide into eight equal balls, and squish slightly with your hands to make large, flat ovals, about twice the size of an egg.

Beat the remaining two eggs in a bowl, loosened with a splash of milk. Put the seasoned flour in another bowl, and the breadcrumbs in a third.

Dip an egg in the flour so it's lightly covered, then place inside the sausagemeat oval. Use your hands to squish the sausagemeat around the egg – you may need to patch up some gaps. Repeat with the remaining seven eggs.

Roll the sausagemeat-covered eggs in flour, followed by the beaten egg, then finally in the breadcrumbs. Put to one side.

Fill a large, deep pan with the oil and heat until it reaches 160°C on a cook's thermometer, or until a cube of bread sizzles and turns golden in around 60–70 seconds. Fry the eggs, two at a time, for 8–9 minutes, until golden and crispy. Remove with a slotted spoon, and drain on kitchen paper.

To make the sauce, combine all the ingredients in a small bowl, and season with salt and pepper to taste. Serve alongside the eggs.

CULAR D

From the start of the Industrial Revolution, right up until the 1950s, London was choked by thick fog. The pollution had a devastating effect on people's health: some 12,000 people are thought to have died as a result of a particularly nasty smog in 1952. But the fog also became symbolic of London, and lent the city an eerie charm. Monet, who painted countless pictures of the murky clouds swirling above the Thames, even went so far as to declare, 'Without fog London would not be beautiful.'

The fog had many nicknames, including 'London particular' and 'pea-souper', due to its yellow-greenish tinge, which reminded people of split pea soup. In 1956, the Government passed the Clean Air Act, and the fog slowly lifted. Thankfully, this comforting soup remained.

SERVES 4–6

30g butter
1 large onion, chopped
1 celery stick, chopped
3 sprigs of thyme, leaves removed and finely chopped
400g split peas, green or yellow
2 bay leaves
2 litres ham or chicken stock
500g cooked ham hock or gammon, shredded
salt and freshly ground black pepper

Heat the butter in a large casserole dish or saucepan, add the onion, celery and thyme, and fry for about 10 minutes, until golden and soft. Add the split peas and stir gently, until completely coated in the butter. Add the bay leaves and stock, bring to the boil and skim off any scum that rises to the surface.

Reduce the heat and simmer, uncovered, for 45–60 minutes, until the peas have broken down and thickened the soup. Season to taste – lots of fresh black pepper makes it sing. If you like, you can purée the soup to make it velvety smooth, but I like it thick and rustic. Add the shredded ham to the pan and serve the soup in bowls with crusty bread.

SMOKED SALMON AND SWEET POTATO FISHCAKES WITH SPICY GARLIC YOGHURT

Many people think the Scots invented smoking, but it was actually Jewish imm the East End we have to thank for this cora delicacy. Sweet potato and salmon work brilli together in fishcakes, especially with a whisper from red chilli. These make a good dinner party sta served with salad or tender green vegetables.

MAKES 4 LARGE OR
8 SMALL FISHCAKES

400g sweet potatoes, peeled and
    chopped into 2cm chunks
250g lightly smoked salmon
    fillets, flaked; or smoked salmon,
    roughly chopped
2 spring onions, white and green parts,
    finely chopped
½ red chilli, finely chopped
grated zest of ½ lemon
1 heaped tablespoon finely chopped
    fresh coriander leaves
50g plain flour
1 egg, beaten
100g dried breadcrumbs
4 tablespoons vegetable oil
salt and freshly ground black pepper

For the spicy garlic yoghurt
200ml natural yoghurt
½ garlic clove, crushed
2 teaspoons harissa paste

Put the sweet potato chunks into a large saucepan filled with salted boiling water. Bring back to the boil and simmer for about 15 minutes, or until tender. Drain, return to the pan and mash roughly – it doesn't need to be completely smooth. Leave to cool slightly.

Put the salmon into a large bowl. Add the spring onions, chilli, lemon zest and coriander, along with the mashed potato, and stir to combine. Season well with salt and pepper, then use your hands to form the mixture into fishcakes. If the mix seems very wet, add 1–2 tablespoons of flour. Pop into the fridge for at least 30 minutes to firm up.

Put the flour in a shallow bowl, the egg in another bowl, and the breadcrumbs in a third bowl. Dip the fishcakes into the flour, followed by the egg, then the breadcrumbs, making sure each cake is thoroughly coated. You can now return them to the fridge until needed.

To make the spicy yoghurt, combine the yoghurt and garlic in a small bowl, and swirl in the harissa.

When you're ready to eat, heat the oil over a medium heat in a frying pan, then add the fishcakes. Cook for about 5 minutes, until golden brown underneath, then carefully flip them over. Fry for another 3–5 minutes until golden on the bottom. Serve with a dollop of the yoghurt on the side.

ARTERS & SMALL PLATES P69

the art of salmon
igrants in
-coloured
ntly
f heat
ter,

l of run-down
s of flats, there is an
ved roof and pale pink
just like a plump piece of
mon. Welcome to H. Forman & Son, one of the oldest
salmon smokeries in the world.

'Smoked salmon shouldn't taste of smoke,' insists
Lance Forman, the company's passionate owner, as he
hands me a piece of salmon to try. 'It's a preserving
technique, not a flavour. But so many producers overload
the smokiness. It disguises the fact their fish is bad
quality, or not very fresh.'

Smoked salmon was once a luxury: the posh canapé
at parties, the special treat on the Christmas table. But
since the 1970s, when the first salmon farms opened
in Britain, it has become cheap and commonplace. Rip
open a packet today, and it's likely to taste greasy, heavy,
and so intensely smoky that the taste will swim around
your mouth for the rest of the day. But Forman's 'London
Cure' is different. As soon as I pop it in my mouth, I am
overwhelmed by its delicate flavour – rich but somehow
soft, with only a wisp of smoke. No wonder every high-
class restaurant from The Ivy to the Ritz has this on
the menu.

Smoked salmon is not just a job for Forman, it is
an obsession. His great-grandfather Aaron 'Harry'
Forman was a Russian immigrant, one of thousands of
Jews from Eastern Europe who fled persecution around
the end of the nineteenth century and ended up in East
London. Smoked salmon was a tradition they brought
with them – not because it was a delicacy, but because
it was an easy way to preserve fish in the days before
refrigeration. 'At first, they shipped in wild salmon in
barrels of brine from the Baltic,' says Lance. 'But one day
they went to Billingsgate Fish Market, and they saw all
that beautiful fresh salmon from Scotland laid out before
them. The rest is history.'

Harry founded his smokery in Stepney, at the heart of
the Jewish community, around 1905. In the beginning,
his fish was enjoyed mostly by fellow immigrants, who
put the vivid orange slices in their bagels, closed their
eyes and remembered the taste of home. Then Harry
and his son Louis had the bright idea of hawking their
product around restaurants and food halls like Harrods.
Before long, smoked salmon had become a favourite

H. Forman and Son's new London home.
(E.J. Westmacott/Alamy)

SALMON IS NOT JUST A JOB FOR FORMAN, IT IS AN OBSESSION.

British treat, and smokeries leapt up faster than salmon up a waterfall – particularly in Scotland, where salmon farming is big business. As recently as the 1970s, there were twelve other Jewish smokeries in the East End. Now Forman's is the last surviving.

Freshness is at the heart of Forman's battle for salmon supremacy. Five days a week, at 4am, a refrigerated truck arrives at the factory with trays of gleaming salmon driven straight down from Scotland. 'We have a rule that the fish must have been in the water no more than forty-eight hours before we get our hands on it,' says Lance. 'I think of us like a bakery, making fresh loaves each morning.' First, the fish is cleaned and filleted. Then it is sprinkled with fat crystals of rock salt and left for twenty-four hours to draw out some of the moisture. Many producers skip this stage 'because when you salt fish, you lose ten per cent of the body weight – and that's ten per cent of their profit. So they put the fish in brine, or even just inject it with salt water. When it's time to smoke, the fish is so wet, it absorbs too much of the smoke. That's also why it tastes greasy.'

After being salted, the fish is hung in vast kilns and gently cold-smoked over oak until it reaches rich, succulent perfection. Finally, it will be skilfully carved

by hand, rather than machine – one worker, Darren, holds the Guinness world record for slicing a side of smoked salmon, finishing the job in 1 minute and 11 seconds – wrapped in crinkly greaseproof paper and sent out for customers to enjoy. Forman's 'London Cure' is so unique that it was recently granted the coveted European protected (PGI) status. This means, like Champagne, Parmesan cheese or Serrano ham, it can only be produced in its home region. It is the first London food to have been added to the scheme; not even London gin has the honour.

A few years ago, Forman's nearly faced extinction when it came to light that the land on which the business stood had been earmarked for the 2012 London Olympic Games – slap bang, in fact, in what is now the Olympic Stadium. After a fight, the company agreed to move, and the flamboyant fish-shaped building, on the edge of the River Lea, was its compensation. It is a very different building, in a very different London, to the one Aaron Forman knew in 1905. But the smoked salmon remains proudly the same.

Stour Road, London, E3 2NT

Salmon fillets prior to smoking on Fish Island. (Jason Alden/Bloomberg via Getty Images)

CRAB DOUGHNUTS

The Chiltern Firehouse in Marylebone is such a celebrity magnet, it's in hotter demand than The Priory rehab clinic. With the likes of Jennifer Lawrence, Madonna and David Beckham in attendance, us civilians are unlikely to bag a table – which is a shame, because chef Nuno Mendes' rich savoury doughnuts, stuffed with crab, are addictive. Luckily, I've developed a simple version you can make at home. If you find the idea of savoury doughnuts perplexing, these are just as good rolled in sugar or filled with jam.

MAKES ABOUT 25

100g butter
170ml milk
500g strong white bread flour
7g sachet fast-action dried yeast
40g caster sugar
1 teaspoon salt
2 eggs, plus 2 egg yolks, beaten
grated zest of 2 lemons
vegetable or sunflower oil, for frying
    (you will need around 2 litres), plus
    extra for greasing

For the filling
300g white crabmeat
juice of 1½ lemons
4 tablespoons crème fraîche
2 tablespoons tomato purée
3 tablespoons finely chopped fresh
    dill (optional)
½ red chilli, finely chopped
½ garlic clove, crushed

Heat the butter with the milk in a small saucepan over a low heat, until the butter has melted and the mixture is warm, but not boiling.

Mix the flour, yeast, sugar and salt together in a large bowl. Pour in the butter and milk mixture, the eggs and the lemon zest. Stir until it comes together into a dough. Knead in a stand mixer fitted with a dough attachment on a low speed for 8–10 minutes, or by hand for 10–12 minutes, until you have a soft, smooth and glossy dough.

Put the dough in a lightly oiled bowl, covered with oiled cling film or a damp tea towel, making sure the cover doesn't touch the dough. Leave in a warm place for about 1 hour, until the dough has doubled in size.

Grease two baking trays. Tip the dough out onto a lightly floured surface and roll until about 1cm thick. Use a 5cm straight-sided cookie cutter to stamp out as many rounds as possible, then gather up the scraps, roll it out again, and cut out as many more doughnuts as you can. Place onto the baking trays, cover and leave for another 30–60 minutes, until they've puffed up a little more.

Fill a large, deep pan with the oil and heat until it reaches 160°C on a cook's thermometer, or until a cube of bread sizzles and turns golden in around 60–70 seconds. Cook the doughnuts in batches, so you don't overcrowd the pan. Carefully lower them in, and fry for about 2–3 minutes on each side, until a sultry golden brown. Drain on kitchen paper.

Combine all the ingredients for the filling in a bowl. Slice through the doughnuts horizontally, but not all the way through, and spoon in a generous amount of filling.

PAN-FRIED SCALLOPS WITH BEETROOT, APPLE AND HAZELNUTS

I begged this recipe off
whose handful of Lond
favourite places to eat.
Spanish flavours, such
more British ingredient
in Spain, but when I m
with it,' says José. Ser
of cold sparkling wine.

SERVES 4 AS A STARTER OR 2 AS A
MAIN COURSE

4 small beetroots (candied beetroots
  look pretty)
1 sharp apple, such as Granny Smith
juice of 1 lemon
3 tablespoons extra virgin olive oil,
  plus extra
1 tablespoon hazelnut oil (optional)
few sprigs of tarragon, leaves stripped
  and finely chopped
95g ibérico ham or pancetta slices
12–16 scallops
2 tablespoons finely chopped chives
50g hazelnuts, toasted and
  roughly chopped
salt and freshly ground black pepper

Peel the beetroots and slice them very thinly (use a mandoline if you have one).
Slice the apple into quarters, skin on, and remove the core, then finely slice into
half-moons. Put the beetroot and apple slices into a bowl, and squeeze a little of
the lemon juice over the apple to stop it browning.

Make a dressing by whisking the rest of the lemon juice with plenty of salt and
pepper in a small bowl. Gradually whisk in the olive oil and hazelnut oil, if using.
Stir in the tarragon.

In a pan with a little olive oil, fry the ham or pancetta over a medium heat until
crisp. Remove with a slotted spoon, crumble into pieces and set aside.

Use a piece of kitchen paper to wipe out all but about a teaspoon of the fat from
the pan and increase the heat to high. When really hot, add the scallops and sear
quickly for 30–60 seconds on each side, until golden and just cooked.

Divide the beetroot and apple slices between serving plates and drizzle with
the dressing. Top with the scallops and crispy ham. Scatter over the chives and
hazelnuts and serve.

...unny days, when the tide is out, you may spot ...eople digging in the damp sand of the Thames foreshore. Here, on the river's edge, these 'mudlarks' uncover oyster shells, fragments of animal bone and broken plates – a sort of edible history of the city, washed up only briefly before the river takes it back into its wet embrace.

London was born because of the Thames. The Romans needed a British port, and found a site where the river was narrow – so a bridge could be built – and the ground not too marshy. Soon, the Tamesis, as they called it, was full of ships from all corners of the Roman empire, many loaded with exotic new ingredients. Cherries, peas and walnuts are just a few of the foods that the Thames ushered into the British larder, changing how we ate forever.

By Tudor times, London was the largest city in the world, and the Thames' fish-rich waters fed the wealthy and poor alike. 'What should I speak of the fat and sweet salmon daily taken in this stream and that in such plenty … as no river in Europe is able to exceed it,' rhapsodised John Stow in 1598. 'But what store also of barbels, trouts, chevens, perches, smelts, breams, roaches, daces, gudgeons, flounders, shrimps eels, etc. are commonly to be had therein?' Despite the fact that much of the city's sewage was dumped straight into it, the putrid Thames was also the poor's only source of water. Small wonder the river acquired an almost religious significance. 'Old Father Thames', the people dubbed it, and images of this wise, bearded Neptune-like figure sprouted all over the city, from a triumphant bronze statue at Somerset House to a tiny face on Kew Bridge. You can still see them today.

As Britain's economy boomed, London became the world's foremost trading hub, and the river was its lifeblood. By the start of the eighteenth century, some 7,000 ships blew in and out every year, carrying mouthwatering goods from all over the world: sugar and rum from the Caribbean, tea and spices from Asia, oranges from Spain, and a curious new vegetable called corn from the Americas. By 1700, London's rickety wharves handled 80 per cent of Britain's imports and 69 per cent of exports. The central stretch of river known as The Pool was the busiest in the world – so chaotic and crowded that visitors could sometimes barely see the water. As one William Camden marvelled: 'A man would say, that seeth the shipping there, that it is … a very wood of trees disbranched to make glades and let in light, so shaded it is with masts and sails.'

By the late eighteenth century, the river was so congested that some ships had to wait an entire week in South London before they were given the green light to sail up to The Pool. Something had to be done. The solution was the building of London's great docks, such as Millwall and West India, in what was then the wasteland of the Isle of Dogs in East London. These enormous quays cost millions and were seen as a modern wonder of the world. When a German prince visited in 1828, he felt 'awe at the greatness and might of England'. In the huge warehouses by the docks, he declared, there was 'sugar enough to sweeten the whole adjoining basin and rum enough to make half of England drunk'.

As Britain's empire collapsed, London's importance as a trade centre faded, and by 1980 all the great docks were closed. Father Thames is quieter now, his tide of merchant ships replaced by a trickle of passenger ferries. You can't blame him: after all, he is very old.

THE ST LAWRENCE IS WATER, THE MISSISSIPPI IS MUDDY WATER, BUT THE THAMES IS LIQUID HISTORY.

MP John Burns, 1929

Nineteenth century illustration of the West India Docks, London. (Oxford Science Archive/Print Collector/Getty Images)

OYSTERS WITH RHUBARB SALSA

Londoners have always been obsessed with shellfish. In the 1700s, huge cartloads of oysters, cockles, winkles and whelks rumbled every day from England's south coast to the city. Back then, oysters were far from the luxury item they are today: taverns would put out bucketloads of the salty shellfish as a free snack to encourage punters to drink a few more pints, while street sellers sold them by the dozen (Samuel Johnson, author of *A Dictionary of the English Language,* famously used to pop out during writing breaks to buy a few oysters for his pampered cat, Hodge). Dig around the Thames foreshore at low tide and you'll uncover countless fragments of long-devoured oysters: as Drew Smith writes in his book *Oyster: A Gastronomic History,* 'the shells went under the floorboards as insulation and into the lime for building the city of London'.

Many of London's best-known restaurants – Wheeler's of St James, Bentley's, J Sheekey – began life as oyster bars. This is a simple but impressive way to serve oysters at home. The tartness of the rhubarb really lifts the oysters' flavour.

SERVES 4 AS A STARTER

16 fresh oysters, in the shell
1 stalk rhubarb, diced into small
  5mm pieces
1 spring onion, white and green parts,
  finely chopped
1 red chilli, deseeded and
  finely chopped
1 tablespoon lime juice
2 tablespoons soft light brown sugar
1 heaped teaspoon finely chopped
  fresh dill

Using a shucker, open the oyster shells. Discard the top shell and loosen each oyster from the base shell.

To make the rhubarb salsa, combine all the remaining ingredients in a bowl. Taste and adjust the sweet-sour balance to your liking, adding a little more sugar or lime juice if needed.

Put about half a teaspoon of the rhubarb salsa in each oyster shell, and serve. Probably wasted on your cat.

CHEESY CRAYFISH QUICHE

Not many people know it, but beneath the calm surface of the Thames swims an army of spiny assassins. The American Signal crayfish was introduced into UK waters in the 1970s, and the population now numbers in the hundreds of thousands. These tough little critters eat everything they can get their claws on, and have caused serious damage to the river's native creatures. But there is a man single-handedly waging war against these fishy invaders: Bob Ring, also known as 'Crayfish Bob'. A weather-beaten figure in muddy jeans and a battered hat, he sails the Thames on a rickety boat, catching as many of the creatures as he can, then cooking them in a variety of delicious and unusual ways.

This quiche is a signature dish of Bob's, and showcases crayfish's delicate, sweet taste. Fresh crayfish are best if you can get them; you'd need about a kilo to get 150g of meat from the tails and claws.

SERVES 8

For the pastry

240g plain flour, plus extra for dusting
¼ teaspoon cayenne pepper
60g butter, cut into cubes
60g white vegetable shortening, such as Trex, cut into cubes

For the filling

40g butter
½ medium onion, finely chopped
½ red pepper, finely chopped
2 garlic cloves, finely chopped
¼ teaspoon cayenne pepper
150g crayfish meat, cooked
60g mature Cheddar cheese, grated
2 eggs
200ml double cream
2 tablespoons chopped fresh chives, plus extra to serve
dash of hot sauce, such as Tabasco (optional)
dash of Worcestershire sauce
50g Parmesan cheese, grated
salt and freshly ground black pepper

First make the pastry. In a mixing bowl, combine the flour, cayenne pepper, butter and vegetable shortening, and rub with your fingertips until the mixture resembles breadcrumbs. Add a little cold water, bit by bit, until the mixture comes together into a dough – about 6 tablespoons should do it. Wrap the dough in cling film and refrigerate for at least 30 minutes.

Preheat the oven to 200°C/180°C Fan/Gas Mark 6. Lightly grease a 23cm tart tin that is at least 3cm deep. Remove the dough from the fridge and roll out on a lightly floured surface until you have a disc about 5mm thick. Transfer to the tart tin and trim away any overhanging pastry edges. Prick the bottom with a fork, line with baking parchment and fill with baking beans or rice. Cook for 15 minutes, then remove the baking parchment and weights, and cook until golden, another 5–8 minutes.

Reduce the oven temperature to 190°C/170°C Fan/Gas Mark 5. To make the filling, melt the butter in a large frying pan over a low heat. Add the onion, red pepper, garlic and cayenne pepper. Cook gently for about 4 minutes, turning regularly, before stirring in the cooked crayfish meat and cooking for a further 1–2 minutes. Leave briefly to cool, then spread evenly across the pastry shell. Distribute the grated Cheddar across the filling.

Now whisk together the eggs, cream, chives, hot sauce, Worcestershire sauce and plenty of salt and pepper in a bowl. Stir in the Parmesan cheese and pour the mixture into the pastry case.

Bake for 25–30 minutes, until the quiche is lightly set and the top is golden brown. Allow to cool for a few minutes, then garnish with chives, and serve.

CHERRY, GOAT'S CHEESE AND CHICORY TART WITH WALNUT GREMOLATA

Londoners always knew when the cherries arrived. Every summer, from medieval times right up to the 1900s, fruit sellers walked the streets with their fresh bounty from the countryside, crying 'Cherries ripe-ripe-ripe!' or 'Cherries in the ryse!' (a 'ryse' was the stick the cherries were tied to). The journalist Henry Mayhew's 1851 investigation, *London Labour and the London Poor*, features a street seller with an interesting theory as to the fruit's popularity. 'Poor people,' he explained, 'like a quantity of any fruit, and no fruit is cheaper than cherries at 1d. a pound, at which I have sold some hundreds of pounds weight… Then boys buy, I think, more cherries than other fruit; because, after they have eaten 'em, they can play at cherry-stones.'

Cherries are rarely more delicious than when scoffed fresh, but they are also brilliant in savoury dishes. I love them paired with creamy goat's cheese in this easy tart, perfect for a light summer lunch. When I bought a big bag of cherries from a roadside fruit seller in East London to test this recipe, he sighed heavily as he handed them over. 'Cherries, cherries, cherries,' he grumbled. 'It's all people ever buy.'

SERVES 4–6

1 tablespoon olive oil, plus extra for greasing
2–3 heads of chicory, halved lengthways
1 teaspoon caster sugar
juice of ½ lemon
320g ready-rolled puff pastry
150g soft goat's cheese, crumbled
150g cherries, de-stoned and halved

For the gremolata
handful of basil leaves
grated zest of ½ lemon
40g walnuts
2 tablespoons olive oil
salt and freshly ground black pepper

Preheat the oven to 200°C/180°C Fan/Gas Mark 6. Lightly grease a baking tray with oil.

Heat the oil in a frying pan. Fry the chicory halves for a few minutes on each side until golden and soft. Sprinkle over the sugar and squeeze over the lemon juice, then drain briefly on kitchen paper.

Unroll the puff pastry sheet on the baking tray. Use a sharp knife to score a 1cm border around the edge, making sure not to cut through the pastry. Prick the centre with a fork a few times. Scatter over the goat's cheese, then add the chicory halves, and tumble over the cherries.

Blitz the gremolata ingredients in a food processor, or use a pestle and mortar, then drizzle over the tart. Season well with salt and pepper.

Bake for 20–25 minutes until crisp and golden.

ROASTED PARSNIP, SQUASH AND POMEGRANATE SALAD

Sally Clarke is an unsung food hero. When she opened Clarke's restaurant in West London in 1984, her simple, seasonal food was a far cry from the cheffy foams and drizzles being splattered and swirled on plates everywhere else, and inspired countless chefs in London and beyond. This is a classic Sally salad, as robust as it is fresh.

SERVES 6 AS A STARTER OR 4 AS A MAIN COURSE

2–3 parsnips, chopped into
  3–4cm chunks
1 small squash, such as
  butternut, peeled and chopped into
  3–4cm chunks
2 medium red onions, quartered
1 tablespoon chopped fresh rosemary
3 tablespoons olive oil, plus an extra
  splash for drizzling
200g salad leaves, such as radicchio,
  watercress, chicory or baby spinach
200g walnuts, chopped into
  small pieces
250g ricotta, sliced or crumbled
salt and freshly ground black pepper

For the dressing
1 small pomegranate
2 tablespoons olive oil

Preheat the oven to 200°C/180°C Fan/Gas Mark 6.

Put the parsnips, squash, onions and rosemary in a close-fitting baking tray and season generously with salt and pepper. Add the 3 tablespoons of olive oil and jumble together until well coated.

Roast for 35–45 minutes, turning the vegetables about halfway through, until golden and tender (you should be able to pierce them easily with a small knife). If the onion slices start to look dry and crisp before the other vegetables are ready, simply remove them and leave to one side.

While the vegetables are roasting, make the dressing. Cut the pomegranate in half and knock the seeds out by holding each half upside down over a bowl and banging it with a rolling pin. Squeeze out all the juice into the bowl too, and mix with the oil, plus plenty of salt and pepper.

Place the salad leaves in a bowl with the walnuts and drizzle with a splash more oil, and season with sea salt and pepper. Toss together gently and divide between serving plates. Place the roasted vegetables on top, making sure that the different colours and shapes are evenly distributed. Pour over the pomegranate dressing and scatter over the ricotta.

SPICY WATERMELON SALAD WITH CORIANDER AND PEANUTS

I have a special place in my heart for Chick 'n' Sours, a down-and-dirty fried chicken joint that specialises in fried chicken and sour cocktails. Yet the cleverest dish on the menu is the watermelon salad. Tangy, spicy, fresh and sweet, all at the same time, it's a perfect complement to rich meat, and so much better than a bowl of limp lettuce and watery tomatoes. Try it at your next barbecue.

SERVES 4 AS A SIDE

500g watermelon, chopped into
   2cm cubes
5 spring onions, finely sliced
generous handful of fresh coriander,
   roughly chopped
generous handful of fresh mint,
   roughly chopped
70g roasted salted peanuts,
   roughly chopped

For the dressing
1 long red chilli, roughly chopped
½ garlic clove, peeled
2 tablespoons palm sugar or soft dark
   brown sugar
25ml fish sauce
60ml freshly squeezed lime juice
   (about 4 limes)

To make the dressing, place all the ingredients in a food processor or blender and whizz until smooth.

Put the watermelon cubes in a bowl, toss with the dressing and leave for 5 minutes.

Add the spring onions, coriander and mint, and toss together until combined. Transfer to a serving dish using a slotted spoon, then sprinkle over the peanuts.

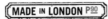

ROASTED BONE MARROW WITH PARSLEY AND LEMON SALT

When Fergus Henderson opened his restaurant St. John in 1994, he shone a light on the simple, sturdy joys of old-fashioned British food. With dishes like beef mince on toast, and bread and butter pudding, a meal at St. John is a bit like the best school dinner you've ever had. Henderson is particularly passionate about eating animals in their entirety, including the bits that make many people squeal.

Over the years, everything from pig's tail to ox heart has trotted onto St. John's tables. His signature dish is roasted marrow, served quivering in the bone, with great chunks of bread to spread it on and a piquant parsley salad. My version features a quick herby salt, to sprinkle on top of the marrow. Like Henderson's salad, it zips through the richness perfectly.

SERVES 4 AS A STARTER

4 beef marrow bones (preferably veal), at least 12cm in length
100g flaky sea salt
grated zest of 1 lemon
2 heaped tablespoons flat-leaf parsley leaves
slices of buttered bread, to serve

Preheat the oven to 230°C/210°C Fan/Gas Mark 8.

Place the bones, cut side up, on a baking tray. Roast for about 15 minutes, until the bone marrow is soft and bubbling, but hasn't completely melted.

While the marrow is roasting, blitz the salt, lemon zest and parsley together in a food processor or blender until fine, then transfer into a small serving dish.

Serve the bone marrow with the salt, and lots of buttered bread.

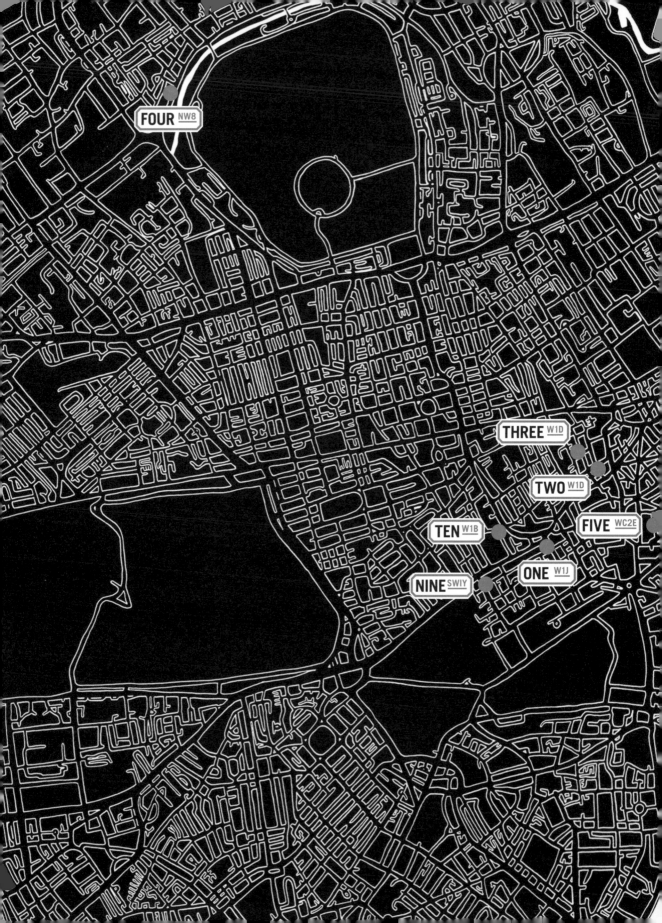

BEST RESTAURANTS

saviniatcriterion.co.uk

With its glistening gold-tiled ceiling and marble columns, The Criterion is easily the most beautiful dining room in London. Its dramatic appearance is due to the Victorian architect Thomas Verity, more famous for designing lavish London theatres. In Sir Arthur Conan Doyle's Sherlock Holmes stories, it is at The Criterion that Dr Watson first hears of the gifted detective; a plaque on the wall commemorates the moment. Since 2015, the restaurant has been under Italian ownership, so you'll tuck into distinctly un-Victorian dishes like seafood risotto or tagliatelle alla Bolognese under the sparkling chandeliers.

2. Kettner's
29 Romilly St, Soho,
W1D 5HP
kettnerstownhouse.com

Romance and scandal hang in the air at Kettner's, which was opened in 1867 by a chef of Napoleon III. Oscar Wilde and his young lover, Lord Alfred Douglas, sipped champagne here, while Edward VII brought his actress mistress Lillie Langtry for foie gras and flirtation. Like Wilde, Kettner's eventually fell from grace, becoming part of a pizza chain, then a middling French brasserie. The building is now owned by members' club Soho House, who have restored the restaurant to its former glory, and even added a few bedrooms for guests to stay in.

3. L'Escargot
48 Greek St, Soho,
W1D 4EF
lescargot.co.uk

London's oldest French restaurant was founded in 1896, when it was known as Le Bienvenue. Owner Georges Gaudin was famous for his snails, which he reared in the basement, and in the 1920s he renamed his eatery in honour of them. A plaster statue of Gaudin triumphantly riding a golden snail, holding a ribbon emblazoned with the motto 'slow but sure', sits above the restaurant's entrance.

4. Oslo Court
Charlbert St,
NW8 7EN
oslecourtrestaurant.co.uk

Compared to the other eateries on this list, Oslo Court is a baby; it hasn't even celebrated its 40th birthday. But this peculiar restaurant, hidden away at the bottom of a nondescript residential tower block, is a unique 1980s timewarp. Nostalgic diners dab their eyes with pink frilly napkins as they tuck into retro delights like melon with Parma ham and 'chicken Princesse'; later on, what must be the last dessert trolley in London death-rattles across the deep-pile carpet, tempting guests with pavlovas and profiteroles. A guilty pleasure.

5. Rules
34–35 Maiden Ln,
WC2E 7LB
rules.co.uk

A rhapsody in red and gold, Rules has been feeding steak and pies to Londoners since 1798. Despite its old-fashioned appearance – all crisp white tablecloths, gilded mirrors and dusty paintings – it is less stuffy than other historic London restaurants, with a relaxed dress code and occasional playful touches on the traditional British menu (Kate Middleton cocktail, anyone?). The bar upstairs is one of London's hidden gems, with smooth martinis that are as easy to sink into as the plush sofas.

The pleasures of the table have always been central to London life; we eat out more than residents of any other city in the country. Some of our most beloved restaurants are older than America (and the food they serve hasn't changed much, either). Here are ten of the city's golden oldies.

6. Simpson's in the Strand
100 Strand,
WC2R 0EW
simpsonsinthestrand.co.uk

Not to be confused with Simpson's Tavern, this bastion of old-fashioned English cooking started life as a smoking room and chess club in 1828. Famous faces including Vincent Van Gogh and Charles Dickens have munched grouse and swirled brandies in the elegant oak-panelled space; the list of female luminaries is somewhat smaller, as until 1984 women could only eat in a separate dining room upstairs. The restaurant's tradition of serving meat from 'carving trolleys' wheeled to diners' tables can supposedly be traced back to its chess-playing past, as it minimised disruption to guests' games.

7. Simpson's Tavern
Ball Court, 38½ Cornhill,
EC3V 9DR
simpsonstavern.co.uk

'Would you like a sausage with that?' is the catchphrase at Simpson's, which has slumbered at the end of a dark cobbled alley off Cornhill since the 1700s. One of London's last traditional 'chophouses', it is a carnivores' paradise of roasted meat, steak puddings and, yes, supplementary sausages. Diners cram into narrow wooden stalls, each with its own overhead brass rail – a throwback to times when gentlemen had top hats and bowlers to hang up.

8. Sweetings
39 Queen Victoria St,
EC4N 4SF
sweetingsrestaurant.co.uk

It's only open between 11.30am and 3pm, shuts at the weekends and refuses to take bookings, but Sweetings is an institution among city workers. The restaurant began life in the 1830s as a fish merchant, and specialises in simply cooked fish and seafood. Order a plate of oysters and the house drink, Black Velvet, an addictive mix of champagne and Guinness, served in a pewter tankard.

9. Wilton's
55 Jermyn St
St James's
SW1Y 6LX
wiltons.co.uk

Wilton's logo is a top-hatted lobster clutching a glass of champagne in one claw and a cane in the other, which tells you all you need to know about how big your bill's going to be. Founded as an oyster stall in 1742, it became a bricks-and-mortar restaurant a century later, and has a loyal clientele of red-faced aristocrats, snooty foreign dignitaries and minor European nobles. If you don't have a royal bank balance at your disposal, the pre-theatre menu is good value.

10. Veeraswamy
Victory House
99 Regent St,
W1B 4RS
veeraswamy.com

Accessed through a tiny doorway in the heart of bustling Piccadilly, Veeraswamy is the oldest surviving Indian restaurant in the UK. It was founded in 1926 by Edward Palmer, a retired army officer with exotic heritage; his grandfather was a British general who married an Indian princess. The restaurant has fed curries and naan to everyone from Winston Churchill to Charlie Chaplin, and has sweeping views over Regent Street.

CORONATION CHICKEN

In June 1953, Queen Elizabeth II was crowned at Westminster Abbey, and Rosemary Hume, founder of Le Cordon Bleu cookery school, was asked to cater for the celebratory banquet. Her creamy 'coronation chicken', studded with fruit and a fragrant hint of spice, achieved what few dishes do – it became an instant classic.

Over the years, coronation chicken has degenerated into a cheap sandwich filler, lurid yellow and usually found in a tub in the reduced section at the supermarket. Make it yourself, and you have a meal that is truly fit for a queen. I like to serve this as a sort of open sandwich, piled on a thick slice of bread, and crowned with a tangle of watercress. It's also excellent on top of salad.

SERVES 4

4 skinless, boneless chicken thigh
    fillets, about 300g
1 bay leaf
thumb-sized knob of ginger
½ teaspoon black peppercorns
1 tablespoon butter
3 spring onions, white and green parts,
    finely chopped
½ green chilli, finely chopped
2 teaspoons medium curry powder
100ml mayonnaise
100ml natural yoghurt
1 tablespoon mango chutney
1 tablespoon tomato purée
juice of ½ lemon
1 mango, cut into small cubes
30g flaked almonds
small handful of fresh coriander,
    finely chopped
watercress, to garnish, optional
salt and freshly ground black pepper

Bring a large pan of water to the boil, then reduce the heat until simmering gently. Add the chicken thighs, bay leaf, ginger, peppercorns and 1 teaspoon of salt. Cover, and poach for about 15 minutes, or until cooked through. Remove the chicken, shred into small pieces and set aside to cool.

Melt the butter in a frying pan over a medium heat. Add the spring onions and chilli and fry for 2–3 minutes, until softened. Add the curry powder and cook for a further 1 minute, then scrape the whole lot into a large mixing bowl.

Add the mayonnaise, yoghurt, mango chutney, tomato purée, lemon juice, mango, almonds and coriander to the bowl and stir to combine. Mix in the shredded chicken, and season with salt and pepper to taste. Garnish with watercress, if you like.

CAULIFLOWER SHAWARMA WITH SPICED BUTTER, POMEGRANATE AND PINE NUTS

Traditionally, the English have not been very good at cooking vegetables, preferring to lavish their attention on a good chunk of meat. 'A foreigner,' wrote a shocked German visitor to London in 1767, 'will be surprised to see what flesh eaters the English are.' But recently, vegetables have become the star of the show, with the city's chefs showcasing dazzling new ways to cook nature's bounty.

At Middle-Eastern-inspired restaurant Berber & Q, secreted underneath the railway arches in Hackney, the star dish is not lamb kebabs or spicy Moroccan sausages, but a whole roasted cauliflower, beautifully charred and dressed with rose petals, tahini, pine nuts and an intensely spiced butter.

Head chef Josh Katz recommends cooking this on the barbecue, but being an apartment dweller with little outside space, like so many Londoners, I usually pop it in the oven. Serve as part of a mezze spread with flatbreads and dips.

SERVES 2–4 AS A SIDE

1 large cauliflower

For the tahini dressing
80g raw tahini
juice of ½ lemon
1–2 garlic cloves, crushed
½ tablespoon salt

For the spiced butter
40g butter, softened
1 garlic clove, crushed
juice of 1 lemon
1 tablespoon ground cinnamon
1 tablespoon sumac
1½ teaspoons ground cumin
½ teaspoon allspice
pinch of ground nutmeg
seeds from 1–2 green cardamom
    pods, crushed
1½ tablespoons fresh coriander,
    finely chopped

Trim away the outer cauliflower leaves, leaving a few on – they add a lovely crunch once they've crisped up. Put the cauliflower in a large pan filled with enough salted water to cover it, and bring to the boil over a high heat. Once the water is boiling, turn the heat down slightly and simmer for around 8–10 minutes, just until the cauliflower is partially cooked.

While the cauliflower is boiling, prepare the dressing. Whisk the ingredients together in a large bowl and gradually add spoonfuls of cold water, mixing until you have a smooth, silky sauce that is runny enough to drizzle.

To make the spiced butter, combine the butter, garlic, lemon juice and spices, either in a food processor or blender, or by hand. Mix in the chopped coriander.

Take the cauliflower out of the water and brush all over with the butter, making sure to get it into every crevice. Reserve a little of the butter for basting later.

If using a barbecue, heat until it is searing hot and place the cauliflower directly on the grill, cooking until the edges start to blacken. Don't worry about 'burning' – that charred taste is what you're aiming for. Turn the cauliflower throughout to ensure that it gets colouration all over, brushing occasionally with the leftover butter.

To serve

1 tablespoon pomegranate molasses

2 tablespoons pomegranate seeds

1½ tablespoons pine nuts, toasted

1 green chilli, finely sliced

1½ tablespoons fresh flat-leaf parsley, finely chopped

1 teaspoon dried rose petals (optional)

If using an oven, preheat to 250°C/230°C Fan/Gas Mark 9, and put a baking sheet or large casserole dish inside to warm up. Place the cauliflower on the sheet and cook for around 8–10 minutes. If you want more colour/char, put it under a hot grill for 5 minutes.

Once the cauliflower is cooked, remove from the heat and transfer to a plate. Spoon over the tahini sauce and pomegranate molasses, and finish the dish by sprinkling the pomegranate seeds, pine nuts, chilli and parsley over the top. Scatter with the rose petals, if you like.

AFTERNOON TEA

AFTERNOON TEA IS A QUINTESSENTIAL LONDON PLEASURE.

THE TRADITION OF TUCKING INTO TEA AND CAKE IN THAT PECKISH PERIOD BETWEEN LUNCH AND DINNER IS SAID TO HAVE BEEN POPULARISED BY LADY ANNA RUSSELL, THE DUCHESS OF BEDFORD, IN THE EARLY NINETEENTH CENTURY. THE HUNGRY DUCHESS' AFTERNOON SOIRÉES BECAME THE TALK OF THE TOWN, AND BEFORE LONG EVERY LONDON SOCIALITE WITH A TEAPOT WAS IMITATING HER.

THERE IS A RICH VARIETY OF POSH HOTELS WHERE YOU CAN ENJOY AFTERNOON TEA, BUT HOSTING YOUR OWN PARTY ALWAYS FEELS MORE IN THE SPIRIT OF LADY ANNA'S CREATION.

LONDON CHEESECAKE

A bit of a mystery, this. Nobody quite knows where it came from and it doesn't remotely resemble a cheesecake. It seems to have popped up in the 1950s and 60s, and is essentially a flaky pastry with a rich, Bakewell-tart-style filling of frangipane and jam. You can skip the desiccated coconut topping if you like, but it does add a certain retro charm.

SERVES 12

50g butter, at room temperature, plus
    extra for greasing
50g caster sugar
50g ground almonds
½ teaspoon almond extract (optional)
1 egg, beaten
2 x 320g pack ready-rolled puff pastry
5–6 tablespoons raspberry jam
150g icing sugar
desiccated coconut,
    to decorate (optional)

Preheat the oven to 200°C/180°C Fan/Gas Mark 6. Lightly grease a large baking tray with butter.

To make your frangipane, put the butter and sugar in a large mixing bowl. Beat with a wooden spoon, or an electric hand whisk, until pale and fluffy. Add the almonds, almond extract (if using), and egg, and beat vigorously for another 30 seconds or so, until combined.

Unroll one pack of pastry on a floured surface and cut into twelve equal squares. Transfer the squares to the baking tray, spaced slightly apart.

Put a blob of jam in the centre of each of the eight squares, then spread up to a teaspoon of frangipane on top, leaving plenty of space around the edges. Don't be tempted to add lots of filling as it will just leak out.

Unroll the remaining pack of pastry and cut into twelve squares again. Pop these squares on top of the jammy squares, and press firmly down at the edges to seal. If the filling does squash out, don't worry – just dab the excess away with kitchen paper.

Bake for 15–20 minutes, until golden. Leave on the tray for a few minutes, then transfer to a wire rack to cool.

Put the icing sugar in a bowl and add 1–2 tablespoons of boiling water, stirring vigorously, to form a thick, smooth paste. When the pastries are cool, spread the icing on top and sprinkle with coconut if using.

WOOD STREET CAKE

This is a wonderful fruit cake. It's lighter than Christmas cake but still stuffed full of warming spices, and topped with an unusual rosewater icing. The name comes from Wood Street, not far from St Paul's Cathedral. In the seventeenth century, the street was famous for its inns and taverns, and it is possible the cake was the signature dish of one of these establishments. Originally, it would have been made with yeast, but it's less dense when made with baking powder, a marvellous invention which revolutionised the way the British made cakes when it arrived in the 1800s.

The cake has a royal connection: it is mentioned in the memoirs of a noblewoman, Lady Halkett, who helped the future King James II escape London during the Civil War. She managed to sneak the prince out of court and put him on a boat to France by dressing him in women's clothes, but not before she purchased for him 'a Wood-street cake, which I knew he loved'. I rather like the image of the pensive young royal, bobbing up and down as he crossed the Channel, a slice of this cake in his hand for comfort.

SERVES 12

225g plain flour
1 teaspoon baking powder
50g ground almonds
225g caster sugar
1 teaspoon ground mixed spice
2 teaspoons ground cinnamon
1 teaspoon ground nutmeg
½ teaspoon ground cloves
½ teaspoon salt
225g butter, at room temperature,
    plus extra for greasing
4 eggs
3 tablespoons milk
200g sultanas
100g currants
200g raisins

For the icing
2 egg whites
450g icing sugar
2 tablespoons rosewater

Preheat the oven to 170°C/150°C Fan/Gas Mark 3. Grease and line a 20cm cake tin with a double layer of baking parchment.

Put the flour, baking powder, ground almonds, sugar, spices, salt, butter, eggs and milk into a large mixing bowl, and use an electric hand whisk to beat for about a minute until you have a smooth mixture. Stir in the fruit, then spoon the mix into the prepared tin.

Bake for 1 hour, then cover the top with foil and cook for another 40–60 minutes, until risen and golden and a skewer inserted into the centre comes out clean. Don't worry if the cake cracks a little – we all do occasionally.

Leave the cake to cool while you make the icing. Put the egg whites into a bowl and lightly whisk by hand or with an electric mixer until they start to foam. Stir in a little of the icing sugar, just a few tablespoons. Beat the mixture, adding the remaining icing sugar very gradually, until you have a thick and glossy icing that stands in soft peaks. Stir in the rosewater, then spread the icing roughly over the cooled cake. Let the icing set before serving.

MAIDS OF HONOUR TARTS

Legend has it that these dainty little tarts were invented at Richmond Palace in South London during the reign of Henry VIII. One day, the greedy king stumbled on his second wife Anne Boleyn and her ladies enjoying a plateful, and decreed that the recipe should be kept under lock and key in an iron box, so that only he could enjoy them.

Fast-forward to the 1850s, when a young Richmond baker called Robert Newens cajoled a court lady to share the coveted recipe with him, and set up a teahouse selling the tarts. The original bakery was sadly bombed to pieces during the Blitz, but the family built a handsome new café which still serves the treats today. The Original Maids of Honour tearoom guards its recipe as closely as Henry, but here is my version.

Best enjoyed in kingly quantities on the sofa, in front of a period drama.

MAKES 12

For the pastry
250g plain flour
125g cold butter, plus extra
    for greasing
80g icing sugar, plus extra for dusting
1 egg
½ teaspoon vanilla extract (optional)

For the filling
100g cream cheese
grated zest of 1 lemon
1 egg, lightly beaten
1 heaped tablespoon ground almonds
50g caster sugar
¼ teaspoon ground nutmeg

To make the pastry, put the flour and butter in a mixing bowl and rub together with your fingertips until you have a mixture that resembles coarse breadcrumbs. Add the icing sugar, egg and vanilla extract, if using, and bring together into a dough. Tip the dough out onto a floured work surface and knead briefly until smooth. Wrap in cling film and refrigerate for at least 30 minutes, or until needed.

Preheat the oven to 200°C/180°C Fan/Gas Mark 6. Lightly grease a 12-hole fairy cake tin.

On a well-floured surface, roll out your dough until it is about 3mm thick; it will be quite sticky. Use a 7cm cutter to cut out twelve rounds and press them into the prepared tin.

For the filling, whisk together the cream cheese, lemon zest, egg, ground almonds, caster sugar and nutmeg until smooth. Fill the pastry cases with the filling mixture, so they are full but not overflowing – a dessertspoon or so each should do it. You may have a little of the filling left over.

Bake for approximately 20–25 minutes, until the tarts have puffed up and are golden and firm. Leave to cool in the tin for 10 minutes before transferring to a wire rack to finish cooling. Don't worry if they sink and crack a little.

Dust with icing sugar before serving.

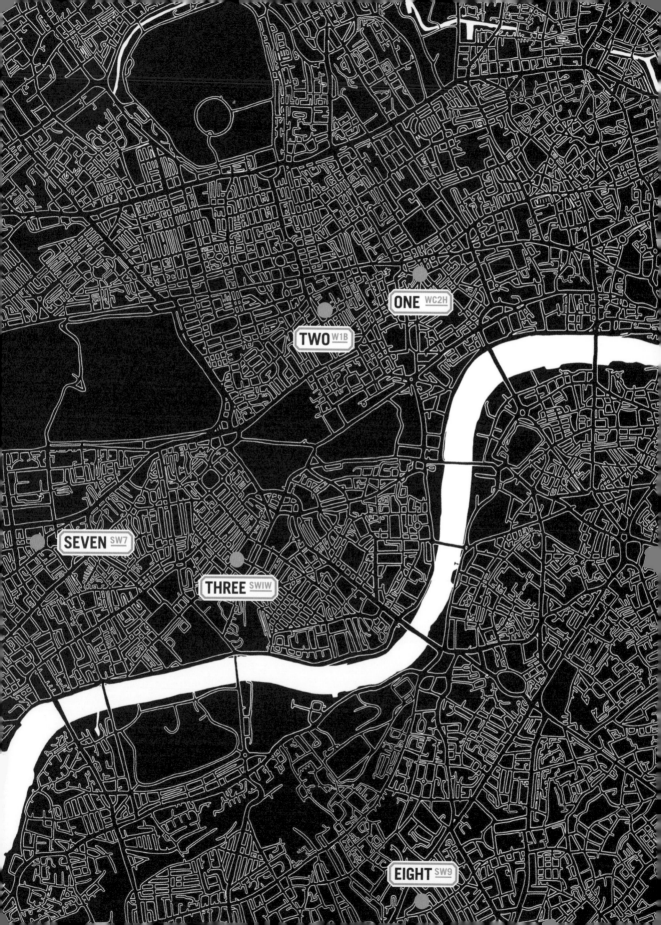

ONE WC2H

TWO W1B

SEVEN SW7

THREE SW1W

EIGHT SW9

1. Bread Ahead

8 Southwark St, SE1 1TL,
plus locations in Covent Garden,
Chelsea and King's Cross
breadahead.com

Sweet-toothed visitors are spoiled for choice at Borough Market, but those in the know head straight to the Bread Ahead stall for the out-of-this-world doughnuts. Baker Justin Gellatly describes his signature treats as 'pillows of joy'; anyone who has bitten into his oozing blackberry with cardamom jam, or salted caramel with honeycomb and vanilla doughnuts would surely like to fall asleep on a pile of them.

2. Crumbs and Doilies

1 Kingly St,
W1B 5PW
crumbsanddoilies.co.uk

You'll get a sugar rush just looking at the menu at this cupcake emporium, tucked away in the foodie mecca that is Soho's Kingly Court. Owned by YouTube baking superstar Cupcake Jemma, it offers around fifty unusual cupcake flavours, from buttered popcorn to cinnamon toast. They even offer delivery.

3. Dominique Ansel

17–21 Elizabeth St
Belgravia,
SW1W 9RP
dominiqueansellondon.com

The first European outpost of Dominque Ansel's celebrated New York bakery. People queue for the famous 'Cronut' – a sinfully delicious mash-up of a croissant and doughnut – but I love the bakes created especially for London. Try 'After the Rain', a quivering jasmine mousse tart topped with mint leaves, inspired by the city's fresh, fragrant atmosphere after a downpour.

4. E5 Bakehouse

Arch 395, Mentmore Terrace,
E8 3PH
e5bakehouse.com

The team at this bakery-cum-café are passionate about proper old-fashioned bread, made with locally milled organic flour and no nasty chemicals. Celebrity chefs are among their many fans: Michel Roux Jr once said that the Hackney Wild loaf (a tangy sourdough) 'turns me on'. You don't get better than that.

5. Fabrique

Arch 385, Geffrye St, E2 8HZ
plus locations in Covent Garden,
Notting Hill and Fitzrovia
fabrique.co.uk

This Scandi-style bakery sells the best cinnamon buns outside Sweden: rich, soft and crunchy with sugar crystals. There are four branches in London, but my favourite is the flagship café under the railway arches at Hoxton. The exposed brick walls and curving tin roof give it a hip industrial feel; I especially like the fact you can see the huge stone ovens used by the bakers at the back.

6. Lily Vanilli

6 The Courtyard
Ezra St,
E2 7RH
lilyvanilli.com

You'll find this bright and airy bakery just a few steps from the hustle and bustle of Columbia Road Flower Market. Owner Lily only opens on Sundays, but has a cult following for her stylish bakes, often using unusual flavour combinations: think fig and strawberry tarts sprinkled with edible flowers, or black sesame and blood orange cake bites. Best visited in summer, when you can wander over with your arms full of fresh flowers and relax in the sunny courtyard.

London's most famous bakery is, of course, the one on Pudding Lane, where the Great Fire of London started in 1666. Thankfully, its modern bakeries are legendary for rather more mouth-watering reasons: buttery cakes, cloud-like meringues, and fat loaves of bread just begging to be slathered in butter and devoured with cheese in a park.

7. Maître Choux

15 Harrington Rd
Kensington, SW7 3ES
maitrechoux.com

The eclairs at this upmarket Kensington patisserie are so slender and beautiful, they look like they should be gracing a catwalk. Master pâtissier Joakim Prat is a dab hand at unusual flavour combinations, too – try the violet and wild berries, which models fetching lilac-coloured icing. A single eclair will set you back a fiver, but they really are works of art.

8. The Old Post Office Bakery

76 Landor Rd,
SW9 9PH
oldpostofficebakery.co.uk

When a German student called Karl Heinz Rossbach arrived in London in the early 1980s, he was depressed he couldn't find anywhere selling the organic wholegrain bread loaves he had grown up with. So he decided to start making his own, using an old bathtub as his mixing bowl. Visit the Clapham shop, or seek out Post Office breads at markets across London.

9. Rinkoff's

222–226 Jubilee St,
E1 3BS
rinkoffbakery.co.uk

An old-fashioned Jewish bakery in the heart of the East End, run by the same family since 1911. It sells traditional challah breads, bagels and pastries, but fifth-generation Rinkoff Jennifer also loves experimenting with playful modern bakes, such as lurid rainbow bagels. Don't go home without a slab of the creamy baked cheesecake.

10. Violet Bakery

47 Wilton Way,
E8 3ED
violetcakes.com

San Francisco-born baker Claire Ptak brought a dose of California cool to East London when she opened her bakery in 2010. Her bakes are driven by seasonal ingredients, often using wholegrain flours and the natural sweetness of seasonal fruit rather than refined sugars. There are few more pleasant ways to spend a lazy Saturday morning than sitting in this cosy bakery with a cup of tea and a prune and spelt scone, watching Claire and her team roll out dough in the open kitchen.

TOTTENHAM CAKE

There is a sweet story surrounding the origin of this old-fashioned traybake. It was created in the 1800s by a Quaker baker called Henry Chalkley in Tottenham, North London, as a cheap treat for local children. The vivid pink icing was traditionally made using mulberries from trees in the Quaker burial ground. I use the rather more easily found (and less creepy) raspberries, plus a splash of food colouring. It is an excellent cake for bake sales or school fêtes; children seem to find the fat pink squares simply irresistible.

SERVES 12

225g butter, at room temperature,
   plus extra for greasing
225g caster sugar
4 eggs, beaten
1 teaspoon vanilla extract
grated zest of ½ orange
300g self-raising flour
2 teaspoons baking powder
3 tablespoons milk

For the topping
120g raspberries
300g icing sugar
few drops of pink food
   colouring (optional)
2 tablespoons desiccated coconut

Preheat the oven to 180°C/160°C Fan/Gas Mark 4. Grease and line a 30 × 20cm rectangular traybake tin with baking parchment.

Using an electric mixer or wooden spoon, cream together the butter and sugar, until light and fluffy.

Slowly mix in the eggs, a little at a time, then stir in the vanilla extract, followed by the orange zest. Fold in the flour and baking powder with a large metal spoon, then stir in the milk so the mix is a little looser (add a splash more milk if it seems very stiff).

Transfer the mixture to the prepared tin and bake in the oven for 30–35 minutes, until golden brown and springy to the touch. Leave to cool in the tin before carefully removing.

For the topping, place the raspberries and 2 tablespoons of water in a small saucepan over a medium heat and cook for about 5 minutes, or until starting to break down and become jam-like. Use the back of a spoon to gently press the raspberries through a sieve into a small bowl – you should get about 5 tablespoons of juice.

Mix the juice with the icing sugar until you have a thick, smooth icing. Add a few drops of food colouring if you'd like it pinker. Spoon over the cake, and smooth over using a palette knife. Scatter with the coconut and slice into squares.

LEMON AND LAVENDER YOGHURT SCONES

Despite its homely appearance, the soft and fluffy scone is the bedrock upon which afternoon tea is constructed. I give mine a sophisticated twist with a smattering of lavender and a bright burst of lemon zest, but you could also keep these plain. Serve warm with jam or honey and reckless quantities of clotted cream.

MAKES 8–10

270g plain flour, plus extra for dusting
2 teaspoons baking powder
¼ teaspoon salt
70g cold butter, cut into small cubes,
    plus extra for greasing
60g caster sugar
100ml natural yoghurt
20ml milk
1 egg, plus 1 extra egg, beaten, to glaze
1½ teaspoons dried lavender
grated zest of 1 lemon

Preheat the oven to 220°C/200°C Fan/Gas Mark 7. Lightly grease a baking tray with butter.

Combine the flour, baking powder and salt in a large bowl. Add the butter and rub in with your fingers, until the mixture resembles breadcrumbs. Stir in the sugar and make a small well in the centre.

In a jug or a small bowl, combine the yoghurt with the milk, 1 egg, lavender and lemon zest. Pour into the well in the dry mix. Use a knife to mix everything together, then quickly use your hands to form a soft dough. It will seem quite wet and sticky, but don't worry. The most important thing is to be gentle; like most Brits, scones hate to be overworked.

Separate the mixture into about 8–10 even-sized balls and place on the prepared baking sheet, flattening them very slightly with the palm of your hand. Brush the tops with the beaten egg, then bake for around 15 minutes, until the scones have risen and are golden brown.

TWININGS:
THE HOME OF TEA

Every morning, a young woman called Martha threads her way up the bustling Strand to her job as a 'tea ambassador' at Twinings Tea Shop. As she pushes open the door, she shouts 'Good day!' to the ancient ghost of Mary Little, who ran Twinings for over two decades in the eighteenth century. 'They say she loved the business so much, she just can't let go,' Martha says cheerfully. 'All the girls who work in the store have a soft spot for her. She is like our mascot.'

It's little wonder Mary wants to keep an eye on the shop, for it is one of the oldest and most fascinating in London. From the outside, it is so tall and skinny, barely wider than its doorway, that you wonder if the two buildings either side of it will one day squash it into dust. Above the door lounges a golden lion and two life-sized statues of moustachioed Chinese men – a nod to the Asian provenance of the very first teas – who calmly survey the traffic carnage below. Slip inside and a long, narrow room is revealed. Paintings of bewigged and frock-coated members of the Twining family adorn

the walls, while wooden shelves crammed with hundreds of types of tea run along almost the entire length of the store. Their names are so romantic that as you browse the shelves, you feel like you are reading a poem or a spell: midnight oolong; jasmine jade butterfly; high-grown nilgiri; rosy fig.

Of the 165 million cups of tea sipped in Britain every day, many of them will be Twinings. The company is the world's second largest producer of tea, selling nearly 200 blends to over 115 countries. But its story began in this tiny building in 1706, when a young man called Thomas Twining rebelled against his family.

The Twinings were weavers, and it had been expected that Thomas would follow in his ancestors' footsteps. Instead, he bought this site on the Strand and opened it as a coffee house. The canny Thomas, however, quickly noticed the rising popularity of an exciting new drink from China. The first ships carrying tea had arrived in London in the 1650s. Charles II's Portuguese wife, Catherine of Braganza, hosted tea parties with her ladies,

ch. Loupot
30

TWINING

Edition "les belles affiches" Création 1930

and the delicate drink quickly became a status symbol for the upper echelons of society – the caviar or foie gras of its day. Just 100g of tea cost £160 in today's money, so to be invited around for tea and gossip was a great honour. The writer and raconteur Samuel Johnson once took wicked pleasure in drinking twenty-five cups of tea at a society lady's house, without contributing a word to the conversation.

Thomas started buying the finest tea leaves he could get his hands on, and before long, lords and ladies, bishops and royalty, were flocking to his temple of tea. Sir Christopher Wren, the architect of St Paul's Cathedral, bought his tea here, as did Jane Austen. By 1717, Thomas' success enabled him to buy three adjacent houses, which he knocked together to create a glamorous tea shop-cum-café (this is why the shop is such a peculiar shape). It is a mark of how good Thomas' tea was that illustrious customers would fall into great debt to get their hands on it. William Wordsworth and his sister Dorothy at one point owed over £4000 for tea, which they regularly ordered great chests of to their Lake District home. The artist William Hogarth had a neat solution when he ended up in similarly hot water. 'The story goes that in exchange for having his slate wiped clean, he agreed to paint a portrait of Thomas. I think we did rather well out of that deal,' says Stephen Twining, the tenth-generation heir to the business, and in whose family's possession the painting now lies.

The story of Britain is steeped in tea. Our foreign policy, our culture, our manners have all been shaped by it. Despite the name, the nineteenth-century Opium Wars with China were largely fought over access to tea; the colonisation of India was intertwined with Britain's need to plant tea there, so we could finally break China's monopoly on the precious leaves. The Twining family has often stirred the teapot of history themselves. In 1784, tea was taxed so heavily, at 119 per cent, that smuggling was rife. It was Thomas' grandson, Richard Twining, who persuaded the prime minister, William Pitt the Younger, to slash the tax to 12.5 per cent and put the smugglers out of business. 'That was the beginning of tea becoming affordable to all. It was Richard, really, who made us a nation of tea drinkers' says Stephen.

The art of blending is at the heart of the business. Twinings does not grow its own tea, for then it would be forced to use even poor-quality leaves, ravaged by storms or drought. Instead, every year, the company's ten or so master blenders scour the world for the best leaves available, and turn them into the perfect cup. It has been this way ever since the 1700s, when Thomas would buy leaves at auction in London and create personal blends for his customers, all written down in his great leather book. Earl Grey tea is said to have been created in the shop when the prime minister, Earl Grey, asked Richard Twining to recreate a citrus-scented tea he had been given by a Chinese diplomat. In 1837, Queen Victoria granted Twinings its first royal warrant (you can see the faded certificate in the little museum at the back of the store), and it has supplied the royal family with their own personal blends ever since. The exact make-up of the Queen's tea is a carefully guarded secret – although at least, unlike some famous customers, she probably pays her bill.

216 Strand, London, WC2R 1AP

IT IS A MARK OF HOW GOOD TWININGS TEA WAS THAT ILLUSTRIOUS CUSTOMERS WOULD FALL INTO GREAT DEBT TO GET THEIR HANDS ON IT

GIN AND LEMON DRIZZLE CAKE

Gin is the spirit of London, here captured in cake form. Juniper berries are the key botanical used to make Mother's Ruin. Crush a few in your hand and sniff; they smell just like the spirit.

SERVES 8–10

200g butter, at room temperature,
    plus extra for greasing
200g caster sugar
4 large eggs
200g self-raising flour
½ teaspoon baking powder
grated zest of 2 lemons
1 teaspoon juniper berries
    (about 10), crushed
pinch of salt
2–3 tablespoons gin

For the drizzle
50ml gin
juice of 2 lemons
125g demerara or caster sugar

Preheat the oven to 180°C/160°C Fan/Gas Mark 4. Grease a 900g loaf tin with butter and line with baking parchment.

Beat together the butter and sugar using an electric mixer, until pale and fluffy, then stir in the eggs, one a time.

Sift in the flour and baking powder, add the lemon zest, juniper berries and salt. Mix with a large metal spoon until well combined. Add just enough gin to make the mixture a dropping consistency – about 2 tablespoons should do it.

Spoon the mixture into your prepared loaf tin, and bake in the oven for about 45–50 minutes, until lightly golden and a skewer inserted into the centre of the cake comes out clean.

For the drizzle, quickly mix together the gin, lemon juice and sugar in a bowl until you have a thick syrup. Use a skewer or cocktail stick to make lots of little holes in the top of the cake, and spoon the syrup over, waiting a few seconds for the cake to absorb each spoonful before adding more. It will seem as though you have a lot of liquid, but the thirsty cake will drink it all in. Leave to cool in the tin before turning out.

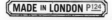

DARK AND STICKY GINGERBREAD

Will Your Worship buy any gingerbread, very good bread, comfortable bread?
Bartholomew Fair by Ben Jonson (1614)

Bartholomew Fair was a vast, rowdy carnival, which took place in London from medieval times right up to 1855, when the authorities closed it down. Thousands of people flocked to eat, drink and be merry while watching such peculiar entertainments as an elephant that could uncork bottles with its trunk, a blindfolded pig that told the time, and – according to one astonished observer – 'lively little crocodiles hatched from eggs by steam'.

The fair was particularly famous for its gingerbread, which was sold by dedicated gingerbread bakers such as 'Tiddy Doll', an eccentric fellow who wandered around in an elaborate ostrich feather hat crying, 'Here is your nice gingerbread, your spice gingerbread! It will melt in your mouth like a red-hot brick-bat!'

In the early days of the fair, gingerbread took the form of chewy biscuits, often moulded into nifty shapes and decorated with gilt. Over time, it evolved to become the wet sticky kiss of a cake we know and love today.

SERVES 9

300g plain flour
2 teaspoons bicarbonate of soda
1 heaped tablespoon ground ginger
1 teaspoon ground cinnamon
½ teaspoon ground cloves
225g butter, plus extra for greasing
140g soft dark brown sugar
160g black treacle
160g golden syrup
2 large eggs, beaten
150ml milk
4 pieces stem ginger from a jar (about 80g), drained and finely chopped

Preheat the oven to 170°C/150°C Fan/Gas Mark 3. Grease a 20cm square tin with butter and line with baking parchment.

In a large bowl, combine the flour, bicarbonate of soda and all the spices.

Melt the butter, sugar, treacle and golden syrup together in a saucepan over a low heat, then pour over the dry ingredients and mix to combine. Stir in the eggs and milk; it will be quite a runny mixture. Gently stir through the stem ginger, then pour into your prepared tin.

Bake for 45–55 minutes, until a skewer or cocktail stick inserted into the centre of the cake comes out clean. Leave to cool in the tin before cutting into squares.

BLOOMSBURY SEED CAKE

With its museums, grand houses and leafy squares, Bloomsbury has long been a magnet for the bookish upper classes. Between 1900 and 1930, it was the stomping ground of the Bloomsbury Set, a loose group of artists and intellectuals who were as famous for their torrid romantic affairs as their art.

The Bloomsbury set loved to eat, seeing long dinner parties and lazy afternoon teas as the perfect opportunity for debate, gossip … and a little flirtation. They actually couldn't cook for toffee themselves (Virginia Woolf once baked her wedding ring into a suet pudding), so were dependent on servants. Grace Higgens was the cook and housekeeper of Woolf's sister, Vanessa Bell. She arrived at Vanessa's London home in 1920 when she was just sixteen, and at first failed to impress with her culinary skills – Vanessa exasperatedly described her as 'very lovely and quite incompetent'. But Grace learnt quickly, and ended up staying with the Bell family for over fifty years, dividing her time between London and their country home, Charleston, in East Sussex.

Virginia had a difficult relationship with food, becoming as thin as a bird when suffering from bouts of the mental illness that plagued her throughout her life, but she had a soft spot for Grace's baking. She once wrote the cook a letter asking for a recipe, because 'I can't get any cakes made except yours that I like to eat'. This old-fashioned seed cake is loosely adapted from one of Grace's recipes. People tend to love or hate the earthy aniseed flavour of caraway seeds, so if you're not keen, replace them with poppyseeds.

SERVES 8–10

180g butter, at room temperature, plus extra for greasing
180g caster sugar
3 eggs
grated zest of 1 lemon
60g mixed peel, roughly chopped
2 scant teaspoons caraway seeds
180g self-raising flour
70g ground almonds
½ teaspoon baking powder
2–3 tablespoons brandy, rum or milk

Preheat the oven to 170°C/150°C Fan/Gas Mark 3. Grease a 900g loaf tin with a little butter and line with baking parchment.

Using an electric mixer or wooden spoon, cream the butter and sugar together until light and fluffy, then beat in the eggs, one at a time. If the mixture looks like it is curdling, stir in a tablespoon of the flour.

Stir in the lemon zest, mixed peel and caraway seeds. Sift in the flour, ground almonds and baking powder, then mix with a large metal spoon until combined. Stir in the brandy, rum or milk.

Spoon the mixture into your prepared loaf tin and bake in the oven for about 1 hour, until a skewer or cocktail stick inserted into the centre of the cake comes out clean. Make sure your wedding ring isn't baked inside.

WIMBLEDON STRAWBERRY AND CREAM CAKE

It's estimated that some 2,000kg of strawberries, along with 7,000 litres of fresh cream, are devoured every day of the Wimbledon championships in July. If you're not lucky enough to nab tickets to the tennis, this cake should cheer you up. The yoghurt makes the sponge beautifully soft and moist.

SERVES 12

200g butter, at room temperature, plus extra for greasing
300g caster sugar
pinch of salt
5 eggs, lightly beaten
150ml natural yoghurt
1 teaspoon vanilla essence
350g self-raising flour
½ teaspoon baking powder
1–3 tablespoons whole milk

For the filling
300ml double cream
2 tablespoons caster sugar
6 tablespoons strawberry jam
400g strawberries, hulled and sliced in half

Preheat the oven to 180°C/160°C Fan/Gas Mark 4. Grease two 20cm sandwich tins with butter and line with baking parchment.

Using an electric mixer or wooden spoon, cream the butter, sugar and salt together until pale and fluffy.

Add the eggs and gradually beat into the mixture. Stir in the yoghurt and vanilla essence, then sift in the flour and baking powder, and mix with a metal spoon. Add enough milk until you have a 'dropping' consistency – that is, when a spoonful of the batter just slides off the spoon.

Divide the mixture between the two tins and cook for 30–35 minutes, until golden and springy on top and a skewer or cocktail stick inserted into the centre comes out clean. Leave to cool.

To make the filling, put the cream and sugar into a large bowl and whip until you have soft peaks. Spread the jam over the bottom of one of the cooled cake halves, followed by about half the cream. Add a layer of the sliced strawberries, then sandwich the second sponge on top. Spread the remaining cream on top of the cake, then decorate with the remaining strawberries in whatever style you like – I like them tumbled untidily on top, rather than in a neat pattern.

BOURBON BISCUITS

In the 1960 and 70s, my grandfather worked at the Peek Freans biscuit factory in Bermondsey, South London. Taking broken or burnt biscuits home was a perk of the job; my father and his siblings have fond memories of Grandpa Jock walking through the front door with boxes of rejected treats for them to devour.

Built in 1866, Peek Freans was the first mass manufacturer of biscuits in Britain. The air surrounding the factory was thick with the smell of sugar and butter, and Bermondsey was popularly known as 'Biscuit Town'. Many iconic British biscuits, such as the Bourbon and Garibaldi, were invented at the factory, before it closed its doors forever in 1989.

This recipe for homemade bourbons is my tribute to Grandpa Jock. With their grown-up dark chocolate filling, they are so much better than Bourbons from a packet, and will make your house smell as mouthwatering as that sugary Biscuit Town air, all those years ago.

MAKES ABOUT 20

For the biscuits

200g butter, at room temperature
80g caster sugar, plus extra for
   scattering (optional)
20g soft dark brown sugar
2 eggs, lightly beaten
300g plain flour
100g cocoa powder
1 teaspoon baking powder

For the filling

50g dark chocolate
100g butter
150g icing sugar
50g soft dark brown sugar
1 teaspoon milk
20g cocoa powder

For the biscuits, cream the butter and sugars together in a large bowl with a wooden spoon until soft and fluffy. (Alternatively, use an electric mixer.)

Mix in the eggs, then sift in the flour, cocoa and baking powders, and stir to combine until the mixture comes together into a smooth dough (it's easiest to use your hands eventually). If the dough feels a little sticky, add more flour, but try not to add too much or the dough will become tough. Wrap the ball of dough in cling film and refrigerate for at least 30 minutes.

Preheat the oven to 180°C/160°C Fan/Gas Mark 4. Line two large baking trays with baking parchment.

Roll the dough out on a lightly floured surface, until you have a rectangle about 60 × 40cm and the thickness of a pound coin. Trim away any rough edges, then use a sharp knife to cut the dough into small rectangles. You can make your bourbons as big or small as you like, but I usually aim to make each one about 7cm long and 3cm wide. You could also use a circular cutter. You should end up with about 40 biscuits.

Transfer the biscuits onto the trays, leaving a small gap between each one. Use a fork or a cocktail stick to make little dots along the length of the biscuits, in the classic Bourbon pattern, and pop in the fridge for about 15 minutes to allow the dough firm up.

Put the trays in the oven and cook for about 8–12 minutes, until the biscuits are just firm to the touch. Scatter over a few teaspoons of caster sugar, if you like, and leave to cool on the trays.

To make the filling, melt the chocolate in a heatproof bowl set over a pan of just-simmering water, then remove the bowl from the pan and leave to cool slightly.

Beat the butter in a large bowl with a wooden spoon until soft, then gradually sift in the icing and brown sugars, beating until you have a fluffy consistency (add a teaspoon of milk to bring the mix together if necessary). Sift in the cocoa powder, pour in the melted chocolate, and stir to combine.

Sandwich the cooled biscuits together with the chocolate filling. Enjoy with a cup of tea.

MASON:
THE QUEEN

...n the front of Fortnum ...es something special. ...wooden figures ...th-century clothes emerge. They ...ssrs Fortnum and Mason, the founders of the company. One holds a tea tray, the other a candelabra. The two men face each other, bow graciously, then return to rest in the darkness. It is a ritual that strikes at the heart of what Fortnum & Mason is all about: elegance, dependability, and above all, Britishness.

I have probably lost days of my life in Fortnum & Mason. Its beguiling turquoise-and-gold façade never fails to lure me in, especially at Christmas, when the gleaming windows are transformed into a magical display of treats. Inside, you will find ornate tea tins and jars of jewel-coloured jam; candied fruits and musical biscuit tins that trill when opened. Everything is stupidly expensive, but you can't help but buy, because this is not just a shop, it's an institution, a place that has fed kings and queens, explorers and soldiers, prime ministers and artists. My father took my mother here on one of their first dates, not to buy anything, but simply because that hushed, lush atmosphere of indulgence is such an experience, and something everyone should soak up at least once.

The story of Fortnum & Mason is wedded to the story of Britain. It was founded in 1707, the very same year that Scotland and England joined together to become the United Kingdom. William Fortnum was a footman at the court of Queen Anne, and one of his responsibilities was to empty the candlesticks at the end of every day. He took the half-burnt ends home, melted them down and turned them into fresh candles to sell to the ladies of the court. He persuaded his landlord, Hugh Mason, to go into business with him, and thus the shop was born.

Although today Fortnum's is a store cupboard of sturdy British victuals – biscuits to dunk in your tea and marmalade to slather on toast – it began as an emporium of more exotic treats, raided from all corners of the ever-expanding British empire. There were spices from India, cocoa beans from the Americas, plus truffles and bonbons from Italy and France. And of course there was tea, an exciting new drink from China that nimble new ships known as 'tea clippers' raced around the world to deliver, trying to keep up with demand.

New and exciting foods were one strand of Fortnum & Mason's appeal to the upper classes; the other was convenience. Long before the development of microwaves and frozen pizzas, Fortnum's realised that people would pay through their snooty aristocratic noses for pre-prepared food. The Scotch egg is said to have been invented by the store as a portable snack for lords and ladies travelling to their country estates. Most famously, Fortnum's developed its wicker hampers, embossed with the F&M logo, which still sell in the hundreds of thousands today. An 1849 catalogue showcases a vast range of luxury treats for hampers – mangoes, truffles, veal ragout, lobster and wild duck – none of which required any cutting or cooking. These gourmet hampers became a staple at posh British summer sporting events, such as the Henley Regatta or the Epsom Derby. Charles Dickens wrote amusedly of one Derby: 'Look where I will... I see Fortnum & Mason. All the hampers fly wide open and the green downs burst into a blossom of lobster salad!'

The Royal family has famously patronised Fortnum's

THIS IS NOT JUST A SHOP, IT'S AN INSTITUTION, A PLACE THAT HAS FED KINGS AND QUEENS, EXPLORERS AND SOLDIERS, PRIME MINISTERS AND ARTISTS.

The exterior of the ever-elegant Fortnum & Mason . Part of a series of images taken to celebrate Fortnum's 250th birthday. (Brian Seed/Getty Images)

since the shop was founded, but the grocer's also made brisk business from bureaucrats and soldiers in foreign fields. These far-away Brits craved a taste of home, and boxes stuffed with hams and fruit cake flew out all over the world, to the damp rainforests of Borneo or the muddy trenches of France. In the Crimean War, Queen Victoria sent the store a sharply worded order 'to dispatch without delay' a supply of concentrated beef tea to Florence Nightingale's hospital in Turkey. Using good food to nurse the sick to better health was a forte of Fortnum's: at one point, the Piccadilly shop had an entire section dedicated to invalids, where worried relatives could buy calves' foot jelly and energy-boosting sweets.

When you walk into Fortnum's today, it seems quaint and old-fashioned. But the store has always been an innovator. In the mid-eighteenth century, Fortnum's launched a fetching rose-coloured honey that was so unique, huge crowds of people gathered to gawp at the jars in the window. In the 1920s and 30s, there was a service where people could send in a sample of their tap water, and Fortnum's tea masters would concoct the perfect blend for that particular strain of H_2O. Not every invention was a hit, however. 'In the nineteenth century we sold meat lozenges, a bit like fruit pastilles,' Dr Andrea Tanner, the store's historian, says. 'We recommended them for people going on long journeys or working long shifts: in particular, if you were a Member of Parliament and had an all-night sitting.' Somehow, the idea didn't catch on; a food so functional and prosaic clearly had no appeal to Fortnum's gourmand customers.

What did catch on was afternoon tea. The store's tea salon is one of the most popular places in London to enjoy the British tradition of scones, cakes and dainty crustless sandwiches, escorted to the table by steaming pots of tea. The joy of afternoon tea is that it is a meal that cannot be rushed, a precious thing in the hectic modern world. Sometimes, when I am feeling stressed, I go to Fortnum's with a friend, and the outside world falls away for a few hours while we sate ourselves with sugar and gossip. It is a ritual which freezes the clock.

181 Piccadilly, St James's, London, W1A 1ER

LON-DINNER

FISH AND CHIPS, PIE AND MASH, RICH STEWS WITH FLUFFY DUMPLINGS...

LONDON'S TRADITIONAL FARE IS THE DEFINITION OF COMFORT FOOD. BUT AS THE CITY HAS BECOME GLOBALISED, WE HAVE ADOPTED NEW DISHES AND INGREDIENTS: BLISTERINGLY HOT CHILLIES, FRAGRANT LEMONGRASS AND EXOTICALLY NAMED GRAINS NOW TUMBLE EXCITEDLY THROUGH RESTAURANT MENUS. DIFFERENT CUISINES MEET AND MINGLE HERE, IN THE HANDS OF BRILLIANT CHEFS.

A CITY THAT USED TO BE MOCKED FOR ITS UNIMAGINATIVE CUISINE HAS BECOME ONE OF THE WORLD'S FOREMOST DINING DESTINATIONS. AND WE STILL DO REALLY GOOD FISH AND CHIPS.

UFFED
S

At first glance, New Malden looks like any other genteel English suburb: terraced houses, tennis courts, churches and supermarkets. But this quiet patch of South-west London is actually home to the biggest population of ex-pat Koreans in the whole of Europe. Peer a little closer and you'll spot Korean restaurants, a Korean karaoke bar and Korean shops selling the area's very own Korean newspaper.

Quite how sleepy New Malden attracted a community of 20,000 Koreans is a mystery, though the fact that both the South Korean ambassador and Korean electronics firm Samsung were once based here probably had something to do with it. But what is clear is that 'Little Korea' opened Londoners' eyes (and mouths) to the wonder of Korean food. The below recipe is not authentic, but it's a great way to use all those spicy, salty Korean flavours in an easy week-night dinner. Gojuchang is a fermented chilli paste and a staple in Korean food; you can pick it up in Asian grocery stores and in some supermarkets.

SERVES 4

4 medium aubergines
2 tablespoons vegetable or sunflower oil
2 tablespoons sesame oil
6 spring onions, white and green parts, finely chopped
1 red pepper, finely chopped
4 garlic cloves, finely chopped
thumb-sized knob of fresh ginger, grated
1 teaspoon chilli flakes
500g lamb mince
4 tablespoons gojuchang
3 tablespoons soy sauce
1 tablespoon rice wine vinegar
2 teaspoons honey
2 teaspoons tomato purée
handful of coriander, roughly chopped, to serve (optional)
salt and freshly ground black pepper

Preheat the oven to 200°C/180°C Fan/Gas Mark 6.

Cut the aubergines in half lengthways, leaving the tops on, and score the surface of the flesh with a knife. Put into a roasting tray, skin side down. Drizzle over the vegetable or sunflower oil and season with salt and pepper. Cook for 30–35 minutes, until golden and soft. Leave to cool slightly.

While the aubergines are cooking, heat the sesame oil in a large frying pan, and fry the spring onions and red pepper for about 5 minutes, until soft. Add the garlic, ginger and chilli flakes and cook for 30 seconds, then add the lamb mince. Cook, stirring frequently, for 5 minutes, until the meat starts to brown. Stir in the gojuchang, soy sauce, vinegar, honey and tomato purée, and cook for a further 5–10 minutes, until the lamb is cooked through and the liquid mostly absorbed.

Scoop out the flesh of the aubergines, leaving a border about 1cm thick, and roughly chop. Stir into the lamb mixture. Season with salt and pepper, then spoon the mix into the aubergine shells and bake for 10 minutes.

Serve with a sprinkling of coriander leaves, if using.

CACIO E PEPE

If you're visiting Borough Market, you can't miss Padella: it's the tiny pasta restaurant with the long queue of people snaking like a wiggly strand of spaghetti out the door. It really is worth the wait. For just six or seven pounds, you can tuck into a perfect plate of handmade ravioli or pappardelle, while the chefs roll and twirl fresh pasta dough before your eyes.

The signature dish at Padella – and the one that everyone raves about – is the cacio e pepe. Literally translated as 'cheese and pepper', it is one of the simplest and tastiest things you will ever eat. The fat strands of pasta are skimpily clad in a creamy sauce made from pungent cheese and a blizzard of black pepper, magically emulsified by just a splash of cooking water. This is an ideal quick supper when the cupboards are bare.

SERVES 4

400g spaghetti or other long pasta
1 tablespoon butter
2 teaspoons black peppercorns, crushed
200g hard Italian cheese, plus extra to serve (I like a mix of Parmesan and Pecorino Romano)

Cook your pasta according to the packet instructions, until al dente. Drain, but keep back about 300ml of the cooking water, and let it cool slightly.

Melt the butter in a large frying pan and add the crushed peppercorns. Cook for a minute, stirring, until the peppercorns start to smell fragrant.

Add about 200ml of the reserved pasta water and mix thoroughly with the butter and pepper. Take off the heat. Add the spaghetti and the cheese and toss furiously with tongs or two spoons, until you have a silky-smooth, creamy sauce (add a little more water if you need to). Divide between serving bowls and scatter over the extra cheese.

LINA STORES:
LONDON'S FAVOURITE ITALIAN DELI

London is an amorphous city; like the river that flows through its heart, it is rarely still. Buildings spring up and are pulled down; restaurants open to great fanfare one week and are shuttered up the next. But one tiny shop has lasted, quietly and proudly, for three-quarters of a century.

Lina Stores is an iconic Italian delicatessen in Soho. Few passers-by can resist the lure of its pretty tiled exterior and peppermint-striped awnings. Inside, a cornucopia of Italian goods awaits them: there are fat bags of pasta in every shape under the Tuscan sun; a counter heaving with cured meats, from wine-red bresaola to soft, spicy 'nduja; dried bunches of oregano all the way from Sicily; oozing orbs of mozzarella. At the tiny marble counter in the window, visitors sip espresso, close their eyes to the rain outside and pretend they're under the beating sun of Puglia or Sicily.

The store was founded in the 1940s by an Italian woman known only as Lina. 'We don't know very much about her,' the shop's manager Marina Dentamaro tells me, 'but she was exceptionally passionate about food. We still use many of her suppliers, because the quality is just that good.'

In the 1940s, Soho was like New York's Little Italy. Many Italian families lived and worked there, and it was full of Italian cafés and delis. Today, the area has changed hugely, and Lina is the oldest surviving deli of its kind. When founder Lina decided to return to Italy, she sold the shop to a couple called Giovanni and Rosa Filippi, who eventually passed it on to their daughter Gabriella. The store is still owned by the same family, with Gabriella's son-in-law Massimo at the helm. 'All around us there are chains, from coffee bars to Mexican restaurants,' says Marina, nodding at the door that leads into Brewer Street. 'But we are still independent, and of that we are very proud.'

The shop has endured because of the quality of its products. The floor is often covered with cardboard boxes, but it's hard to object when they are crammed with goodies imported from all over Italy. Meat comes from Vernasca in northern Italy, where the Filippi family are from. A supplier in Sicily produces olives and antipasti solely for the shop. A small quantity of truffles come in just once or twice a year, 'because we only want the really good ones'. Particularly popular are Lina's sunshine-yellow fresh pastas, filled with everything from pumpkin to veal. They are made every day in the ramshackle kitchen below the shop floor, to an old family recipe.

There has been change over the years, of course. The shop used to be full of homesick Italians, craving the flavours of home; today, most customers are English. Trends shift, too. Customers used to pop in for risotto rice and prosciutto, but at the moment they're asking for guanciale, a rich cured meat made from pig cheeks. 'As soon as Nigella Lawson or another famous chef uses an Italian ingredient on television, people will start asking us for it,' says Marina with a grin.

Nigella is one of many famous faces known to frequent the shop, though the staff are almost tiresomely discreet about their celebrity fans, however much you nudge them in the hope of salacious gossip about pasta fetishes. 'We treat them just like any normal person, chatting about the ingredients and how to cook them. That's the kind of service that makes people like us. That's why they come back.'

18 Brewer Street, Soho, London, W1F 0SH

INSIDE, A CORNUCOPIA OF ITALIAN GOODS AWAITS...

Soho's Lina Stores, the much-loved Italian delicatessen. (Sam Mellish/-Getty Images)

MACARONI CHEESE WITH ROASTED MUSHROOMS AND GARLIC-THYME CRUMBS

Tucked under the railway arches in Bermondsey, you'll find not one but two brilliant street food markets. Maltby Street is the more famous: a narrow alley strung with colourful bunting and packed with traders offering everything from Sri Lankan pancakes to cocktails made with local gin. A short walk away is Druid Street, where you'll find the brilliant street food stall Return of the Mac. It specialises in indulgent, British-inspired twists on the cheesy pasta dish. This herby, mushroom-studded recipe is inspired by a particularly fine pot I once inhaled there. Three cheeses might sound excessive, but they provide the perfect combination of flavour and melting gooiness.

SERVES 4–6, DEPENDING ON HOW MUCH CHEESE YOU CAN HANDLE

250g mixed mushrooms, preferably wild, quartered
2 tablespoons olive oil
1 tablespoon finely chopped fresh thyme leaves
350g macaroni pasta
50g butter
50g plain flour
½ teaspoon English mustard powder
600ml milk
100g mature Cheddar cheese
100g Gruyère cheese
50g Parmesan cheese
salt and freshly ground black pepper

For the garlic-thyme crumbs
1 tablespoon olive oil
1 tablespoon butter
1 garlic clove, finely chopped
2 sprigs of fresh thyme, leaves picked and finely chopped
50g fresh breadcrumbs

Preheat the oven to 220°C/200°C Fan/Gas Mark 7. Toss the mushrooms with the oil and the thyme leaves, plus a good grinding of salt and pepper. Transfer to a baking tray and roast, tossing once, for about 20 minutes, until golden brown. Leave to one side.

While the mushrooms are roasting, cook the macaroni in a pan of salted boiling water until tender, then drain. This is also a good time to make the garlic-thyme crumbs. Heat the oil and butter in a saucepan over a medium heat, then add the garlic, thyme and breadcrumbs. Cook until crispy, then put to one side.

To make the white sauce, melt the butter in a large pan. Cook for a minute, then add the flour and mustard powder, and cook for a further minute, stirring constantly. Slowly whisk in the milk until the sauce is smooth and lump-free. Bring to the boil, then reduce the heat and simmer until the consistency of thick custard, about 5–10 minutes. Mix in all the cheese, then take off the heat and wait for the cheese to melt, stirring occasionally to help it along.

Add the drained pasta and the roasted mushrooms to the pan, and mix in. Season with salt and pepper to taste. Divide between serving bowls and sprinkle over the garlic-thyme crumbs.

BILLINGSGATE FISH STEW

Every so often, my friends and I get [up?] Saturday to go to Billingsgate, London['s fish?] market. We are horribly grumpy when we [enter?] the doors at 5am, but soon cheer up once all the glistening fresh fish is laid out before us.

Billingsgate was once the biggest fish market [in the?] world, though it was more famous for the foul-mouth[ed?] women who worked there. The 'fishwives' smoked, dra[nk?] and frequently got into fights, much to the amusement of spectators. An 1830 cartoon called 'Billingsgate: Tom and Bob taking a Survey after a Night's Spree' shows two young gentlemen gawping as bare-breasted fishwives grapple furiously in the street.

The fishwives of Billingsgate are sadly no more, but the bustling market is still one of London's most unique experiences. This stew is my go-to recipe when I've come back with a good Billingsgate catch. It's very forgiving: if you don't have mussels or prawns, throw in whatever you fancy.

SERVES 4

2 tablespoons olive oil
1 onion, finely chopped
2 garlic cloves, finely chopped
200ml white wine
400ml fish stock
400g can chopped tomatoes
2 tablespoons tomato purée
2 tablespoons chopped fresh rosemary
pinch of sugar
pinch of chilli flakes
2 white fish fillets, such as cod or hake
    (about 150g each), skin removed
200g raw tiger prawns
300g mussels, cleaned and de-bearded
200ml double cream
juice of ½ lemon
salt and freshly ground black pepper

Heat the oil in your largest saucepan or casserole dish over a medium–high heat. Add the onion and cook until softened and starting to turn golden, about 7 minutes.

Add the garlic plus a generous grinding of salt and pepper, and fry for a further minute or two. Pour in the white wine. Bring to the boil, then add the stock, tomatoes, tomato purée, rosemary, sugar and chilli flakes. Turn down the heat and simmer for about 10 minutes or so, so the flavours can get to know each other as well as wrestling fishwives.

Add the fish fillets to the pan, making sure they are immersed in the liquid. Cover and cook for about 6 minutes. Stir in the prawns, then add the mussels on top. Cover and cook for another 5 minutes or so, until the mussel shells have popped open and the prawns have turned pink.

Take the pan off the heat and remove the mussels with a slotted spoon. Break the white fish into chunks with the back of a spoon, if it hasn't already fallen apart. Stir in the cream and lemon juice. Divide the stew between serving bowls and top with the mussels. Lovely with a big wedge of garlic bread.

LON-DINNER P142

ED FISH

There are more fish and chip shops in London than there are red telephone boxes, but the classic fast-food is not as hard to knock up at home as you might think. Starting the chips in a pan of cold oil is a trick I learned from the domestic goddess herself, Nigella Lawson. It sounds mad but you end up with chip nirvana: fluffy on the inside and crisp on the outside. For the true British experience, serve your fish and chips under a thick blanket of vinegar and salt, with (slightly cold) mushy peas.

For the chips

600g floury potatoes, preferably Maris Piper, peeled and chopped into roughly 1cm wide chips

vegetable or sunflower oil, for frying (you will need about 1 litre)

For the fish

75g plain flour, plus 2 tablespoons extra

25g cornflour

1 teaspoon baking powder

½ teaspoon salt

125ml cold beer

2 thick white fish fillets, such as cod or hake (about 150g each)

freshly ground black pepper

First, fry your chips. Put the chopped potatoes in a wide, deep pan over a high heat, and cover with the oil. Bring to the boil, then cook for about 20 minutes, until the chips are golden and crunchy. Make sure you give the pan a gentle stir about 10 minutes in, to loosen any chips that have stuck to the bottom or sides. Ideally, you want the temperature of the oil to stay below 160°C. You can check this with a cook's thermometer, but if you don't have one, just keep an eye on the pan and turn down the heat if the chips are browning too quickly. Remove the chips with a slotted spoon, transfer to an ovenproof dish and pop into a low oven to keep warm. Leave the oil over a medium heat.

Make your batter by combining 75g flour, cornflour, baking powder, salt and a hefty grinding of black pepper in a large bowl. Pour in the beer and whisk to combine until you have a batter the consistency of thick double cream – add a splash more beer or cold water if needed.

Now, turn up the heat under the oil. It needs to be a little hotter for cooking the fish – about 180°C on a cook's thermometer, or when a drop of batter sizzles and crisps up instantly.

Pat any excess moisture from your fish fillets with kitchen paper, then gently roll in the 2 tablespoons of extra flour. Shake off any excess, then dip into the batter so they are completely coated. Carefully lower the fish into the oil and fry for 6–10 minutes, until the fillets are golden and crispy. Scoop out, drain on kitchen paper, then serve with the chips.

FISH AND CHIPS:
A LONDON LOVE STORY

The story of fish and chips begins hundreds of years ago, when Jewish refugees from Europe settled in London. These newcomers brought with them the tradition of frying fish in flour, and by the 1700s fried fish had become a popular fast food. Charles Dickens mentions a 'fried fish warehouse' in his novel *Oliver Twist*, while the future American president Thomas Jefferson described eating 'fried fish in the Jewish fashion' on a visit to the capital.

Many fried fish sellers worked on the streets, carrying the fish in heavy wooden trays on leather straps that bit into their necks. It was a hard life; the stink of frying fish made them unpopular tenants, so they lived in slums. Accidents were common. In 1837, a London newspaper reported 'the frightful death by burning' of one Mrs Rebecca Mendes, a 'Jewess' whose fish pan caught fire. Other sellers plied their trade in pubs, where customers could quickly turn nasty. One fish seller reported mournfully in the 1840s: 'I've had my tray kicked over for a lark in a public house, and a scramble for my fish, and all gone, and no help and no money for me.'

Like all great love stories, it took a while for fish and chips to come together. The practice of frying delicate slivers of potato to make chips probably came via another group of immigrants – the Huguenots from France and Belgium – but quite how fish and chips ended up on the same plate is a mystery. What we do know is that around 1860, a Jewish immigrant called Joseph Malin opened what was probably the first fish and chip shop in the country in London's East End. The 'good companions', as Winston Churchill dubbed them, have been a cornerstone of British life ever since.

For years, eating fish and chips was looked down upon by the upper classes as an unhealthy vice of the lower orders, like gin or dog-fighting. One newspaper even investigated reports that babies in poor families had died from being fed fish and chips instead of a 'proper' diet. But the dish provided quick, cheap nourishment for working families, many of whom had no time to cook after punishing shifts in factories and mines. Slowly, helped by the growth of the rail network and advances in refrigeration techniques – which meant fresh fish could be easily transported around the country – fish and chips battered its way into the hearts of every Englishman. By the time the Second World War erupted, the dish was considered so important for the country's morale that it was one of the few foods not rationed. It even played a small role during the D-Day landing: British soldiers identified each other by calling the word 'Fish'; if an ally heard it, they would cry back, 'Chips!'.

Ironically, the same appetite for foreign foods that made fish and chips such a success has slowly chipped away at its popularity. The rise of pizza, kebabs and curry means there are now around 10,500 fish and chip shops in the UK, down from a high of 35,000 in 1929. Yet the English retain a special affection for the old-fashioned chippy, with its murky jar of pickled eggs behind the counter and the tastebud-tickling tang of vinegar that hangs in the air. In London, there are so many that practically everyone has a different favourite. Michael Jackson favoured the upmarket The Sea Shell in Marylebone, where he once had a mushy pea fight with David Gest. I myself go mushy for Soho's Rock and Sole Plaice, founded in 1871 and the oldest surviving chippy in London. Its fish and chips are great, but I love it mostly because the owners squeezed not one but two fish puns into the name.

LONDON IS A CITY OF IMMIGRANTS, SO IT IS NO SURPRISE THAT OUR MOST FAMOUS DISH SWAM TO US ACROSS THE SEA.

A very British scene: a sign for fish and chips in a traditional London pub window. (Pawel Libera/Getty Images

THE FRIED FISH SHOP.

SHEEKEY'S FISH PIE

J Sheekey is a grande dame of the London restaurant scene. It was founded in the 1890s, when Lord Salisbury gave a trader called Josef Sheekey permission to flog shellfish from a stall in St Martin's Court – just as long as he kept a few treats back for the aristocrat's thespian parties. The restaurant's ties with theatreland have remained as tight as a closed oyster. The wood-panelled walls are smothered with photographs of actors, and famous faces including Keira Knightley and Ewan McGregor have been spotted in the more secluded booths. This fish pie is Sheekey's most iconic dish.

SERVES 4

200g boneless cod fillet (or a white chunky fish such as halibut), skinned and cut into rough 3cm chunks
200g salmon fillet, skinned and cut into rough 3cm chunks
200g smoked haddock fillet, skinned and cut into rough 3cm chunks
½ small bunch of flat-leaf parsley, chopped

For the sauce
50g butter
50g plain flour
125ml white wine
500ml fish stock
90ml double cream
1 tablespoon English mustard
1 teaspoon Worcestershire sauce
juice of ½ lemon
½ teaspoon anchovy extract or 1 anchovy fillet (optional)

For the topping
50g butter
50ml milk
1kg floury potatoes, peeled, boiled and mashed (King Edward work well)
20g fresh white breadcrumbs
10g Parmesan cheese, grated
salt and freshly ground black pepper

To make the sauce, melt the butter in a heavy-bottomed saucepan over a low heat. Gently stir in the flour and cook for a few minutes. Gradually add the wine, stirring well, then slowly pour in the stock until you have a silky smooth sauce. Bring to the boil and simmer gently for up to 10 minutes.

Add the cream and briefly bring to the boil again. Stir in the mustard, Worcestershire sauce, lemon juice and anchovy extract or anchovy (it will slowly melt into the sauce). Season with salt and pepper to taste.

Gently fold the fish and parsley into the hot sauce, and pour into a large pie dish to about 3cm from the top of the dish. Leave to cool slightly.

Preheat the oven to 190°C /170°C Fan/Gas Mark 5.

Make the topping by mixing the butter and milk into the mashed potato and season with salt and pepper. Spread the potato over the pie, and use a fork to make a pattern on top, if you like.

Bake in the oven for 30 minutes. Scatter over the breadcrumbs and Parmesan, and bake for a further 10 minutes until golden.

SHEEPS' FEET AND STRAWBERRIES: LONDON AND ITS MARKETS

London was born as a market. The Romans built the city on the edge of the Thames so the rushing river could transport goods to and from the empire. By medieval times, London was an intricate patchwork of different markets, each with their own speciality. Farringdon was the place for watercress; Spitalfields for potatoes; Queenhithe for grain. The very names of London's tangled streets are epitaphs to long-lost markets: Bread Street, Fish Street Hill, Honey Lane.

London market traders are famously boisterous. The fifteenth-century poem 'London Lickpenny' tells the story of a young man from Kent who visits the capital. Wherever he walks, he is beset by bullish stallholders who shout at him to buy their 'hot sheeps' feet' and 'ripe strawberries'. Wander into a busy East End fruit and veg market today, with the traders bellowing 'Five apples for a pound!' in your face, and you'll probably feel similarly overwhelmed.

Over time, many markets withered away, but a handful have survived. The great meat market of Smithfield in Farringdon has a lengthy history of bloodshed, for it was here that heretics and rebels were traditionally executed in front of jeering crowds. On Tuesdays and Fridays, cattle, sheep and other animals were brought from the countryside to be sold. The noise and the filth were captured by Charles Dickens in *Oliver Twist*:

> Countrymen, butchers, drovers, hawkers, boys, thieves, idlers, and vagabonds of every low grade, were mingled together in a mass; the whistling of drovers, the barking dogs, the bellowing and plunging of the oxen, the bleating of sheep, the grunting and squeaking of pigs, the cries of hawkers, the shouts, oaths, and quarrelling on all sides; the ringing of bells and roar of voices, that issued from every public house; the crowding, pushing, driving, beating, whooping and yelling; the hideous and discordant din that resounded from every corner of the market; and the unwashed, unshaven, squalid, and dirty figures constantly running to and fro.

Smithfield could be as dangerous as it was squalid. On one occasion, a man was 'severely trampled on and gored' by an excitable bull. In the 1860s, the livestock market was closed, and a grand building with a wrought-iron roof was erected for butchers to ply their trade in. This incarnation of Smithfield trots on today, and has witnessed some extraordinary scenes. During the Second World War, the scientist Max Perutz secreted himself away in one of the vast cold stores underneath the market. Here, he experimented on a shatter-proof form of ice, dreaming that Allied air bases might be floated on it in the Atlantic Ocean.

Fish from the Atlantic came ashore at Billingsgate, a tiny open-air market on the river near Lower Thames Street. It was famous for its violent, sharp-tongued female vendors: in a 1736 dictionary, a 'Billingsgate' is defined as a 'scolding, impudent slut'. The market eventually outgrew the space, and since 1982 it has been in a purpose-built warehouse in the Docklands.

For fruit and veg, Londoners turned to Borough Market – the oldest market in the city, dating back to the eleventh century – or Covent Garden. Today Covent Garden is a bland shopping and restaurant complex, the fruit and veg sellers having shipped out in the 1970s to New Covent Garden Market in Vauxhall, but it really did begin life as a garden; the monks of Westminster Abbey grew their vegetables here. In the 1630s, the Earl of Bedford ordered the architect Inigo Jones to redesign

THE VERY NAMES OF LONDON'S TANGLED STREETS ARE EPITAPHS TO LONG-LOST MARKETS: BREAD STREET, FISH STREET HILL, HONEY LANE.

Early morning deliveries at a busy Covent Garden Market in the 1920s. (FPG/Getty Images)

the square as an elegant Italian-style piazza, and forty years later the Earl's avaricious son started to lease the land out to market traders. The square was famous for its spankingly fresh fruit, vegetables and flowers. An eighteenth-century painting by Balthazar Nebot shows pink-cheeked women delighting passers-by with their overflowing baskets.

Much of the produce was brought in from the countryside, but some was grown in London's own gardens: Ealing, then just a tiny village on the outskirts, had some 250 market gardens by 1800. Not everyone was convinced by London-grown goods. 'All [vegetables] that grow in the country about London, cabbage, radishes and spinnage [sic], being impregnated with the smoke of sea-coal, which fills the atmosphere of the town, have a very disagreeable taste,' sniffed a Frenchman in 1772. More exotic items were shipped

in from abroad. 'The supplies of fruit and vegetables sent to this market, in variety, excellence, and quantity, surpass those of all other countries. There is more certainty of purchasing a pineapple here, every day of the year, than in America and Calcutta, where the pines are indigenous,' marvelled John Timbs in 1855.

Today, with supermarkets on every corner, the traditional London market is an endangered species. But there is a flicker of hope in the recent growth of dedicated street food markets, whose succulent burgers and fragrant noodle soups draw office workers out in their droves come lunchtime. Markets like Dinerama in Shoreditch and Kerb in Camden are a world away from the cattle trading of old Smithfield. But in their ability to bring Londoners together, buying and selling and shouting and shuffling, the metropolis' enterprising market spirit lives on.

Fishmongers pose amongst their stalls at the old Billingsgate Market, around 1918. (Guildhall Library and Art Gallery/Getty Images)

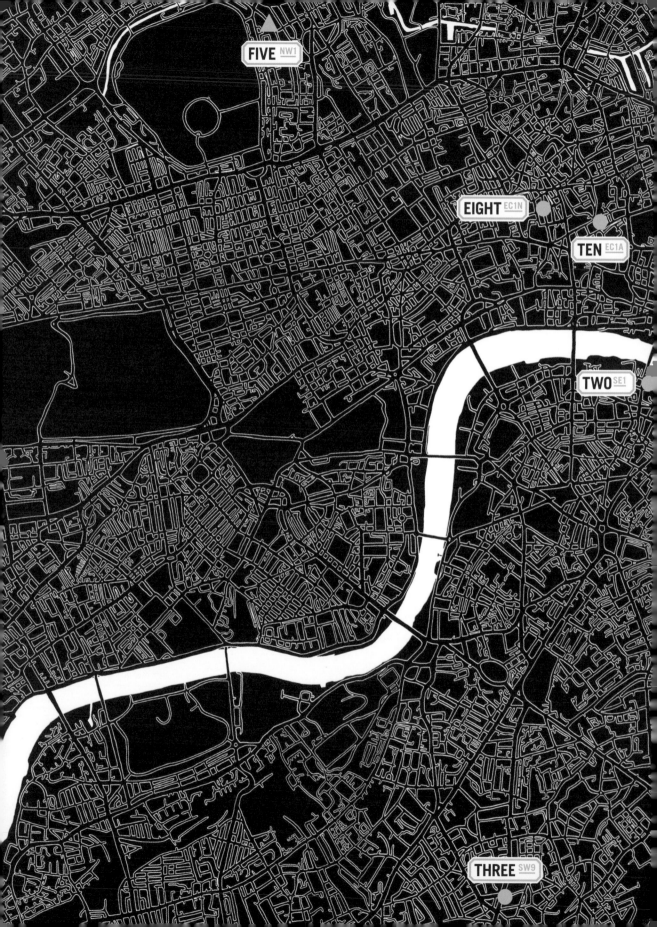

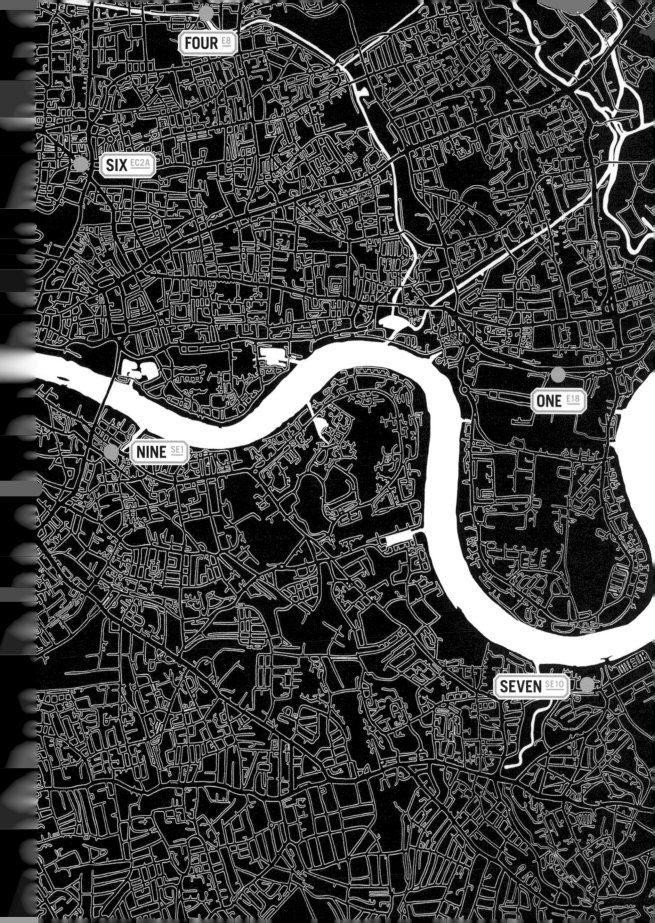

LONDON'S BEST FOOD MARKETS

1. Billingsgate Fish Market

Monday–Saturday, 4–8.30am
Trafalgar Way, Poplar,
E14 5ST
billingsgatefishmarket.org

'It has seen out the Normans and the Plantagenets, the Lancasters and the Yorkists, the Tudors and the Stuarts, the Orangists and the Georges; it has supplied fish to all of them,' wrote George Dodd of Billingsgate Fish Market in 1856. Haggling for the freshest fish starts at 4am, so you'll need to set your alarm clock early, but the experience is unforgettable.

2. Borough Market

Monday–Saturday
8 Southwark St,
SE1 1TL
boroughmarket.org.uk

Underneath the arches of London Bridge station, in the shadow of Southwark Cathedral, is the city's oldest and most famous food market. Historically a fruit and veg market, it is now home to over 100 traders offering everything from freshly baked bread to exotic spices. There is also plenty of street food, if you'd rather stuff your face than stock your cupboards. Best visited on weekdays when it's a little quieter.

3. Brixton Market

Brixton, SW9
brixtonmarket.net.

The buzz at Europe's biggest Afro-Caribbean market is intoxicating. Once you've stocked up on yams and plantains on Electric Avenue, head to Brixton Village and Market Row. This historic collection of covered arcades is crammed full of charming cafés, restaurants and shops; stop off for Chinese dumplings at Mama Lan's, then treat yourself to a bag of bonbons at retro confectioner's Sweet Tooth.

4. Broadway Market

Saturday
Broadway Market,
Hackney, E8 4QJ
broadwaymarket.co.uk

Broadway Market was once a drovers' road, where thousands of animals were driven from the countryside into the city's markets. Today, it is a popular weekend market where street food vendors selling haggis toasties and iced Vietnamese coffee sit side by side with old-fashioned cake stalls and pie and mash shops. A perfect place to wander on a Saturday morning.

5. Camden Market

Camden Lock Pl,
NW1 8AL
camdenmarket.com

It's more famous for bad clothes and tacky jewellery than food, but the edible offerings at this sprawling, raucous market go from strength to strength each year. There's fish and chips, vegan burgers, and even an entire café dedicated to cereal (120 brands and counting). Finish with an ice cream from Chin Chin Labs, a futuristic ice cream parlour where scoops are frozen to order by clouds of liquid nitrogen.

Whether they're flogging fish or dealing with the equally slippery business of stocks and shares, markets have long been at the heart of London life.

6. Dinerama

Thursday–Sunday
19 Great Eastern St,
EC2A 3EJ
streetfeast.com

Set up by restaurateur Jonathan Downey in 2012, Street Feast takes derelict and unused spaces and transforms them into vibrant night markets. Dinerama is the first and best: a former East London truck depot, now two levels of street food stalls and bars. Particularly glorious in summer, when the roof slides away to let the sunshine in, and Londoners let their hair down (and belts out) till the early hours.

7. Greenwich Market

Greenwich Market,
SE10 9HZ
greenwichmarketlondon.com

What it lacks in size, Greenwich Market makes up for in quaintness. Covered on top and cobbled underfoot, it offers a tasty mix of street food and craft stalls. There are some pleasant cafés in the little alleys winding away from it, too.

8. Leather Lane Market

Monday–Friday
Leather Ln,
EC1N 7TJ

There has been a market on this busy street for over four centuries, though you're unlikely to find leather these days. Street food stalls pop up every weekday lunchtime, luring hungry office workers with falafel wraps and freshly baked sourdough doughnuts. You'll also find good-value fruit and veg stalls, and some of London's best coffee shops.

9. Maltby Street Market

Saturday and Sunday
41 Maltby St, Ropewalk,
SE1 3PA
maltby.st

You'll smell Maltby Street Market before you see it; the waft of spices and sizzling meat from the street food vendors who gather here is irresistible. Start the day with a custard doughnut from St John's, then head to The Cheese Truck for an oozing grilled cheese sandwich.

10. Smithfield Market

Monday–Friday, 2–8am
Buyers Walk W Market,
EC1A 9PS
smithfieldmarket.com

The largest meat market in the UK, Smithfield opens its doors at 2am. It is traditional for the local pubs to start serving drinks a few hours later, so Smithfield's porters, or 'bumarees', can enjoy a little liquid refreshment after (or during) their shifts.

DEEP-FRIED SEA BASS WITH THAI SALAD

A cult London dish, from chefs Andy Oliver and Mark Dobbie at the Thai-inspired Som Saa. Even if you've seen it a million times on Instagram or Twitter, nothing will prepare you for how good this is: violent bursts of sweet, hot, sour and salt, calmed only by clouds of fragrant herbs. A gastronomic firework.

SERVES 2–4
AS PART OF A SHARED MEAL

1 tablespoon sticky Thai white rice, for the toasted rice, to garnish
6 dried red chillies, for the roasted chilli powder
vegetable or sunflower oil, for frying (you will need at least 1 litre)
1 whole sea bass (about 500–600g), gutted and scaled, but head, fins and tail left on
3 tablespoons light soy sauce
pinch of caster sugar
2 dried red chillies, crumbled, to garnish

For the salad
2 sticks of lemongrass, finely sliced
4–5 shallots (preferably Thai red), thinly sliced
2 spring onions, thinly sliced
3–4 fresh or frozen kaffir lime leaves, cut into very fine strips
small handful of fresh mint, chopped
small handful of fresh coriander, chopped
small handful of fresh sawtooth coriander or Thai parsley, washed and thinly sliced (optional)

For the dressing
5 tablespoons lime juice (about 3 limes)
1½ tablespoons caster sugar
4 tablespoons fish sauce

To make the toasted rice, put the rice into a dry frying pan or wok and toast over a medium heat until golden, about 5 minutes. Transfer to a mortar and pestle and pound until crushed into a powder. Set aside.

To make the roasted chilli powder, add a splash of vegetable or sunflower oil to the pan, and cook the chillies until dark red and crisp, about 10 minutes. Remove with a slotted spoon and drain on kitchen paper. Crush the chillies in a mortar and pestle to form a fine powder, you should have about 1 tablespoon. Set aside.

Heat the oil in a deep, wide saucepan or wok to 180°C on a thermometer, or until a cube of bread sizzles and turns golden within 60 seconds. Score the sea bass with three or four angled cuts on each side, then roll it in the soy sauce and sugar. Drop the fish, slightly curled if you can (it looks better on the plate), into the oil and fry for about 8–10 minutes, until the skin is crispy and the flesh a deep golden brown.

While the fish is frying, prepare the salad. Combine the lemongrass, shallots, spring onions, lime leaves, mint, coriander and sawtooth coriander, if using, in a mixing bowl.

Now make the dressing. Mix together the lime juice and sugar until the sugar is dissolved, then add the fish sauce, 3 tablespoons of water and your tablespoon of chilli powder. Taste and adjust the seasoning: it should be hot, sour and slightly salty. Set aside.

Once the fish is cooked, carefully remove from the pan and allow to drain and cool on kitchen paper for 1 minute. Place the fish on a large plate or in a wide bowl and pour one-third of the dressing over it. Add the remaining dressing to the salad in the mixing bowl, toss, and serve the salad over the top of the crispy fish.

Garnish with the toasted rice and the two dried chillies, crumbled into fragments.

SOME LIKE IT HOT: THE STORY OF CURRY

In 1810, Britain's first curry restaurant opened in London. Founded by the Indian entrepreneur Sake Dean Mahomed, 'The Hindoostane Coffee House' on George Street was advertised in *The Times* as a place where worldly gentlemen could relax with a hookah pipe and enjoy 'India dishes, in the highest perfection, and allowed by the greatest epicures to be unequalled to any curries ever made in England'.

Fast-forward two centuries and Britain's love affair with Indian food is still burning hotter than your mouth after a particularly feisty vindaloo. Today, there are some 9,000 curry houses within the UK, nearly half of which are in the capital. So integral is Indian food to our culture that in 2001, foreign secretary Robin Cook described chicken tikka masala as Britain's national dish, an example of the way the country 'absorbs and adapts external influences'.

London's curry heartland is Brick Lane, a historic East London street where over fifty curry houses jostle for space with sari shops and Asian grocers, and the smell of spices and freshly cooked naan hangs thick in the air. These no-frill joints offer the full British curry house experience: flocked wallpaper the same violent shade of red as the curries, tinny Indian music, and drunken customers daring each other to try the hottest thing on the menu. The greasy, saucy dishes you'll find here bear almost no resemblance to curries in South Asia – but authenticity and the British curry have never exactly bothered to make friends.

The story of London and Indian food is entangled with the queasy history of empire. The English first gained power in India in the seventeenth century, and the bureaucrats and soldiers who served there developed a taste for the spicy local food – a welcome change, one imagines, from the bland flavours of British food at the time. By the 1800s, London shops like Sorlie's Perfume Warehouse in Piccadilly and Payne's Oriental Warehouse in Regent Street were importing chutneys, spices and pickles, so that old 'India hands' could recreate their favourite curries. One can only imagine the distress of homely British cooks, more used to serving up roast chicken or rice pudding, on being loftily instructed by their masters to prepare a biryani for dinner. They weren't very good at it: instead of fragrant, nuanced spice mixes of turmeric, cumin and coriander, most cooks reached for curry powder, plus, inexplicably, apples and sultanas. In 1845, Edmund White wrote despairingly that British curries were 'nothing more nor less than a bad stew'.

It wasn't until after the Second World War that curry houses became part of the fabric of British life. Throughout the nineteenth century, South Asian sailors or 'lascars' were employed on British boats. Most came from the port city of Sylhet, in what is now Bangladesh. They were given the lowliest jobs, feeding coal into boilers or working the machinery in the airless engine rooms, often until they died of heat and exhaustion. Unsurprisingly, many lascars abandoned ship the second their tired feet set down in London, and by the 1940s there was a thriving Sylheti community in the East End.

After the Second World War, Sylhetis bought bombed-out fish and chip shops or cafés and reopened them, serving curry on the side for their Indian customers. Eventually, the Londoners who staggered in after a heavy session at the pub realised that a spicy bowl of chicken madras was even better than fish and chips for soaking up booze, and the shops gradually transformed into takeaways and curry houses. Though the British invariably talk of 'going for an Indian', more than 80 per cent of the UK's curry houses are run by Bangladeshis – and most of them can trace their heritage back to that one city, Sylhet.

The British-style curries you'll find in Brick Lane

Taj Stores in Brick Lane, 1978. (Michael Fresco/Getty Images)

are curious bastard creatures: saucy, spicy and a world away from the softer, more herb-heavy curries of South Asia. Chefs quickly realised that Brits have very different spice tolerances, so every day they cook up a huge vat of all-purpose 'base sauce', made from onions, carrots, garlic and ginger. With a few quick additions, this sauce is transformed into dishes of varying heat levels. Add yoghurt and almonds and you have the creamy, mild passanda. Throw in extra chilli and a dash of vinegar and you have the fiery vindaloo. These are dishes unrecognisable to most Bangladeshis or Indians. So, too, is the British habit of chugging down at least five pints of lager while eating them. Drinking beer with curry is actually thought to have started in Veeraswamy's restaurant in Regent Street, when Prince Axel of Denmark

turned up with a keg of Carlsberg lager to wash down his duck vindaloo.

Over the past few years, as the British palate has grown more sophisticated, upmarket Indian restaurants have started popping up in London. At The Cinnamon Club in Westminster, you might spot a famous politician as you tuck into seared sea bass fillet on spiced red lentils with coconut ginger sauce. In 2014, the Indian restaurant Gymkhana, where the 'mixed grill of the day' will set you back £42, was named the best restaurant in Britain. But there is still a special place in most Londoners' heart for the traditional curry house – just as there is always room in our bellies for that last onion bhaji.

BRICK LANE CURRY

Brick Lane is a fascinating slice of London history, a microcosm of the ever-shifting patterns of immigration in the city. Successive groups of dispossessed people made their home in this former East London slum, until they were rich enough to move on to more salubrious surroundings. In the 1600s, it was where Huguenots fleeing religious persecution settled; a few centuries later, Jewish and Irish migrants appeared. Finally, in the past 100 or so years, the Bangladeshi community moved in, which is how the street became the curry capital of the UK.

Most Londoners will tell you there is better-quality curry to be had outside the cheap-and-cheerful curry houses of Brick Lane, but a meal here is a rite of passage. You only need edge a toe into the street and you'll be pounced upon by eager restaurateurs, each trying to beat the deals offered by their neighbours ('A curry and a pint for seven pounds! Two pints! Three pints and a samosa!'). I once tried to zip through Brick Lane as a shortcut and ended up with a tikka masala in front of me before I even realised what was happening.

I make no claim for this being a remotely authentic South Asian dish; it is a quintessential British-style curry, spicy and saucy, and designed to be mopped up with a naan bread bigger than your head.

SERVES 4

3 tablespoons ghee or butter
2 small onions, sliced
6 garlic cloves, roughly chopped
thumb-sized knob of fresh ginger, roughly chopped
2 green chillies
1 tablespoon mild or medium chilli powder
2 teaspoons ground cumin
1 teaspoon ground coriander
½ teaspoon ground fenugreek
½ teaspoon turmeric
½ teaspoon ground black pepper
4 vine tomatoes (about 400g), finely chopped
1 tablespoon tomato purée
1 tablespoon honey, plus a little extra to taste (optional)
½ teaspoon salt
800g chicken breast or boneless, skinless thighs, chopped into chunks
150ml chicken stock
60ml crème fraîche or double cream
juice of ½ lemon
1 teaspoon garam masala
handful of fresh coriander, chopped, to serve (optional)

In a large pan over a medium heat, melt the ghee or butter. Cook the onions, stirring frequently, until soft and golden brown, about 15–20 minutes. Add the garlic and ginger and cook for 1 minute, then scrape the whole lot into a blender. Add the chillies and 4 tablespoons of water, and blitz to make a thick purée.

Add the ground spices to the pan and cook for about 30 seconds, until they release a fragrant aroma. Add the onion purée, the chopped tomatoes, tomato purée, honey, salt, chicken and stock. Bring to the boil, then reduce the heat until simmering, and cook, uncovered, for 20 minutes, until the chicken has cooked through.

Stir in the crème fraîche or cream, the lemon juice and garam masala. Tomatoes differ in sweetness, so taste and add a little more honey if you think it's needed. Garnish with the chopped coriander.

JERK ROAST CHICKEN

The 1940s and 50s saw a huge wave of immigration from the West Indies to London, after the British Government advertised for foreign workers to help rebuild the country following the Second World War. Jamaican jerk chicken is now as popular as fish and chips or pie and mash, and with good reason – its combination of mouth-blasting spice, sweetness and salt is irresistible. Here, I've given the classic British roast chicken a jerk makeover, with another famous Jamaican dish, rice and peas, making a guest appearance as stuffing. If you can't get hold of Scotch bonnet chillies, use three or four long red chillies instead. This is good served with roasted sweet potatoes and greens.

SERVES 4

1 whole chicken (about 1.8kg)
4 large sprigs of fresh thyme

For the jerk marinade
5 spring onions, white and green parts, roughly chopped
2 shallots, roughly chopped
3 garlic cloves
thumb-sized knob of fresh ginger
2–3 Scotch bonnet chillies (include the seeds for extra spiciness)
½ teaspoon ground nutmeg
½ teaspoon ground cinnamon
1 teaspoon salt
1 tablespoon fresh thyme leaves
1 tablespoon ground allspice
2 tablespoons soft dark brown sugar
2 tablespoons dark soy sauce
grated zest and juice of 2 limes
freshly ground black pepper

For the stuffing
100g long-grain rice
2 spring onions, white and green parts, finely chopped
2 sprigs of fresh thyme
200ml coconut milk
200g can kidney beans, drained and rinsed

Put all the ingredients for the marinade into a food processor or blender, along with a generous grinding of fresh black pepper. Whizz until you have a thick purée.

Put the chicken in a close-fitting tray. Using a sharp knife, make a few slashes in the chicken, including the legs, and rub the marinade all over. This is easiest done with your hands, but Scotch bonnets are incredibly hot, so make sure you don't touch your eyes. Use your fingers to loosen the skin from the breast a little and push some of the marinade underneath. Cover with foil and refrigerate for at least 6 hours, or overnight.

Preheat the oven to 200°C/180°C Fan/Gas Mark 6. Put the rice, spring onions and thyme sprigs in a medium saucepan and add the coconut milk along with 50ml of water. Stir and bring to the boil. Cover, reduce the heat to low and cook for 15–20 minutes, until the rice is tender. Stir in the kidney beans and cook for a further 2–3 minutes.

Stuff the rice into the chicken's cavity. Cover the chicken with foil again and roast for 70 minutes, then remove the foil and baste the chicken with any juices that have collected in the pan. Cook for another 20–30 minutes, until the bird is a gorgeous crispy brown and the juices run clear from the thickest part when pierced with a knife. Leave to rest, covered, for at least 10 minutes before carving.

SUNSHINE ON A PLATE: HOW CARIBBEAN FOOD CAME TO LONDON

It's often said that London is less a city than a ragged patchwork of villages, each with their own distinct character. The most distinct of all is Brixton. Step out of Brixton Underground station and within seconds you will be swallowed by the biggest, most bustling Afro-Caribbean market in Europe. Ladies in patterned dresses load their bags with mangoes and plantains; stalls wobble under mountains of fiery Scotch Bonnet chillies and tins of creamy ackee, Jamaica's national fruit; trays of dried fish, crusty with salt, waft their pungent scent; and in the butchers' shops, fat legs of goat wait to be simmered into curry. For the truly adventurous, there are even giant African snails – supposed to be eaten, but mostly bought by curious children (and the odd adult) as pets.

Brixton has been the heart of Britain's Caribbean community since 1948, when the SS *Empire Windrush* brought some 500 people, mostly Jamaican men, to help rebuild Britain after the ravages of the Second World War. Many of the new arrivals had no job or accommodation, and ended up living temporarily in an old air-raid shelter under Clapham Common. The nearest job centre was in Brixton, and so this run-down patch of South London became their home.

The image of the *Windrush*'s passengers filing off the gangplank has come to symbolise a turning point: the beginning of mass immigration, and the birth of modern Britain. But life was tough for the new arrivals. Racism was rife; signs saying 'No blacks, no dogs, no Irish' sprouted like mould on the windows of rental properties and bed and breakfasts. The weather was incessantly cold and rainy. And compared to the sunshine flavours of Caribbean cuisine, British food was unfamiliar and insipid.

Defining Caribbean food is almost impossible, for it is stamped with the footprint of every nationality that landed on those sandy shores. Indian slaves introduced spices and flatbreads; Asian immigrants brought rice; African slaves planted vegetables like okra and yams;

and the English and French sprinkled everything with garlic and thyme. The resulting melting pot of flavours is a giddy carousel of sweet, sour, salty, spicy and fresh. Small wonder that British cuisine – still choked by the yoke of post-war rationing – was one of the hardest things for the newcomers to adjust to. Many West Indians begged family back home to send them their favourite ingredients: 'We all had our little pots of condiments and pepper sauce from home to liven up the food, which was served to us in seemingly enormous but bland quantities,' recalled Sula Chance, a Trinidadian nurse who arrived in London in 1964.

Soon, enterprising immigrants started to import food from the Caribbean, transforming Brixton into a vibrant

A stall at Brixton market in 1969, packed full of freshly imported produce. (RDImages/Getty Images)

marketplace where you could get a taste of Tobago or St Lucia or Jamaica or all of them at once.

Unlike Chinese or Indian food, it has taken a long time for Caribbean food to be embraced by the British public – perhaps because the Caribbean community cooked for themselves, rather than trying to adapt their food to appeal to outsiders. But recently London has woken up and smelt the chilli. In Brixton Village, hungover students and hungry tourists queue outside Fish, Wings and Tings to get their hands on Jamaican-style jerk chicken. At The Rum Kitchen in Notting Hill, another area where many West Indians settled, diners devour plates of crunchy saltfish fritters and sip cocktails to the mellow strains of reggae.

Like New York's Brooklyn, Brixton has changed almost beyond recognition since the 1950s. Rows of slum housing have been knocked down for shiny new flats; in Brixton's famous arcades, the Caribbean shops selling goats' heads now sit cheek-by-jowl with posh boutiques selling £100 rugs, coffee shops and even a 'champagne and cheese' bar. There are mutterings about rising rents and gentrification, and many West Indian families have sadly moved out to the suburbs. But to walk through Brixton is still to glimpse a tiny corner of the Caribbean, transplanted and nurtured under London's grey skies.

CHICKEN COOKED IN MILK WITH SAGE AND MUSTARD

Unlikely as it seems, London was once full of cows. Before the development of railways and refrigeration, it was difficult to bring milk in from the country without it turning sour, and so every spare patch of grass, yard or even shed was given over to cattle rearing. In 1850, there were around 20,000 cows in the city, with Islington, Hackney, Edgware Road and Mile End home to some of the biggest populations. London was famous for its milkmaids, hundreds of whom walked the streets shouting 'Milk below!' up to customers' windows. It was back-breaking work: the women travelled as many as 19 miles a day, with two huge pails of milk suspended from a heavy wooden pole slung across their shoulders. In more salubrious areas, cows would be dragged to residents' front doors to be milked, so the customers could check their milk wasn't being diluted with dirty water or whitened with chalk.

The freshest milk came from St James's Park, where for centuries a small herd of cows grazed peacefully under the watchful eyes of the 'Mall milkmaids'. For a penny, growing children and sickly young ladies could enjoy a mug of warm, frothing milk, straight from the udder. The women who tended the cows had supposedly been given the right to sell milk by a former king – sometimes said to be Charles II, sometimes James I, both of whom probably had an eye for comely young milkmaids. There were cows in the park until 1905, and even after the animals were booted out, the milkmaids' descendants continued to sell the white stuff from a kiosk for another seventeen years.

The technique of cooking chicken in milk comes from Italy, but there seems no more suitable way to honour London's milk-rich past, especially when you bring in classic English flavours like mustard and sage. This is not a looker of a dish – the sauce splits as it cooks, so you end up with lots of little curds – but the milk makes the chicken incredibly tender. Serve with rice or mash and buttered greens.

SERVES 4

2 tablespoons sunflower or
  vegetable oil
8 bone-in, skin-on chicken legs
  and/or thighs
1 onion, finely sliced
600ml whole milk
7 garlic cloves, peeled and left whole
2 teaspoons fennel seeds,
  lightly crushed
4 cloves, crushed
4 tablespoons Dijon mustard
peel of 1 lemon, cut into large strips
12 large sage leaves, roughly torn
salt and freshly ground black pepper

Preheat the oven to 180°C/160°C Fan/Gas Mark 4.

Heat the oil in a large, heavy-based casserole dish with a lid. Season the chicken pieces with salt and pepper, and fry for about 5 minutes on each side until browned (you may have to do this in batches). Remove the chicken and put to one side, then add the onion. Fry for 10 minutes, until the onions are nicely softened. Return the chicken to the pan and add the remaining the ingredients, with a little more salt and pepper, and bring to the boil.

Transfer the casserole dish to the oven, and partially cover it with the lid. Cook for 1½ to 2 hours, until the sauce is thickened to your liking. Fish out the lemon peel and serve.

THE IVY'S SHEPHERD'S PIE

The Ivy, one of London's most famous restaurants, was founded in 1917 by an Italian immigrant called Abel Giandellini. Back then, it was just a humble café where Soho's theatre fraternity could let their hair down after a performance. The name was coined by the saucy French actress Alice Delysia, a former chorus girl at the Moulin Rouge. When Giandellini apologised to her for a spate of building works at the restaurant, she replied, 'Don't worry, we will always come to see you,' then trilled at him a line from a popular song: 'We will cling together like The Ivy'.

Since then, politicians, royalty and their hangers-on have all clung to the Ivy, which blossomed into a London institution. With its wood-panelled walls and stained-glass mullioned windows, it is one of the most elegant dining rooms in London. For me, the most distinctive thing about it is the smell. As soon as you enter, you are buffeted by the comforting, old-fashioned aroma of meat and potatoes, a testament to how many people are ordering the famous shepherd's pie. This is The Ivy's own recipe.

SERVES 6

2 tablespoons vegetable
  or sunflower oil
250g lean rib of beef mince
250g lean lamb mince
4 shallots, peeled and finely chopped
3 sprigs of fresh thyme, leaves picked
  and chopped
150g button mushrooms,
  finely chopped
2 medium carrots, peeled and
  finely chopped
1 tablespoon tomato purée
200g can chopped tomatoes
150ml (about 1 glass) red wine
2 tablespoons Worcestershire sauce
300ml veal, beef or chicken stock
3 sprigs of fresh oregano, leaves picked
  and chopped
salt and freshly ground black pepper

For the topping
1kg potatoes (ideally King Edward
  or Maris Piper), peeled and cut into
  even-sized pieces
50g butter

Heat a tablespoon of the oil in a large frying pan and cook the meat, stirring continuously, for about 5 minutes, until light brown in colour. Pour off the excess liquid and put the meat to one side.

In the same pan, heat the remaining oil and gently fry the shallots, thyme, mushrooms and carrots for about 8 minutes, until softened. Add the mince with the tomato purée and cook for about 5 minutes, then add the tomatoes and red wine, and reduce for about 10 minutes. Add the Worcestershire sauce and stock. Bring to the boil and simmer for 30 minutes. Season with salt and pepper, adding more Worcestershire sauce if required, then stir in the oregano. Set aside.

Preheat the oven to 180°C/160°C Fan/Gas Mark 4.

Cook the potatoes in boiling salted water for around 15 minutes or until soft, then drain and return to the pan over a low heat to remove any excess moisture. Using an old-fashioned masher or a potato ricer, thoroughly mash the potatoes, then mix them with the butter, and add salt and pepper to taste.

To assemble and serve, put the meat mixture into an ovenproof dish. Top with the mashed potato (you can pipe this if you have the time), and bake for around 30 minutes until the top of the pie is a nice golden colour. Serve with seasonal vegetables.

FRAGRANT LAMB, APRICOT AND ALMOND RICE

In 1997, chef couple Sam and Sam Clark opened a restaurant inspired by their travels in Spain and northern Africa. The result, Moro, has enchanted Londoners ever since. Although I love trying new restaurants, I am rarely happier than when sat at Moro's long zinc bar, unable to decide between dunking more freshly baked sourdough into a pool of herbaceous olive oil, or saving room for the sherry and raisin ice cream.

This recipe is loosely inspired by the Clarks' lamb stuffed with saffron rice, jazzed up with almonds and apricots. It is a tribute to the fragrant flavours Londoners learned to love at their table.

SERVES 4

50g butter
2 large onions, finely sliced
400g lamb leg steaks, cut into
    bite-sized pieces
2 garlic cloves, finely chopped
1 teaspoon cumin seeds, crushed,
    or ground cumin
5 green cardamom pods, cracked
4 black peppercorns, crushed
300g basmati rice
550ml lamb or chicken stock
generous pinch of saffron threads,
    soaked in 50ml boiling water for
    10 minutes
2 cinnamon sticks, or 1 heaped
    teaspoon ground cinnamon
75g dried apricots, quartered
40g flaked almonds, toasted
handful of fresh mint and/or coriander,
    chopped, to serve
natural yoghurt, to serve
salt and freshly ground black pepper

Heat the butter in a large saucepan over a medium heat. Add the onions and cook, stirring occasionally, for 15 minutes, until completely softened. Remove and put to one side.

Season the lamb with salt and pepper and add to the pan. Cook for 4–6 minutes, turning occasionally, until browned. Add the garlic, cumin, cardamom pods and peppercorns, and cook for a minute or so until fragrant.

Return the onions to the pan, then add the rice and stir to coat. Add the stock, saffron and its soaking water, and the cinnamon, then return the lamb to the pan. Stir, and salt generously. Bring to the boil, then reduce the heat to low, cover and cook for 15–20 minutes, until all the water has been absorbed and the rice is cooked through.

Stir through the apricots and the almonds. Serve scattered with the fresh herbs and a drizzle of yoghurt.

PORK LAAP

One of the best things about London is that you can try food from virtually every corner of the world, however far-flung or little-known. Saiphin Moore is the owner of the Lao Café, which celebrates the food of Thailand's northern neighbour Laos, and this fresh, tangy stir-fried pork salad is her family's version of laap – or as the Thais call it, larb. You can make this in less than half an hour, so it's a perfect midweek meal.

SERVES 4

2 tablespoons white rice, for the toasted rice (optional)
2 tablespoons vegetable or sunflower oil
½ red onion, finely chopped
6 garlic cloves, finely chopped
2 thumb-sized knobs of galangal or ginger, finely chopped
2 lemongrass stalks, very finely chopped
500g mince pork
2 teaspoons chilli flakes
1 heaped teaspoon finely chopped lime leaves, fresh or dried
3 tablespoons fish sauce
juice of 5 limes
bunch of fresh mint (about 30g), finely chopped
bunch of fresh coriander (about 30g), finely chopped
½ bunch of fresh Thai basil, finely chopped

If making the toasted rice, add the rice to a dry frying pan or wok over a medium heat and cook until golden, about 5 minutes. Transfer to a mortar and pestle and pound until crushed into a powder, and set aside.

Heat the oil in the pan. Add the onion, garlic, galangal or ginger and lemongrass, and fry for a few minutes until the onion is softened and starting to turn crispy.

Add the mince and cook, breaking up lumps with a wooden spoon, for 5–7 minutes until cooked.

Take off the heat and stir in the chilli flakes, lime leaves, fish sauce, lime juice and all the fresh herbs. Taste, and add a little salt if required. Scatter over the toasted rice, if using, and serve.

PIE AND MASH:
THE FOOD THAT BUILT LONDON

In the dank, dark streets of Victorian London, where gas lamps flickered in the fog, there were street food sellers offering almost every delicacy imaginable. You could buy hot potatoes topped with butter and salt; piquant pickled whelks; bunches of watercress from the countryside, so fresh they were still damp at the roots. But most popular of all were the piemen, whose cries of 'Penny pies, all 'ot, all 'ot!' could be heard all over the city.

Londoners have always had a penchant for pies; the damp, chilly weather here makes us crave something warm and comforting. In 1844, the first dedicated pie and mash shop opened in South London, and slowly, more and more piemen moved off the streets into permanent premises. Here, the working classes could enjoy a cheap, hearty meal before they headed to the docks or the markets or the construction sites. Modern London was built on a foundation of pie and mash.

There used to be hundreds of pie and mash shops, stretching all the way from Shepherd's Bush to Bermondsey, with a few on the fringes of Essex and Kent. Today, less than thirty remain, mostly in the South and East End. Burgers, kebabs and pizzas have stolen pie and mash's crown as the fast food of choice. But there are still true believers. David Beckham has been spied popping into a shop near where he grew up in East London, while for over two decades, a band of Londoners known as 'The Pie and Mash Club' have spent their Friday lunchtimes trundling to different pie shops, attempting to outdo each other in the number of pies they can devour. 'Our record-holder is Chris Charalambous with a massive ten pies,' founder Nick Evans says seriously. 'It is an achievement we may never see bettered.'

There is a ritual to visiting a pie and mash shop. The second you step in, the person behind the counter will lift a towel off the metal tray of freshly baked beef pies and bark grumpily at you: 'Large or small?' The pie is plopped on the plate, followed by a dollop of creamy mashed potato. Finally, you will be asked the question that horrifies tourists and makes old East Enders wriggle with glee: 'Do you want eels with that?'

Pies, mash and eels are London's holy trinity. The Thames was once full of eels, a cheap and plentiful source of food for the poor. In 1853, a doctor called Charles David Badham wrote: 'London, from one end to the other, teems and steams with eels, alive and stewed; turn where you will; hot eels are everywhere smoking away.' Demand was so high that extra supplies were specially imported from Holland. The Dutch ships docked just outside Billingsgate Fish Market, and traders would row out to take their pick from the writhing vats of live eels. Eel pies were once as popular as beef, but the traditional way to eat eels in a pie and mash shop is stewed or 'jellied' – that is, boiled until they set into a gelatinous mess. Even those customers who don't like eels will still ask for their pies to be doused in 'liquor', a greenish, parsley-flecked sauce traditionally made from the eels' leftover stewing water, which is made to a different recipe in every shop. I never find it tastes of much, but pie and mash somehow doesn't feel quite right without it.

Although the food they serve is humble, many pie and mash shops are beautiful places. With their marble counters, engraved mirrors and gleaming white tiles, they are a masterclass in simple elegance. Each has its own character. At F. Cooke in Hackney you'll find the traditional sawdust-strewn floor (for spitting eel bones or bits of gristle out on) and tiles in a gloriously queasy shade of custard yellow. Then there is G. Kelly in Bethnal Green, with its wooden benches and walls plastered with images of local boxing heroes. The fairest of them all is M.Manze in Walthamstow, which was recently granted Grade II status for its 'exceptional' interior. The shop's carved mahogany booths and hand-blown lamps have stood untouched ever since it opened its doors in 1929. Until a few years ago, when burglars broke in and stole it, Manze's even had the original antique brass till. One local was so outraged by the theft that he spearheaded a campaign on Facebook to try and find it; over 60,000 people shared his plea for the tills safe return, so far in vain. Like I said: Londoners' love for pie runs deep.

STEAK AND ALE PIE WITH THYME-MUSTARD PASTRY

Pie and mash is a classic London dish, and steak and ale is the king of the fillings. It's even better when the tender beef is nestled within a thyme- and mustard-spiked pastry.

Here, I like to use a beer called porter, which was invented in London in the 1700s. Strong and dark, it gained its name due to its popularity with 'porters', the burly men whose job was to lug goods on and off ships and carry them around the city. Stout is actually descended from porter, so if you can't find porter, a bottle of Guinness will work just as well. And if you're raising your eyebrows at the inclusion of Marmite, don't worry; the pie won't taste like breakfast. A spoon of the spread just adds an extra layer of savoury deliciousness.

SERVES 6

60g plain flour
800g braising beef, chopped
  into chunks
knob of butter
2–3 tablespoons vegetable or
  sunflower oil
200g bacon, chopped into small pieces
2 large onions, roughly chopped
2 carrots, roughly chopped
1 stick of celery, finely chopped
150g chestnut mushrooms, halved
  or quartered
5 sprigs of fresh thyme, leaves picked
  and finely chopped
2 bay leaves
500ml porter or stout
200ml beef stock
½ teaspoon Marmite (optional)
1 tablespoon soft dark brown sugar
1 tablespoon balsamic vinegar
salt and freshly ground black pepper

For the thyme-mustard pastry
600g plain flour
300g butter, cut into cubes
1 tablespoon finely chopped fresh
  thyme leaves
1 tablespoon English mustard powder
1 tablespoon wholegrain mustard
1 egg, beaten, to glaze

Preheat the oven to 160°C/140°C Fan/Gas Mark 3. Put the flour in a bowl, along with salt and a generous grinding of pepper, and mix together. Taking a piece at time, roll the beef in the flour until coated, and set aside, shaking off any excess.

Melt the knob of butter with 2 tablespoons of oil in a large casserole dish or ovenproof pan over a high heat, then add the beef. Fry for 2–3 minutes, then turn and fry the other side for 1–2 minutes, until the meat is golden brown all over (you don't want to crowd the pan, so you may need to do this in batches). Remove the beef and put to one side.

Add another drizzle of oil to the pan, if needed, and fry the bacon for 3 minutes or so, until crispy. Remove and put to one side.

Turn the heat down to medium. Add the onions and fry gently for 10 minutes or so, until soft and starting to turn golden. Add the carrots and celery and cook for 5 minutes.

Return the beef chunks and bacon to the pan, and add the mushrooms, thyme and bay leaves. Pour in the porter or stout and the stock. The liquid should cover the meat, so add a splash more water if needed. Stir in the Marmite, if using, sugar and balsamic vinegar. Season with pepper and a little more salt.

Bring to the boil, cover and transfer to the middle shelf of the oven for 2 hours. Uncover the stew and cook for a further 1½ hours, or until thickened slightly.

Set the stew aside to cool (it will also be fine in the fridge overnight) and get to work on the pastry. Sift the flour into a large mixing bowl and add the cubes of butter, plus a generous pinch of salt. Use your fingertips to rub the butter and flour together until the mixture resembles breadcrumbs. Stir in the thyme leaves and the mustard powder. Mix 120ml of cold water with the wholegrain mustard and

add just a tablespoon or two at a time, until the mixture binds together and you can knead it into a firm dough (you may not need all the water). Wrap the pastry in cling film and leave to chill in the fridge for at least 30 minutes, or overnight.

When it's time to cook the pie, preheat the oven to 200°C/180°C Fan/Gas Mark 6. Grease a large, family-sized pie dish (approximately 25cm).

Take about a third of the pastry and put to one side. This will be your lid. Roll out the remaining pastry using a rolling pin until you have enough to line the pie dish, then put it into place in the dish. Spoon the stew into the pastry-lined dish using a large slotted spoon – you don't want all the gravy.

Brush the edges of the pastry with the beaten egg. Roll out the rest of the pastry until you have enough to cover the dish (you may have a little left over). Lift on top of the pie and push down gently to seal. Use a knife to make a few small slits in the pastry. Decorate with the excess pastry, if you like – I use a biscuit cutter to make little leaf decorations – then brush the pastry with the rest of the beaten egg.

Cook in the oven for 35–45 minutes, until golden brown. Serve with buttery mash and seasonal veg of choice.

AROMATIC BEEF PHO

London has been home to a significant Vietnamese community since 1975, when the Vietnam War ended. Boatloads of refugees who feared persecution from the new Communist government made the perilous journey to Hong Kong, then under British rule, and were eventually allowed to settle in the UK.

Vietnamese restaurants are now everywhere, and pho – the fragrant noodle soup that is often considered the national dish of Vietnam – has become very popular. This recipe is from Uyen Luu, whose family came to London when she was a small child. She now runs a wildly popular Vietnamese supper club. You will need a very large pan, or perhaps use two.

SERVES 8, GENEROUSLY

2 tablespoons sea salt
600g oxtail
1.5kg beef shin, flank or rib
700g beef bones
2 litres chicken stock
1 large onion, peeled and both
    ends trimmed
200g fresh ginger, peeled
    and halved
1 daikon, or 2 large
    carrots, peeled
20 star anise
½ teaspoon cloves
2 cinnamon sticks, preferably
    Vietnamese or Chinese
3 cassia bark sticks, or use
    2 more cinnamon sticks
1 teaspoon coriander seeds
1 teaspoon fennel seeds
1 teaspoon black peppercorns
2 black cardamom pods
4 pieces of dried orange
    peel (optional)
3 teaspoons rock salt,
    or sea salt
50g rock sugar, or 20g
    granulated sugar

Bring a very large pan of water to the boil with the sea salt. Add the meat and bones and boil until scum forms on the surface, about 10 minutes. Remove from the heat and discard the water. Wash the meat and bones in cold water, rinsing off any scum, and set aside. This will give you a clearer broth.

Wash the pan, add 3 litres of fresh water and bring to the boil. Return the meat to the pan and bring to a gentle simmer. Skim off any scum and fat from the surface with a spoon, and pour in the chicken stock.

Heat a griddle pan over a high heat (do not add oil). Char the onion and ginger on both sides. Add to the broth with the daikon or carrot.

Put all the spices and the orange peel, if using, in a piece of muslin and tie with twine to seal. Add to the broth with the salt and sugar. Simmer for at least 2 hours with the lid on. Check occasionally and skim off any scum and fat from the surface.

After 2 hours, remove the beef from the pan and allow it to rest slightly, then slice it thinly and store in a sealed container until serving. Leave the bones and oxtail in the pan and simmer for at least another hour. Remove the oxtail and shred the meat from the bones, putting the meat to one side with your sliced beef. Remove all the other bones from the pan. Add the bouillon, fish sauce and plenty of black pepper to the pan, to taste.

3 teaspoons pork or
   vegetable bouillon
4 tablespoons fish sauce
1 red onion, thinly sliced
small handful of fresh
   coriander, finely chopped
2 spring onions, thinly sliced
1kg dried pho noodles
freshly ground black pepper

To serve on the side
a selection of fresh Thai
   sweet basil and/or coriander,
   sliced bird's eye chillies,
   beansprouts, lime wedges,
   fish sauce, hoisin sauce,
   Sriracha chilli sauce and
   chilli oil

In a small bowl, mix together the red onion, coriander and spring onions.

Cook the noodles according to the packet instructions. Divide the cooked noodles between big, deep soup bowls. Place the cooked meat on top and sprinkle with the red onion mixture. Bring the broth to boiling point, then pour ladlefuls of it over the noodles to submerge them.

Serve the garnishes and condiments on the side, so guests can add them to their pho as desired.

Adapted from *My Vietnamese Kitchen* by Uyen Luu (Ryland Peters and Small, 2013)

BAO BUNS WITH STICKY PORK AND PICKLED CARROTS

I first tasted the Chinese steamed buns called bao at a street food market in East London, and have been fighting an addiction ever since. I'm not alone. London has gone so mad for these fluffy pillows that the best restaurant offering them (the prosaically-named Bao) always has huge queues outside.

Making your own bao takes a little time, but watching the buns swell up like proud little clouds is very satisfying. Classic Chinese bao get their snowy white colour from bleached flour, but I tend to use plain, as it's what I have in the cupboard. You'll need a steamer and a plentiful supply of chopsticks or wooden skewers to prop the buns open as they rise.

MAKES 10

For the quick pickled carrots
3 medium carrots
60ml rice wine vinegar
1 tablespoon caster sugar
½ teaspoon salt

For the bao
450g plain flour
7g sachet fast-action dried yeast
3 tablespoons caster sugar
1½ teaspoons baking powder
½ teaspoon salt
50ml milk
1 tablespoon vegetable or sunflower oil, plus extra for greasing/brushing

For the pork
600g pork belly, chopped into 3cm pieces
2 tablespoons vegetable or sunflower oil
100ml dark soy sauce
3 tablespoons light soy sauce
3 tablespoons hoisin sauce

To make the pickled carrots, peel the carrots, then use the peeler to cut them into long, thin slices. Put the vinegar, sugar and salt in a bowl, tip in the carrots and mix to combine. Refrigerate until needed, draining any excess liquid from the bowl just before serving.

To make the bao dough, put the flour, yeast, sugar, baking powder and salt in a large bowl, and mix to combine. Add 200ml of warm water, the milk and oil and bring together into a dough. Knead for 10 minutes by hand, until smooth and not too sticky, or for about 8 minutes in a stand mixer using the dough hook attachment. Put the dough into a large oiled bowl. Cover with a damp tea towel or oiled cling film, and leave in a warm place for about 1 hour, until doubled in size.

Lightly flour a clean work surface and tip out the dough. Give it a quick knead, then divide into ten pieces (about 70g each). Roll the pieces into balls, then use a rolling pin to roll out each ball into an oval about 12 × 8cm. Brush each oval with oil, then place an oiled chopstick or skewer horizontally across the centre. Fold the dough over the chopstick. Place the bao, with the chopsticks inside, on a baking sheet lined with baking parchment. Cover and leave to rise for 1 hour.

While the bao are rising, make the pork filling. Bring a saucepan of water to the boil and cook the pork belly pieces for 15 minutes. Drain, reserving 200ml of the cooking water.

Heat the oil in a large saucepan or casserole dish and cook the pork belly for a few minutes on each side, until browned. Add both of the soy sauces and hoisin sauce, sugar, ginger, garlic, five-spice powder and star anise, plus the 200ml of reserved

30g dark brown sugar
thumb-sized knob of fresh ginger,
    finely grated
2 garlic cloves, grated
1 teaspoon Chinese five spice
2 star anise

To serve (optional)
coriander, roughly chopped

water. Bring to the boil, then turn down to a simmer and cook for 1 hour, until the belly is tender. Just before you want to serve, whack the heat up to high and boil to reduce the sauce until thick and shiny.

To cook the bao, heat a large steamer over a medium–high heat, and line with a circle of baking parchment. Pull the chopsticks out of the buns, then steam the buns for 10–12 minutes, until swollen and fluffy (you will probably need to do this in batches, depending on the size of your steamer).

Prise the buns open (use a knife if they're stuck together), and fill with the pork and the carrot pickle. Sprinkle over the coriander and enjoy.

SAMUEL PEPYS' RABBIT RAGU

As a child, I loved learning about the Great Fire of 1666: how it broke out in a bakery on Pudding Lane, raged for four days and destroyed over 13,000 homes. But most of all, I adored the story of diarist Samuel Pepys, who buried wine and 'Parmazan cheese' in the garden to try and save them from the flames.

Pepys was an unabashed glutton whose diary gives a fascinating insight into the food of seventeenth-century London, so it seemed only fitting to create a recipe in tribute to him. Here, I've combined his precious red wine and Parmesan with a favourite meat of his, rabbit. If you can resist eating this straight away, it tastes even better the day after.

SERVES 4–6

2 tablespoons olive oil, plus
  extra if needed
200g bacon, roughly chopped
4 tablespoons plain flour
1 rabbit, jointed into pieces
  (about 700–900g)
2 onions, finely chopped
1 large carrot, finely chopped
2 sticks of celery, finely chopped
4 garlic cloves, finely chopped
1 tablespoon fresh chopped thyme
  leaves, plus extra to garnish
1 sprig of fresh rosemary
1 heaped teaspoon fennel seeds
2 bay leaves
300ml red wine
400ml chicken stock
400g can chopped tomatoes
grated zest and juice of 1½ lemons
knob of butter
120g Parmesan cheese, grated
salt and freshly ground black pepper

Heat the oil in a large casserole dish over a medium heat, then add the bacon. Fry until golden and crispy, then lift out and put to one side.

Put the flour in a large bowl and season generously with salt and pepper. Toss the rabbit meat in the flour, then add to the pan and fry for a few minutes on both sides, until browned. Remove and set aside with the bacon.

Add the onions, carrot, celery, garlic, thyme, rosemary, fennel seeds and bay leaves to the pan, along with a splash more oil if needed, and fry for 5 minutes. Return the bacon and rabbit to the pan, then add the wine, chicken stock and the tomatoes. Season with plenty of salt and pepper. Bring to the boil, then reduce the heat to low so it's just gently simmering. Cover with a lid and cook for 2–3 hours, until the rabbit is tender and falling off the bone.

Remove the rabbit from the pan and shred the meat using two forks, discarding all the bones. Return the meat to the pan and whack up the heat until the sauce has reduced by half – be patient, this could easily take 20 minutes. Stir in the lemon zest and juice, the butter and half the Parmesan. Garnish with thyme leaves and the rest of the Parmesan. Serve tossed through a big bowl of pasta or with rice.

PUDDING

'"TO COME IN PUDDING TIME" IS AS MUCH TO SAY, TO COME IN THE MOST LUCKY MOMENT IN THE WORLD,' WROTE AN EXCITED FOREIGN VISITOR TO LONDON IN THE SEVENTEENTH CENTURY.

LONDON COOKS ARE MASTERS OF SUGAR. IN THE 1500s, THE ROYAL KITCHEN WOULD MAKE QUEEN ELIZABETH I ASTONISHING SCULPTURES FROM MARZIPAN, IN THE SHAPE OF EVERYTHING FROM CHESSBOARDS TO ST PAUL'S CATHEDRAL.

TODAY'S CHEFS AND BAKERS ARE JUST AS CREATIVE, CRAFTING CHOCOLATE PUDDINGS WITH GLORIOUSLY MOLTEN CENTRES, AND JELLIES THAT JIGGLE AND GLEAM. DINNER IN LONDON NEVER FEELS COMPLETE WITHOUT AN INDULGENT DESSERT. IT IS THE CUSTARD-DRENCHED FULL-STOP TO THE EVENING.

PEACH MELBA

Peach melba is so much more than the sum of its parts. The combination of fresh peaches, raspberry sauce and ice cream looks like a stupendously gaudy sunset, and it tastes like the essence of summer.

The dish was invented by the celebrated French chef Auguste Escoffier at the Savoy hotel in the 1890s in honour of the Australian opera singer Dame Nellie Melba, who was performing at the nearby Royal Opera House in Covent Garden. I like to poach the peaches in wine instead of the traditional water, because … why not?

SERVES 4

300ml white wine
200g caster sugar
peel of 1 lemon
4 ripe peaches, halved and
    stones removed
250g raspberries
1 tablespoon icing sugar
vanilla ice cream, to serve

Heat the wine, sugar and 200ml of water together in a saucepan, stirring regularly, until the sugar has dissolved. Add the lemon peel. Bring to the boil, then turn the heat down to reach a gentle simmer. Add the peaches, cut side down, and poach until tender, about 10 minutes, or a little longer if your peaches aren't quite ripe.

Remove the peaches with a slotted spoon, reserving the poaching liquid. When the fruit has cooled down, remove and discard the skins – they should slip off easily, like Dame Nellie flinging off a fur – and refrigerate the peaches until needed.

Purée the raspberries with 4 tablespoons of the poaching liquid in a food processor or blender. Strain through a sieve into a bowl to get rid of the seeds. Stir in the icing sugar and taste, adding a little more sugar if it's too sharp.

To serve, put two peach halves in each serving bowl with a big scoop of ice cream and drizzle with the raspberry sauce.

PEAR AND ALMOND TART

When the River Café opened in 1987, it introduced Britain to the joy of Italian food. Ruth Rogers and Rose Gray's fresh, rustic cooking sent the public off on a feverish hunt for pancetta and mascarpone, while their kitchen became a training ground for star chefs including Jamie Oliver and Hugh Fearnley-Whittingstall. Many of London's best restaurants have the River Café's DNA flowing through them.

This simple tart is the epitome of River Café style. Grating the pastry sounds strange, but it's actually much easier than rolling it out.

SERVES 8

For the pastry
230g plain flour
pinch of salt
150g cold butter, cut into small cubes
70g icing sugar
2 egg yolks

For the filling
4 ripe pears, peeled, halved and cored
175g butter, softened
175g caster sugar
125g blanched whole almonds
  or ground almonds
1 egg, plus 1 egg yolk

For the pastry, 'rub' the flour, salt and butter in a food processor until the mixture resembles coarse breadcrumbs. Add the sugar, then the egg yolks, and pulse. The mixture will immediately combine and leave the sides of the bowl. Remove from the processor, wrap in cling film and chill in the fridge for at least 1 hour.

Preheat the oven to 180°C/160°C Fan/Gas Mark 4.

Grate the pastry coarsely into a 22cm loose-bottomed flan tin with high sides (about 3cm), then press it evenly into the sides and base. Line with baking parchment, fill the tin with baking beans or rice, and bake for 20 minutes until very light brown. Remove the paper and beans and leave to cool, then place the pears in the pastry case, face down.

Reduce the oven temperature to 150°C/130°C Fan/Gas Mark 2.

For the filling, cream the butter and sugar using an electric whisk or stand mixer until the mixture is pale and fluffy. If using whole almonds, put them in a food processor and chop until fine. Add the almonds to the butter and sugar mixture and stir to combine, then beat in the eggs. Spoon the mixture over the pears. Bake for 45–55 minutes.

Adapted from *The River Café Cookbook* (Ebury Press, 1995)

PIMM'S TRIFLE WITH LEMON CURD CREAM

Pimm's was invented in London in the 1800s and has become the ultimate English summer drink. The thought of a cool, refreshing glass of Pimm's after work is often the only thing that gets many Londoners through the hot and sticky days of August, when the tube is like hell, only hotter and more crowded. I like to use Pimm's in trifle, where it brings a sprightly fruitiness to all that custard and cream.

SERVES 8–10

5 sheets of gelatine
260ml Pimm's
300ml lemonade
50g caster sugar
juice of 1 orange
250g sponge cake (such as Madeira)
500g strawberries, washed and hulled, plus an extra handful, sliced, to serve (optional)
700ml good-quality custard
600ml double cream
200ml mascarpone
4 tablespoons icing sugar
3 heaped tablespoons lemon curd
grated zest of 1 lemon
mint leaves, to serve (optional)

Put the gelatine leaves in a bowl of cold water and leave to soften for 5 minutes.

Meanwhile, make the jelly. Gently heat 200ml of the Pimm's with the lemonade, caster sugar and orange juice in a saucepan over a medium heat, until the sugar has melted and the mixture is just about to bubble. Squeeze the water out of the gelatine, add the sheets to the Pimm's mixture and stir until melted. Transfer the mixture to a bowl and put into the fridge for about 2 hours, until the jelly is nearly set.

Cut the cake into thin slices, around 1cm thick, and use them to line the bottom of a large glass bowl. Pour over the remaining Pimm's and leave to soak for a few minutes. Quarter the strawberries lengthways and scatter over the top.

Take your cooled jelly from the fridge and pour it over the strawberries and sponge. Return to the fridge for 1 hour so to allow the jelly to firm up further.

Pour the custard over the jelly, then whip the cream, mascarpone and icing sugar in a bowl until it forms soft peaks. Gently mix in the lemon curd and the lemon zest and spoon onto the custard.

Decorate the trifle with the sliced strawberries a few leaves of mint if you like. Chill in the fridge until ready to serve.

IT'S PIMM'S O'CLOCK! LONDON'S FAVOURITE SUMMER DRINK

A tall glass of Pimm's, festooned with fruit and clinking with ice, exerts a powerfully symbolic pull on Londoners. Just one sip evokes a fantasy of the perfect English summer: cricket and tennis matches in the park, languid riverside picnics and sunburnt noses. As soon as the temperature starts to rise, we whisper excitedly to our friends: 'Shall we order a Pimm's?' And we drink it everywhere, in pub gardens, at barbecues and on our balconies, until suddenly autumn comes and our thirst for Pimm's melts away, just like the ice in the glass.

London's affair with Pimm's stretches back generations. And like so many things in this city, it all started with oysters. In the 1820s, James Pimm, a farmer's son from Kent, ran an oyster bar near the Bank of England. As shellfish was so cheap and plentiful, the city was flooded with identikit oyster bars, and Mr Pimm needed something to set his venue apart. Like a modern nightclub owner trying to lure in punters with a free welcome drink, he came up with a refreshing, gin-based drink to wash the shellfish down. He called it 'Pimm's No. 1 cup'.

Nobody quite knows what Pimm put into his drink; even today, only a handful of Pimm's workers are said to know the exact mix of herbs and spices involved (they are known as the 'Pimm's Six' and aren't allowed to travel on the same plane, for fear the secret could be lost). But this tawny nectar was an instant hit – the prosecco of its day, if you will. It probably didn't hurt that Pimm marketed the drink as an aid to digestion; the hypochondriac Victorians loved nothing more than to be told alcohol was medicinal. Ever the entrepreneur, Pimm developed different 'cups' using different base spirits, such as No. 2 (whisky) and No. 3 (brandy), to appeal to different customers, though only the original is widely available today. Clearly, you weren't going to get away with ordering a pint of beer at Mr Pimm's joint.

By the mid-nineteenth century, Pimm was selling the drink to other bars, and in 1865 the business was sold. Soon, a wine merchant called Horatio David Davies bought the rights to the brand. He went on to become the mayor of London and, with somewhat dubious ethics, used his connections to make Pimm's No. 1

JUST ONE SIP EVOKES A FANTASY OF THE PERFECT ENGLISH SUMMER.

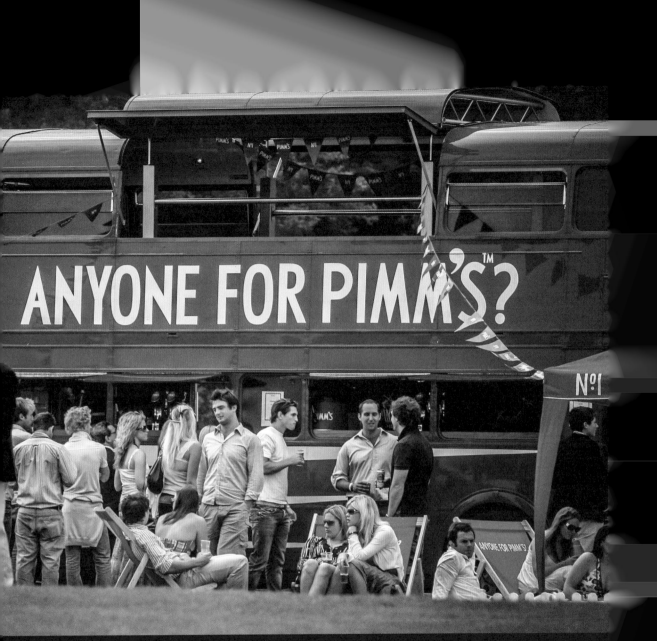

ANYONE FOR PIMM'S™?

No1

A Pimm's bus attracts the crowds at Guards Polo Club in Windsor, 2007. (coldsnowstorm/istock

the glamorous society drink of choice. The drink has long traded off its upper-class, oh-so-English character; in the 1960s, the firm ran a competition offering a 'lordship of the manor' to one lucky drinker. Pimm's No. 1 Cup is now an indispensable part of posh summer events such as the Henley Regatta or Wimbledon, where some 230,000 glasses of Pimm's are consumed each year.

There is an art to making Pimm's. Firstly, it should be potent, no weaker than one part Pimm's to three parts lemonade. The British take this very seriously. In 2014, a newspaper sent a squad of undercover journalists to Wimbledon to analyse the alcohol content of the Pimm's

offering. They reported in breathless horror that it was only half as strong as officially recommended. Secondly, Pimm's is not an excuse to use up the mushy kiwis and peaches languishing in the fridge – you'll end up with fruit salad in a glass. A handful of chopped strawberries and cucumber, a slice of lemon and a sprig of mint are the only adornments Pimm's needs. That, and perhaps a few oysters on the side.

WHITE CHOCOLATE AND SAFFRON POTS

With its fiery red colour and heady fragrance, saffron seems such an exotic spice. But in the Middle Ages, England was actually the world's biggest producer of saffron crocuses, exporting the spice all over the globe. Even more surprisingly, saffron was produced in London: the powerful Bishops of Ely owned a sumptuous palace in Holborn and grew an impressive array of crocuses in the grounds. The Bishops' gardens are long gone, but there is a single remaining thread of that history in the name of a road: Saffron Hill. This is a very easy dessert, with just a delicate hint of that enticing saffron flavour.

SERVES 4–6

3 sheets of gelatine
400ml double cream
200ml milk
70g caster sugar
½ teaspoon saffron threads, plus a
    little extra for decoration (optional)
100g white chocolate, finely cut into
    shards, plus a little extra
    for decoration

Put the gelatine leaves in a bowl of cold water and leave to soften for 5 minutes.

Gently heat the cream, milk, sugar and saffron in a large saucepan, until the sugar has dissolved and the mixture is just below simmering point. Add the chocolate, then take the saucepan off the heat and let stand for 10 minutes, until the chocolate has melted. Give the mixture a stir, then pour through a sieve into a fresh bowl to get rid of the saffron threads.

Squeeze the water out of the gelatine, and add the sheets to the warm cream mixture, stirring to dissolve. Divide the mixture between teacups, glasses or ramekins. Refrigerate for at least 3 hours or overnight. Decorate each cup with shards of white chocolate, and a few strands of saffron, if you like.

ST EMILION AU CHOCOLAT

The most divine dessert, and so very easy. This chocolate pot of dreams comes from Quo Vadis, a charming restaurant in theatreland, headed by the exuberant chef Jeremy Lee. He took the recipe from food writer Elizabeth David, and he loves it so much that he says it's unlikely to ever come off the menu. If you're feeling adventurous, swap the cognac for whisky or rum.

SERVES 6–8, DEPENDING ON THE SIZE OF YOUR GLASSES

16 macaroons, or similar crunchy biscuits such as amaretti
70ml cognac, plus extra
110g butter, at room temperature
110g caster sugar
150ml whole milk
225g good-quality dark chocolate, at least 70% cocoa solids
1 egg yolk

Crumble the biscuits into small pieces and divide them between the glasses or cups, holding a few pieces back to decorate the tops, if you like. Add a splash of cognac to each glass.

Put the butter and sugar in a bowl and beat using an electric whisk or wooden spoon, until pale and fluffy.

Heat the milk in a pan and bring to a gentle simmer. Remove from the heat, tip in the chocolate and mix gently but thoroughly until the chocolate is completely melted.

Add the egg yolk to the butter and sugar mixture, then slowly pour in the hot chocolate and milk. Mix together, then divide between the glasses, onto the biscuits. Sprinkle the last few biscuit crumbs over the top and dampen with a tiny splash of cognac. Refrigerate until ready to serve – overnight is best.

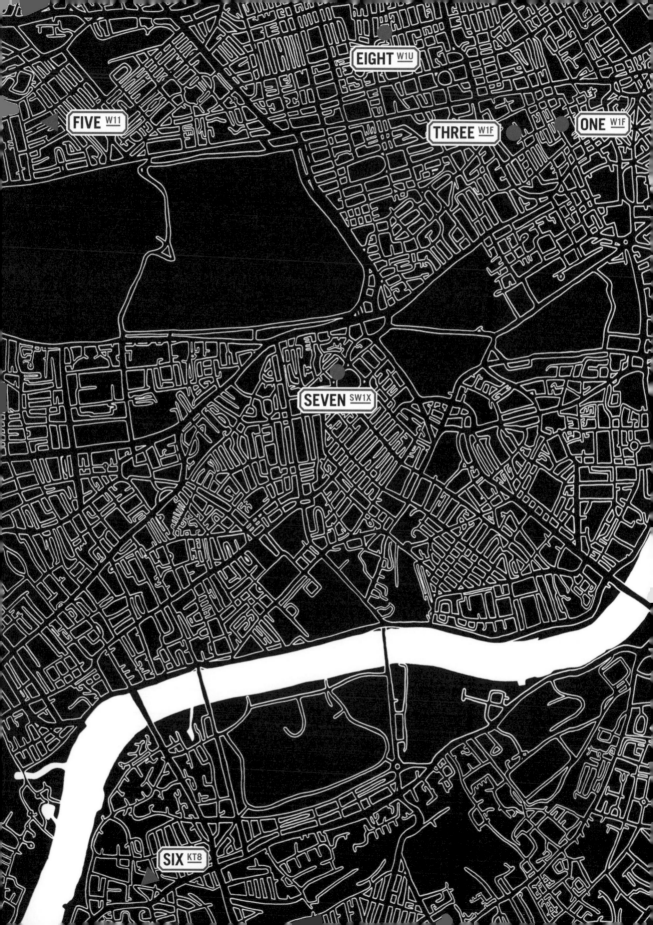

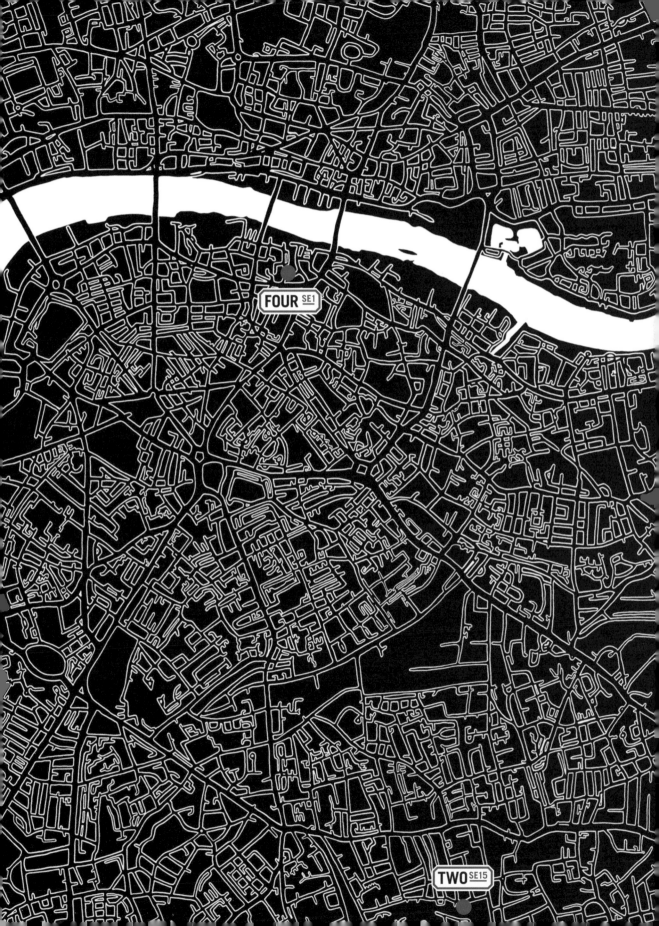

FOUR SE1

TWO SE15

LONDON FOR CHOCOLATE LOVERS

1. Blow your mind with extraordinary flavours

143 Wardour St, Soho, W1F 8WA
plus other locations in Camden
and the City
paulayoung.co.uk

Rhubarb and pink peppercorn; honey and pine nuts; prune and goat's cheese… Master chocolatier Paul A. Young's unique flavour combinations are unrivalled. They're also some of the most beautiful chocolates in the city.

2. Explore a chocolate museum

187 Ferndale Rd, Brixton,
SW9 8BA
thechocolatemuseum.co.uk

Founded by Frenchwoman Isabelle Alaya, who also owns the delightful chocolate shop Melange in Peckham, this is a small but fascinating museum stuffed full of artefacts relating to the history of chocolate. Don't leave without trying the delicious hot chocolate at the café.

3. Gawp at London's wackiest chocolate creations

30–32 Foubert's Pl, Carnaby,
W1F 7PS
choccywoccydoodah.com

If Willy Wonka was secretly running a chocolate shop in London, Choccywoccydoodah would be it. This temple to chocolate has a cult following for its fantastical creations – think lurid green chocolate frogs, chocolate bars studded with chunks of bacon, and teetering cakes topped with everything from grinning chocolate skulls to rearing horses.

4. Indulge at a chocolate-themed restaurant

2–4 Bedale St,
SE1 9AL
hotelchocolat.com

In the heart of Borough Market is Rabot 1745, a restaurant/cocktail bar owned by upmarket chocolate brand Hotel Chocolat. Unsurprisingly, the menu is a chocoholic's delight: start with a cocoa martini, then move on to chocolate-glazed sticky ribs and chips with cacao ketchup.

Along with beef, beer and anything deep-fried or topped with pastry, chocolate is one of those foods Londoners have a serious soft spot for. Thankfully, there are plenty of places where they can get their cocoa fix.

5. Make your own chocolates

59 Ledbury Rd,
W11 2AA
meltchocolates.com

Chocolate shops don't come any more gorgeous than Melt, a sleek and airy space in Notting Hill where you can watch the chocolatiers creating beautiful treats in the open kitchen. Sign up for one of Melt's courses and spend an hour learning how to craft perfect bonbons and truffles.

6. See a royal chocolate kitchen

Hampton Court Palace,
East Molesey, KT8 9AU
hrp.org.uk

In 2013, workers at Hampton Court Palace stumbled across a hidden room. Behind the locked door was a seventeenth-century 'chocolate kitchen', where the royal chocolatier, Thomas Tosier, crafted cups of hot chocolate for King George I. The kitchen has now been brought exquisitely back to life.

7. Sip hot chocolate in a secret garden

5 Motcomb Street, SW1X 8JU
plus other locations in Chelsea,
Marylebone and Covent Garden
rococochocolates.com

Rococo was founded by a young punk called Chantal Coady in 1983, after she was sacked from Harrods' chocolate department for dyeing her hair a fetching mix of green and red. Hidden away at the back of her Belgravia store is a Moroccan-inspired courtyard garden, where you can enjoy an indulgent hot chocolate amid the aroma of jasmine and mint plants.

8. Visit the fashionistas' favourite chocolate shop

37 Marylebone High St, W1U 4EQ,
plus concessions in Harrods
and Selfridges
eu.marcolini.com

Pierre Marcolini describes himself as a 'haute chocolatier' and counts models like Diane Kruger among his clientele. Unsurprisingly, his glossy Marylebone store feels more like a fashion boutique than a sweetshop. His signature treats are the jewel-like chocolate hearts; try the scarlet ones filled with raspberry dark chocolate ganache.

CHOCOLATE AND MISO CARAMEL TART

One of London's best street food stalls is Fatties Bakery, which you'll find at various markets throughout the city. Its owner is Chloe Timms, a real-life sugar fairy who makes the most glorious, gooey caramel treats. The combination of caramel and the Japanese bean paste miso was something I first tried at her stall, and it is just inspired – think salted caramel, but with a richer, more complex flavour. This dessert is my tribute to Chloe. You can serve it squidgy and warm from the oven, but I prefer it fridge-cold, with a dollop of crème fraîche.

SERVES 8

For the pastry
220g plain flour
150g cold butter, cut into cubes
30g icing sugar
20g cocoa powder
2 egg yolks

For the filling
100g butter
90g soft dark brown sugar
80g white miso
397g can sweetened condensed milk
½ teaspoon salt (optional)

For the topping
80g butter
100g dark chocolate
1 egg, plus 2 egg yolks
3 tablespoons caster sugar

To make the pastry, put the flour, butter, icing sugar and cocoa powder into a large bowl and use your fingertips to gently rub the mixture together until it resembles fine breadcrumbs. Add the egg yolks and mix with a knife to form a dough. You may need to add 2–3 tablespoons of water to bring the mixture together. Squidge the pastry together with your hands and give it a quick knead on a floured work surface to create a smooth ball. Wrap in cling film and put into the fridge to chill for at least 30 minutes.

Preheat the oven to 180°C/160°C Fan/Gas Mark 4.

Roll out the pastry on a lightly floured surface to a thickness of about 5mm, then transfer to a 23cm loose-bottomed tart tin. Press the pastry firmly into the tin, then trim away any overhanging edges. Prick the bottom with a fork, line with baking parchment and fill with baking beans or rice. Cook in the oven for 15 minutes, then remove the paper and beans and return to the oven for 5 minutes. Leave to cool slightly.

To make the caramel filling, melt the butter, sugar and miso in a saucepan over a low heat, whisking occasionally, until combined. Add the condensed milk and bring to a simmer. Cook for 3–5 minutes, stirring constantly, until you have a thick, golden-brown caramel (be careful it doesn't burn). Remove from the heat and taste. If you're not getting much of an umami hit (miso brands can vary in intensity), add ½ teaspoon of salt. Spoon into the pastry case and put into the fridge for about 1 hour.

To make the chocolate topping, melt the butter and chocolate in a heatproof bowl over a pan of gently simmering water. Take off the heat and leave to cool slightly.

Whisk the eggs, egg yolks and sugar using an electric hand-whisk until pale and fluffy, about 5 minutes, then gently fold in the melted butter and chocolate. Pour over the caramel and bake for 20–25 minutes, until set.

DEEP-DISH COOKIE WITH A MOLTEN CHOCOLATE CENTRE

Chef Neil Rankin's restaurant Temper is famous for its succulent charcoal-grilled meats, but for me, this indulgent dessert is the real star of the menu. Essentially an underbaked cookie, Neil loves the recipe because it stirs 'memories of early baking, and the mistakes we make'. I love it because it means I can legitimately eat an entire panful of cookie dough.

SERVES 4–6

140g plain flour
½ teaspoon baking powder
½ teaspoon salt
120g butter
40g light brown sugar
100g caster sugar
½ teaspoon vanilla extract
1 egg
vanilla ice cream, to serve

For the chocolate centre
3 tablespoons butter, plus a little extra
397g can sweetened condensed milk
pinch of salt
4 tablespoons cocoa powder, sifted
1 teaspoon vanilla extract

First, make the chocolate mixture, which will become the gooey centre of your cookie. In a medium heavy-based saucepan, heat the butter, condensed milk, a pinch of salt and the cocoa powder, stirring constantly with a wooden spoon, until the mixture comes to the boil. Make sure you watch the pan like a hawk and regularly scrape the bottom, as it can burn very easily.

Reduce the heat to low and cook for another 10–15 minutes, still stirring constantly, until the mixture is thick and shiny. Stir in the vanilla and mix vigorously again. Pour the mixture onto a small buttered plate, and chill in the fridge for at least 2 hours.

Preheat your oven to 220°C/200°C Fan/Gas Mark 7. In a small bowl, whisk together the flour, baking powder and salt.

In a large bowl, beat together the butter and sugars until light and fluffy. Add the vanilla extract and eggs and beat until combined. Add the flour mixture to the wet ingredients and beat again until just combined.

Cover the base of a 20cm ovenproof frying pan with a thick layer of the mixture (about 1cm) and press down a small circle in the centre.

Use a cutter to cut out a circle of the chilled chocolate, then place it in the centre of the mix. You might need to use a spoon or knife to lever it off the plate. Spoon another 1cm layer of the cookie mixture on top and spread evenly, so the chocolate is completely covered.

Place the pan in the oven and cook for about 10 minutes, or a little longer if you'd prefer your cookie to be less runny. Serve straight away, hot and still in the pan, with a dollop of ice cream on top.

SMOKED SALT BROWNIE WITH BUTTERSCOTCH SAUCE

'What is London's best brownie?' is a controversial question. My favourites are those sold by chocolatier Paul A. Young at his beautiful shops around the city. They have a dense, moist fudginess that, for me, is the essence of a proper brownie.

When I started writing this book, one of the first things I did was ask Paul if he'd give me a special twist on his classic recipe. He came up with this 'dessert brownie', served in a rich puddle of butterscotch sauce. If you can't find smoked salt, ordinary sea salt will do, but try and use big, crunchy flakes – the little bursts of saltiness are delicious.

SERVES 9

150g butter, plus extra for greasing
260g light muscovado sugar
75g golden syrup
1½ teaspoons smoked sea salt
½ teaspoon freshly ground black pepper (optional)
250g good-quality dark chocolate, at least 70% cocoa solids, broken into small pieces
4 eggs
75g plain flour
vanilla ice cream, to serve

For the butterscotch sauce
100g butter
100g light muscovado sugar
1 teaspoon smoked sea salt
100ml double cream

Preheat the oven to 180°C/160°C Fan/Gas Mark 4. Grease a 20cm square tin with a little butter and line with baking parchment.

In a medium saucepan, melt the butter, sugar, golden syrup, salt and black pepper, if using, until combined. Take the pan off the heat, add the chocolate, and leave for a few minutes until the chocolate is fully melted. Give everything a good stir to combine.

Use a whisk to mix the eggs, one at a time, into the mixture. Add the flour and whisk in.

Pour the batter into your lined tin. Bake for 30–35 minutes, until the brownie has set at the edges but is still a little moist in the centre. Leave to cool in the tin for at least 20 minutes before cutting into squares.

To make the butterscotch sauce, combine the butter, sugar and salt in a small saucepan. Cook until all the ingredients are melted and combined. Bring to the boil, then reduce the heat to low and simmer for 5 minutes, stirring occasionally, until you have a thick, gooey sauce. Take off the heat and stir in the cream.

Serve the brownies warm with the butterscotch sauce and ice cream.

PADDINGTON'S BREAD AND BUTTER PUDDING

Bread and butter pudding is a classic British dessert. This recipe was inspired by Paddington, the little bear who arrives in London from 'deepest, darkest Peru' and has a penchant for marmalade sandwiches. When Paddington's creator Michael Bond died in 2017, many forlorn Londoners left jars of marmalade by the statue of the bear that stands at Paddington station.

SERVES 6

60g butter, plus extra for greasing
10 slices of stale white bread,
    crusts removed
5 tablespoons chunky marmalade
2 tablespoons mixed peel,
    roughly chopped
300ml milk
200ml double cream
3 eggs
50g caster sugar
1 teaspoon ground cinnamon
½ teaspoon ground nutmeg
grated zest of 1 orange
2 teaspoons demerara sugar

Lightly grease a medium ovenproof baking dish, about 25 × 20cm. Butter each slice of bread, then spread five of the slices thickly with marmalade. Put the slices together, so you have five marmalade sandwiches, and slice into triangles. Arrange the triangles in overlapping rows in the baking dish, and scatter over the mixed peel.

Whisk the milk, cream, eggs, caster sugar, cinnamon, nutmeg and orange zest together. Pour over the bread and leave to soak for at least 30 minutes.

Preheat the oven to 180°C/160°C Fan/Gas Mark 4. Sprinkle the demerara sugar over the top of the pudding, and bake for 35–45 minutes, until golden and puffy.

RULES: LONDON'S OLDEST RESTAURANT

London's oldest restaurant does not wear its age lightly. Instead, it piles on the diamonds, throws on a silk stole and shouts 'I've been here since 1798, bitches!' at the top of its voice. To enter Rules is to step back 200 years: one minute you are in the tourist bustle of Covent Garden, the next you are in a fantasy of a Victorian gentleman's English country home, all wood-panelled walls, thick red and gold carpets and the heavy smell of suet and gravy.

This Victorian gentleman must have been a kleptomaniac, for Rules' history is quite literally layered on the yellowing walls. There are busts in alcoves, ornate mirrors hung with dried hops, signed letters from celebrity fans, and antlers upon antlers upon antlers, the crumbling vestiges of long-ago hunts. There are paintings of long-dead beauties, demented clocks that seem to chime at completely irregular times, and occasional delightful flashes of campness. One wall is entirely given over to a painting of Margaret Thatcher, dressed in armour like Joan of Arc, with her gartered leg waggling reprovingly in the foreground.

The restaurant's history is as rich as its famous steak and kidney pudding. It was founded as an oyster bar by a rakish young man called Thomas Rule, and has survived nine English monarchs and two world wars with only two changes of ownership (the current owner is John Mayhew, whose Rolls-Royce, 'Bubbles', can sometimes be seen parked outside). The list of who has dined at Rules reads like a roll-call of British history: everyone from Charles Dickens to Charlie Chaplin to Madonna has sipped a cocktail on its red velvet couches. Graham Greene celebrated his birthdays here, while John Betjeman loved Rules so much that when it was threatened with demolition, he wrote a letter of protest, calling it 'unique and irreplaceable'. And the philandering Edward VII would sneak through a secret door, in what is now the stylish first-floor bar, to have his royal way with the actress Lillie Langtry.

It would be so easy for Rules to become a tourist trap, dishing up brown plates of roast beef and shepherd's pie and charging a lustful king's ransom for them. But the food is sublime: traditional British dishes that hug you like a fur coat on a winter's night. There is wild boar pie, the meat slowly cooked in red wine until it falls tenderly apart; melt-in-the-mouth steak and kidney pudding; perfectly cooked Dover sole, pearlescent and soft, swimming in oyster sauce. Game is a speciality:

Mayhew owns an estate in the High Pennines, and once a year his prized herd of belted Galloway cattle makes it onto Rules' fine china. Wine is mostly French and poured with great ceremony at the table by the bow-tied waiters, a delightfully inscrutable bunch who all appear to be auditioning for the role of snooty butler in an Oscar Wilde play.

Yes, you will find tourists at Rules, cooing over the gravy boats on lace doilies and snapping pictures of the fluffy golden syrup pudding. But you'll also find young couples on their first date; elegant ladies enjoying one too many of the bar's superlative martinis; and jowly, red-cheeked gentlemen sinking bottles of claret that will be immediately dumped onto company expense accounts. It is a London institution, and the only place, I often think, that deserves to be exempt from the smoking ban. A few wreaths of atmospheric cigar smoke would be the finishing touch to that delightfully old-fashioned atmosphere; a magic circle to ward away the modern world.

34–35 Maiden Lane, London, WC2E 7LB

GOLDEN SYRUP AND APPLE STEAMED PUDDING

Along with pigeons and irate taxi drivers, one thing London has never been short of is canny businessmen. Golden syrup was invented in the 1880s when Abram Lyle, the owner of a sugar factory, decided to try selling the sticky golden liquid that was a natural by-product of refining sugar. Tate & Lyle's golden syrup became a household staple, and the original factory still stands proudly on the banks of the Thames today. You can't miss it: there's a giant version of the iconic green-and-gold syrup tin mounted on the wall.

I love using golden syrup in an old-fashioned steamed pudding, where its unabashed sweetness is balanced by nuggets of sharp apple. It takes a little while to put together, but a pudding bubbling away on the hob, filling the kitchen with the scent of butter and sugar, is a truly delightful thing. If you prefer to eat out, head to London's oldest restaurant, Rules – their golden syrup pudding is the best in the city (see pages 224–225).

SERVES 4

7 tablespoons golden syrup

grated zest of 1 lemon, plus juice of ½ lemon

120g butter, at room temperature, plus extra for greasing

120g golden caster sugar

2 eggs

120g self-raising flour

400g cooking apples (about 2 large apples), cored and chopped into small cubes

pinch of salt

1 tablespoon whole milk, plus more if needed

custard, to serve

Butter the inside of a 900ml pudding bowl or basin and put the golden syrup into the bottom. Add the lemon juice, and stir with a spoon to combine.

In a large mixing bowl, or using a stand mixer, cream the butter and sugar together until soft and fluffy. Gradually add the eggs, beating well until mixed in.

Using a large metal spoon, stir in the flour, followed by the lemon zest, apples and the pinch of salt, until everything is combined. Add the milk, or a little more if needed, until you reach a 'dropping' consistency – that is, the mix will slowly slide off if you hold the spoon upside down. Spoon the mixture into the pudding bowl.

Cover the bowl with a lid or a tight layer of baking parchment, followed by a layer of foil, securing each layer with string. It's a good idea to make a little handle with more string, so you can remove the pudding easily later.

Put the pudding on top of a trivet or upturned saucer in a large saucepan and pour in boiling water so the water comes about halfway up the sides of the bowl (make sure the foil and paper don't touch the water, or your pudding will end up soggy). Bring to the boil, then cover with a lid, turn the heat down to low and steam for 2 hours.

Remove the bowl from the pan and turn the pudding out onto a warm serving plate. Serve with custard.

THE RITZ'S PLUM CHRISTMAS PUDDING

Every year, the chefs at The Ritz hotel make 2,000 of these Christmas puddings by hand. They are so popular that a guest once had a pud flown to Los Angeles by private plane. It is a proper old-fashioned Christmas pudding: rich, dark and boozy. If you don't own all the different alcohols, or don't want to buy them, feel free to make up the quantities with whatever you have to hand.

MAKES 1 LARGE (1.7-LITRE) PUDDING

200g sultanas
200g currants
200g raisins
40g glacé cherries, chopped
40g mixed peel
50g prunes, chopped
85g plain flour
35g ground almonds
120g fresh white breadcrumbs
85g soft dark brown sugar
1 tablespoon salt
10g crystallised ginger, finely chopped
½ teaspoon mixed spice
½ teaspoon ground nutmeg
½ teaspoon ground cinnamon
½ large cooking apple (about 70g), chopped
½ small carrot (about 45g), grated
grated zest and juice of 1 large orange
grated zest and juice of 1½ lemons
1 tablespoon golden syrup
1½ teaspoons cognac
25ml Guinness or other stout
25ml bitter ale
1 tablespoon madeira or sherry
2 teaspoons rum
1 egg
1 tablespoon shredded suet
1 tablespoon milk

Mix the dried fruit, flour, ground almonds, breadcrumbs, sugar, salt, ginger and all the ground spices together in a large bowl.

In another bowl, add the apple, carrot, citrus zest and juice, golden syrup and all the alcohol, and stir to ensure everything is thoroughly mixed. Slowly mix the wet ingredients into the dry, making sure nothing is crushed.

Pour the mixture into a clean tub or bowl and leave at room temperature for 3 days.

On the third day, mix in the egg, suet and milk. Lightly grease a 1.7-litre pudding bowl and place a small disc of foil or baking parchment on the base. Tip the pudding mix into the bowl and press down firmly with a spoon. Cover the pudding with a circle of baking parchment, tied securely with string or twine. Repeat with a layer of foil. It's also sensible to tie a piece of string or twine across the top to make a handle. Store in the fridge for 1 more day.

To cook the pudding, put the bowl in a large steamer of boiling water and cover with a lid. If you don't have a steamer, put the bowl in your largest saucepan, on top of a trivet, upturned saucer or small plate (this stops the pudding overcooking on the bottom). Fill the saucepan with boiling water, so it comes halfway up the side of the bowl, and cover with a tight-fitting lid, so no steam escapes. Cook the pudding on a gentle simmer for 8 hours, topping up the boiling water now and again if needed.

Allow the pudding to cool, then give it a fresh cover of baking parchment and foil. Store in a cool, dry place until Christmas Day.

To heat, steam for 2 hours as before, and turn out onto a plate. Douse with gently warmed brandy, light with a match, and bring to the table to the 'ooohs' and 'aaahs' of your guests.

EASY CARAMELISED NUT ICE CREAM

Caramelised nuts are the taste of London in winter. Almost the very second the weather turns chilly, vendors selling these addictive, sugar-crusted morsels pop up all over the city. This recipe transforms the nuts into a lovely crunchy dessert. The ice cream couldn't be easier, as there is no need for an ice cream maker or churning of any kind; just pop the mix in a freezer and return later with your largest spoon.

SERVES 8

100g caster sugar
100g almonds, halved
600ml double cream
397g can of condensed milk
1½ teaspoons ground cinnamon

Line a baking sheet with baking parchment and put to one side.

Place the sugar and 50ml of water into a small saucepan over a medium–high heat. Bring the mixture to the boil, stirring to dissolve the sugar, then add the almonds. Cook, stirring frequently, for 8–12 minutes until the sugar crystallises – it will go thick and grainy, like sand. Keep cooking, stirring vigorously, as the sugar slowly melts into a deep golden-brown caramel. Stir to coat the nuts, then quickly remove the pan from the hob (it can burn very quickly) and spread the nuts onto the baking sheet.

Once the nuts are cool, break up any that have clumped together. Roughly smash about half of the nuts with a pestle or the end of a rolling pin.

To make the ice cream, pour the cream, condensed milk and cinnamon into a large bowl and beat with an electric mixer or hand-whisk until stiff peaks form. Stir in the caramelised almonds, then transfer the mix to a large plastic tub and freeze until solid – at least 6 hours, or preferably overnight. This is good on its own, or with apple crumble or pie.

ST CLEMENT'S MERINGUE PIE WITH A GINGER CRUST

'Oranges and lemons/sing the bells of St Clement's'. So goes the old English nursery rhyme, referring to the distinctive bells of many famous churches within the City of London. Here, I've taken the classic British dessert lemon meringue pie, and given it a St Clement's twist.

SERVES 6–8

For the ginger pastry crust
200g plain flour, plus extra for dusting
pinch of salt
100g cold butter, cut into small cubes
2 tablespoons icing sugar
2 tablespoons crystallised ginger, very
  finely chopped
1 egg yolk

For the lemon orange curd
grated zest and juice of 4 lemons
grated zest and juice of 2 oranges
30g cornflour
3 egg yolks
170g caster sugar
20g butter

For the meringue
4 egg whites
200g caster sugar

To make the pastry crust, put the flour and salt into a large bowl. Add the butter and use your fingertips to gently rub the mixture together, until it resembles fine breadcrumbs. Stir in the sugar and ginger, then add the egg yolk and 2 tablespoons of water. Using a knife, stir the mix so the crumbs bind together into a dough. Add a splash more water if needed, but be cautious – you don't want the pastry to be too wet.

Using your hands, squidge the pastry together and give it a quick knead on a floured work surface to create a smooth ball. Wrap it in cling film and refrigerate for at least 30 minutes.

Preheat the oven to 180°C/160°C Fan/Gas Mark 4.

Roll out the pastry on a lightly floured surface to a thickness of about 5mm, then use it to line a 23cm tart tin. Press the pastry firmly into the tin, then trim away any overhanging edges. Prick the bottom with a fork, line with baking parchment and fill with baking beans or rice. Cook in the oven for 15 minutes, then remove the paper and beans and cook for a further 5–8 minutes, or until the pastry is golden. (Leave the oven on.)

To make the curd, put the citrus zest and juice in a saucepan along with 50ml of water. Stir in the cornflour until the mixture is smooth, and bring to the boil. Turn down the heat to medium–low, then mix in the egg yolks, caster sugar and butter. Keep cooking, whisking constantly, for about 7–10 minutes, until the mix is thick like a custard. Take off the heat and leave to cool for 5 minutes, then spoon into the tart case. If you like, you can now refrigerate until needed.

To make the meringue, put the egg whites into a large bowl and whisk until stiff peaks form. Add the sugar, 1 tablespoon at a time, until you have a stiff, glossy mixture. Spoon over the lemon curd, using your spoon to create a lovely swirl effect.

Bake in the oven for about 15 minutes, until the meringue is lightly browned on top. Leave to cool slightly before serving, to allow the curd to set.

LATE-NIGHT LONDON

LONDON IS AT ITS MOST ATMOSPHERIC AFTER NIGHTFALL, WHEN DARKNESS POOLS IN THE LABYRINTHINE ALLEYS AND FOXES SKULK ON STREET CORNERS.

UNDER THE THIN LIGHT OF STURDY VICTORIAN STREET LAMPS, CHATTERING CROWDS POUR OUT OF THE THEATRES, PUBS AND CLUBS, ON THE HUNT FOR A LATE-NIGHT SNACK.

WHETHER YOU FANCY A SIT-DOWN MEAL WITH PANORAMIC VIEWS OVER THE GLITTERING CITY OR A CHEEKY STOP-OFF AT A FRIED CHICKEN SHOP BEFORE CALLING A CAB, SUSTENANCE IS NEVER FAR AWAY.

BURNT COURGETTE TZATZIKI

When The Palomar opened in 2014, I thought it sounded hellish. A restaurant throbbing with loud music, and where the chefs wear baseball hats and down shots with the customers, seemed like a pointed challenge to British reserve. But curiosity eventually got the better of me, and I'm glad it did, because the second you take your seat at the buzzing kitchen bar, you're at the best party in town. Diners jiggle on their seats to Abba and James Brown, while the chefs fire out plate after plate of stunning Middle Eastern-inspired food.

The siren glow of Palomar's red neon sign often lures me in late at night for a glass of wine and a platter of punchy dips, scooped up with big hunks of bread. This is my version of their addictive tzatziki, which replaces the conventional cucumber with golden, crunchy courgette.

SERVES 4–6 AS A STARTER

1 large courgette, chopped into
   1cm chunks
400ml natural yoghurt
juice of 1 lemon
1 garlic clove, crushed
small handful of fresh mint, chopped
1 teaspoon sumac
1 tablespoon extra virgin olive oil, plus
   extra to serve
handful of almonds, toasted, to garnish
salt and freshly ground black pepper

Heat a griddle or frying pan until very hot. Add the courgette chunks and cook, turning regularly, until tender and charred. Remove from the heat, sprinkle with a little salt, and leave to cool.

Put the yoghurt, lemon juice, garlic, mint, sumac, ½ teaspoon of salt and 1 tablespoon of the oil into a bowl and stir to combine. Mix in the courgettes, and add salt and pepper to taste. Garnish with the toasted almonds and another drizzle of oil, and serve with lots of bread for dipping. Dancing while eating is strictly optional.

EAST END BAGELS

Bagels were brought to London, just as they were to New York, by Jewish immigrants from Eastern Europe. Many Jews settled in the poor East End, where you'll still find two of the best bagel places in town. There is fierce local debate over whether Beigel Shop ('the yellow one') or Beigel Bake ('the white one') is better. Both are open twenty-four hours a day and are particularly popular after midnight, when post-party Londoners pile in and devour bagels with the kind of religious contentment that only comes with a very heavy carb fix.

Making bagels at home isn't difficult, but I do recommend using a stand mixer, because the dough is very stiff to knead by hand. The resulting bagels are chewy, tender and all the tastier because you don't have to wobble your way home in the dark after eating one.

MAKES 8

500g strong white bread flour
7g sachet fast-action dried yeast
3 tablespoons malt syrup or honey
oil, for greasing
1 teaspoon bicarbonate of soda
1 egg white
sesame seeds or poppyseeds (optional)
salt

Mix the flour, yeast and 2 teaspoons of salt in a large mixing bowl. In a small bowl or jug, dissolve 2 tablespoons of the malt syrup or honey in 280ml of warm water, and stir. Pour into the bowl containing the flour.

If you are using a stand mixer, knead on a low speed with the dough hook attachment for about 7 minutes. If you are doing it by hand, bring the mixture together using a wooden spoon, then turn out onto a clean work surface and knead until you have a smooth, stiff dough – about 10 minutes.

Put the dough in a lightly oiled bowl, covered with either oiled cling film or a damp tea towel. Leave in a warm place until doubled in size, about 1–1½ hours.

Line a large baking tray with lightly greased baking parchment. Take the dough out of the bowl and divide it into eight equal pieces. Roll each piece into a ball, then flatten very slightly with the palm of your hand. Make holes in the bagels. I find the easiest way to do this is to dip your index finger into flour, then use it to make a hole in the centre of each bagel. Insert the index finger of your other hand into the hole so the fingers meet, then twirl the bagel around your fingers to widen the gap, until it's about the size of a fifty pence piece. Place on the baking trays, cover and leave for another 30 minutes, until they have puffed up a little more.

Preheat the oven to 220°C/200°C Fan/Gas Mark 7. Heat a large pan of water until simmering, then add the remaining malt syrup or honey, the bicarbonate of soda and a heavy pinch of salt. Boil the bagels, a few at a time, for 1 minute, turning them over halfway through. Remove from the water with a slotted spoon and drain on kitchen paper. Don't panic if the bagels look as wrinkly as newborn babies after a bath – the creases magically disappear in the oven.

Brush the tops of the bagels with the egg white, and dunk into a bowl of sesame seeds or poppyseeds, if using. Return them to the lined trays. Bake for 20–25 minutes, until golden on top. Slice open and fill with cream cheese and salmon, or salt beef and mustard.

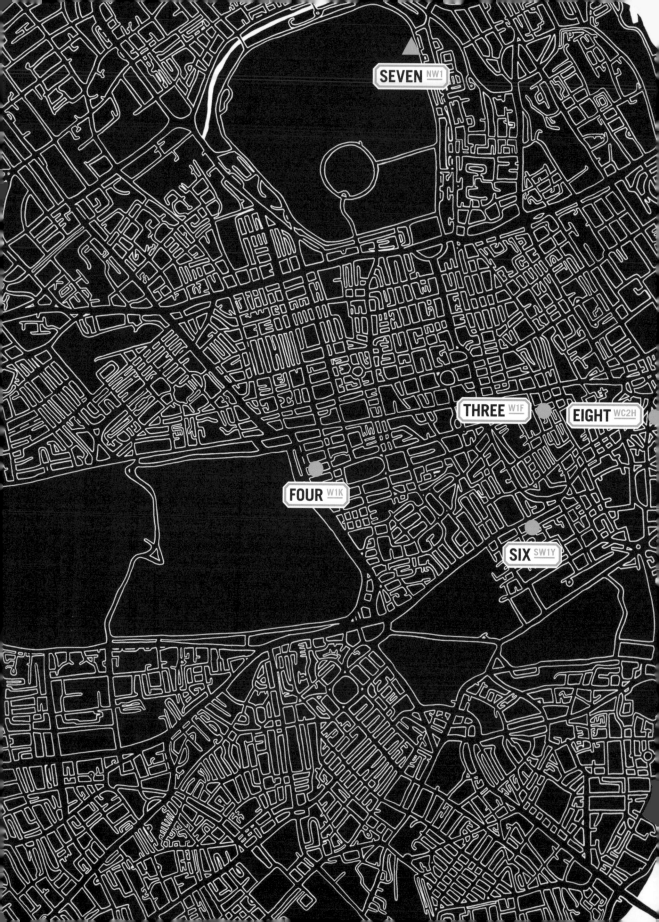

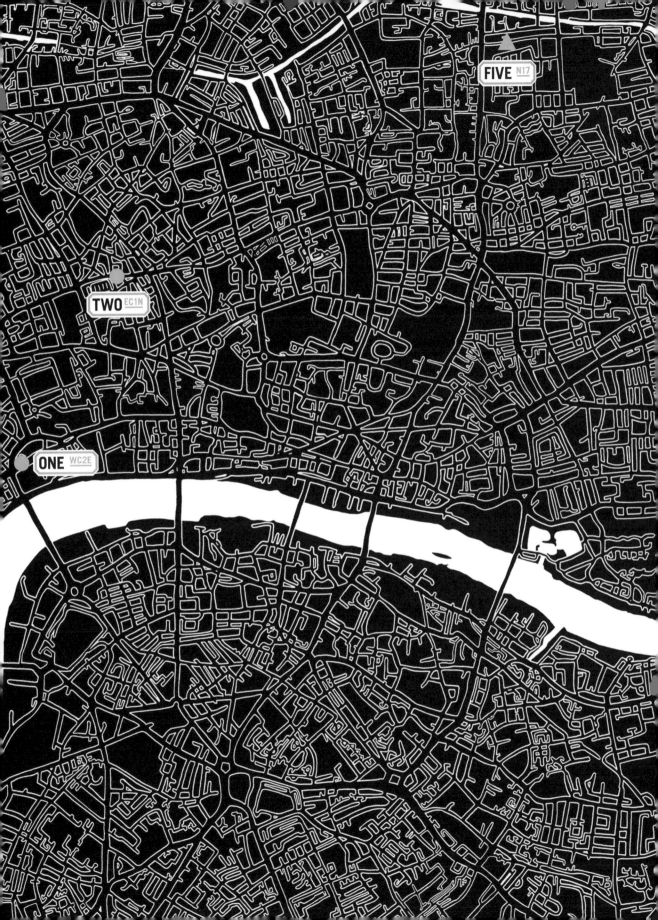

A GUIDE TO...
LONDON FOR CHEESE LOVERS

1. Have a cheese and fizz party

22 Wellington St, WC2E 7DD
plus other locations in Brixton,
Greenwich and Southwark
champagneplusfromage.co.uk

Civilisation has surely peaked with Champagne + Fromage, a small chain of cafés dedicated to cheese and fizz, aka the two best things in life. Take your pick of fifty top-quality French cheeses, plus excellent charcuterie, bread and, of course, champagne.

2. Devour the ultimate cheese toastie

Leather Lane Market
Tue–Fri, 12–2pm
grillmycheese.co.uk

Street food stall Grill My Cheese sells indulgent grilled cheese sandwiches that will make you weep with pleasure, even as your belt pings off in protest. Don't miss Baby Got Mac, a sourdough toastie piled high with oozing cheese, macaroni, pulled pork and barbecue sauce.

3. Dive into the city's best fondue

161 Wardour St, Soho,
W1F 8WJ
stmoritz-restaurant.co.uk

A giant vat of bubbling cheese is just the ticket on a chilly London night. St Moritz, the oldest Swiss restaurant in the capital, is the unchallenged king of fondue. They even do a chocolate one for dessert.

4. Go retro with a cheese trolley

43 Upper Brook St,
Mayfair,
W1K 7QR
le-gavroche.co.uk

Once a restaurant staple, the cheese trolley has sadly been relegated along with vol au vents and corned beef to the graveyard of food fashion. At Michelin-starred Le Gavroche, however, a groaning cheese trolley is still making the rounds, delighting diners with its magnificent selection of over forty cheeses.

You don't need to go to Paris to find good cheese;
London is a paradise for fans of fromage.

5. Learn the art of cheesemaking

33 Queen St,
N17 8JA
wildescheese.co.uk

When Philip Wilton lost his job as a management consultant, he decided to follow a very different passion: cheese. Now he runs Wildes, a teeny urban dairy on an industrial estate in the north of the city. Sign up for a course and he'll show you how to make cheese at home with little more than a bowl, a cloth and a colander.

6. Sample the Queen's cheese

93 Jermyn St, St James's,
SW1Y 6JE
paxtonandwhitfield.co.uk

The official cheesemonger to Her Majesty The Queen, Paxton & Whitfield can trace a gooey thread all the way back to 1742, when a young man named Stephen Cullum started selling cheese from a stall in Aldwych. Winston Churchill once declared Paxton & Whitfield the only shop where a 'gentleman' would buy his cheese.

7. Try blue cheese ice cream

93–94 Camden Stables,
NW1 8AH
thecheesebar.com

Fancy cheese for your starter, main course and dessert? Then head to The Cheese Bar, a restaurant that's even cheesier than your dad's dancing. Don't miss the oozing 'mozzarella sticks' – deep-fried cheese with a tomato sauce for dipping – or the blue cheese and honey ice cream.

8. Visit the home of the British cheese revolution

17 Shorts Gardens, WC2H 9AT
plus other locations in Borough
Market and Bermondsey
nealsyarddairy.co.uk

Randolph Hodgson is a big cheese in the food world. He founded Neal's Yard in Covent Garden in 1979 and was one of the first retailers to champion artisan British cheese. His three London shops offer a dazzling array of products from dairies across the UK. Try St Jude's, a creamy raw milk cheese made in Suffolk.

BIG BEN BURGER

I'm going to risk offending our American friends and say it: London leads the world in burgers right now. Walk through Soho or Shoreditch late on a Saturday night, and the smell of plump beef patties and sticky onions is inescapable. Gourmet burger restaurants like Honest Burger, MeatLiquor and Dirty Burger are all doing sensational things to meat in a bun, and Londoners can't get enough.

This recipe is my tribute to the city's burger bonanza. Like all true Brits, it turns its nose up at plain-old ketchup; instead, there's a quick burger sauce made with HP, the classic English brown sauce with the Houses of Parliament on the bottle. Slathering the patties with mustard before cooking so they get a rich, tangy crust is an idea that originated in the States. I think it works even better with punchy English mustard.

SERVES 4

For the burgers
500g good-quality beef mince,
   ideally 20% fat
1 small onion, very finely chopped
1 teaspoon salt
4 teaspoons English mustard
freshly ground black pepper

To serve
4 thick slices mature Cheddar cheese
4 tablespoons HP sauce
2 tablespoons mayonnaise
1 tablespoon ketchup
4 soft burger buns, halved
4 gherkins, sliced
1 large tomato, sliced
½ iceberg lettuce, shredded

In a bowl, mix the beef mince, onion, salt and plenty of fresh black pepper. Divide into four pieces, and with wet hands, roll each one into a ball. Gently squish each one into a patty, about 10cm wide. If you have time, put them in the fridge for at least 30 minutes; this will help the burgers firm up and stop them disintegrating when cooked.

Heat your barbecue, or a griddle pan over a medium–high heat. Smear ½ teaspoon of mustard over the top of each burger, and cook, mustard-side down, for 3 minutes, until there is a good crust on the underside of the burger. Smear another ½ teaspoon of mustard over the top of each burger, then flip and cook to your liking – another 2–3 minutes is about right if you want them rare, 4–5 minutes for well done. A few minutes before your burgers are ready, add a slice of cheese on top of each one so it begins to melt.

Remove the burgers onto a plate and leave to rest for a few minutes. In a small bowl, make your burger sauce by mixing the HP sauce, mayonnaise and ketchup, then smear it over the bottom of the buns. Add the gherkin slices. Slide the burgers on top, then add a tomato slice and a small handful of iceberg lettuce on each one. Squish on the top halves of the bun, and serve.

STEAK TARTARE

There are few London restaurar[...] much as Bob Bob Ricard. With its [...] buttons on every table, and flamboya[...] Orient Express, redesigned by Liberace a[...] while on a massive bender – it is ostentatiou[...] most absurd, gleeful way. A late-night, gossipy [...] in one of Bob Bob's cosy booths will set right most [...] wrongs in the world, just as long as you don't look at [...] your bank balance the next day. This is my version of the [...] restaurant's Imperial steak tartare. They top it with foie gras and caviar, but it tastes just as divine without such oligarchical accoutrements.

SERVES 2

300g best-quality fillet steak
1 shallot, finely chopped
2 anchovies, finely chopped
2 heaped teaspoons finely chopped
   flat-leaf parsley
1 tablespoon cornichons,
   finely chopped
1 tablespoon capers
1 tablespoon Worcestershire sauce
5 drops Tabasco
2 teaspoons Dijon mustard
squeeze of lemon juice
1 scant teaspoon brandy (optional)
salt and freshly ground black pepper

To serve
caviar, foie gras, or just good
   old-fashioned parsley

Finely chop the steak ¬ you are aiming for really small pieces, like coarse mince. Put into a bowl, and use a fork to mix in the remaining ingredients. Add salt and pepper to taste, then use your hands to gently mould the mixture together into two burger-like shapes.

Leave for at least 20 minutes (raw beef tastes better when it's not straight from the fridge) before garnishing with your chosen additions. This is best served with something crunchy, like pumpernickel bread, or, for the ultimate treat dinner, a big pile of homemade chips.

RGE:
IAL

ts that make me smile as
'press for champagne'
t decor – think
nd Prince
s in the
dinner

'Butchery is a dying trade,' says Richard Turner sadly, as he takes off his apron. 'It's a really full-on, physical job – blood, guts, hauling around carcasses. Nobody wants to do that any more; they want to go on a reality TV programme and become famous. They want an easier life.'

Londoners have always loved their meat. The Worshipful Company of Butchers, one of the city's many ancient trade organisations, can trace its beginnings all the way back to 975AD. Each London neighbourhood traditionally had its own butcher, who was at the heart of the community. In the eighteenth and nineteenth centuries, when a couple got married, there was a peculiar tradition for butchers' apprentices to serenade them by banging marrow bones on cleavers. One can't help but think the bride and groom would probably rather have had a pack of free sausages.

These days, however, most people get their meat from the supermarket, and independent butchers are disappearing faster than the last burger at a summer barbecue. Opening a butcher's at such a time seems mad, but that's exactly what Richard Turner and James George did.

Turner is a chef by trade, who has a reputation as London's main 'meat man'. He has stakes (and steaks) in various meaty restaurants, including barbecue joint Pitt Cue and chop specialist Blacklock, and is passionate about quality British meat, reared humanely and without being pumped full of hormones or antibiotics. He was working at the steak restaurant group Hawksmoor when he received an email from George, a butcher who supplied a pub he used to work in. 'He asked me if I fancied going into business with him, and opening an old-fashioned butcher – proper meat from British breeds. And I did.'

In 2013, the pair opened Turner & George, in a old Victorian butcher's shop in Clerkenwell. Step inside and you will feel as though that original butcher's never closed. There are the original cream and brown-coloured

IF YOU ARE EVER IN NEED OF A LAMB'S KIDNEY, A PIG'S HEAD OR AN OXTAIL, THIS IS THE PLACE TO COME.

The exterior of Turner & George, Clerkenwell. (Photo by Tom Gold)

tiles; shining meat hooks; and a counter piled high with plump rib-eye steaks and marbled slabs of home-cured bacon. The pair buy their meat from small, independent farms across Britain, and age much of it, especially the beef, in the cellar underneath the shop, for five to seven weeks. 'We want our customers to have a piece of meat that they can really taste, and you just don't get that without dry-ageing,' explains George. 'When meat is fresh it will be tough, full of water and lacking in any real depth of flavour. Ageing helps to break down the muscles, and as water evaporates, the flavour intensifies. It's akin to how beef used to taste before industrial farming.'

Turner and George are passionate about eating the whole animal, nose to tail; if you are ever in need of

a lamb's kidney, a pig's head or an oxtail, this is the place to come. But it is the prime cuts that most customers come in for: a juicy steak or a fat lamb chop. George loves a 'nice, thick rib-eye steak from one of our rare-breed cattle, usually Red Poll or Belted Galloway'. Turner has a soft spot for Highland cattle, those quaint beasts with the long horns and flowing coats. 'They live all year round and forage, eating moss and clover and grass, which means they have a really distinctive flavour,' he says. 'But you also can't get a Highland to slaughter in under three years. It will taste good, because time is on its side.'

399 St John Street, Clerkenwell, London, EC1V 4LD

PROPER FRIED CHICKEN WITH A HERBY CRUST

Fried chicken shops are ubiquitous in London. Sadly, a late-night chicken stop tends to taste of grease and bad decisions, so it's worth knowing how to make the good stuff at home. The trick to crisp yet juicy fried chicken is to heat the oil to exactly the right temperature: 170°C, if you have a cook's thermometer. The fresh herbs and lemon here are unconventional, but they cut nicely through the heaviness of the chicken.

SERVES 4

300ml buttermilk
grated zest of 2 lemons
2 garlic cloves, crushed
2 teaspoons salt, plus extra to serve
8 skin-on chicken pieces on the bone,
    (a mixture of thighs and drumsticks)
200g plain flour
3 tablespoons cornflour
1 teaspoon paprika
½ teaspoon freshly ground
    black pepper
1 heaped tablespoon very finely
    chopped fresh rosemary, plus extra
    to garnish (optional)
1 heaped tablespoon very finely
    chopped fresh thyme, plus extra
    to garnish (optional)
vegetable or sunflower oil, for frying

Mix the buttermilk, lemon zest, garlic and 1 teaspoon of salt in a large bowl, and add the chicken, making sure the marinade coats all the meat. Cover the bowl and pop it in the fridge for at least 4 hours, or preferably overnight.

In a separate large, shallow bowl, combine the flour, cornflour, paprika, pepper, rosemary, thyme and the remaining teaspoon of salt. Take the chicken from the fridge and use kitchen paper to wipe off some of the excess buttermilk. Roll the chicken pieces one by one in the herby flour mixture until evenly coated.

Fill a large, wide pan with the oil and heat until the oil is very hot – 170°C on a thermometer, or until a cube of bread sizzles and turns golden within 60 seconds when dropped into the oil. Carefully add the chicken, in batches of two or three pieces at a time to avoid overcrowding the pan. Fry until crisp and golden, usually 9–14 minutes, depending on the size of your chicken joints. If you have a thermometer, poke it into the chicken's thickest part – it is cooked at 75°C. Alternatively, cut open a piece of chicken and make sure the juices are running clear.

Place the cooked chicken pieces in an ovenproof tray lined with plenty of kitchen paper, and keep warm in a low oven while you finish cooking the remaining chicken. Serve sprinkled with extra salt, and with a few herb sprigs to garnish, if you like.

CRISPY CHINESE-STYLE ROASTED DUCK WITH PANCAKES

The classic Chinatown dish is roast duck, wrapped in paper-thin pancakes, with a sticky drizzle of hoisin sauce. It's not difficult to recreate at home, but you need to start the day before; letting the bird dry out in the fridge is the secret to obtaining that really crisp skin.

SERVES 4

1 whole duck (about 2kg)
2 tablespoons soy sauce
2 tablespoons honey
2 teaspoons salt
1 teaspoon Chinese five-spice powder

To serve
Chinese pancakes
hoisin sauce
cucumber and spring onions,
   thinly sliced

Prepare the duck the day before you want to eat it. Slide your fingers underneath the skin and wiggle to loosen it away from the breast meat, working your way down the bird. Put the duck on top of a wire rack in the sink, and pour over a kettleful of boiling water. This will tighten the skin, so it gets extra crispy. Leave the duck to sit for a moment, until most of the water has dripped off, then transfer to a roasting tray, patting the bird all over with kitchen paper to remove the excess moisture.

Combine the soy sauce, honey, salt and five-spice powder in a small bowl, then rub this mixture all over the duck, inside and out. Put the duck, uncovered, in the fridge overnight.

The next day, preheat the oven to 180°C/160°C Fan/Gas Mark 4.

Put a roasting tray half filled with water at the bottom of the oven (this will catch the fat from the duck as it drips), then place the duck straight onto a wire rack above. Roast for about 2 hours, until golden and crispy. If you're worried the duck is burning, you can cover it with foil, but you want it to be really crispy.

Once cooked, let the duck stand, covered, for at least 10 minutes. Shred it into small pieces, and serve with the pancakes, hoisin sauce and sliced vegetables, so everyone can assemble their own.

CHINATOWN: LONDON'S IMPERIAL CITY

Chinatown at night, when Londoners descend on the area's cheap-and-cheerful restaurants. (Amy Davies/Digital Camera Magazine/Getty Images)

The first time you stumble across Chinatown is magical. One minute you are in Leicester Square, in the heart of London's entertainment district – all colossal cinemas, gaudy casinos and fast-food outlets. But venture just a few steps north and you'll suddenly find yourself passing through an intricately decorated Chinese gate.

Here, in a jumble of narrow streets strung with glowing red lanterns, there are restaurants with crispy bronzed ducks hanging in their windows, tiny Chinese medicine shops offering cures for every ailment imaginable, and the smell of spices and rosewood. This is the biggest and most centrally located Chinatown in Europe, so impressive that some refer to it as 'The Imperial City'. Every day, locals and tourists alike arrive to fill their bellies with cheap-and-cheerful Chinese food. Few know that there was once another Chinatown in London, with a far less appetising reputation.

Britain began trading with China in the seventeenth century, and it wasn't long before Chinese sailors arrived in the capital. They settled in the impoverished slums of the East, mostly in Limehouse, and Pennyfields in Poplar. This growing community of foreigners terrified the Victorians. Their feverish imaginations painted the area as a murky underworld of opium dens and gangs, presided over by moustachioed Chinese crime lords with a penchant for deflowering English maidens. Late Victorian and early twentieth-century novels are saturated with Chinaphobia. Sax Rohmer's Fu Manchu novels feature a Chinese mastermind who plots the downfall of Western civilisation from his base in East London. Sir Arthur Conan Doyle's Sherlock Holmes stories paint a hellish picture of opium dens, where 'one could dimly catch a glimpse of bodies lying in strange fantastic poses, bowed shoulders, bent knees, heads thrown back, and chins pointing upward'. Newspaper headlines shrieked of 'Yellow Peril' and 'The Lure of the Yellow Men!'.

The reality was rather less titillating. Firstly, the Chinese community was small: by 1914, there were only around 300 people and thirty Chinese businesses. Secondly, rather than drug smuggling and murder, most made their living in the rather cleaner business of laundries. Spotless as their hands were, the community's time in East London was short-lived. By the end of the

A Chinese shop in Limehouse, the site of the original Chinatown
(Historic Graphica Collection/Heritage Images/Getty Images)

Second World War, heavy bombing and a decrease in the number of ships docking in the area had driven the Chinese away. Walk around Limehouse today, and only a few street names – Ming Street, Mandarin Street – give a clue that they were ever there.

So how did modern-day Chinatown spring up? In the 1960s, Soho was notoriously seedy, filled with dive bars and brothels, so rents were cheap. English soldiers returned from service in the Far East with a taste for Chinese food, and resourceful Chinese immigrants began to open restaurants. There are now over eighty eateries crammed into the area, offering everything from dumplings to Chinese custard tarts. Few of London's 12,000-strong Chinese community still live there (rents aren't so cheap anymore), but Chinatown is still very much the heart of the community. It is here that London's traditional Chinese New Year celebrations take place. Watching colourful dragon and lion puppets weave and roar their way through the streets is an unmissable

restaurants have sprung up far beyond the confines of Soho. In truth, many of them offer better fare than the 'all you can eat' buffets of Chinatown. At A Wong in Pimlico, diners tuck into an elaborate ten-course 'Taste of China' menu, kicking off with a delicate scallop salad and finishing with a lychee granita. At upmarket Hutong, on the 33rd floor of The Shard skyscraper, the Peking Duck will make you weep with pleasure even as it nibbles £60 from your wallet. Compare this to Chinatown's Wong Kei, often dubbed the rudest restaurant in Britain, where staff have been known to mock customers who can't use chopsticks and chase them down the street if they don't leave a tip. (I must note here that Wong Kei's waiters have softened their behaviour of late, though I'd eat my bamboo hat if they ever pulled a chair out for you.) But even if we're verbally abused over our sweet and sour chicken balls, there is something about Chinatown that draws Londoners back time and time again. Perhaps an evil mastermind is at work after all.

DUCK AND WAFFLE WITH MUSTARD MAPLE SYRUP

Way up in the sky, on the 40th floor of a towering skyscraper, Duck & Waffle has an unbeatable view of London. It's also open 24/7, so you can watch the sun rise as you tuck into a hearty breakfast. This is the signature dish: a crispy confit duck leg, served on a fluffy waffle, with a fried egg and a sticky pool of spiced maple syrup.

SERVES 4

4 duck legs
500g duck or goose fat
4 duck eggs
oil, for greasing
butter, for frying

For the duck cure
60g coarse salt
60g caster sugar
grated zest of 2 oranges
pinch of ground cinnamon
1 clove
1 star anise
2 pink peppercorns
10ml brandy

For the waffle
180g plain flour
10g caster sugar
1 teaspoon baking powder
½ teaspoon bicarbonate of soda
pinch of salt
180ml buttermilk
35g butter, melted
1 small egg

For the mustard maple syrup
200ml maple syrup
25g yellow mustard seeds
1 teaspoon English mustard powder
2.5cm piece of cinnamon stick
1 sprig of fresh thyme

The day before cooking, mix all the ingredients for the cure in a large bowl, then add the duck legs and make sure they are thoroughly coated. Cover, and leave in the fridge overnight.

The next day, preheat your oven to 140°C/120°C Fan/Gas Mark 1. Take out the duck legs and brush off all of the cure. Place in an ovenproof casserole dish and cover with the duck or goose fat. Put into the oven and cook for approximately 3 hours, or until the meat just falls off the bone. Allow to cool in the fat.

To make the waffle mix, put the flour, sugar, baking powder, bicarbonate of soda and salt into a bowl and whisk together. In another bowl, whisk together the buttermilk, melted butter and egg, then pour this into the flour mixture and whisk until just combined. The mixture will be quite thick. Put into the fridge until you are ready to make your waffles.

Combine all the ingredients for the maple syrup in a saucepan and bring to the boil. Take off the heat and leave to cool to allow the flavours to infuse. Remove the cinnamon and thyme sprig, but leave the mustard seeds, as they add a nice dimension when bitten into.

When ready to serve, preheat the oven to 180°C/160°C Fan/Gas Mark 4, and turn on your waffle iron. Heat an ovenproof frying pan over a high heat, and add the duck legs, skin side down. Once the skin starts to crisp, turn the legs over and put into the oven for 8–10 minutes, or until crisp.

While the duck legs are in the oven, make your waffles. Brush the hot waffle iron with oil and pour a ladleful of batter into each mould. Spread it all around, as the mix is very thick and won't spread on its own. Cook for about 3 minutes, or until golden and cooked through.

Put another frying pan over a medium–low heat. Melt some butter in the pan and gently break in the duck eggs. Fry until the whites are set, spooning the hot butter over the yolk right at the end.

Serve a duck leg on top of each waffle, with an egg on top of the duck and the maple syrup on the side.

Adapted from *Duck & Waffle* by Dan Doherty (Mitchell Beazley, 2014).

HOMEMADE DONER KEBABS

We have Turkish and Greek immigrants to thank for the London institution that is the kebab. The first kebab house opened in the north of the city in 1966. Now, no Friday night pub session is complete without wobbling to the nearest takeaway and devouring a kebab drowned in so much garlic sauce it would send a vampire running for the nearest night bus. They're more than just drunk junk food, however: for London's immigrant communities, the kebab shop is a hallowed place where they can sit, talk and enjoy a solid meal for just a few pounds.

The traditional doner kebab, scraped off the revolving 'elephant's leg', is often greasy and unpleasant. But a good one – all tender meat, soft bread and crunchy salad – is unbeatable. You can make your own version by cooking lamb mince in a loaf tin, a little like an American meatloaf, then slicing it. I like to stuff the lamb into a pitta bread with a bright homemade coleslaw, but if you want the classic kebab house experience, serve with lettuce, pickled chillies and garlic sauce instead.

SERVES 4

1 teaspoon vegetable or sunflower oil, for greasing
½ onion
600g lamb mince, preferably 5% fat
2 garlic cloves, crushed
1 teaspoon salt
2 teaspoons ras el hanout
¼ teaspoon freshly ground black pepper
½ teaspoon ground cinnamon
1½ teaspoons ground cumin
pitta breads or wraps, to serve
chilli and garlic sauce, to serve (optional)

For the coleslaw
¼ red cabbage, very thinly sliced
¼ white cabbage, very thinly sliced
1 large carrot, roughly grated
3 spring onions, very thinly sliced
handful of fresh mint and/or coriander, chopped
4 tablespoons natural yoghurt
2 tablespoons mayonnaise
1 heaped tablespoon harissa paste
juice of ½ lemon
1 tablespoon red wine vinegar
1 teaspoon caster sugar
½ teaspoon salt

Preheat the oven to 200°C/180°C Fan/Gas Mark 6. Lightly grease a 900g loaf tin with the oil.

If you have a food processor, whizz the onion until very finely chopped; if not, grate it. Put the onion into a large bowl with all the other ingredients and mix thoroughly. Transfer to the loaf tin and press down firmly with the back of a spoon or your hands – you want it to be very compressed.

Cook for 35 minutes, then carefully drain off any fat or oil from the tin, and set aside for 10 minutes to cool down slightly. Turn the meat out and slice into thin strips.

To make the coleslaw, mix together all the ingredients in a large bowl and toss to combine.

Serve the sliced lamb with the coleslaw, pitta breads and sauces, if using, o everyone can dig in and make their own kebabs.

SPICY LAMB CHOPS WITH KACHUMBER

Tayyabs is not the place for a relaxing night out. This cheap-and-cheerful East London curry house is so busy, there is always a queue for tables, and so noisy that you'd be forgiven for thinking you'd accidentally ordered the apocalypse instead of a biryani. But there is something intoxicating about the restaurant's hectic energy, and the food really is worth it. This is my version of Tayyabs' legendary Punjabi-style lamb chops, served sizzling from the grill. They're perfect paired with a fresh, zingy Indian salad known as kachumber.

SERVES 2

4 lamb chops
lemon wedges, to serve

For the marinade
1 teaspoon cumin seeds
1 teaspoon black peppercorns
4 tablespoons natural yoghurt
1 tablespoon lemon juice
1 teaspoon salt
1 tablespoon tomato paste
1 teaspoon red chilli powder
1½ teaspoons garam masala
2 garlic cloves, crushed
thumb-sized knob of ginger, grated
1 green chilli, finely chopped

For the kachumber
4 tomatoes, finely chopped
½ onion, finely chopped
½ cucumber, finely chopped
½ green chilli, deseeded and
    finely chopped
½ teaspoon salt
small handful of coriander leaves,
    finely chopped
juice of ½ lemon
½ teaspoon garam masala

In a dry frying pan over a medium heat, gently fry the cumin seeds and peppercorns for just a few minutes, tossing regularly, until they start to smell fragrant and jump around in the pan. Crush in a pestle and mortar and put into a large bowl.

Add all the remaining ingredients for the marinade into the bowl and mix to combine. Add the lamb chops and rub the marinade all over, making sure you get it into every crevice of the lamb. Cover the bowl and refrigerate for at least 4–5 hours.

Meanwhile, make the kachumber. Simply mix together all the ingredients in a bowl and put to one side until needed (note that tomatoes taste much better when not fridge-cold).

Take the chops out of the fridge at least 30 minutes before you want to eat them – this gives them the chance to come up to room temperature. Preheat the grill to a moderately high heat, and cook the chops for 8–12 minutes, turning at least once, until they are cooked to your satisfaction (I like them well done and starting to develop a nice char on the outside).

Serve the chops with the kachumber on the side and lemon wedges for squeezing over.

CAPITAL DRINKS

LONDON HAS ALWAYS WORSHIPPED AT THE SHRINE OF THE GRAPE, THE GRAIN AND THE HOP.

THE CITY'S INHABITANTS, WROTE THE FRENCH POET PAUL VERLAINE DISAPPROVINGLY IN 1873, WERE 'NOISY AS DUCKS … EVERLASTINGLY DRUNK'.

I LIKE TO THINK MODERN LONDONERS ARE A LITTLE MORE RESTRAINED – THOUGH ALL BETS ARE OFF AT THE WEEKEND.

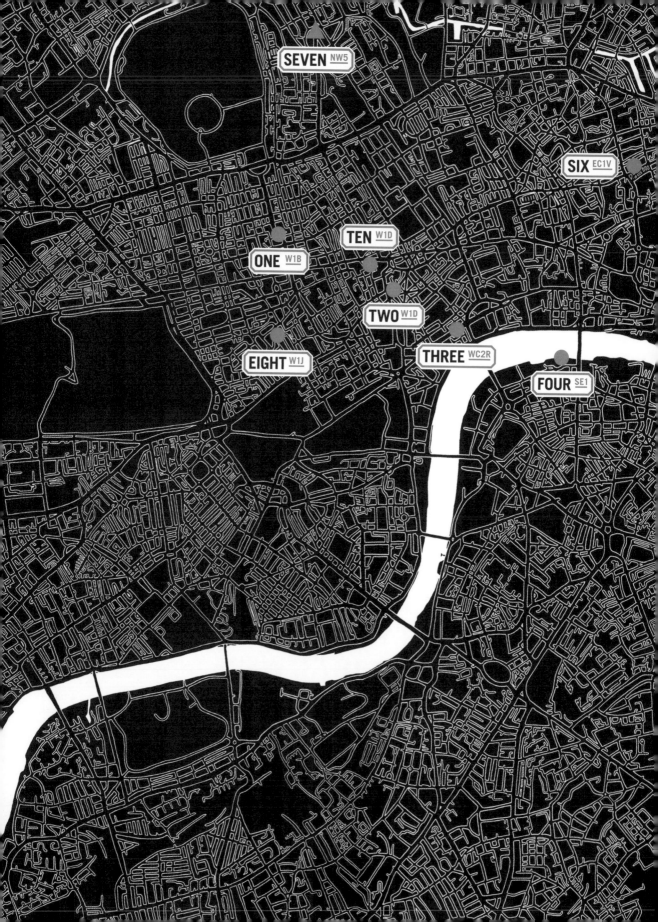

A GUIDE TO...
LONDON'S BEST COCKTAIL BARS

1. Artesian
1C Portland Pl,
W1B 1JA
artesian-bar.co.uk

Drinks served in gilded pineapple or Lego elephants, clouds of smoke that smell like tangerine or opium, ingredients that range from mushroom to frankincense... Artesian takes cocktails to a new level. Go with an open mind, and don't ask for a Cosmopolitan.

2. Bar Termini
7 Old Compton St,
W1D 5JE
bar-termini.com

The Italian-inspired Bar Termini does just two things, coffee and cocktails, and it does them both superbly. Stand up, Italian-style, and enjoy a speedy £1 espresso, or nab one of the coveted twenty-five seats and enjoy owner Tony Conigliaro's legendary Negronis.

3. Beaufort Bar
99 Strand,
WC2R 0EU
fairmont.com/savoy

The Savoy hotel is famous for the American Bar, where Frank Sinatra and Marlene Dietrich once tippled, but I've always preferred its darker, more intimate sibling. A cocktail at the Beaufort will set you back at least £15, but the Art-Deco-inspired room, with its colour scheme of jet-black and softly glowing gold, is unequalled for opulence and glamour.

4. Dandelyan
20 Upper Ground,
SE1 9PD
morganshotelgroup.com/Mondrian

The plush bar at the Mondrian hotel is run by award-winning bartender Ryan Chetiyawardana, whose drinks take inspiration from the wild world of botanicals. Nestle into the baby pink sofas and gaze out over the Thames.

5. Frank's Café and Campari Bar
95A Rye Lane,
SE15 4ST
frankscafe.org.uk

The tenth floor of a run-down multi-storey car park doesn't sound the most enticing place to spend an evening, but this South London bar, only open during the summer months, is a London institution. The Italian-style cocktails are top-notch, but you're really here for the panoramic view across the London skyline.

Let the New Yorkers sulk into their martinis; London has the best cocktail scene in the world. Wherever the night takes you, there's a perfect bar in which to get shaken and stirred.

6. The Gibson
44 Old St,
EC1V 9AQ
thegibsonbar.london

A tin bar where the subdued 1920s atmosphere – think bowler hats hanging on the wall and a pianist tinkling Etta James tunes – is offset by thrillingly creative drinks served in flamboyant drinking vessels, from lightbulbs to glass pipes.

7. Ladies and Gentlemen
2 Highgate Rd,
NW5 1NR
ladiesandgents.co

A disused underground lavatory transformed into a cocktail bar sounds ridiculous, but this tiny North London drinking hole is a real find. Owner William Borrell's lovingly crafted drinks focus on seasonal fruits and herbs, often gathered from nearby allotments. He's even managed to squeeze in a mini distillery, in the form of a copper still which produces just twelve bottles of gin a day.

8. Mr Fogg's Residence
15 Bruton Ln,
W1J 6JD
mr-foggs.com

A deliciously madcap bar inspired by *Around The World in Eighty Days*. The gimmick is that you have stumbled into Victorian explorer Phileas Fogg's home, so every surface is covered with stuffed animals, tattered flags and oil paintings of unattractive fictional ancestors. Embrace the silliness with the sharing punch, served in a huge wooden globe.

9. Nightjar
129 City Rd,
EC1V 1JB
barnightjar.com

A 1920s-style basement speakeasy, where the hooch is strong and the jazz is loud. Order a Josephine Baker, an intoxicating mix of brandy, rum and passion fruit, with a little kick from African alligator pepper. London's night owls flock to Nightjar, so it's wise to book ahead.

10. The Vault at Milroy's
3 Greek St, Soho,
W1D 4NX
thevaultsoho.co.uk

This gem of a bar is hidden beneath Milroy's, one of London's finest whisky shops, and you'll need to slip through a secret door concealed behind a bookcase to enter. Unsurprisingly, whisky is the star of the menu – try the gently spiced Nobility cocktail, made with bourbon and cardamom.

BREAKFAST MARTINI

I love marmalade, and I love cocktails, so it's no wonder I've got an affinity for this fruity little number. The drink was invented at the Lanesborough hotel by Salvatore Calabrese, a dashing Italian barman who was introduced to marmalade by his English wife and sensibly decided that such a delicious ingredient was wasted on bread. I'm too much of a wimp to actually drink this at breakfast, but it's often my go-to first cocktail in the evening, before I head out to meet friends in the city. Its mix of sharpness and sweetness somehow sets you up perfectly for whatever the night has in store.

SERVES 1

1 heaped teaspoon marmalade
40ml gin
20ml Cointreau or triple sec
1 tablespoon orange juice
2 tablespoons lemon juice
strip of orange zest, to garnish

Put the marmalade and gin in a cocktail shaker and stir vigorously with a spoon until the marmalade dissolves. Add all the other ingredients, except the orange zest, and plenty of ice. Shake vigorously, strain into a martini glass and garnish with the strip of orange zest.

JAMES BOND'S MARTINI

An Arctic-cold martini, served in that elegant V-sign of a glass, is one of the purest pleasures in life. James Bond would certainly agree. Over the course of Ian Fleming's novels, the hard-drinking spy downs over thirty of these potent cocktails; in fact it's a miracle he ever aims a gun correctly.

There are many London bars in which you can enjoy a martini worthy of 007, but all serious Bond buffs make a pilgrimage to Dukes Bar, part of the genteel Dukes Hotel in Knightsbridge, where the martinis are neither shaken nor stirred. Instead, a bartender will wheel over a glamorous martini trolley filled with ice-cold bottles taken straight from the freezer, then pour them with a flourish into a chilled glass. The resulting drink is strong, dry and more than a touch dangerous – much like Bond himself.

SERVES 1

few dashes dry vermouth
very cold vodka or gin, ideally from
   the freezer
strip of lemon zest

Take a chilled glass and pour in a few dashes of dry vermouth. Swirl the glass so the vermouth coats the inside, then fill the glass with vodka or gin. Gently twist the lemon zest over the drink, so the citrus oil sprays over the surface, then drop into the glass. Drink immediately. Think carefully before making another.

CHOCOLATE
ESPRESSO MARTINI

In the 1980s, so the story goes, a misbehaving model walked into a Soho bar and demanded a drink that would 'wake me up and **** me up'. The bartender glanced at his booze bottles, then glanced at the coffee machine, and the espresso martini was born. I've swapped the usual coffee liqueur for crème de cacao, to give the drink a velvety chocolate edge.

SERVES 1

25ml espresso
30ml vodka
30ml dark crème de cacao
ice cubes
coffee beans, to serve (optional)

Combine all the ingredients, except the coffee beans, in a cocktail shaker with plenty of ice, and shake vigorously to combine.

Strain into a chilled cocktail glass, and garnish with three coffee beans placed next to each other, if desired.

SMOKING BISHOP PUNCH

Charles Dickens loved punch. At his family's London home, 48 Doughty Street, he often hosted lavish dinner parties, where the free-flowing punch bowl was as big an attraction as the novelist himself. In *A Christmas Carol* the reformed Scrooge invites his beleaguered employee Bob Cratchit to get merry 'over a Christmas bowl of Smoking Bishop'. Smoking Bishop was a warm port punch, a little like mulled wine, but with a rich, almost marmalade-like quality from roasted oranges. It fills the house with the most marvellously Christmassy smell.

SERVES 10

30 cloves
5 oranges, plus extra orange slices
    to serve
1 lemon
750ml bottle red wine
750ml bottle ruby port
4 cinnamon sticks, plus extra to serve
¼ teaspoon ground nutmeg
½ teaspoon mixed spice
200g caster sugar, or to taste

Preheat the oven to 180°C/160°C Fan/Gas Mark 4.

Push five cloves into each orange and lemon. This is easier if you use a knife to make small incisions in the fruit first.

Put the fruit in a close-fitting oven dish or tray and roast for about 1–1½ hours, until starting to brown (you may need to turn the fruit halfway through, to ensure they colour evenly). Leave to cool slightly.

Put the wine, port and all the spices into a large pan. Squeeze the juice from the oranges and lemons into the pan. They might still be quite hot, so be careful (ideally, use a juicer with handles). Don't worry if lots of fruit pulp drops into the pan. Put over a medium heat until piping hot, but don't let it boil.

Strain the punch through a sieve into a clean pan, to get rid of all the fruit pieces and cinnamon sticks. Return to the heat and stir in the sugar (you may wish to do this gradually, tasting after each addition, so you can decide when you've added enough). Serve in mugs or glasses, with a cinnamon stick and orange slice in each one.

CARNIVAL RUM PUNCH

One of the biggest events on the London calendar is the Notting Hill Carnival. A vibrant celebration of the city's West Indian community, it grew out of a series of festivals held in the late 1950s and 60s as an attempt to improve race relations in the city, and now attracts around one million people every year. The steel bands and dancers, in their beautiful costumes and headdresses, are unmissable. So is this cocktail.

MAKES ABOUT 2 LITRES (IT'S A CARNIVAL, AFTER ALL)

500ml gold rum
500ml pineapple juice
500ml orange juice
juice of 5 limes
6 dashes of Angostura bitters
caster sugar, to taste (optional)

To serve
ice cubes
slices of orange and/or lime
handful of fresh mint leaves
freshly grated nutmeg (optional)

In a large jug, combine the rum, fruit juices and bitters, then taste. This is one of those marvellous drinks that is easily customised according to your own preference: add more lime juice if you prefer a sourer cocktail, or sugar if you'd prefer something sweeter.

Divide between ice-filled glasses, and top each one with a slice of orange and/or lime, a scattering of mint leaves, and a grating of fresh nutmeg if desired.

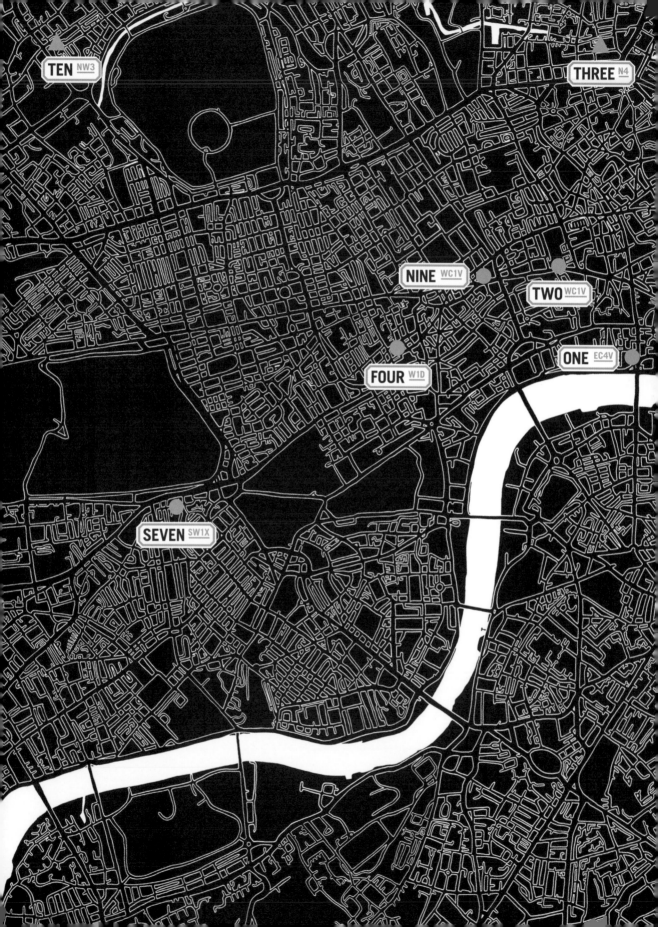

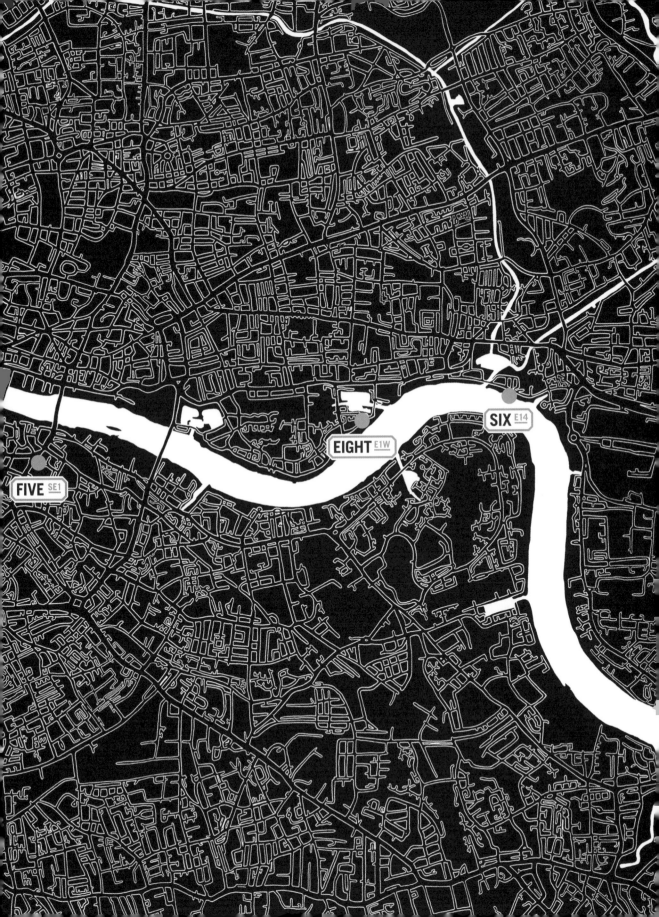

FIVE SE1

EIGHT E1W

SIX E14

A GUIDE TO...
LONDON'S BEST PUBS

1. The Blackfriar
174 Queen Victoria St,
EC4V 4EG

This wedge-shaped pub, squeezed awkwardly into a chaotic junction by Blackfriars Bridge, always looks a little out of place: no wonder the vast monk statue above the doorway appears to be giggling. The pub was built in about 1875 on the site of a Dominican monastery, but was remodelled in 1905 into a madcap Art Nouveau masterpiece. Inside, the walls are covered in extravagant copper friezes of jolly monks fishing, collecting fruit and (for some reason) trundling along a pig in a wheelbarrow. Don't miss the church-like marble dining room with its mosaiced gold ceiling and ominous mottoes emblazoned on the wall, like 'A good thing is soon snatched up' and 'Finery is foolery' – a rather serious outlook while you're munching pie and chips.

2. The Cittie of Yorke
22 High Holborn,
WC1V 6BN

With its soaring wooden-beamed ceiling and mullioned windows, the Cittie of York looks like somewhere King Henry VIII would have enjoyed a flagon of ale while eyeing up (or feeling up) a buxom bar wench. But despite medieval roots, this vast pub's olde-worlde interior was actually created in the 1920s. Lawyers from the adjoining Gray's Inn often mutter furtively with clients inside the cosy wooden booths.

3. The Faltering Fullback
19 Perth Rd, Finsbury Park,
N4 3HB
falteringfullback.com

The perfect pub for a summer's day. Grab a pint, then head upstairs to explore the magical urban garden, which resembles a ramshackle treehouse spread over three levels. There are countless nooks and crannies to sit in, and (if you can find your way back downstairs to order) decent Thai food to soak up all the booze.

4. The French House
49 Dean St, Soho,
W1D 5BG
frenchhousesoho.com

For much of the twentieth century, this dark and cosy pub encapsulated the democratic spirit of Soho. Run by a bohemian French family called the Berlemonts, it welcomed everyone from poets to prostitutes. The French Resistance met here, while Welsh poet Dylan Thomas accidentally left the handwritten manuscript of Under Milk Wood under a chair after a heavy drinking session. Today, the pub still sticks to the Berlemont rule that beer can only be served in half-pints, a decree supposedly introduced after a rowdy gang of French sailors used their pint glasses to clop each other on the head.

5. The George Inn
The George Inn Yard,
75–77 Borough High St,
SE1 1NH
george-southwark.co.uk

In the seventeenth and eighteenth centuries, the area around London Bridge was crammed full of galleried coaching inns, where tired travellers and their horses could rest. The George, with its white-painted balcony, is the last surviving example. Everyone from Princess Margaret to Elizabeth Taylor has enjoyed a drink in the dark warren of rooms. Winston Churchill cheekily brought his own bottle of port, though the aggrieved landlady did charge him steeply for corkage.

The London pub is a unique and sacred space. Whether it's a gloomy old-fashioned boozer or a modern, brightly lit temple to craft beer, the pub is a place that people from all walks of life can call their home. Sometimes you drink in solitude, with only the crossword for company; at other times you shout about politics with your neighbours until the landlord taps you on the shoulder and politely asks you to leave. In the summer, you can sip a pint in a sun-drenched beer garden; in the winter, you can huddle with a whisky by the roaring fire. Whatever the occasion, whatever your mood, there is a pub for you. There are so many pubs in this city – thousands upon thousands – each with its own rich history and character, so choosing the 'best' is a nigh-on impossible task. Here, then, are ten of my personal favourites. Just don't tell everyone about them.

6. The Grapes

76 Narrow St
Limehouse,
E14 8BP
thegrapes.co.uk

This higgledy-piggledy East End boozer has stood precariously on the edge of the Thames in Limehouse for over 500 years; Charles Dickens described it as resembling 'a faint-hearted diver, who has paused so long on the brink that he will never go in at all'. If you're lucky, you might spot the distinguished landlord, Sir Ian McKellen. The staff he carried as Gandalf in the *Lord of The Rings* films sits behind the bar.

7. The Nag's Head

53 Kinnerton St,
SW1X 8ED

Don't even think about using your mobile at this historic Knightsbridge watering hole – landlord Kevin has a fearsome reputation for shouting at customers who break his no-phones policy. Instead, take a seat at the incredibly low bar and admire the quirky palimpsest of clutter on the wood-panelled walls, from faded newspapers and horse brasses to rusty instruments and the odd vintage penny-slot machine. The pub is tucked away down a sleepy backstreet, so it's a devil to find the first time – but once you have, you won't want to drink anywhere else.

8. The Prospect of Whitby

57 Wapping Wall, Wapping,
E1W 3SH
greeneking-pubs.co.uk

A noose swings eerily outside London's oldest riverside tavern, a dark tribute to the pirates and smugglers who drank here until they were caught by the Royal Navy and hanged at nearby 'Execution Dock'. Once known as the 'Devil's Tavern', the pub was built around 1520, more than three decades before Shakespeare was born. The interior is deliciously atmospheric, with wood-panelled walls, original flagstone floor and marine paraphernalia including ships' wheels and masts.

9. The Princess Louise

208 High Holborn,
WC1V 7EP
princesslouisepub.co.uk

Her beer selection isn't the best, and she's a little too popular for her own good, but Londoners can't resist the knock-out that is The Princess Louise. A classic example of a late Victorian boozer, the place is a pub-lover's fantasy of engraved glass panels, beautiful tiled flooring and an intricately carved mahogany bar, lorded over by a vintage clock. Even the men's urinals are made of marble.

10. The Spaniards Inn

Spaniards Rd, Hampstead,
NW3 7JJ
thespaniardshampstead.co.uk

Legend has it that highwaymen used to sip brandy by the windows of this sixteenth-century pub, watching and waiting for wealthy travellers to pass by. Today, it's a favourite refreshment spot for walkers on nearby Hampstead Heath, who sink jugs of Pimm's in the large garden. Superstitious locals whisper of ghostly sightings, including a lady in white and a lovelorn landlord. Sometimes, the hooves of highwayman Dick Turpin's beloved horse, Black Bess, are heard pattering outside.

SPICED HOT CHOCOLATE

Londoners adore chocolate: a recent study found that we eat more chocolate on a daily basis than any other city in Britain. Our love affair began in the sixteenth century, when the very first cocoa beans arrived from the New World. Hot chocolate became a fashionable drink among the upper classes, and dedicated 'chocolate houses', such as The Cocoa Tree in Pall Mall, bubbled up all over the city. Although they sound charming, in practice many chocolate houses were rowdy gentlemen's clubs, where gambling and violence were rife. In 1717, an argument at the Royal Chocolate House got so out of hand that three men were killed.

The hot chocolate enjoyed by our ancestors bears little resemblance to the powdery sweet stuff sold today. It was rich and dark, and often flavoured with exotic ingredients, from chilli to jasmine flowers. The recipe below will give you a taste of those decadent times.

MAKES ENOUGH FOR 2 BIG MUGS
OR 4 DAINTY GLASSES

400ml milk
50ml double cream (optional)
50g dark chocolate (at least 70%
    cocoa solids)
1 tablespoon cocoa powder
1½ tablespoons soft dark brown sugar
¼ teaspoon ground nutmeg
1 cinnamon stick or ½ teaspoon
    ground cinnamon
¼ teaspoon mild chilli powder
    (optional)
1 teaspoon vanilla extract

Combine all the ingredients in a pan and bring gently to the boil, stirring to combine. Lower the heat, so the mixture is barely bubbling, and cook for another 5 minutes or so. Remove the cinnamon stick, if using, and stir vigorously with a whisk to create a lovely froth. Strain through a sieve and serve.

TOM COLLINS

A sprightly gin cocktail, ideal for hot summer days. There are many rival stories about its genesis, but I like the theory of cocktail historian David Wondrich, who believes it was created at Limmer's hotel in Mayfair during the nineteenth century. Limmer's was memorably described in 1862 as 'the most dirty hotel in London', but its bar was extremely popular with raffish aristocrats, due in no small part to its wickedly potent gin punches. Wondrich thinks that the Tom Collins grew out of a drink called the 'John Collins', which was named for Limmer's head waiter. Perhaps those squiffy gentlemen were too far gone to correctly remember poor John's name.

SERVES 1

60ml London dry gin
30ml lemon juice
2 teaspoons caster sugar
ice cubes
soda water, to top up
lemon wedge, to garnish

Mix the gin, lemon juice and sugar together in the bottom of a tall glass. Fill the glass two-thirds full with ice, top up with soda water, and gently stir to combine. Garnish with the lemon wedge.

BEECH LEAF GIN

The word 'foraging' conjures up idyllic images of picking blackberries in the countryside, but there is a treasure trove of wild edibles in London, too. This is a green city, with over eight million trees and 3,000 parks and open spaces; if you know what to look for, you're bound to find something tasty.

One of the best things to forage in London is beech tree leaves. Beech trees are everywhere, but few people realise that you can use their leaves, much like you do sloes, to make a delicious liqueur. Simply stuff them in a jar with a bottle of cheap-ish gin, and a few weeks later you'll have a unique green-hued drink with a fresh, delicate flavour – the essence of spring in a glass. The secret is to collect the leaves when they are very, very young, around early May. They should be lime green, soft and so thin they are almost translucent. This is good drunk neat over ice, but even better with ice-cold tonic and a wedge of lemon. You can also top it up with fizz.

MAKES 700ML

enough young beech leaves (washed) to fill a large jar
700ml bottle London dry gin
120g caster sugar

First, sterilise your jar. You can either wash it in hot, soapy water and leave in a 140°C/120°C Fan/Gas Mark 1 oven for about 15 minutes until dry, or just put the jar through the highest setting on the dishwasher.

Pack the jar densely with the beech leaves, making sure to remove any twigs, then pour in the gin. You want the gin to completely cover the leaves; any exposed to the air will go brown and nasty. Add the sugar, then seal the jar and give it a good shake. Leave in a cool, dark place for 2–3 weeks.

Strain the gin through a piece of muslin (or a sieve at a push) into a sterilised bottle. You can drink this straight away, but it tastes better if you let it mature for a few more weeks, or even longer.

'DRUNKEN PEOPLE FROM MORNING TILL NIGHT...': THE GIN CRAZE

When you pick up a glass of gin, you are clasping on to a spirit that nearly destroyed London.

It may sound like an exaggeration, but the gin craze that broke out in the eighteenth century caused unprecedented social breakdown, and was responsible for the deaths of thousands of men, women and children. The trouble began with the accession of the Dutch king William III to the English throne in 1688. Imports of spirits from other countries, such as French brandy, were limited, while a sweetish Dutch spirit called 'genever', made from juniper berries, was encouraged. Londoners quickly acquired a taste for this exotic new tipple, and started making their own, even more potent version: gin.

Some gins were of decent quality, distilled in proper factories by companies that still exist today; Greenall's and Gordon's, bottles you will spot in many British bars, can both trace their roots to the eighteenth century. But most gin was rough, throat-burning stuff, brewed in back rooms and cellars, and adulterated with unsavoury additions such as turpentine and sulphuric acid. All it offered was the ability to make people pulverisingly drunk – and poor inner-city Londoners, seeking a cheap escape from the squalor and misery all around them, embraced it like a lover.

By 1723, one in four homes in London's poorest areas, like the slum of St Giles, housed a rudimentary gin operation, or 'dram shop'. In back rooms, on piles of dirty straw, gin-addled Londoners lay for hours until they were capable of struggling to their feet and wobbling over to the next shop. Street vendors offered ladles of the stuff for a halfpenny. 'The whole town of London swarmed with drunken people from morning till night,' wrote the courtier Lord Hervey. It has been estimated that the average person downed between one and two pints of gin per week.

Women seemed particularly fond of gin, as the spirit's feminine nicknames – 'Mother's Ruin', 'Madame Genever' – suggest. Their heavy consumption of the spirit had grim consequences. The Royal College of Physicians noted that the babies of gin-drinking mothers appeared 'weak, feeble and distemper'd', suffering, presumably, from what we would now recognise as foetal alcohol syndrome. Even healthy children had no escape from the spirit: tired mothers would spoon gin into their babies' mouths to quiet them. In 1751, the artist William Hogarth created his famous print Gin Lane, designed to show the grim impact of gin on the city. In the foreground, a half-naked woman is sprawled, too drunk to notice her baby is tumbling to its death over a stairwell. Hogarth wasn't being sensationalist: in a famous case not many years before, a young Londoner named Judith Dufour strangled her own baby and sold its clothes for gin money.

It took a long time to crush the city's addiction. Between 1729 and 1751, Parliament passed eight 'Gin Acts', introducing higher taxes and expensive licenses for retailers. But gin peddlers always found ways around the restrictions. One enterprising fellow, Captain Dudley Bradstreet, installed a cat-shaped sign outside his house, which had a lead pipe concealed underneath the cat's paw. Customers went up to the sign and whispered, 'Puss, give me two pennyworth of gin!' They popped a coin into the cat's mouth, and the captain poured a trickle of gin down the pipe. The customers would catch the gin in a cup or – probably more likely – drink it straight from the pipe. Bradstreet's idea was widely copied, creating, essentially, a network of vending machines for addicts.

The nail in Madame Genever's coffin was the disastrous harvest of 1757. Fearing a shortage of food, the government banned the use of corn and other grains to make spirits. The ban was overturned a few years later, but London had begun to dry out.

Today, London is in the grip of another 'gin craze', though thankfully a rather more civilised one. In 2009, a small gin distillery called Sipsmith opened – the first in London since 1820 – and a new wave of independent ginmakers rippled throughout London and beyond. There are gin bars, dedicated 'gin tours', and even a gin-themed hotel, The Distillery, where room service will deliver you a 'sharing martini' to sip in your pyjamas. Paris can keep its champagne, and New York its Manhattans. It is gin that flows through Londoners' veins.

Drunkenness and debauchery: 'Gin Lane' by William Hogarth, 1751. (Three Lions/Getty Images)

THE QUEEN MOTHER COCKTAIL

The Royal family really do enjoy their booze. The late Queen Mother was particularly fond of this gin cocktail, as is her daughter, who supposedly drinks it every day as an aperitif before lunch. It is an elegant, though very potent drink.

SERVES 1

80ml Dubonnet
40ml gin
juice of ½ lemon
ice cubes
strip of lemon zest, to serve

Shake the Dubonnet, gin and lemon juice together in a cocktail shaker with plenty of ice. Strain into a chilled martini glass and garnish with a strip of lemon zest. Sip regally.

LONDON CALLING

This refreshing little number was invented by my fellow Londoner and gin fiend, the drinks writer Kay Plunkett-Hogge. It is dead simple, and dangerously drinkable.

SERVES 1

50ml London dry gin
10ml elderflower cordial
sparkling wine, chilled, to top up

Pour the gin and elderflower cordial into a champagne glass. Stir to combine, then top up with the sparkling wine.

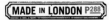

DUSKY BRAMBLE

A lot of grim cocktails came out of the 1980s (Sex on the Beach, anyone?) but the Bramble cocktail was not one of them. A bright concoction of gin, lemon and blackberry liqueur, it was invented at Soho watering hole Fred's Club by the bartender Dick Bradsell, who was inspired by childhood memories of blackberry picking. My more sultry, autumnal version replaces the gin with whisky; its woody, earthy notes have such an affinity with blackberries. I like to curl up with this in front of the fire, with a good book and a few squares of dark chocolate.

SERVES 1

60ml whisky
30ml lemon juice
20ml crème de mure
20ml sugar syrup*
4 blackberries
ice cubes
fresh rosemary sprig, to garnish

* You can buy simple syrup, but it's
   cheap and easy to make. Simply heat
   one part sugar and one part water in
   a saucepan for a few minutes, until
   the sugar has completely dissolved.
   Leave to cool before using. The
   syrup will keep, covered, in the
   fridge for at least a month.

Put all the ingredients except the rosemary sprig into a shaker with lots of ice. Shake vigorously, then strain into a tumbler glass filled with ice. Garnish with the rosemary sprig (I like to hold the sprig briefly over a flame – it adds a slightly smoky, more aromatic dimension to the drink).

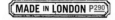

TEA AND LEMON CRUSH

Tea is the archetypal London drink. In the 1800s, tea ships or 'clippers' would race to bring the first of the new season's leaves from China to London, with people placing extravagant bets on which ship would be the fastest. (One of the last tea clippers, the *Cutty Sark*, is on display in Greenwich; I gaze out at it through my window most mornings, with a steaming brew cupped in my hand).

In the summer I love to use tea in a refreshing icy drink like this, inspired by the Italian granita. Although iced drinks and desserts seem to have originated in continental Europe, Londoners have long been partial to them; King Charles II served ice cream at court in 1671, while at the King's Cross canal museum, you can admire a huge Victorian ice well, built to cater to the growing demand for the cold stuff. I like to make this with English breakfast tea, but you can experiment with other flavours, too.

SERVES 6

130g caster sugar
3 tea bags of your choice
juice and zest of 3 large lemons

Put the sugar and teabags together in a large pan with 600ml of water. Gently heat, stirring occasionally, until the sugar has dissolved (about 10 minutes). Remove the teabags and stir in the lemon juice and zest. Pour the liquid into a large, shallow baking dish or tray and leave to cool for 30 minutes.

Transfer the dish to the freezer. After 40–60 minutes, you will see chunky ice crystals blooming around the edges. Use a fork to mash the frozen edges and stir them into the centre. Leave for a further 30 minutes, then mash the crystals again. Repeat this process every half hour, at least two or three times more, until the mixture is entirely frozen into a pile of glittering ice crystals. Cover and leave in the freezer until needed.

Take the granita of the freezer 10 minutes or so before you need it, roughly ruffling the crystals with a fork again. To serve, divide the granita between glasses. For a more liquid refreshment, add a splash of water or lemonade and sip it with a straw, or spoon it straight into your mouth like a sorbet.

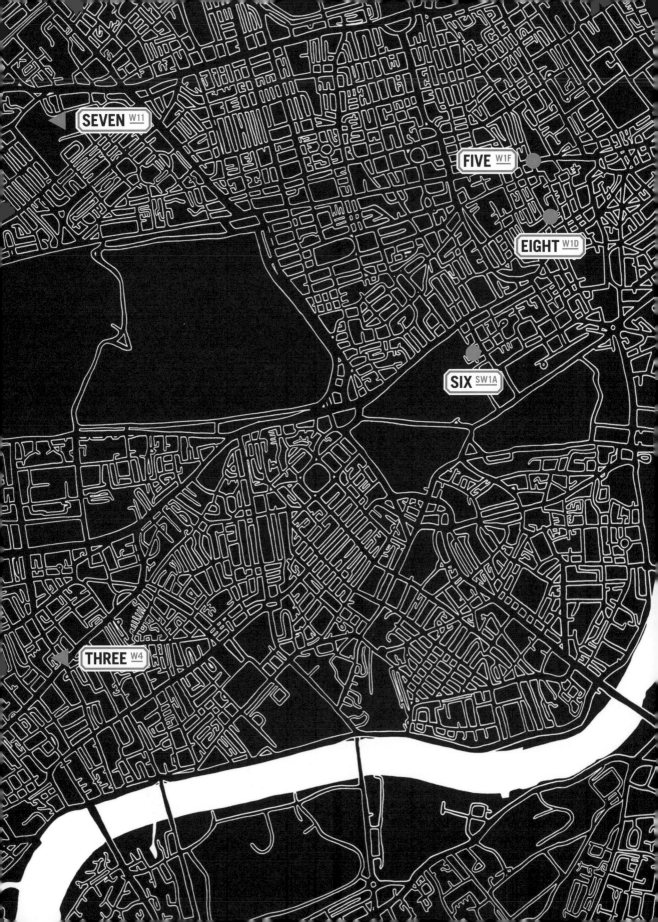

SEVEN W11

FIVE W1F

EIGHT W1D

SIX SW1A

THREE W4

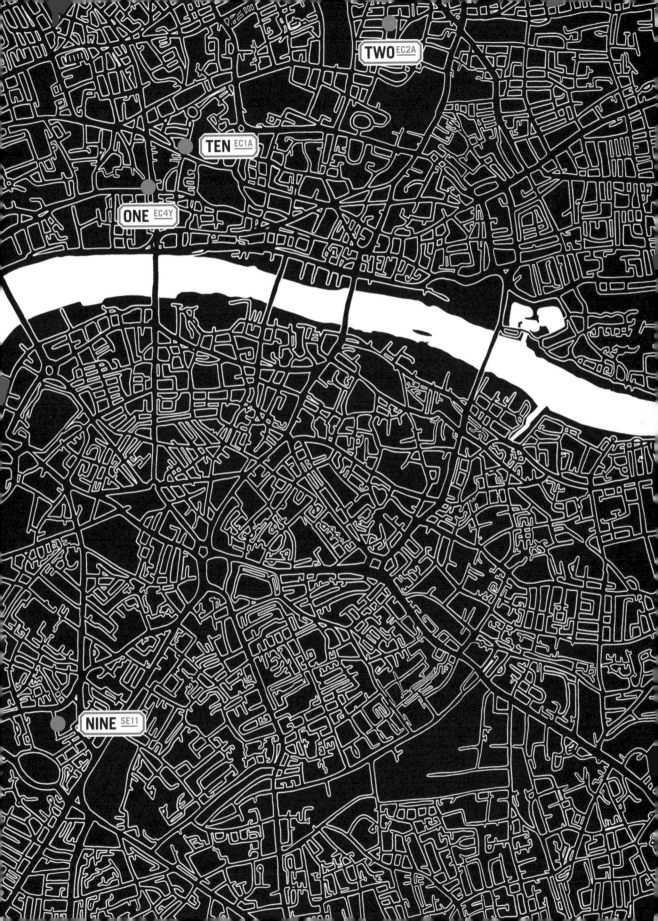

LONDON FOR GIN LOVERS

1. Create your own gin

22–24 Bride Ln,
EC4Y 8DT
cityoflondondistillery.com

Like the idea of having your own unique gin? Visit the City of London distillery to experience the art of gin-making first-hand. A tutor will guide you through the properties of different botanicals, from citrus peel to pink peppercorns, then it's up to you to create the perfect blend. You'll even design your own label.

2. Drink cocktails by candlelight

63 Worship St,
EC2A 2DU
whistlingshop.com

The prize for London's most atmospheric cocktail bar must surely go to Worship Street Whistling Shop, a subterranean drinking den inspired by the Victorian gin palaces and 'dram shops' of old. Despite the candles and old-fashioned gas lamps flickering in the darkness, the drinks are decidedly modern, with many featuring cutting-edge techniques and exotic ingredients. Try the Japanese-inspired Ibaraki cocktail, a refreshing concoction of gin and cherry blossom tea.

3. Enjoy a tutored tasting

83 Cranbrook Rd, Chiswick,
W4 2LJ
sipsmith.com

When it opened in 2009, Sipsmith was the first new gin producer in London for nearly 200 years. It has a particularly gorgeous distillery, dominated by three copper stills (the giant kettles used to make gin) named Prudence, Patience and Constance. Visit the distillery and a Sipsmith gin expert will lead you through a tasting of the range, from sweet, jewel-hued sloe gin to the dangerously smooth overproof.

4. Explore London's gin-soaked past

ginjourney.com

Skip the boring red bus tour and sign up for the 'Gin Journey', a lively tour of London's gin hotspots. A chauffeur will drive you between distilleries and bars, as you listen to the dark story of Mother's Ruin while sipping a never-ending stream of gin samples and cocktails. Stocking up on painkillers beforehand is recommended.

5. Join the London Gin Club

22 Great Chapel St, Soho,
W1F 8FR
thelondonginclub.com

Tables book up weeks in advance at this cosy Soho bar, which offers over 300 tempting gins from all over the world. Try them neat, in cocktails, or in a 'tasting flight' of gin and tonics, each served with an unusual garnish. Join the club as a member and you'll get discounts in the bar, plus access to exclusive tastings and events.

Londoners have had an unquenchable thirst for gin ever since the very first bottles arrived from Holland in the seventeenth century. It's time to get in the spirit.

6. Sip James Bond's martini

35 St James's Pl, St James's,
SW1A 1NY
dukeshotel.com

Martinis are taken very seriously indeed at Dukes Hotel, where natty white-jacketed bar staff trundle around a dedicated martini trolley and make the drink theatrically at your table. Small wonder that James Bond author Sir Ian Fleming supposedly came up with the 'shaken not stirred' catchphrase here. A martini won't leave you with much change from £20, but it's an experience at the top of the London bucket list.

7. Stay in a gin hotel

186 Portobello Rd,
W11 1LA
the-distillery.london

London's eighteenth-century gin addicts would have thought they'd died and gone to heaven if they'd stumbled across The Distillery, a four-floor temple to gin in Notting Hill. Owned by local gin brand Portobello Road, it is home to a tasting and distilling room, two gin bars and – right at the top – three bedrooms where you can sleep off your hangover. That's if you can resist the gin cocktails in the minibar…

8. Stock up your home bar

74 Old Compton St, Soho,
W1D 4UW
gerrys.uk.com

'Off licence' doesn't do justice to Gerry's of Soho, London's premier booze shop. In this tiny, ramshackle building you'll find all sorts of gin, from classics like Gordon's to limited-edition bottles flavoured with elderflower or rhubarb, plus plenty of other weird and wonderful libations you won't be able to resist taking home.

9. Tour a historic distillery

20 Montford Pl,
SE11 5DE
beefeaterdistillery.com

Beefeater is the oldest gin distillery in the city, with a recipe dating back to the nineteenth century. The gin is named for the Tower of London's red-clad guardians, the Yeoman of the Guard or 'Beefeaters', and is a classic 'London Dry' style – clean and crisp, with a heady kick of juniper. Pop in for a quick tour (including the small but excellent museum on the history of gin), then kick back with a G&T in the bar.

10. Visit a Victorian gin palace

126 Newgate St,
EC1A 7AA
viaducttavern.co.uk

In the nineteenth century, when gin was slowly becoming respectable once more, beautiful pubs known as 'gin palaces' flourished in London. The Viaduct Tavern, with its engraved glass screens and floor-to-ceiling paintings of pouting women, is the finest remaining example. Note the wooden booth at the back: it's where landladies of old would dole out 'gin tokens', so their untrustworthy staff couldn't pocket customers' cash.

BIBLIOGRAPHY & INDEX

BIBLIOGRAPHY

Ackroyd, Peter, *London: The Biography*, Chatto & Windus (2000)

Brown, Pete, *Shakespeare's Local: Six Centuries of History Seen Through One Extraordinary Pub,* Macmillan (2012)

Collinson, Lizzie, *Curry: A Tale of Cooks and Conquerors*, Oxford University Press (2007)

Colquhoun, Kate, *Taste: The Story of Britain Through Its Cooking,* Bloomsbury (2008)

Crystal, Paul, *Tea: A Very British Beverage,* Amberley Publishing (2014)

Dickson Wright, Clarissa, *A History of English Food*, Random House (2011)

Hope, Annette, *Londoners' Larder*, Mainstream Publishing (1990)

Levene, Alysa, *Cake: The Short, Surprising History of our Favourite Bakes*, Headline (2011)

Majumdar, Simon, *Eating for Britain: A Journey into the Heart (and Belly) of a Nation*, John Murray (2010)

Marriott, John, *Beyond the Tower: A History of East London*, Yale University Press (2011)

Ondantje Rolls, Jans, *The Bloomsbury Cookbook: Recipes for Life, Love and Art*, Thames and Hudson (2014)

Phillips, Mike and Trevor, *Windrush: The Irresistible Rise of Multi-Racial Britain*, HarperCollins (1998)

Porter, Roy, *London: A Social History*, Penguin (2000)

Velten, Hannah, *Beastly London: A History of Animals in the City*, Reaktion Books (2013)

White Jerry, *London in the 18th Century: A Great and Monstrous Thing*, Bodley Head (2012)

Williams, Olivia, *Gin Glorious Gin: How Mother's Ruin Became the Spirit of London*, Headline (2015)

A

A Wong 250
afternoon tea 10, 103, 135; *see also* cakes; pastries; scones; tarts (sweet); tea
Albion 53
alcohol *see* cocktails; drinks
Algerian Coffee Stores 34
almonds
 caramelised ice cream 229
 lamb and apricot rice 178
 and pear tart 200
apples
 golden syrup steamed pudding 226
 with scallops, beetroot and hazelnuts 77
apricots lamb and almond rice 178
Aromatic Beef Pho 186
Artesian 264
aubergine Korean stuffed 140
Austen, Jane 122

B

Bacon Naan with Chilli Tomato Jam 41
bakeries 10, 112–13
baking 19
bananas and coffee smoothie 36
Bao Buns with Sticky Pork and Pickled Carrots 190
Bar Termini 264
bars 17, 264–5; *see also* individual bars
Bartholomew Fair 126
Beaufort Bar 264
Bedford, Lady Anna Russell, Duchess of 103
Beech Leaf Gin 283
beef
 Big Ben burger 242
 pho 186
 steak and ale pie 182
 steak tartare 243
Beefeater 295
beer 17
 steak and ale pie 182
 battered fish and chips 148
beetroot with scallops 77
Beigel Bake 235
Beigel Shop 235
Bell, Vanessa 127
Bentley's Oyster Bar & Grill 61, 82
Berber & Q 10, 98

Betjeman, John 224
Big Ben Burger 242
Billingsgate Fish Market 18, 156, 162
 fish stew 147
biscuits Bourbon 130
 Black Rice and Coconut Porridge 26
Blackfriar, The 278
Bloomsbury Seed Cake 127
blueberries and vanilla compote 56
Blumenthal, Heston 14
Bob Bob Ricard 243
Bond, Michael 221
bone marrow roasted with parsley and lemon salt 91
Borough Market 10, 143, 156, 162, 212
Bourbon Biscuits 130
Bradstreet, Capt Dudley 284
bread
 bacon naan with chilli tomato jam 41
 bagels 235
 bao buns 190
 bread and butter pudding 221
 cheese and Marmite rolls 53
 Chelsea buns 40
 coconut with lemon curd cream cheese and rhubarb 37
 crab doughnuts 74
 fig and feta pide 25
 smoked eel toasted sandwich 64
 treacle soda 61
 see also scones
Bread Ahead 112
breakfast 21
 bacon naan with chilli tomato jam 41
 black rice and coconut porridge 26
 burnt honey grapefruit with cardamom-ginger yoghurt 22
 cheese and Marmite rolls 53
 duck and waffle with mustard maple syrup 254
 Earl Grey pancakes with blueberry and vanilla compote 56
 omelette Arnold Bennett 10, 47
 one-pan English 52
 prawn omelette with chilli sambal 45
Breakfast Martini 267
Brick Lane 166–7
 curry 170
British Empire 11, 134, 166
Brixton 11, 162, 174–5
Broadway Market 162

Burnt Courgette Tzatziki 234
Burnt Honey Grapefruit with Cardamom-Ginger Yoghurt 22
butchers 244–5

C

Cacio e Pepe 143
Café Royal 14
cakes
 Bloomsbury seed 127
 gin and lemon drizzle 124
 gingerbread 126
 Tottenham 116
 Wimbledon strawberry and cream 129
 Wood Street 106
Camden Market 162
Caravan 37
Caribbean food 11, 171, 174–5
Carnival Rum Punch 275
carrots pickled 190
Catalyst 34
Catherine of Aragon 11
Catherine of Braganza 11, 122
cauliflower 10
 shawarma with spiced butter, pomegranate and pine nuts 98
Champagne + Fromage 240
Chaplin, Charlie 95, 224
Charles II, King 11, 28
cheese 240–1
 crayfish quiche 84
 fig and feta pide 25
 goat's cheese, cherry and chicory tart 85
 lemon curd cream cheese 37
 macaroni cheese with roasted mushrooms 146
 and Marmite rolls 53
Cheese Bar, The 241
Chelsea Buns 40
Cherry, Goat's Cheese and Chicory Tart with Walnut Gremolata 85
Chick 'n' Sours 90
chicken
 Brick Lane curry 170
 cooked in milk with sage and mustard 176
 coronation 96
 fried with a herby crust 246
 jerk roast 171
chicory cherry and goat's cheese tart 85

chillies
    butter 44
    sambal 45
    tomato jam 41
Chiltern Firehouse 74
Chinatown 250–1
Chinese food 190, 249, 250–1
Choccywoccydoodah 213
chocolate 212–13
    deep-dish cookie 217
    espresso martini 270
    and miso caramel tart 216
    St Emilion au chocolat 209
    smoked salt brownie 220
    spiced hot 280
    white chocolate and saffron pots 206
chophouses 14
Churchill, Winston 95, 144, 150, 240, 279
Cinnamon Club, The 167
Cittie of Yorke, The 278
Clark, Sam and Sam 178
Clarke, Sally 89
Climpson & Sons 34
cocktails 17, 264–5
    breakfast martini 267
    chocolate espresso martini 270
    James Bond's martini 268
    see also gin
coconut
    black rice porridge 26
    bread with lemon curd cream cheese and
        poached rhubarb 37
coffee 28–9
    and banana smoothie 36
    shops 34–5
coleslaw 255
coriander with watermelon salad 90
Coronation Chicken 96
Corrigan, Richard 61
courgettes tzatziki 234
Covent Garden 156–7
Crab Doughnuts 74
Craft 10
crayfish cheesy quiche 84
cream cheese lemon curd 37
Cricks Corner 34
Crispy Chinese-Style Roasted Duck with
    Pancakes 249
Criterion, The 14, 94
Crumbs and Doilies 112

curry 166–7
    Brick Lane curry 170

D

Dalston 17
Dairy 19
Dandelyan 265
Dark and Sticky Gingerbread 126
Davies, Horatio David 204–5
Deep-Dish Cookie with a Molten Chocolate
    Centre 217
Deep-Fried Sea Bass with Thai Salad 164
desserts 197
    bread and butter pudding 221
    caramelised nut ice cream 229
    chocolate and miso caramel tart 216
    deep-dish cookie with chocolate centre
        217
    golden syrup and apple steamed pudding
        226
    peach Melba 199
    pear and almond tart 200
    Pimm's trifle with lemon curd cream 201
    Ritz's plum Christmas pudding 228
    St Clement's meringue pie with ginger
        crust 231
    St Emilion au chocolat 209
    smoked salt brownie with butterscotch
        sauce 220
    white chocolate and saffron pots 206
Dickens, Charles 17, 95, 134–5, 150, 224,
    271
Dinerama 17, 157, 163
Dishoom 41
Distillery, The 284, 295
Dobbie, Mark 164
Dominique Ansel 112
doughnuts crab 74
dried fruit
    plum Christmas pudding 228
    Wood Street cake 106
drinks 17, 261, 278–9
    carnival rum punch 275
    smoking bishop punch 271
    spiced hot chocolate 280
    see also beer; cocktails; coffee; gin;
        Pimm's; tea
Druid Street market 146
duck 10

Chinese-style roasted with
    pancakes 249
    and waffle with mustard maple syrup
        254
Dukes Bar 268, 295
Dusky Bramble 290

E

E. Pellicci 48–9
E5 Bakehouse 112
Earl Grey Pancakes with Blueberry and
    Vanilla Compote 56
East End Bagels 235
Easy Caramelised Nut Ice Cream 229
Edward VII, King 14, 94, 224
eels 15, 180
    smoked toasted sandwich 64
eggs
    omelette Arnold Bennett 10, 47
    poached with sausage, yoghurt and chilli
        butter 44
    prawn omelette with chilli sambal 45
    Scotch with mustard mayonnaise 65
Electric Coffee Company 34
Elizabeth I, Queen 197
Empire Windrush, SS 11, 174
English mustard powder 19
Escargot, L' 94
Escoffier, Auguste 199

F

F. Cooke 180
Fabrique 112
Faltering Fullback, The 279
Fatties Bakery 216
Federation Coffee 35
Fig and Feta Pide 25
fish
    and chips 11, 148, 150–1
    sea bass with Thai salad 164
    Sheekey's fish pie 155
    see also Billingsgate Fish Market; eels;
        smoked salmon; seafood
Fish, Wings and Tings 175
Fortnum & Mason 65, 134–7
Fragrant Lamb, Apricot and Almond Rice
    178
Frank's Café and Campari Bar 264
French House, The 279

fruit 156–7
blueberry and vanilla compote 56
cherry, goat's cheese and chicory tart 85
coffee and banana smoothie 36
fig and feta pide 25
honey grapefruit with cardamom-ginger yoghurt 22
lamb, apricot and almond rice 178
peach Melba 199
pear and almond tart 200
smoking bishop punch 271
St Clement's meringue pie with ginger crust 231
strawberry and cream cake 129
watermelon salad with coriander and peanuts 90
see also apples; coconut; dried fruit; lemons; pomegranate; rhubarb

G

G. Kelly 180
Gavroche, Le 241
George II, King 40
George III, King 40
George Inn, The 279
Gerry's of Soho 295
Gibson, The 265
gin 17, 284–5, 294–5
beech leaf 283
dusky bramble 290
and lemon drizzle cake 124
London Calling 288
Queen Mother cocktail 287
Tom Collins 282
goat's cheese cherry and chicory tart 85
golden syrup 19
Golden Syrup and Apple Steamed Pudding 226
Gordon, Peter 44
grapefruit burnt honey with cardamom-ginger yoghurt 22
Grapes, The 278
Gray, Rose 11, 200
Great Fire of London 14, 194
Green, Dr Matthew 28–9
Greene, Graham 224
Greenwich Market 163
Grill My Cheese 240
Gymkhana 167

H

H. Forman & Son 70–1
ham and split pea soup 68
Hampton Court Palace 212
Hansen, Anna 45
Harris, Stephen 61
hazelnuts with scallops, beetroot and apple 77
Henderson, Fergus 91
Henry VIII, King 10, 11, 109
Higgens, Grace 127
Hodgson, Randolph 240
Hogarth, William 122, 284
Homemade Doner Kebabs 255
honey burnt grapefruit 22
Honey and Co. 25
Hutong 250

I

ice cream caramelised nut 229
immigration 11, 150, 171, 174
Indian food 166–7
Italian culture 29, 48–9, 144–5; *see also* pasta
Ivy, The 10
shepherd's pie 177

J

J Sheekey 82, 155
Jacksons of Piccadilly 56
James Bond's Martini 268
James II, King 106
jams chilli tomato 41
Jefferson, Thomas 150
Jerk Roast Chicken 171
Jewish food 11, 69, 70–1, 150, 235
Jonathan's Coffee House 28

K

Kaffeine 35
Katz, Josh 98
kebabs 255
Kensington Place 11
Kerb 157
Kettner's 94
Kirby, Miles 37
Korean Stuffed Aubergines 140

L

Ladies and Gentleman 265
lamb
apricot and almond rice 178
chops with kachumber 258
doner kebabs 255
shepherd's pie 177
Langtry, Lillie 94, 224
Lao Café 179
Lawson, Nigella 144, 148
Leather Lane Market 163
Lee, Jeremy 209
lemons
and gin drizzle cake 124
and lavender scones 117
tea slushy 291
Lily Vanilli 112
Lina Stores 144–5
Lloyd's Coffee House 28
London Calling 288
London Cheesecake 105
London Gin Club 294
London Particular (Split Pea and Ham Soup) 68
Lyle, Abram 226

M

Macaroni Cheese with Roasted Mushrooms and Garlic-Thyme Crumbs 146
Maids of Honour 10, 109
Maître Choux 113
Malin, Joseph 11, 150
Maltby Street Market 146, 163
M. Manze 180
Marcolini, Pierre 213
markets 15–17, 146, 156–61; *see also* Billingsgate Fish Market; Borough Market
Marmite and cheese rolls 53
Mayhew, Henry 15, 85
Mayhew, John 224
mayonnaise spicy mustard 65
meat *see* beef; chicken; duck; lamb; pork; rabbit; Smithfield Market; Turner & George
Melba, Dame Nellie 199
Melt 212
milk with chicken, sage and mustard 176
Model Market, Lewisham 17

Modern Pantry, The 45
Monmouth Coffee Company 35
Moore, Saiphin 179
Moro 178
Mr Fogg's Residence 265

N

Nag's Head, The 278
Neal's Yard 240
New Malden 140
Newens 109
Nightjar 264
Noble Rot 61
Nopi 26
Notting Hill Carnival 275
nuts
    hazelnuts with scallops, beetroot
        and apple 77
    peanuts with watermelon salad 90
    pine nuts with cauliflower sharwarma 98
    walnut gremolata 85
    see also almonds

O

Old Post Office Bakery, The 113
Oliver, Andy 164
Omelette Arnold Bennett 10, 47
One-Pan English Breakfast 52
Oslo Court 94
Ottolenghi, Yotam 26
oysters 204
    with rhubarb salsa 82

P

Paddington's Bread and Butter
    Pudding 221
Padella 15, 143
Palomar, The 234
Pan-Fried Scallops with Beetroot, Apple
    and Hazelnuts 77
pancakes Earl Grey with blueberry and
    vanilla compote 56
Parle, Stevie 10
parsley with roasted bone marrow 91
parsnips and squash and pomegranate
    salad 89
pasta 15
    cacio e pepe 143

macaroni cheese with roasted
    mushrooms 146
pastries London cheesecake 105
Paxton & Whitfield 240
Peach Melba 199
Peak Freans 130
peanuts with watermelon salad 90
Pear and Almond Tart 200
peas and ham soup 68
Pepys, Samuel 194
pie and mash shops 10, 14, 180–1
pies
    shepherd's 177
    steak and ale 182
Pimm's 204–5
    trifle with lemon curd cream 201
pine nuts and cauliflower shawarma 98
Pizarro, José 77
Poached Eggs with Spicy Sausage, Yoghurt
    and Chilli Butter 44
Polpo 14
pomegranate
    and cauliflower shawarma 98
    and parsnip and squash salad 89
pork
    laap 179
    sticky with bao buns and pickled
        carrots 190
    see also bacon; ham; sausages
porridge black rice and coconut 26
potatoes chips 148, 150; see also sweet
    potato
poultry see chicken; duck
prawns omelette with chilli sambal 45
Princess Louise, The 279
Proper Fried Chicken with a Herby Crust
    246
Prospect of Whitby, The 279
Providores and Tapa Room, The 44
Prufrock Coffee 35
pubs 17, 278–9
puddings see desserts

Q

Queen Mother Cocktail, The 287
Quo Vadis 209

R

rabbit ragu 194
Rabot 1745 212
Ramsay, Gordon 14
Rankin, Neil 217
restaurants 14, 94–5; see also individual
    restaurants
rhubarb
    poached with coconut bread and cream
        cheese 37
    salsa 82
rice
    black and coconut porridge 26
    lamb, apricot and almond 178
Ring, Bob 84
Rinkoff's 113
Ritz's Plum Christmas Pudding, The 228
River Café 11, 200
Roasted Bone Marrow with Parsley and
    Lemon Salt 91
Roasted Parsnip, Squash and Pomegranate
    Salad 89
Rock and Sole Plaice 150
Rococo 212
Rogers, Ruth 200
Roman Empire 11, 78
Roseé, Pasqua 28, 36
Royal family 11, 135; see also
    individual monarchs
Rules 94, 224–5, 226
Rum Kitchen 175

S

saffron 206
St Clement's Meringue Pie with
    a Ginger Crust 231
St Emilion au Chocolat 209
St. John 91
St Moritz 241
salads
    parsnip, squash and pomegranate 89
    Thai 164
    watermelon with coriander
        and peanuts 90
salmon see smoked salmon
salsas rhubarb 82
salt 19
Samuel Pepys' Rabbit Ragu 194
sandwiches smoked eel toasted 64

sauces
   butterscotch 220
   chilli sambal 45
sausages with poached eggs, yoghurt and
   chilli butter 44
Savoy Hotel 10, 47, 199, 264
scallops pan-fried with beetroot, apple and
   hazelnuts 77
scones lemon and lavender 117
Scotch Eggs with Spicy Mustard
   Mayonnaise 65
sea bass deep-fried with Thai salad 164
Sea Shell, The 150
seafood
   crab doughnuts 74
   crayfish quiche 84
   prawn omelette with chilli sambal 45
   scallops with beetroot, apple and
     hazelnuts 77
   see also oysters
Sheekey's Fish Pie 155
Shepherd's Pie 177
Simpson's in the Strand 95
Simpson's Tavern 95
Sipsmith 284, 294
Smithfield Market 156, 163
Smoked Eel Toasted Sandwich 64
smoked salmon 70–1
   and sweet potato fishcakes
Smoked Salt Brownie with Butterscotch
   Sauce 220
Smoking Bishop Punch 271
Soho 144, 295
Som Saa 164
soups
   beef pho 186
   split pea and ham (London
     Particular) 68
Spaniards Inn, The 278
Spiced Hot Chocolate 280
Spicy Lamb Chops with Kachumber 258
Spicy Watermelon Salad with Coriander
   and Peanuts 90
Split Pea and Ham Soup 68
squash and parsnip and pomegranate
   salad 89
Steak and Ale Pie with Thyme-Mustard
   Pastry 182
Steak Tartare 243
stews rabbit ragu 194
strawberries and cream cake 129

street food 15, 17, 146, 157
Sugar-Cured Prawn Omelette with Smoked
   Chilli Sambal 45
sweet potato and smoked salmon
   fishcakes 69
Sweetings 95
Sylhetis 166

T

tapas 14
tarts (savoury)
   cheesy crayfish quiche 84
   cherry, goat's cheese and chicory 85
tarts (sweet)
   chocolate and miso caramel 216
   Maids of Honour 10, 109
   pear and almond 200
Tayyabs 258
tea 11, 29, 120–3
   Earl Grey pancakes 56
   and lemon slushy 291
Temper 217
Thames River 78–9
Timms, Chloe 216
Tom Collins 282
tomatoes chilli jam 41
Tottenham Cake 116
Treacle Soda Bread 61
Turner & George 244–5
turtle soup 14
Twinings 56, 120–3

U

Uyen Luu 186

V

vanilla and blueberry compote 56
Vault at Milroy's, The 265
Veeraswamy 95, 167
vegetables 156–7
   burnt courgette tzatziki 234s
   cauliflower shawarma 98
   chicory, cherry and goat's cheese tart 85
   coleslaw 255
   kachumber 258
   Korean stuffed aubergines 140
   parsnip, squash and pomegranate
     salad 89

pickled carrots 190
   scallops with beetroot 77
   split pea and ham soup 68
   see also potatoes
Viaduct Tavern 295
Victoria, Queen 122
Vietnamese food 11, 186
Violet Bakery 113

W

walnuts gremolata 85
watermelon salad with coriander
   and peanuts 90
Wheeler's of St James 82
White Chocolate and Saffron Pots 206
White Mulberries 35
Wilde, Oscar 14, 94
Wildes 241
William III, King 284
Wilton's 95
Wimbledon Strawberry and Cream
   Cake 129
Wolseley, The 22
Wong Kei 250
Wood Street Cake 106
Woolf, Virginia 127
Wordsworth, William 122
Worship Street Whistling Stop 294
Wren, Sir Christopher 122

Y

yoghurt
   cardamom-ginger 22
   with poached eggs and sausage 44
   spicy garlic 69
Young, Paul A. 212, 220

ABOUT THE AUTHOR

Leah Hyslop is a food writer
and editor. She spent many years
working at *The Telegraph*, and is
now Food Director of Sainsbury's
magazine. She lives in East London,
where she is the proud mother of
a vast collection of cake tins.

Leahhyslop.com

© Nassima Rothacker

CREDITS

Publisher Jon Croft
Commissioning Editor Meg Boas
Project Editor Emily North
Art Director and Designer Marie O'Mara
Cartography Firewater Gallery *firewatergallery.com*
Photographer Martin Poole *martinpoolephotography.com*
Food Styling Kim Morphew
Food Styling Assistant Lola Milne
Photographer's Assistant Sophie Fox
Copyeditor Rachel Malig
Proofreader Kate Wanwimolruk
Indexer Zoe Ross

ACKNOWLEDGEMENTS

This is not just a book of recipes, but of stories. I'm grateful to all the brilliant
chefs, restaurateurs and characters who shared their time and talent with me.
Thanks to my brilliant agent, Juliet Pickering at Blake Friedmann, and to the
team at Absolute – Jon, Meg, Emily and Marie, you made my words come to
life. A hat tip to my friends and family, for valiantly eating all the pies. And to
Martin and Kim, the dream team, for the brilliant pictures, food styling and
tips on how to beat a claw machine.

Finally, thanks to London – you're like that chaotic, beautiful, hot mess of
a friend we all have that we moan about. But deep down, there's nobody else
we'd rather kick back and have a drink with. Cheers!

ABSOLUTE PRESS

Bloomsbury Publishing Plc

50 Bedford Square, London, WC1B 3DP, UK

BLOOMSBURY, ABSOLUTE PRESS and the Absolute Press logo
are trademarks of Bloomsbury Publishing Plc

First published in Great Britain, 2018

A catalogue record for this book is available from the British Library.

Library of Congress Cataloguing-in-Publication data has been
applied for.

ISBN

    HB: 978-1-4729-4905-9
    eBook: 978-1-4729-4904-2
    ePDF: 978-1-4729-4915-8

2 4 6 8 10 9 7 5 3 1

Printed in China by C&C Offset Printing Co., Ltd.

Bloomsbury Publishing Plc makes every effort to ensure that the
papers used in the manufacture of our books are natural, recyclable
products made from wood grown in well-managed forests. Our
manufacturing processes conform to the environmental regulations
of the country of origin.

To find out more about our authors and books visit
www.bloomsbury.com and sign up for our newsletters.